NATURAL RESOURCE ECONOMICS

THIRD EDITION

NATURAL RESOURCE ECONOMICS

AN INTRODUCTION

THIRD EDITION

BARRY C. FIELD
UNIVERSITY OF MASSACHUSETTS AMHERST

WAVELAND
PRESS, INC.
Long Grove, Illinois

For information about this book, contact:
Waveland Press, Inc.
4180 IL Route 83, Suite 101
Long Grove, IL 60047-9580
(847) 634-0081
info@waveland.com
www.waveland.com

Cover photo: Johnny Adolphson, Shutterstock

To Martha

Contents

SECTION I
INTRODUCTION 1

SECTION II
BUILDING BLOCKS 33

SECTION III
GENERAL NATURAL RESOURCE ISSUES   77

SECTION IV
NATURAL RESOURCE ANALYSIS 119

Section V
APPLIED NATURAL RESOURCE PROBLEMS   161

SECTION VI
NATURAL RESOURCES IN INTERNATIONAL PERSPECTIVE 391

Preface

One of the major themes of human concern as we negotiate the new millennium is how we should shape and manage our relationship to the natural world. On one side of the issue are those who believe that we are exhausting and degrading natural resource endowments to such an extent that the future welfare of the human community itself is threatened. On the other are those who believe that the technological and institutional challenges of natural resource scarcity can be overcome given sufficient amounts of human effort and ingenuity. Most people are probably somewhere in the middle: concerned but hopeful.

Wherever one stands on the ecological spectrum, it is clear that future outcomes depend to a great extent on the human decisions that are made about resource use. Natural resource economics represents one way of framing and analyzing these decisions. By "analyze" we mean developing an understanding of why resource decisions are made the way they are and how they might be improved upon. Natural resource economics focuses on resource valuation, economic incentives, and the institutional arrangements that will give us the utilization and conservation decisions we want.

The basic structure of the book is to start out with a few preliminaries, then cover some fundamental principles of economics, discuss how these principles apply to the general question of natural resource use, and then move to a series of topical chapters—each of which treats a particular natural resource. Finally, the last two chapters examine natural resource issues as they are encountered in developing countries and the impacts of globalization on the utilization and conservation of natural resources. There may be too many chapters to cover in a single semester course. In this case it should be easy to cover the basics, and then select the applications chapters that instructors and students find most interesting and relevant.

Each chapter ends with a summary, list of key words, some questions for further discussion, a brief reference to websites that might be useful, and a short list of selected readings. Neither the selected readings nor the website lists are comprehensive; given the massive proliferation of websites and the large scientific literature on natural resource issues, the lists at the end of each chapter can cite only a tiny fraction of the material that students might find interesting and informative. They are meant simply as a way to help students get their feet in the door, should they want to push further with any of the ideas of the chapter.

In this sense the book is a companion to another work, *Environmental Economics: An Introduction*, by Barry C. Field and Martha K. Field (McGraw-Hill, 7th edition, 2017). The latter treats issues of environmental pollution and the management of environmental quality in the same fashion, and has found a wide audience. It is used primarily for introductory courses, but on occasion also for more advanced courses. My hope is that the present work will find the same niche.

■ Highlights of the Third Edition

The third edition preserves the basic structure of the earlier editions. All the tables and figures have been updated, and many new exhibits have been included. In addition, new material has been added on:

Climate Change and Resources	Chapter 1
Fracking	Chapter 4
Resource Cartels and Boomtowns	Chapter 10
Energy Intensity	Chapter 11
Energy Efficiency Gap	Chapter 11
Reducing Fossil Energy	Chapter 11
Forests and Carbon	Chapter 12
Deforestation	Chapter 12
Aquaculture	Chapter 13
Managing Public Lands	Chapter 14
International Water Issues	Chapter 15
Food Security and Climate Change	Chapter 16
Agriculture and GMOs	Chapter 16
Globalization and Resources	Chapter 21

■ Acknowledgments

Like most textbooks, this book is the result of many years' teaching in the classroom. So my deepest debt is to the thousands of students who have sat in my classes over the years. Without their faces, reactions, and feedback, the book could not have been written, and if I have been able to present the material in a way future students find comprehensible and meaningful, it is all these earlier students who can take most of the credit.

Many thanks to the instructors who adopted previous editions of this text and offered their comments: Richard Brazee, University of Illinois; Penelope Diebel, Oregon State University; Molly Espey, Clemson University; John Janmaat, The University of British Columbia; Dean Lueck, University of Arizona; Andrew Seidl, Colorado State University; Susan Slocum, Utah State University; and John Stranlund, University of Massachusetts Amherst. Special thanks to the staff at Waveland Press, especially Laurie Prossnitz for her superb editing. Finally, love and thanks to Martha, without whom this edition would never have been completed.

About the Author

Barry C. Field is Professor Emeritus of Resource Economics at the University of Massachusetts Amherst. Previously he taught at the University of Miami and The George Washington University. He received his BS and MS degrees from Cornell University, and his PhD from the University of California at Berkeley.

At the University of Massachusetts he has devoted many years to teaching natural resource economics to students at all levels, and has worked to develop an undergraduate major in environmental and resource economics.

Professor Field is the author of numerous articles on resource and environmental economics.

SECTION I

INTRODUCTION

This first section contains two introductory chapters. Chapter 1 offers a brief tour through some of the major natural resource issues facing us today. The objective is to become acquainted with them in commonsense terms before we launch into an analysis of these problems in later chapters. The second chapter covers some of the essential terminology that will be used throughout the book.

1

Important Issues in Natural Resource Economics

In this book we apply some relatively simple, but powerful, economic principles to the study of natural resource conservation and use. We emphasize analysis: why resources are used as they are, and what specific steps can be undertaken to use them at a rate that is socially beneficial for all. It may sometimes seem that the emphasis is more on refining the analytical principles than on applying them in useful ways. To underline the fact that the analytical models are not of interest per se but help us come to grips with real-world problems, we start by taking a brief, descriptive excursion through a number of important contemporary natural resource issues. In other words, we provide an overview of the kinds of problems that are dealt with in natural resource economics before launching into the study of the analytical tools that are brought to bear on them.

■ Climate Change and Natural Resources

The most significant problem faced by humankind in the current era is the change in global climate patterns resulting from air pollutants flowing from the contemporary world economy. The expectations are that by the end of the 21st century, world mean surface temperatures may have risen above historic levels by anywhere from 2 to 10 degrees centigrade, depending on what steps are taken to reduce the human activities that are causing the problem.

Climate Change and Water

One major implication of global climate change is its expected impact on water supplies around the world. According to a recent report of the Intergovernmental Panel on Climate Change (IPCC),[1] some of these water-related consequences will be:

3

- Increases in precipitation in "high latitudes and part of the tropics, and decreases in some subtropical and lower mid-latitude regions."
- Increases in precipitation intensity and variability, which will increase the risks of floods and droughts in many areas.
- Decreases in the amount of water stored in glaciers and snow.

Figure 1-1 depicts how an array of events of this type has already impacted people around the world. Of course, water-related emergencies are not new in history; what is new is the **increased probability** of these phenomena, together with the growth of the human population that will be affected.

One important issue is the balance between urban and rural water use. Agricultural irrigation accounts for about 70 percent of total water withdrawals around the world, and about 90 percent of consumptive water use (i.e., withdrawals that become unavailable for reuse downstream). In water-stressed regions, such as the American West, the apportionment of the available water supply between farmers and city dwellers has become an increasingly acrimonious political and economic battle, which is sure to get worse in coming years.[2]

For the most part, the allocation of water in the United States between different users has been governed by historic patterns of water rights: "riparian" rights in the eastern part of the country and "appropriative" rights in the West. More recently there has been an effort to make greater use of markets to allocate water supplies. Interactions of buyers and sellers, either strictly voluntary or with some degree of public oversight, could be used to address the fact that the marginal value of water often differs, sometimes by a lot, among different users. In chapter 4 we will look more closely at how markets for water might function.

Another water issue, the obverse of this one, is too much water, i.e., floods. Figure 1-2 on p. 6 graphs the number of floods around the world from 1980 to 2011. Clearly there has been a major increase, and there is no reason to doubt that this trend will continue as a result of the meteorological impacts of climate change. The occurrence of floods and the damage they cause are not simply unforeseen weather events with humans as innocent victims. They are indeed events of nature, but their impacts are deeply influenced by decisions people make about how land is used, how and where structures are built, and how land-use regulations impact patterns of settlement. In chapter 14 we will look at, for example, how publicly subsidized flood insurance can tend to encourage people to locate in flood-prone areas.

■ Sustainability

Sustainability has become the prime concept and organizing principle for thinking about the impacts of today's decisions on the future welfare of humans and the nonhuman biosphere. In general, **sustainability** refers to the ability of a system to maintain itself over time. Since natural resource

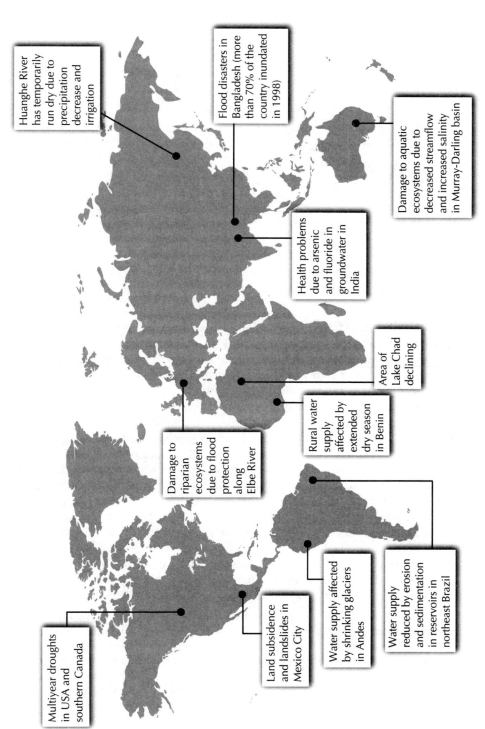

Figure 1-1   Water-Related Emergencies throughout the World

Source: Adapted from Intergovernmental Panel on Climate Change, *Climate Change 2007: Working Group II: Impacts, Adaptation and Vulnerability*, 2007. (https://www.ipcc.ch/publications_and_data/ar4/wg2/en/ch3s3-2.html)

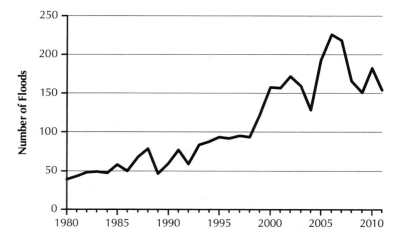

Figure 1-2   Number of Climate-Related Floods around the World, 1980–2011

Source: Data from OFDA/ CRED International Disaster Database, version 13 June 2012.

decisions are almost always time related, it is appropriate to view these decisions through the lens of sustainability.

Sustainability at the Macro Level

The longest-running issue in natural resource economics is undoubtedly the **resource adequacy** issue. Given that contemporary economies use relatively large amounts of many types of natural resources as "inputs" to production and consumption, we must ask ourselves a few serious questions: Will future supplies of these resources be sufficient to support the economic needs of our children, grandchildren, and succeeding generations indefinitely? Or will natural resource shortages ultimately become so severe as to threaten, and perhaps lead to a collapse of, future standards of living?

People who think about the likelihood of an economic collapse induced by natural resource scarcity tend to distribute themselves along a spectrum running from extreme pessimism to extreme optimism. The pessimist side goes back at least to Thomas Malthus, whose famous treatise on population was based on the notion that human population growth would inevitably outstrip the ability of nature to provide sustenance in ever-increasing amounts.[3] The pessimists can point to history to support their view. George Perkins Marsh, in his influential historical study[4] of the relationships of humans to their natural environments, begins with an allusion to the Roman Empire:

> The Roman Empire, at the period of its greatest expansion, comprised the regions of the earth most distinguished by a happy combination of physical advantages. . . . The abundance of land and water adequately supplied every material want, ministered liberally to every sensuous enjoyment. . . . If we compare the present physical conditions, . . . we shall find that more than half of their whole extent . . . is either deserted by civilized man and surrendered to hopeless desolation, or at least greatly reduced in both productiveness and population.

In the early 1970s an influential work supporting the pessimistic view was published titled *The Limits to Growth*.[5] Studies of this type continue to appear.[6]

At the other end of the spectrum are the extreme optimists. Natural resource scarcities will surely occur in the future, they admit. But human beings have the capacity to overcome this challenge, largely by finding substitutes for resources that become scarce and by eventually bringing population growth under control.[7]

Perhaps it is fair to say that most of us lie somewhere between the extremes on this issue: We are concerned, certainly, but there is a sense that this is not a situation that we are incapable of ameliorating to a large extent if the right steps are undertaken. This prompts a further question: How are we to know when real natural resource scarcity is about to put a serious crimp in economic welfare? To be able to forecast accurately when some essential natural resource will become seriously restricted in supply, we need better models incorporating predictions about population growth, the rate of technological change, the rate of new discoveries, and so on. It is very difficult to build economic models that explicitly account for all these factors.

Sustainability at the Micro Level

A "sustainable" decision is presumably one that maintains, or continues, some desirable state of affairs. So the first step is deciding what it is we are trying to maintain. In the case of natural resources the most appropriate thing to sustain might appear to be some measure of physical availability. Thus, for example, sustainable management of a fishery might consist of maintaining a given minimum level of the fish biomass.

Fish, however, are a **renewable resource**; big fish give rise to little fish, and the overall size of the fish stock depends on the balance of births and deaths, including harvesting by humans. Other important natural resources are **nonrenewable**; once "harvested" and used they are gone forever. Here the concept of sustainability is trickier, because it cannot realistically be defined in physical terms; one cannot simultaneously use and preserve a nonrenewable resource.

So sustainability in the nonrenewable case has to be understood in a different way. One way, which we will discuss in chapter 10, is through substitution: As we draw down the stocks of some nonrenewable resource, sustainability can be achieved only by adding something of at least equal value to the production base of an economy. It could be some quantity of a renewable resource, if that were possible, or perhaps some other assets, such as infrastructure capital.

Of course this line of reasoning is easy to understand if we have a way of placing a value on units of the natural resource we are considering. If that resource is traded on a **market**, we could use market values—prices—for this purpose. But in many cases real-world markets are distorted in some way; for example, in cases where they are either subject to a monopoly or to a small number of participating agents, or perhaps through public subsidies.

And for many natural resources, markets may not even exist. Such is the case with the resource called **biological diversity**. One type of biological diversity is **species diversity**, the diversity among collections of species in a given ecosystem. While the total number of animal and plant species in the world is enormous, but unknown, it is known that modern economic development is in fact contributing to substantial species loss: through habitat destruction, harmful alien species, environmental pollution, and the over-harvesting of wild species. One might suppose that species diversity preservation would be largely a biological issue. We will see, in chapter 19, that economic analysis can have interesting and important things to say about diversity preservation.

■ Natural Resources and Property Rights

Natural resources are made available by mother, or father, nature. These resources have value to human beings, and thus humans have an incentive to maintain these values. It is **property rights** that determine, for specific instances, in whose pockets these values will end up. The regimes governing access to natural resources will determine how these resources will be used, or abused.

This is easy to understand from a distributional standpoint; if a single person, or group, can gain ownership of a valuable resource, legally or illegally, that person or group can appropriate the value of that resource. This can have major repercussions directly on the distribution of wealth and on economic growth rates.

Property Rights and Rent Seeking

In natural resource economics we use the term **rent** to refer to the *in situ* (in their natural location) value of a resource.[8] And we use the term **rent seeking** to refer to the efforts that people make to gain property rights over valuable resources and thus to gain access to the rents these resources generate. Exhibit 1-1 discusses a particularly virulent case of rent seeking in Mongolia, as people maneuver to gain access to the value of newly discovered mineral resources.

One type of rent seeking in recent decades has produced **conflict resources,** in which rents from appropriated resources are diverted to fuel civil wars or insurgencies. Thus oil, timber, diamonds and other minerals, agricultural land, and other resources have been used in various parts of the world to finance armed struggle of one type or another.[9]

Rent seeking is pursued not only by individuals and corporate entities but also by national governments, in which case the competition for rents achieves the status of "geopolitics." Current points of contention are the South China Sea and the Arctic Ocean; both involving efforts to secure access to offshore petroleum deposits.

Exhibit 1-1   "Rent Seeking" in Mongolia

In Mongolia, the discovery in the early 2000s of massive deposits of copper and gold have been at the center of a conflict between mining companies and the Mongolian government as both seek control of billions of dollars of potential rent. Concerns over lack of transparency and corruption surrounding the negotiation process and large-scale protests over the distribution of mining royalties resulted in the 2009 establishment of a Human Development Fund (HDF) to distribute mining royalties to citizens as well as stricter government reporting requirements and pledges to disburse funds to citizens in the form of tuition fees, health coverage, and cash handouts.

In addition, revenue collection is typically a sector highly vulnerable to corruption. Complex arrangements are often in place for collecting taxes, royalties, and other revenues derived from extractive operations, based on the local fiscal regime. Corruption can manifest itself in the form of tax evasion committed by extractive companies, or corruption by tax officials themselves, resulting in risks to the country's development prospects.

In Mongolia, revenues derived from selling these resources are collected and divided by the state, but protesters fear that rents are being captured either by individuals or by the local elite for political or private gain. The population of Mongolia is relatively small and wealth is concentrated in a small community of business people with close ties to government. In addition, conflicts of interest and the revolving door phenomenon between the public and the private sectors are widespread in the country, further exacerbating the risk that rents are not being fairly apportioned. . . .

Source: Excerpted from Marie Chene, Transparency International, *Corruption in Natural Resource Management in Mongolia*, Anti-Corruption Resource Center Report No. 354, November 2012.

Property Rights and Open-Access Resources

Another property rights issue affecting many resources is the **open-access** phenomenon. Many important resources—fish in the sea, for example—have traditionally been treated as open-access resources. This means that the resource can be accessed by anybody and harvested according to his or her individual incentives. The fish become the property of whomever gets there first and puts the most effort into catching them. This has repeatedly led to overfishing and reduced fish stocks. Table 1-1 on the following page lists the fisheries of the U.S. that are judged to be overfished.

A new approach to property rights has emerged in response to this situation. Called individual transferable quotas (ITQs), this approach creates marketable property rights in fish. ITQ programs have been put in place in many fisheries throughout the world. They have reduced significantly the likelihood of overfishing and helped to improve overall efficiencies in the fishing industry. However, economic efficiency, a concept we will encounter many times in this book, may not be the only objective of value in some cases. With fisheries, for example, it is important also to consider the health and welfare of existing fishing communities, many of which may have no other means of livelihood.

Table 1-1 Overfished Stocks in the United States, 2014

New England	South Atlantic	Pacific
Atlantic cod – Georges Bank	Red porgy	Canary rockfish
Atlantic cod – Gulf of Maine	Red snapper	Pacific ocean perch
Atlantic halibut	Snowy grouper	Yelloweye rockfish
Atlantic salmon	Blueline tilefish	**Western Pacific**
Atlantic wolfish	**Gulf of Mexico**	Seamount groundfish complex –
Ocean pout	Gray triggerfish	Hancock seamount
Thorny skate	Greater amberjack	Striped marlin – Central Western Pacific
Yellowtail flounder –	Red snapper	**Highly Migratory Species**
Georges Bank	**Caribbean**	Blacknose shark – Atlantic
Yellowtail flounder – Cape	Goliath grouper	Blue marlin – Atlantic
Cod/Gulf of Maine	Nassau grouper	Bluefin tuna – West Atlantic
Windowpane – Gulf of	Queen conch	Dusky shark – Atlantic
Maine/Georges Bank	**Pacific/Western Pacific**	Porbeagle shark – Atlantic
Winter flounder – Southern	Pacific Bluefin tuna	Sandbar shark - Atlantic
New England/Mid-Atlantic		White marlin – Atlantic
Witch flounder		Scalloped hammerhead - Atlantic

Note: Some stocks are fished by U.S. and international fleets.

Source: National Oceanic and Atmospheric Administration Fisheries, *Status of Stocks 2014: Annual Report to Congress on the Status of U.S. Fisheries,* April 2015.

■ Resource Preservation: The Importance of Valuation

Throughout most of history, natural resources were thought to be merely raw materials to be extracted or otherwise physically converted or used to support economic growth and the advancement of material welfare. They were regarded as inputs to fuel the economy and the production of the full range of goods and services desired by consumers.

In this role, extracted natural resources typically move through markets, and in these markets the interaction of sellers and buyers establish prices which can often be interpreted as the value of these resources to society. Thus the markets for petroleum, timber, agricultural land, and commercial fish, for example, if they are reasonably competitive and generate no side effects, establish prices that represent the marginal social values that people place on these items.

In recent times we have recognized another source of natural resource value: the value of natural resources in terms of the **nonextractive** services they provide—scenic values, support for outdoor recreation, biodiversity preservation, and simply the preservation of a meaningful natural heritage.

The opposition between the motives of extraction and preservation produced some monumental conflicts in the 20th century. One of the first and best known was the fight in the early years of the century over converting the Hetch-Hetchy Valley within Yosemite National Park from a scenic natural wonder to a massive dam and reservoir to supply water to San Francisco. A similar fierce debate occurred in the 1960s and 1970s over the construction of a dam in Glen Canyon, Utah, that converted a location of great natural beauty to a large flat-water recreation area. Conflicts continue today: cutting old-growth forests vs. preserving endangered species; drilling for oil in designated wilderness areas; expansion of ski resorts vs. preservation of forest habitat; growth of off-road motor vehicles vs. preservation of natural peace and quiet, and so on.

In the extraction/preservation debate there are a number of important tasks for resource economists. One is to try to look deeply into the basic nature of the choice that confronts society in these cases. Preserved resources are usually unique; extracted resources usually are not. Extraction often results in irreversible changes in natural resource assets; preservation normally does not. In light of these factors, normal principles of rational choice may suggest that we adopt conservative decision strategies that will prolong our natural resource options. We discuss this topic at greater length in chapter 7.

Resource economists also can contribute to this debate by assessing the economic consequences of shifting resources from extractive to preservation uses, especially the consequences in terms of the distribution of costs. Programs to reduce or change the extraction rates of particular resources usually have important impacts on the extractive industries formed for this purpose. Proposals to reduce timber harvesting in a certain region, for example, impact people in transport and mill operations in that locale. Plans to reduce fishery catch rates inevitably lead to cutbacks in employment in the fishing fleet. Very often the costs of preservation programs are disproportionately borne by relatively small groups of people. It is important for economic analysts to identify this situation when it exists and to help provide the data and analysis on which compensation might be devised.

Natural Resource Accounting

Resource valuation is important in order to provide the basis for **natural resource accounting**. This involves estimating the value of ecosystem services provided by a country's natural resource endowment, so that such values can be included along with standard output measures in the national economic accounts. An example of this is the measurement of flood control values produced by many forested areas or the wildlife preservation values produced by public parks or other wildlife refuge areas.

In 2014 the **gross domestic product** (GDP) of the United States was $17,150 billion. This figure is an estimate of the total value of "final" goods and services produced in the economy; that is, goods and services supplied to households and other consumers. Among the countries of the world, increases in GDP are normally associated with growth and progress. They support growing populations and make it possible to enjoy increases in per capita wealth and human welfare.

But conventional GDP measures are deficient in a number of respects. One important problem is that they measure only the value of goods and services that move through markets. So, for example, the value of volunteer work done in the country is not included, nor is the value of work done in the household by members of those households. Another problem is that traditional GDP measures do not allow for **natural resource depletion.** Adjustments are normally made for the depreciation of human-produced capital goods—buildings, equipment, and the like—which, in the normal functioning of an economy, will be used up to some extent. Deducting capital depreciation from gross economic output leads to a measure of net output.

But depreciation may also occur in a society's **natural resource capital.** The production of conventional goods and services requires inputs from the natural environment, both in traditional forms, such as minerals, timber, water, and agricultural land, and in the less widely recognized nontraditional services such as biological diversity, carbon fixation, and nutrient recycling. Natural resources supply important scenic resources that are fundamental to the large outdoor recreation and tourism industries. The resource base from which these goods and services are supplied can clearly be depreciated as a result of their use. Quantitatively, resources such as minerals used today reduce the stock available for future generations. Qualitatively, ecosystems may be impacted so much that they lose productivity, as in the case of soil erosion.

Resource valuation is especially important in countries of the developing world, particularly those whose economies depend heavily on natural resources. **Sustainable development** in these settings requires that the reductions in the value of their natural resource capital be offset by increases in other forms of productive capital. Estimating the value of natural resource stocks is one important task of **ecological economics**, a new discipline that tries to combine the principles of economics and ecology to produce more powerful ways of examining the roles of natural resources and the impacts of economic activity on natural resource systems.

■ Policy Issues

Natural resource policy refers to public actions taken to influence the rate at which natural resources are used. Policy analysis in resource economics normally involves two steps:

1. identification of an **optimal** utilization rate, and
2. determination of steps that can be taken to move society toward the optimum.

Defining the Optimum

"Optimal" means "best" according to some specified criteria. Optimal use rates depend on many factors, such as the value of the resource in alternative uses, rates of natural replenishment, environmental factors, expected demographic and technological trends, and so on. The challenge to those who study these matters is to apply theories and models that capture the important complexities of the real world, but give results that are comprehensible to others.[10]

A number of criteria might be analyzed to identify what is optimal in any specific case. One of these is **social efficiency,** defined as the maximum of **net benefits** (total benefits minus total costs) accrued by members of a society. This is an important concept in later chapters of this book. Another criterion is sustainability, which can be defined in a number of ways but generally refers to maintaining or augmenting some valued index of human or ecosystem welfare. Another is **irreversibility,** meaning to avoid actions that may cut off important future situations, such as the destruction of certain unique natural resources. Still another is **fairness,** in the sense of identifying actions that impact people in ways that are regarded as equitable.

As an example, consider the case of suburban wildlife, especially deer. In many communities deer populations have exploded because of dispersed human development, the presence of good food sources, and the lack of substantial predators. The **benefits** and **costs** of having these wildlife populations have become controversial in many cases, leading to more explicit efforts to identify population numbers that might be called an optimal herd size in specific circumstances. As many communities have found, this is not an easy thing to do. Society is composed of many people and groups, and what is optimal for one may not be for another.

Moving toward the Optimum

Identifying optimal use rates is only part of the problem; the next job is to consider actual use rates and, if they differ, look for ways of moving toward the optimum. There are many possible approaches to accomplish this: public and private, individual and collective, command and control and incentive-based, regulatory and voluntary, and more.

Most economies around the world are based, to a greater or lesser extent, on the use of markets to determine what, and how, goods and services get made and distributed, including goods and services that are resource based. In the first set of chapters we will lay out the simple analytics of market operation, from a conceptual point of view. In the real world, private markets, in which participants represent their own interests,[11] can work very effectively to guide production and distribution. But there are many circumstances where that is not the case, where private markets, left to themselves, lead to the mismanagement of natural resources. When that happens some type of public policy action may be called for.

Policy action usually involves **government action** of one type or another, at the local, state, or federal level. Sometimes it is **regulatory action,** in which resource owners and users are required to perform in certain ways, with penalties if they don't. Examples are regulations on permissible fishing equipment and catch limits, rules on water use for crop irrigation, and rules on clear cutting to protect an endangered animal. These are sometimes called **command-and-control** policies.

Public policies also include fundamental changes in a nation's **economic institutions**. Institutions refer to the underlying organizations, laws, and practices that a society deploys to structure its economic activity. Markets are economic institutions, as are corporations, the body of commercial law, public agencies, and so on. Especially important for natural resource management are property rights, as discussed earlier. Another example of institutional change is the formation of local groups for the purpose of managing important local natural resources.

We will consider these matters again in chapter 7 and will encounter them repeatedly in later chapters dealing with specific resources.

■ Land-Use Issues

In the ebb and flow of public concern about high-profile natural resource issues—like endangered species, mining in national parks, and grazing fees on the public range—it is sometimes easy to overlook one resource problem that is faced virtually every day by communities everywhere: **the use of the land.** Land is a resource in the sense that it is capable of producing distinctive goods and services; it is also a resource because it is the spatial plane on which most human activity takes place. Humans use portions of the earth's surface for myriad purposes: housing, work locations, roads and other transportation corridors, farms, parks, and wilderness areas. Land is also the critical supporting medium for other biological resources of all types.

In most countries of the developed world, decisions on how particular pieces of land will be devoted to particular uses are made through a complex mixture of private land markets and public oversight. Land markets in the United States are extremely well developed, with sophisticated surveying, deed registration, title transfer practices, and courts to adjudicate disputes. But there is a long history of public intervention in land issues, to provide essential public services like roads, to regulate the economic and technical impacts that adjoining or propinquitous parcels of land have on one another, and to manage human impacts on portions of the natural environment. In doing this, communities have developed a large arsenal of regulatory tools, such as zoning, conservation restrictions, subdivision regulations, and outright land purchase.

Exhibit 1-2 discusses a technique used by many states for preserving agricultural land uses. In certain places, agricultural preservation is important for cultural, scenic, and/or food supply reasons and so officials have looked for ways to slow the rate at which agricultural land is converted to other uses, such as home lots. The approach is **development rights purchase,** whereby public authorities purchase only the right to develop from farmers, leaving them with the remaining rights on their land and the freedom to farm the land as they wish. This allows some farmers to

Exhibit 1-2   Development Rights in Land

In a purchase of development rights (PDR) program, a landowner voluntarily sells his or her development rights to a government agency or land trust. The agency/trust pays the landowner the difference between the value of the land in its current use and the land's potential development value.

Example: If a farmer's land is worth $2,000 per acre for agricultural use and $5,000 an acre for development, the farmer can sell his development rights for $3,000 per acre. When the sale occurs, a legal document called a **conservation easement** is created. This easement restricts, in perpetuity, the use of the land to farming, open space, and wildlife habitat. The farmer retains private ownership of the land and can sell it, hold it, or pass it on to heirs.

The concept of selling development rights is tied to private property rights. Landowners in the United States enjoy several rights: water rights, air rights, mineral rights, the right to sell land, the right to develop it, the right to pass it on to heirs, and the right to use the land in different ways. A landowner can choose to separate individual property rights, and can sell, donate, or otherwise encumber these rights. In addition, property rights may be limited by the government through its power of eminent domain, right to zone, use of police power, and right to tax.

There are several conservation easement concepts:

- It is a voluntary program. No one is forced to sell his or her development rights.

- The land remains private property. The landowner is only selling the right to develop the land.

- The land is protected from development in perpetuity through a legal document known as a conservation easement.

continue farming but also to realize a large share of the development value of their lands. This clearly improves their financial position, and the hope is that it will enable them to continue operating their farms. This may be easier because of the tax advantages stemming from sale of the development rights.

It is easy to see how economic analysis plays an important role in cases like this. Local land markets are usually very finely tuned institutions; they normally react quickly to new stimuli (e.g., rumors of a new office building going up in town), and they can be very hard to guide in particular directions because of the substantial incentives they give to participants. The effects of purchasing development rights may be to protect land from development, but not necessarily to ensure the preservation of farming. We look at some of the major dimensions of land economics in chapter 14.

◼ Natural Resources and Globalization

Few economic stories have caught the public's attention and imagination more in recent years than the phenomenon called **globalization**. Globalization appears to involve inexorable, worldwide forces that are fundamentally changing the way people live. Proponents point out the advantages of globalization and the positive impacts it can have on the welfare of people in diverse circumstances around the world. Critics stress the economic and social threats to which many people will be exposed as globalization rolls onward in apparently ever-strengthening waves.

A major, perhaps the major, implication of globalization is increased trade among the nations of the world. In 2012 total global exports—that is, aggregate exports of all countries—amounted to about one-third of total world economic activity. Approximately one-quarter of all global merchandise exports consisted of natural resources, the bulk of which were agricultural goods, fuels, and nonfuel minerals.

Increased trade can be expected to produce higher total output and incomes in the trading countries. Or can it? The economic notion behind trade is the theory of comparative advantage. Countries can specialize in the economic activities they are good at (in the relative, not absolute, sense). By so doing, simple economic theory indicates they can increase their livelihoods above the level they could attain if they were to remain outside the international trading system. For the most part, economic studies confirm the stimulating effect of external trade; countries that trade extensively have healthier economies than those that don't.

But do the higher levels of output stimulated by trade lead to greater stress on natural resources (see exhibit 1-3)? While the theory of compara-

Exhibit 1-3 The Plundering of Nauru

Nauru is a small speck of an island in the western Pacific. Historically it had a population of about 10,000 people, though now it has only about 600 residents. In 1907 mining began on a newly discovered phosphate deposit. The mining was carried out largely by Australian firms, and by the time Nauru gained independence in 1968, more than half of the phosphate had been mined and exported.

Mining continued under local control. Substantial amounts of the resource rents were spent on short-term consumption rather than investments for the long run. Several public funds were set up, including the Nauru Phosphate Royalties Trust, but these funds were not managed wisely, and were subject to appropriation by politically connected individuals. Thus the funds in the public accounts have been substantially dissipated.

Outmigration from Nauru has been strong. Those who remain have ended up with a seriously degraded natural environment, basically a moonscape of old phosphate mines. Here is a stark example where the rents from extracting and exporting a natural resource were not used wisely to overcome the effects of the diminished resource value. Similar cases analogous to this, though perhaps not so extreme, have happened in many other countries where the forces of globalization have overpowered local conservation efforts.

For more on Nauru and other cases of this type see Naazneen H. Barma, K. Kaiser, T. Minh, and L. Viñuela, *Rents to Riches? The Political Economy of Natural Resource-Led Development*, The World Bank, Washington, DC, 2012. Also, a good article on Nauru is "Paradise Well and Truly Lost," *The Economist*, December 22, 2001.

tive advantage says there are mutual gains for countries that engage in trade, it doesn't deal directly with natural resource implications. In fact, it is easy to find cases where increased trade has led to very substantial impacts on resources—some so severe that they may threaten the long-term economic health of the countries involved. Exhibit 1-3 discusses a particularly egregious case of this.

We will discuss these issues at greater length in chapter 21. Suffice it to say here that globalization does not invariably mean the degradation of natural resources. We will see cases where countries have managed their resources sustainably, and in a way that has contributed to achievements in their economic welfare. But we will learn that this doesn't happen automatically; it has to be done with appropriate public oversight and effective regulatory enforcement.

■ Summary

One of the most important forces affecting natural resource management and utilization is global climate change. For example, we can expect new challenges in water supply in many parts of the world, too little in some places and too much in others. Sustainability, in terms of long-term natural resource adequacy, has long been a concern in natural resource use. Many people have predicted that resource scarcities will undermine economic growth, but these have not yet occurred. Opinion about future resource supplies is divided among optimists, pessimists, and those in the middle. Other resource issues are the shift from extractive to nonextractive forms of natural resource use, the determination of optimal rates of use, the study of policies to bring about these optimal rates, the role of natural resources in developing countries, how basic economic institutions such as property rights regimes affect resource-use rates, and the impacts of globalization on natural resources.

Notes

[1] The IPCC is the Intergovernmental Panel on Climate Change, a United Nations-sponsored body charged with bringing together the results of worldwide research on the climate implications of human activity. This fifth major report was published in March 2014: *Climate Change 2014: Impacts, Adaptation, and Vulnerability.*

[2] The battle was the subject of the 1974 film by Roman Polanski called *Chinatown*. The battle still goes on, as evidenced by the 2015 mandated cutbacks in water consumption.

[3] T. R. Malthus, *An Essay on Population*, London, 1798.

[4] George Perkins Marsh, *Man and Nature*, Belknap Press of Harvard University Press, Cambridge, MA, 1965, pp. 7–9.

[5] Donella H. Meadows, et al., *The Limits to Growth: A Report for the Club of Rome's Project on the Predicament of Mankind*, Universe Books, New York, 1972.

[6] An example is Mark Hertsgaard, *Earth Odyssey: Around the World in Search of Our Environmental Future*, Broadway BDD, New York, 1999.

[7] A good early example of the optimist school is the report put out by the Hudson Institute, a think tank specializing in trying to discern future trends; see Herman Kahn, William Brown, and Leon Martel, *The Next 200 Years*, William Morrow, New York, 1976. Other optimist works

are Julian Simon, *The Ultimate Resource 2*, Princeton University Press, Princeton, NJ, 1996; and Sue Anne Batey Blackman and William J. Baumol, "Natural Resources," *The Concise Encyclopedia of Economics*, Library of Economics and Liberty, www.econ.lib.org/library/Encl/Natural Resources.

[8] This is not to be confused with the idea of rent you pay to your landlord for your room or apartment.

[9] For more information about this phenomenon see Ian Bannon and Paul Collier, eds., *Natural Resources and Violent Conflict: Options and Actions*, World Bank, 2003.

[10] In economics a "model" is a simplified way of depicting how important factors (e.g., resource use rates, technical change, population growth) are interrelated and how changes in one factor can affect changes in others.

[11] We are not saying that they think only of themselves; just that they do not operate in the market under false pretenses.

Useful Websites

For general reviews of current natural resource issues, log on to:

- Resources for the Future (http://www.rff.org), a resource and environmental think tank in Washington DC that pioneered the application of economic analysis to these problems
- Environmental Defense Fund (http://www.edf.org), a public interest group that emphasizes economic analysis
- World Resources Institute (http://www.wri.org), for an international perspective
- National Library for the Environment (http://www.sustainable.org/environment/biodiversity/378-national-library-for-the-environment)

Public agencies are good sources of overview material, such as:

- United States Department of the Interior (http://www.doi.gov)
- Natural Resources Canada (http://www.nrcan.gc.ca)
- United Kingdom Department of Environment, Transport, and the Regions (http://www.gov.uk)

Selected Readings

Holecheck, Jerry L., et al. *Natural Resources: Ecology, Economics and Policy*, 2nd ed. New York: Prentice-Hall, 2002.

Howe, Charles W. *Natural Resource Economics*. Malden, MA: Wiley, 1979.

Macdonnell, Lawrence J., and Sarah F. Bates, eds. *Natural Resource Policy and Law: Trends and Directions*. Covelo, CA: Island Press, 1993.

Miller, Alan S. *Gaia Connections: An Introduction to Ecology, Ecoethics, and Economics*. Lanham, MD: Rowman and Allenheld, 1991.

Wu, Jungie, Paul W. Barkley, and Bruce H. Weber, eds. *Frontiers in Resource and Rural Economics*. Washington, DC: Resources for the Future, 2007.

2

Natural Resources and the Economy

An economy is a means by which a group of people provide themselves with adequate, and perhaps improving, levels of material and social welfare. In general, we associate economies with societies defined by national boundaries: the U.S. economy, the Japanese economy, the South African economy, and so on. Sometimes, however, we speak of the global economy, or of subnational economies such as one for a particular region or community.

All individuals play two roles in an economy—producers and consumers. In managing its economy, a society makes critical decisions about goods and services, including how much, when, and where to provide these services and the means through which this will be accomplished. They also make fundamental decisions about how these goods and services will be distributed, who among them will have access to them, and on what terms. In a market-type economy, these decisions result from the voluntary interactions of producers and consumers through market institutions. Such decisions are normally accompanied by varying degrees of public oversight and regulation through governmental institutions of different types.

■ Nature and Economy

Society is surrounded by, or encompassed within, a natural world. There are many ways of describing that natural system in physical terms.[1] At any point in time it can be described by a series of variables specifying the quantitative and qualitative status of the system. The **quantitative** variables consist of stock variables (e.g., acres of forest, tons of marine biomass) and flow variables (e.g., energy striking the surface of the earth, wind speed), while the **qualitative** variables describe important features of the resources (e.g., parts per million of air pollution, salinity and temperature of water) at particular points of time. Biological and physical laws describe how these variables are transformed from one time to another.

A fruitful way of thinking about the natural resource system and its relationship to human welfare is to think of it as a stock of **natural capital** that, in conjunction with other types of inputs, yields useful **goods and ser-**

19

vices. The word "capital" has been used historically in economics to refer to a stock of human-produced artifacts, such as tools, machines, and buildings.[2] The concept of natural capital is useful because it combines the notion of nature-provided inputs with the idea that their quantity and quality can be affected by human actions.

Natural capital, in conjunction with other inputs, produces a wide variety of goods and services. We can discuss these under two rubrics, as depicted in figure 2-1. The arrow labeled (a) depicts the flow of natural resource **products and services** into an economy. **Natural resource economics** is the study of this flow using the analytical tools of economics. We must think of this broadly, as encompassing both traditional extractive uses and the services provided by natural resource preservation. The arrow labeled (b) represents the flow of materials and energy **residuals** back into the natural world. This flow is the main subject of **environmental economics.**

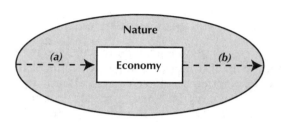

Figure 2-1   Nature and Economy

Which particular parts of the natural world have value depends on the characteristics of the society and economy in question. At any point in time an economic system contains a variety of **technological capabilities** (e.g., different modes of production, distribution, and communication); **economic, legal, and regulatory institutions** (e.g., private business firms, a court system, commercial law, public agencies); and an important array of **demographic factors** (e.g., tastes and preferences, population sizes, skill levels, educational institutions). It is these technological, institutional, and demographic facts that transform arbitrary elements of nature into natural resources. One hundred years ago petroleum was not a natural resource, nor was bauxite or uranium. Seventy years ago, water resources as the provider of recreational services were almost unknown. In recent years **biological diversity** has become an important natural resource. One hundred years from now some feature of the natural world that is currently unknown may have great social value—and may be, in other words, a valuable natural resource.

So the notion of natural resources as portions of the natural world that have value must be understood in the broadest sense. We must recognize that there are dimensions of nature that may become more valuable in the future when human institutions are very different from those of today. Thus social value incorporates what we would regard as the future potentials of the natural world in addition to those portions being used today.

The return flow labeled (b) in the diagram highlights services being provided by nature in the form of a "sink" for the reception of wastes. Some of these wastes may be rendered more benign through changes that are produced by the **assimilative capacity** of the environment. Some may accumulate and produce various types of negative impacts on human welfare and the health of the ecosystems comprising the natural world.

There is clearly a close relationship between natural resource economics and environmental economics. The laws of physics assure us that what is taken in by the economy, in terms of material and energy, must eventually come out. So the decisions undertaken in the context of flow (*a*) will have a lot to do with the problems that have to be addressed under flow (*b*). But convention, and the advantages of dividing the whole subject into several manageable portions, leads us to focus in this book on the resource side of the system.[3]

Some might argue that this way of framing things tends to imply that the worth of the natural world is exclusively, or primarily, in terms of its significance for human beings.[4] Nature, it is sometimes said, has value in and of itself, independent of the wishes of people. We leave it to philosophers to argue about whether nonhuman organisms or entities of the natural world express values for different states of that world. This book is about how human values lead people to make decisions about natural resources. Some of these decisions may involve our preserving elements of the natural world in their undisturbed state, insofar as this can be done. We may be motivated simply by our desire to be good stewards of nature, or by the fear that we don't completely understand how nature affects human welfare. But these decisions express our human values as clearly as does the cutting down of a tree to make 2 × 4's.

Of course the primary concept in natural resource management is **conservation.** Battles have been fought over the meaning and application of this word.[5] It clearly has something to do with saving—or reducing—waste, but historically it has been used to cover everything from dam building, so as to reduce the "waste" implied by water runoff, to a state of moral commitment from which to launch political attacks on all the supposed villains of economic excess. Today we may say that conservation is the idea of using natural resources at a rate that is, in some sense, **socially** optimal. Of course, what is optimal for one person or group is not the same as what is correct for another, but the term does seemingly connote a course of action that finds an appropriate balance among diverse motives and avoids action that leads to waste and excessive damage.

One fault line that continues to run through public discussion is that between resource **development** and resource **preservation.** Development refers to actions that transform natural resources to a greater or lesser extent, presumably with the intent of increasing their contribution to the welfare of human beings. Preservation, on the other hand, connotes putting resources aside in a state of nonuse or in a state such that whatever use is allowed basically maintains the original status of the resource. An important modern version of this term is **scientific preservation,** in which the conflicts over development and preservation are analyzed and illuminated with sound scientific tools, especially the tools of natural science, rather than consigned solely to the emotionally charged arena of the political struggles. The most recent incarnation of this concept is **ecosystem management,** the idea of resource management decisions based on sound principles of ecological science.

■ The Range of Natural Resource Services

A minimal classification of natural resources would perhaps be (1) land resources, (2) water resources, and (3) air resources. But we need to move well beyond this delineation if we are to get a more complete understanding of the number and variety of goods and services that nature provides. As a first step in this direction we distinguish between use values and nonuse values. **Use value** implies that attributes of nature are being utilized in some sense. This sense may be the classic one, such as when water is used to irrigate crops, which are then harvested and consumed. But the sense of use may not involve traditional consumption. White-water rafting and bird watching are activities that use resources in a different sense. Scenic values involve use only in the sense that natural resources are simply present to the senses. **Nonuse values,** on the other hand, are values expressed by human beings simply for the **existence** of natural resources. Existence may be related to prospects for future use, called **option value,** or the desire to leave a healthy ecosystem to future generations, called **bequest value.** People may not be using a resource at present, but may prefer actions that will ensure that the resource is available in the future, should they or future generations wish to utilize it later; in other words, it is worth something to preserve the option. But people also hold true existence values, not linked to present or possible future use. Such values may of course be harder to assess and measure in particular cases, but they are nonetheless real and relevant to the full set of incentives that motivate human decisions.

Table 2-1 contains a catalog of use values. These are broken down into extractive and nonextractive resources. **Extractive resources** are those subject to some process of physical removal from their natural surrounding and perhaps physical transformation during their use. Classic cases include mining ores of various types and harvesting timber and converting it to building materials. Commercial fishing, as well as much recreational fishing and hunting, are also extractive. It is common to use the term **natural resource products** (or **commodities**) to refer to quantities of physical resources that have been removed from nature and made available for use.

Nonextractive resources are those that yield valuable services without being removed from their natural setting. The classic example of a nonextractive resource is resource-based recreation, such as backpacking and river rafting. Many resources produce both extractive products and nonextractive services. Forests may produce both timber and backpacking. Water can be used for municipal and industrial water supplies and for boating.

Another important nonextractive resource service is **ecosystem protection.** One part of a resource system provides support and protection for other parts. Wetlands, for example, are usually integral parts of wider

Table 2-1   Classification of Natural Resources

Natural resource	Natural resource products and services	
	Extractive	Nonextractive
Minerals	Nonfuel (bauxite) Fuel (coal)	Geological services (weathering)
Forests	Forest products (timber)	Recreation (backpacking) Ecosystem protection (flood control, CO_2 sequestration)
Land	Fertility	Space, scenic values
Plants	Food and fiber (agricultural crops, wild food crops) Biodiversity products (medicinal plants)	Erosion control, soil enrichment, scenic values
Terrestrial animals	Food and fiber (farm animals, wild game) Biodiversity products (genetic variability)	Recreational services (bird watching, ecotourism)
Fisheries	Food (saltwater and freshwater fish)	Recreational services (recreational fishing, whale watching)
Water	Municipal and industrial supplies, irrigation	Recreation (boating)
Meteorological services	Energy sources (geothermal)	Energy sources (solar) Global radiation balances Radio spectrum Natural disasters

hydraulic systems, so their retention is important in providing protection for water resources that are subject to direct extraction, such as groundwater aquifers. Forests often provide important services in flood control and the regulation of water quality. Land and water resources in coastal areas provide important services in terms of mitigating storm damage.

The newest resource, biological diversity, is perhaps a special type of extractive resource. Diversity is not a feature of one ecosystem or species or gene, but of a collection of them. But the justification for preservation of diversity is often expressed in extractive terms, as a source of diversity-type products like medicines and plant characteristics. Diversity may also be important in general ecosystem maintenance. Preservation of diversity normally implies a shift away from traditional types of extractive activities.

We normally think of nature as the repository of useful goods and services, but it also supplies negative services; that is, services that may have negative value, at least to human beings. In an average year natural disasters—earthquakes, floods, volcano eruptions—cause enormous damage around the world. Some of these are exacerbated by human impacts on natural resources, e.g., deforestation. In all cases intelligent adjustments are necessary to manage these impacts at acceptable levels.

The dividing line between extractive and nonextractive resources is sometimes ambiguous. Some extractive resources are not necessarily transformed during use or entirely lost to nature. Water that is extracted from an aquifer or river and used for irrigation may flow back into the hydraulic system at a different location, although possibly in diminished quantity and perhaps also degraded in terms of quality. The flow of zoo animals is extractive in the sense that they are removed from their natural habitats, but no physical conversion is involved. Soil fertility may be thought of as extractive in one sense, in that agricultural practices may lead to its temporary or permanent diminution. In another sense it is nonextractive, since appropriate steps can be taken for its maintenance.

■ Modeling Resource Services

There are several other ways of distinguishing among types of natural resource goods and services. In order to discuss them, however, we will adopt a slightly more formal approach. In later chapters we use simple analytical models to examine various natural resource problems. The material that follows in this section gives us a chance to start thinking in ways that are somewhat more formal and abstract, but that preserve the essence of the resource situations we want to study.

Natural resource management decisions are complex because they involve connections and trade-offs between the present and the future. The connections stem from the characteristics of the resource itself, such as its biology or chemistry, and the way they are impacted by human use. Consider a situation in which there are just two time periods, period 0 and period 1. In effect, period 0 could stand for today and period 1 for some time in the future, but to keep it simple think of period 0 as this year and period 1 as next year.[6]

The basic structure of a general resource-use problem can now be set up in the following way. Suppose that there is a certain quantity of a resource available at the beginning of period 0. During that period the resource is "used" in some amount. It is easiest to think of "use" in this case as extraction in the traditional sense. But we can also interpret it in other ways. The other thing that may happen during the first period is some amount of replenishment or growth of the resource, the amount of which depends on the type of resource involved. All these factors contribute to the quantity of the resource available in period 1.

We can express the basic relationship as follows:

Amount of resource available in period 1 (S_1)	=	Amount of resource available in period 0 (S_0)	−	Amount of resource used in period 0 (Q_0)	+	Increment to the resource in period 0 (ΔS)

It is easier to write this expression in terms of the symbols shown in parentheses under each one:

$$S_1 = S_0 - Q_0 + \Delta S$$

The critical term is ΔS, representing the added increment of the resource that becomes available during period 0.[7] By interpreting ΔS in different ways, we can use the basic expression to describe many different types of resources.

Nonrenewable Resources

The most straightforward application of the general expression is a **nonrenewable resource.** For a known deposit of such a resource, we have $\Delta S = 0$; that is, there is no replenishment or increment of the resource. This being the case, the basic accounting expression becomes $S_1 = S_0 - Q_0$; the quantity available in the next period (S_1) is the quantity that was available at the beginning of the present period (S_0) minus the quantity used in this period (Q_0). The classic example is a mineral deposit containing a given quantity of material. It is true that very long-run geological processes may be creating new deposits, but in terms of the time spans that are relevant to generations of human beings, total quantities are effectively fixed in amount.

A resource in one circumstance may be renewable; in another circumstance it may not be. Groundwater is held in underground geological formations, or aquifers. In this case, ΔS is the **recharge quantity,** the quantity that flows into the formation during a year. In some cases ΔS is essentially zero, making that aquifer a nonrenewable resource. In other cases $\Delta S > 0$, making it a renewable resource.

The basic character of a nonrenewable resource changes if we move from considering a single deposit to considering all known deposits. Over a period of time, **exploration and development** can add to the quantity of the known stock. In this case ΔS is the quantity added to existing stocks through discovery and development. In fact this makes the situation quite complex because "new" deposits come in a variety of forms. For example, a deposit can be new in the sense of recent geological discovery, or it may be "new" in the sense that we have a new technology capable of extracting it, as compared to last year when it was geologically known but essentially beyond our reach.

What this tells us is that the distinction between renewable and nonrenewable resources is only partly a physical one. It is also partly an economic one. The decision to put more effort into resource exploration is economic; it uses resources and has certain potentials in terms of benefits. Resource development, based on human actions, can convert cases that seemingly involve nonrenewable resources into cases of renewable resources.

Don't be fooled by the fact that this demonstration includes only two time periods. Of course public and private resource planning will involve multiple time periods, starting now and stretching into the future. Our studies of water, timber, minerals, biodiversity, and other resources will reflect this. Here we use a two-period model simply to demonstrate the logic of the underlying resource decision process.

Recyclable Resources

Certain nonrenewable resources may be **recyclable.** A portion of the resource used in period 0 can be recycled back to add to the available supply in period 1. Here the basic expression may be rewritten as:

$$S_1 = S_0 - Q_0 + \alpha Q_0$$

where α is a percentage indicating the proportion of the first year's use that is returned via recycling. Here two basic decisions are to be made, the utilization rate Q_0 and the recycling ratio α.

Renewable Resources

A **renewable resource** is one that replenishes itself in some fashion. In this case $\Delta S > 0$, so the quantities available in period 1 are affected by the replenishment process. This may be a biological process, as for example in the case of fisheries or timber. For a forest, the amount of wood (in, for example, cubic feet) in year 1 is what existed at the beginning, minus that which was harvested during period 0, plus the biological growth increment of the timber that was not harvested. The size of the growth increment will be related to the size of the population and also to other features of the ecosystem, such as climate.

Most biological growth processes involve **accumulation** to some degree; the resource growth adds to the resource stock. Certain types of renewable resources are nonaccumulating. Consider a free-flowing river, for example. Each year a certain (no doubt fluctuating) amount of water comes down the river; this is a meteorological and geographical fact of life. But it flows by a given point and then is gone. Thus the annual replenishment does not add to any preexisting quantity. In this case our basic relationship changes to the following:

$$S_1 = \Delta S$$

The amount of the resource available in period 1 now does not depend on the rate of use during period 0.

Of course if somebody were to build a reservoir on the river, the situation would change. Now the incoming flow would augment whatever was left in the reservoir from the previous year, changing a nonaccumulating resource into an accumulating one, at least to some degree. Another example of a nonaccumulating renewable resource is the incoming stream of solar energy that strikes the earth each year. The stream itself is nonaccumulating, though of course all the biological processes it makes possible on earth represent accumulating phenomena.

This accounting expression can be applied to land resources, but it will look different according to the exact way we define the resource. If we write the formula for the total land area in a given geographical region, such as a town, the expression is simply $S_1 = S_0$. In other words, the total area is fixed and unchanging (barring political changes in town boundaries). But if we define our resource of interest as, for example, land devoted to a particular use, such as housing developments, wetlands, or land used for agriculture, it would look like

$$S_1 = S_0 - Q_0 + \Delta S$$

where Q_0 is the amount of acreage taken out of that use during the year (e.g., number of acres devoted to new housing development) and ΔS is the amount of land put back into that use (e.g., wetlands restored, if our S variable of interest is acreage of wetlands).

An important feature of some natural resources is **reversibility**, expressed in terms of either quantity or quality. Usage of a natural resource is reversible if it is possible that $S_1 > S_0$. By definition, utilization of a nonrenewable resource is irreversible, at least as long as we are talking about a particular deposit. Most renewable resources are reversible; if extraction is lowered sufficiently, the natural replenishment will cause the stock to increase, at least up to some biological maximum. But many renewable resources, especially biological resources, may have **thresholds** that, once past, render the resource irreversibly changed. The classic case is a population of wildlife in which the number of adults falls below a level sufficient to support reproduction greater than mortality, and hence evolves irreversibly toward extinction. More complex cases occur, for example, where characteristics of species diversity change in an ecosystem sufficiently to set in motion forces that bring about permanent changes in many structural and functional features of that ecosystem.

With renewable resources much policy attention is directed at **habitat improvement.** In terms of the fundamental equation above, this can be interpreted as an effort to affect ΔS, the growth rate of the resource, to achieve a generally higher level of S_0, the initial quantity (population) of the resource.

■ Some Concepts of Economics

This is a book about **economic analysis.** To analyze something means to examine its basic structure and the cause-and-effect relationships that govern the way it works. So to analyze the problems of saltwater fisheries, for example, we will try to understand the basic **bioeconomic** operation of the interconnected system that includes the growth and decline of fish stocks together with the human fishing effort expended on them. When we look at the role of natural resources in economic development and growth, we must try to understand the main linkages between natural resource stocks and such processes as imports, exports, and rates of growth in gross domestic product (GDP).

To pursue these analyses we need to:

1. look at the **data** that tell us what has happened historically and what the current situation is with respect to particular natural resources, and

2. develop simple **analytical models** with which to explore the interconnections among the important elements of each situation.

A **model** in economics is an explanatory construct built up from some underlying principles and concepts and used to examine the behavior of the economy, or some part of it. For example, the market model is built up from underlying principles of supply and of demand. The model we use to look at issues of wildlife management contains both economic and biological concepts. A prime feature of economic models is that they are **abstract.** You got a little taste of that in the preceding section where we explored the differences among types of resources. A model is abstract when it focuses on underlying relationships and leaves out the many factors that are not relevant to understanding those basic relationships. It is not to say that the factors left out are unimportant, only that they are not considered important in the present context. Often factors are omitted to make a model simple and easy to understand.

Natural resource problems vary over a continuum from relatively small, local issues (which are nevertheless of great importance to local communities), to larger regional problems, to all-encompassing national and global issues. The models that economists use to study these problems must range commensurately in terms of scope and applicability. It is standard to divide economics into microeconomics and macroeconomics. **Microeconomics** (or just "micro" as it is often called) proceeds on the basis of detailed models of individual behavior—of consumers, producers, policy makers, and so on. These models are normally "aggregated" up so that we can derive conclusions about the performance of groups of people. Studying how individual households make choices about their use of water in and around the home—so that we might predict the effects, for example, of a tax on water use—is a problem in microeconomics. So is a study of how the logging industry in, say, Oregon, might respond to a new set of regulations on habitat preservation.

Macroeconomics, on the other hand, takes economies as a whole as the basic unit of analysis. A study on how the U.S. economy might respond to higher energy prices would probably be conducted with a macroeconomic model, one that deals directly with relationships among macro variables, such as the overall rate of unemployment, rates of economic growth, and changes in the growth patterns of major industry groupings. Another type of macroeconomic study would be one that looks at the role played by natural resource endowments in a country's historical pattern of economic growth. Still another would be a study to adjust commonly published measures of macroeconomic performance, for example, GDP, to take into account natural resource depletion.

Many resource problems fall between these two types of analysis, and make use of both. One very common natural resource issue is the performance of a local or regional economy that is based to some degree on the exploitation of a natural resource (e.g., logging or mining), a resource that other groups are trying to have preserved in a natural state. A major factor in trying to determine the best course of action in such a case is knowing how the regional economy is in fact affected by changes in the availability of the resource. To get to the bottom of this we may call on both microeconomics (e.g., how will firms, workers, and consumers behave if the rates change) and macroeconomics (e.g., how will developments in the national economy affect demand for the resource). The conclusion to be drawn from this is that many resource issues call for several different types of analyses, so we need to be ready with a full array of tools to carry them out.

Another important distinction that needs to be made is that between **factual statements** and **value judgments.** In economics these are usually referred to as **positive economics** (factual) and **normative economics** (values). If somebody analyzes the rates at which mineral mining has grown over the last century or the way timber prices have trended over the last few decades, he or she is engaged in positive economics; that is, what has actually happened in the use of these resources in these time periods. Similarly, if somebody studies how log prices and interest rates affect the rate of deforestation in some region or how fishers respond to certain restrictions on their harvesting practices, he or she is also engaged in positive economics: how the world actually works, in terms of the interconnections of economic variables and the resulting rates of output, prices, and so on.

Statements as to what people **ought to do,** on the other hand, fall under the heading of normative economics. If an economist recommends limiting the catch season for a certain species of fish or initiating certain policy changes to reduce the rate of soil erosion, he or she is engaging in normative economics because the recommendations require placing value judgments on different outcomes that could result from different types of behavior.

For us to make headway in better managing the world's natural resources, both types of economics are necessary. Policies need to be enacted and pursued, with the explicit or implicit value judgments they contain. But these policies should be based on our best understanding of how economies and natural systems work. Activists, who are anxious to get on with doing something, are often impatient with analysts who are engaged in strictly positive analysis. The prime motivation of the latter is that better knowledge about how things actually work allows better policies to be created.

■ Policy and Politics

In the chapters that follow we use several criteria to evaluate the performance of natural resource-using individuals and firms and of public agencies pursuing natural resource management policies of different types. Issues of **economic efficiency** and **equity** will be encountered, as will the idea of **sustainability** in resource use. We use these criteria from the perspective of society, meaning that we include all interests and values and not just those of a particular individual or subgroup. But of course people differ in terms of values and in terms of the circumstances they find themselves in, so contention and conflict can easily take place over natural resource valuation and policy actions in particular cases. Analysis has to be undertaken from a particular perspective, but what that perspective should be can sometimes be hard to determine. For example, the United States has the responsibility of establishing and enforcing fisheries regulations in its own coastal waters, as other countries do in theirs. Should these policies be evaluated in terms of how well they represent the interests of the U.S. citizenry, or all of North America, or some other unit? The answers one gets may differ, depending on one's perspective. Exhibit 2-1 discusses a particularly interesting example of the problem in Central Asia.

The problem exists also at local and regional levels. Suppose we wish to evaluate the economic efficiency of a local wetlands-protection regulation. Should we evaluate this strictly from the standpoint of the one community where the wetland is located, the region, the state, or the country? In fact a common bumper sticker reads "Act Locally, Think Globally," which seems to imply that we ought to evaluate all local programs like this in global terms. The upshot of this discussion is simply to clarify that when we use criteria like efficiency or equity **from the social standpoint,** we need to be clear about which particular "society" we are talking about.

Exhibit 2-1   The Caspian Sea

The Caspian Sea is a body of brackish water in Central Asia about the size of California. The northern half is quite shallow and is the main home of the Caspian sturgeon fishery, the primary source of the world's caviar. At various points around its borders, and within the sea itself, petroleum deposits have been exploited in the past. Since 2010 the pace of petroleum-related activity, especially natural gas, has accelerated in the region, and there could be a boom in oil exploration and development in the next few decades, depending on developments in Middle Eastern oil fields and the building of pipelines to get the oil and natural gas to export markets.

Large increases in onshore and offshore fossil-fuel development and production will have huge implications for the environmental quality of the region, especially through their impacts on the aquatic environment of the Caspian Sea. The people of the region will be faced with important and difficult issues about the appropriate balance between economic growth and environmental protection. Identifying and achieving this balance will be hard in light of the environmental uncertainties, political realities, and economic aspirations of people in the region. But the Caspian Sea is bordered by five different countries (Azerbaijan, Iran, Kazakhstan, Russia, and Turkmenistan). Suppose we are trying to evaluate the performance of one of them, say Kazakhstan, regarding the use of Caspian resources and, especially, the development of petroleum resources in the Caspian basin. Suppose further that we are evaluating the cost effectiveness of Kazakhstan's planned program for protecting the water quality of the Caspian Sea during its petroleum-exploration activities. If we were to do this solely from the perspective of this one country, we might get a different answer than if we approached it from the standpoint of all the Caspian countries together. But if we do it from the standpoint of Caspian society in general, what particular group of people should we include?

■ Summary

Natural resource economics is the study of how the flow of goods and services derived from natural resources is, and ought to be, managed in today's world. Resource-management problems derive from the underlying technological, institutional, and cultural factors that characterize an economy. Natural resource economics focuses on resource flows into an economy, whereas the flow out of that economy back into nature is studied under environmental economics. There are many types of natural resource goods and services. One way of thinking about the differences among them is to take a basic accounting identity of resource use, $S_1 = S_0 - Q_0 + \Delta S$, and then alter its several terms to describe natural resources with specific characteristics. The most basic distinction between natural resources is that between renewable and nonrenewable resources. Characteristics such as recyclability and reversibility are very important. When we consider natural resource management issues from the perspective of "society," we must recognize that there can be conflicts among subgroups within the whole.

Notes

1 For example, population ecology looks at how collections of related organisms grow and change, while ecosystem ecology focuses on energy flows among trophic levels and how various biotic processes contribute to ecosystem functions.

2 There are other recognized types of capital: working capital, the financial assets that permit the continuity of production and consumption; and human capital, the capacities and capabilities of human beings.

3 Those who would like a similar treatment of environmental economics may want to look at *Environmental Economics: An Introduction*, by Barry C. Field and Martha K. Field, 7th ed., McGraw-Hill, New York, 2017.

4 This is termed the "anthropocentric" point of view.

5 See the well-known monograph of Samuel P. Hays, *Conservation and the Gospel of Efficiency: The Progressive Conservation Movement, 1890–1920*, Harvard University Press, Cambridge, MA, 1959.

6 Natural resource economics is about time, so we need a way of indexing events in different time periods. The convention that we follow throughout the book is to index today, or the present period, with a zero (e.g., q_0). Subsequent periods follow along; next year is indexed with a one (e.g., q_1), the next with a two, and so on.

7 The symbol Δ is often used to denote the change in a variable.

Key Terms

bequest value	nonrenewable resource
biological diversity	normative economics
economic efficiency and equity	option value
ecosystem management	positive economics
economic models	quantitative
existence value	recyclable resource
extractive and nonextractive	renewable resource
microeconomics and macroeconomics	sustainability
natural capital	use values and nonuse values

Questions for Further Discussion

1. Identify several cases where certain features of the natural environment, which were not regarded as natural resources in the past, are now thought of in those terms.

2. How might the basic resource formula be written to represent the occurrence of natural disasters (i.e., characteristics of nature that have negative values rather than positive values)? How about a natural attribute such as soil fertility?

3. Distinguish between use values and nonuse values in natural resource economics.

4. Consider a particular natural resource issue, for example the allocation of scarce water supplies among competing uses in the western United States. Give an example of a positive statement and a normative statement in the context of this problem.

5. Suppose we are studying the extraction rates of copper ore in the United States over the last decade. There are both macro and micro factors that affect these rates. Give several possible examples of each type.

Useful Websites

For a broad perspective on the goods and services produced by natural resources:

- International Society for Ecological Economics
  (http://www.isecoeco.org)
- Sustainable Earth Exchange for Educators; offers links to a wide variety of websites for resources and the environment
  (http://www.class.csupomona.edu/earth.html)

Selected Readings

Adams, David A. *Renewable Resource Policy: The Legal-Institutional Foundations.* Washington, DC: Island Press, 1993.

Hays, Samuel P. *Conservation and the Gospel of Efficiency.* Cambridge, MA: Harvard University Press, 1959.

Herfindahl, Orris C. "What Is Conservation?" in *Three Studies in Mineral Economics.* Washington, DC: Resources for the Future, 1961.

Howe, Charles. *Natural Resource Economics.* New York: John Wiley, 1979, chapter 1.

Poljman, Louis P., ed. *Environmental Ethics: Readings in Theory and Application,* 6th ed. Boston: Wadsworth, 2012.

Randall, Alan, and John C. Bergstrom. *Resource Economics: An Economic Approach to Natural Resource and Environmental Policy,* 3rd ed. Northampton, MA: Edward Elgar, 2010, chapters 2 and 3.

SECTION II

BUILDING BLOCKS

To understand how natural resources are used and to formulate policies that might influence these rates of use in desirable directions, two strands of knowledge must be brought together: knowledge of how natural ecosystems themselves function and knowledge about human behavior. The first comes from scientists such as biologists, ecologists, meteorologists, and earth scientists. The second comes from social scientists such as economists, political scientists, and sociologists. This book emphasizes economics, the science that deals with values, incentives, and institutions governing the allocation of productive resources[1] and the production of goods and services. This section is devoted, therefore, to the study of a number of primary concepts and relationships in economics. Economics is a cumulative subject. The more complex theories and models used to study complicated real-world problems are always built up from the core concepts. Thus the ideas studied in this chapter, though very simple and rather abstract, are vital to the various natural resource models we develop later to look at specific resource issues.

Virtually any human action affecting natural resources use rates has two consequences: on the one side it normally creates goods or services that have value; on the other side it entails costs. This is true whether the action is a private or public firm extracting or otherwise using a natural resource, or whether some organization, such as a government agency, is pursuing an explicit program of preservation. The discussion is organized around these two sides; first we discuss willingness to pay and **demand** on the output side, and then we get into opportunity cost and **supply** on the input side.

Note

[1] "Resources" has two meanings in economics: On the one hand it is short for "natural resources"; on the other it is often used to refer to all inputs, both natural and otherwise, that are used to produce goods and services. The context is usually sufficient to distinguish the meaning being used.

3

Valuing Natural Resources
Willingness to Pay/Demand

valuation
) value
to end
value
to collective

We begin our discussion of economic concepts with the question of **value**: how do we assess the value of a natural resource? Our procedure is first to think about value to an individual, and then **social value**; that is, value to a collection of individuals.

Some people feel that normal human values should not necessarily be applied to nature, that natural objects or events ought to be privileged over merely human artifacts. They might object to applying the same valuation concept to natural things as we would apply to, for example, shoes. This could mean two things: Either humans put too small a value on nature, perhaps out of ignorance, or we should not make decisions about nature by referring to human values. But all human actions imply valuations, either explicitly or implicitly. So the fundamental issue is—whose valuation should count? For the purposes of the analysis in this book the answer to this will be "everybody's in equal measure."

■ Willingness to Pay

To make this notion of value visible so that it can be observed and measured, we use the idea of willingness to sacrifice. The value that a person puts on something is the amount they are willing to sacrifice to obtain that something, which may be a good, service, or state of being. Sacrifice what? It could be anything. For a hermit the best index might be the time needed to produce some item. In a monetized economy it makes most sense to measure it as willingness to sacrifice generalized purchasing power. Thus we use willingness to pay as our fundamental concept: The value a person places on a good or service is what they are willing to pay to get that good or service.

What determines how much a person is willing to pay to obtain something? Clearly individual tastes and preferences are paramount. Some peo-

35

ple are willing to pay a lot to visit the Grand Canyon; others are not. Some people are willing to pay a lot for white-water recreation opportunities; others are not. Some people place a high value on trying to preserve the habitat of unique animal and plant species; others do not. It is obvious also that a person's **wealth** affects the willingness to sacrifice; the greater his or her wealth, the more a person can afford to pay for various goods and services. Willingness to pay, in other words, also reflects **ability to pay**. Willingness to pay also depends on one's knowledge and experience. For a person who has never left the city, for example, a backpacking experience may open up new opportunities and essentially shift a person's preferences.

It is easy to misunderstand the implications of using willingness to pay as a measure of value, or benefits, of an outcome. It does not imply, for example, that the only things that count are money payments in a market. Many people speak of, and genuinely feel, restorative or spiritual qualities of the natural world—in total, or in terms of specific components (bald eagles, majestic firs, tidal pools, silence . . .). For a person holding these values, or someone who is evaluating the quantity of timber he requires to build his house, willingness to pay simply indicates they would be willing to sacrifice something to attain these ends.

Willingness to Pay Illustrated

"Value" can be a word with many interpretations, but in economics it means the worth that a person, or group of people, place on an outcome, such as the possession of a given quantity of some good or service, or more abstractly on some specified state of the world.

Consider an individual and some arbitrary good or service. We need a way of graphically representing that person's willingness to pay for the item in question. We will use simple numbers for illustrative purposes.

Assume that the person has none of the good to begin with. We ask her, or perhaps deduce from watching her spend her money, how much she would be willing to pay for a single unit of a good rather than go without. Suppose this is some number, say, $38 (see figure 3-1). We then ask, assuming she already has one unit of this good, how much she would be willing to pay for a second unit. According to figure 3-1, her answer is $26. In similar fashion, her willingness to pay for each additional unit is depicted by the height of the rectangle above that unit: $17 for unit 3, $12 for unit 4, and so on. These numbers depict a fundamental relationship of economics: the notion of **diminishing willingness to pay**. As the number of units consumed increases, the willingness to pay for additional units of that good decreases.

Quantity data (e.g., consumption, production) often have a **time dimension** such as pounds consumed per month or year, or tons produced per year. To remind ourselves of this, we could index our variables with a time indication, such as Q/t. In the interest of notational simplicity we will sometimes leave out the explicit time designator, but you should remember that it is in the background.

It is not very convenient to work with diagrams that are step-shaped as in the top of figure 3-1. Assume that people can consume fractions of items in addition to integer values (e.g., pounds of potatoes consumed per week). This produces a smoothly shaped **willingness-to-pay curve,** such as the one pictured in the bottom of figure 3-1. In effect the steps in the willingness-to-pay curve have become too small to see, yielding a smooth curve to work with. On this smooth function we have singled out one quantity for illustrative purposes. It shows that the willingness to pay for the third unit is $17.

The concept in use here is more exactly called **marginal willingness to pay** (MWTP). Suppose a person is already consuming two units of this good; according to figure 3-1,

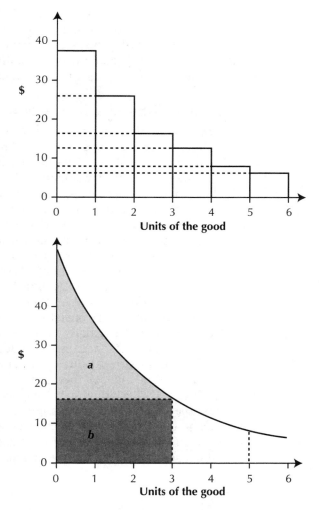

Figure 3-1   The Concept of Willingness to Pay

that person would be willing to pay $17 for a third unit. This is the marginal willingness to pay—in this case, for the third unit. "Marginal" thus describes the additional willingness to pay for one more unit. So the height of the rectangles in the top of figure 3-1 and the height of the curve in the bottom graph show the marginal willingness to pay for this good.

The **total willingness to pay** for a given consumption level refers to the total amount a person would be willing to pay to attain that consumption level rather than go without the good entirely. Suppose the person is consuming at a level of three units; her total willingness to pay for consuming this quantity is $81, which is in fact the sum of the heights of the demand rectangles between the origin and the consumption level in question ($38 for the first plus $26 for the second plus $17 for the third). This corresponds, in the smooth version of the willingness-to-pay function, to the whole area under the marginal willingness-to-pay curve from the origin up to the quantity in question. For three units of consumption, the total willingness to pay is equal to an amount represented by the combined areas *a* and *b*.

Marginal Willingness to Pay and Demand

There is another way of looking at these marginal willingness-to-pay relationships. They are more familiarly known as **demand curves**.[1] An individual demand curve shows the quantity of a good or service that the individual in question would demand (i.e., purchase and consume) at any particular price. For example, suppose a person whose MWTP/demand curve is shown in the bottom part of figure 3-1 is able to purchase this item at a unit price of $17. The quantity he would demand at this price is three units. The reason is that his marginal willingness to pay for each of the first three units exceeds the purchase price. He would not push his consumption higher than this because his marginal willingness to pay for additional quantities would be lower than the purchase price.

An individual's demand/MWTP curve for a good or service is a way of summarizing his personal consumption attitudes and capabilities for that good. Thus, we would normally expect these relationships to differ somewhat among individuals because individual tastes and preferences vary. Figure 3-2 displays several different demand curves. Panel (a) shows two demand curves, one steeper than the other. The steeper one shows a situation in which MWTP drops off fairly rapidly as the quantity consumed increases; the other MWTP, although lower to begin with, goes down less rapidly as quantity increases. These two demand curves could represent the case of one consumer and two different goods or services, or the case of two different consumers and the same good or service.

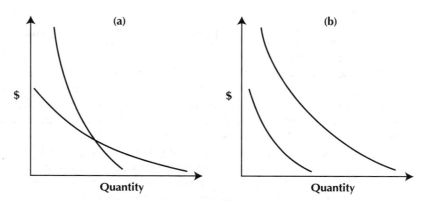

Figure 3-2   Typical Demand/Marginal Willingness-to-Pay Curves

Panel (b) of Figure 3-2 also has two demand curves; they have the same general shape, but one is situated well to the right of the other. The demand curve lying above and to the right shows a good for which the MWTP is substantially higher than it is for the same quantity of the other good. What could account for the difference? They might represent the demand curves of two different people for the same good. But there are other possibilities. How much a person is willing to pay for something obviously depends on how much money she has; more than likely the higher her income, the more she is willing to pay. So the two demand curves in panel (b) could apply to the same individual and the same good, but at two different points in time, the one to the right being her willingness to pay after she has had a substantial increase in income.

There is another way of looking at the two demand curves of panel (b), one that may be very important for the application of these ideas to natural resource assets. People's tastes depend on a variety of psychological and historical factors that are hard to pin down and describe but are nevertheless real. They depend in part on the experiences that people have and the information they gather over time about the qualities of different goods and how they feel about them. So, for example, the demand curve to the right could be the same consumer's demand curve for a good for which his appreciation has increased over time. Perhaps they are demand curves for outdoor wilderness experiences, the one to the left applying before much is known about this type of activity and the one to the right applying after the person has had wilderness experience and learned to enjoy the activity. Other factors that influence a person's tastes are information and psychology; the demand curve on the right might be a person's demand for a good before an announcement of the presence of pesticide residues in it, with the curve on the left being the demand curve after the announcement.

Note that the demand curves are in fact nonlinear rather than straight lines. A straight-line demand relationship would imply a uniform change in the quantity demanded as its price changes. For most goods, however, this is unlikely to be true. At low prices and high rates of consumption, studies have shown that relatively small increases in price will lead to substantial reductions in quantity demanded. At high prices and low quantity demanded, however, price increases have a much smaller effect: They produce much smaller reductions in quantity demanded. This gives us a demand relationship that is convex to the origin; that is, relatively flat at low prices and steep at higher prices. Exhibit 3-1 on the following page discusses this in terms of the demand for gasoline.

Economics is sometimes misunderstood as assuming that people are driven only by thoughts of their own welfare, that they are complete egoists. Because these are individual demand curves, they do indeed summarize the attitudes of single individuals, but this does not imply that individuals make decisions with only themselves in mind. Although some people focus only on themselves, most people are influenced by other powerful motives that affect their demands for different goods, including altruism toward friends and relatives, feelings of civic virtue toward their communities, and a sense

---

Exhibit 3-1   The Demand for Energy for Transportation

People sometimes think of their demands as somewhat fixed, according to their lifestyles. This is often the way people think of their demand for gasoline, for example. Actually, researchers have found these relationships to be somewhat more flexible. In general, as the price of gasoline rises, the total consumption of gasoline declines: Although individual responses differ, depending upon peoples' circumstances and preferences, the total declines.

At relatively low prices, gas consumption is high; because of the low cost of driving, people use their cars with little restraint. At somewhat higher prices, many (though not necessarily all) people begin to think about curtailing unessential driving, perhaps going to the supermarket only once per week rather than two or three times, and riding with somebody else to the movies on the weekend. At still higher prices more thought is given to reducing unessential driving, and at very high prices people have the incentive to carpool, switch to public transit, buy more fuel-efficient vehicles, or, in the long run, move closer to their place of work.

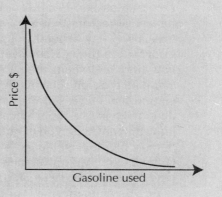

This implies that the demand for gasoline might be shaped as in the diagram. At low and moderate prices, increased prices lead to substantial drops in aggregate consumption because, paradoxically as it might seem, the higher the level of consumption, the easier it is to find ways to cut back. So the demand curve is relatively flat in this range. But at higher prices where most driving is for essential purposes, further price increases lead to smaller drops in consumption, and hence a steeper demand curve.

---

of social responsibility toward fellow citizens. Individual tastes and preferences spring from these factors as well as from more narrow considerations of personal likes and dislikes.

Aggregate Willingness to Pay/Demand for Private Goods

In examining real-world natural resource issues, attention is usually focused on the behavior of groups of people, not single individuals. It could be all people in a single community or region, or all people in the country. It could even be all people in the world. The **aggregate marginal willingness-to-pay curve** is the summation of the marginal willingness-to-pay curves of all the individuals in the group of interest.[2] The aggregate marginal willingness to pay for water by people in California, for example, is the curve that one gets from adding together the individual marginal willingness-to-pay curves for water (in terms of, say, the number of gallons used per month) of all the residents of California.

Figure 3-3 depicts the derivation of a simple aggregate marginal willingness-to-pay curve, in this case by adding together (horizontally) the MWTP

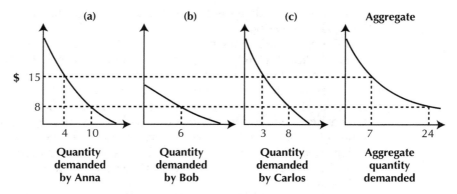

Figure 3-3   Aggregate Demand/Marginal Willingness-to-Pay Curve for a Private Good

curves of each of the three people in this group. A good like this, which can be consumed in separate and possibly different amounts by each of the individuals in a group, depending on their preferences and wealth positions, is called a **private good.** The total amount consumed in this case is simply a sum of the individual quantities consumed. Cantaloupes are a good example, as are cars, fishing trips, and pencils. At a marginal willingness to pay of $8, consumption is 10, 6, and 8 units, respectively, for Anna, Bob, and Carlos. Thus total consumption at $8 is 24. At a marginal willingness to pay of $15, aggregate consumption is 7 units (4 for Anna, none for Bob, and 3 for Carlos).

Aggregate Willingness to Pay/Demand for Public Goods

Many of the goods and services produced by natural resources are not private goods, for which we add together the consumption levels of different people to get total consumption. Rather, they are called **public goods.** A public good is one that when it is made available to one person, automatically becomes available to others as well. A good example is a signal broadcast by a radio station. When the signal is sent out, it is available to anybody within range who has a receiver. Furthermore, this type of public good is available to every individual in essentially the same quantity; in other words, the amount that one person listens does not diminish the amount available to other potential listeners.

Goods and services are defined as public or private in microeconomics by their **technical** characteristics, not by whether they are produced by public agencies or private firms. If a radio station "scrambled" its signal, and then rented unscramblers to subscribers, the signal would then be a private good. Public agencies may provide private goods (publicly provided flood insurance, for example); private firms may provide public goods (the radio station example). And the difference between public and private goods is not that the former has, in some sense, greater social importance than the latter. It is strictly a distinction based on the technical characteristics of the good in question.

To find the aggregate marginal willingness to pay for a public good, we must proceed somewhat differently from the case of a private good. Consider a program designed to reestablish a certain species of wildlife in a region, for example the restoration of the bald eagle in New England. Let the group of people involved consist of three individuals, the same three we mentioned earlier. The individual marginal willingness to pay of each one is listed numerically in table 3-1. Three alternative discrete levels of restoration are identified: "low," "moderate," and "extensive," corresponding, for example, to the number of adult animals that would be expected to survive under each scenario.

Table 3-1   Aggregate Marginal Willingness to Pay (MWTP) for Restoring Bald Eagles

| Extent of restoration | Marginal willingness to pay (MWTP) | | | |
	Anna	Bob	Carlos	Aggregate
Low	50	10	25	85
Moderate	30	5	10	45
Extensive	10	0	5	15

The MWTPs for Anna, Bob, and Carlos are as shown. For example, Anna would be willing to pay $50 for a light restoration program, and $30 more if it were increased to a moderate level, and so on. Bob has a lower marginal willingness to pay than Anna, and Carlos lies between the other two in terms of MWTP. The restoration of the bald eagle is a public good, in the sense just described. If it were carried out for one person it would be available to others as well. To find the aggregate marginal willingness to pay in this case, we add together the individual MWTPs corresponding to given "output" levels (in this case different levels of restoration). This is done in the last column of table 3-1.

Figure 3-4 on the next page shows the derivation of the aggregate marginal willingness to pay in graphical terms. In contradistinction to the private good, where the aggregate MWTP is found by adding individual curves horizontally (i.e., adding quantities of the three individuals corresponding to the same MWTP), we instead add the individual curves together vertically (i.e., the marginal willingness to pay of the three individuals corresponding to the same quantities on the horizontal axes).

Willingness to Pay and Benefits

We now come to the idea of **benefits.** Benefits is one of those ordinary words to which economists have given a technical meaning. The word "ben-

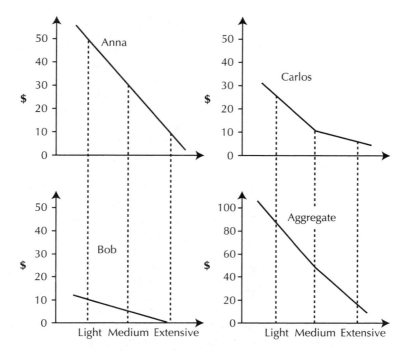

Figure 3-4   Aggregate Marginal Willingness to Pay/Demand for a Public Good

efits" clearly implies being made better off. If someone is benefited by something, her position is improved—she is better off. Conversely, if benefits are taken from her, she is worse off. How do we confer benefits on somebody? We do this by giving her something she values. How do we know that she values something? We know by the fact that she is willing to sacrifice, or willing to pay, for it. Thus, the benefits that people get from something are equal to the amount they are willing to pay for it.

The logic behind this definition of "benefits" is quite strong. It means we can use ordinary demand curves to measure the benefits accruing to people from given quantities of a good or service. For example, figure 3-5 on the following page shows two demand curves, and on the horizontal axis two quantity levels are indicated. Suppose we wish to estimate the total benefits of increasing the availability of this item from quantity q_1 to quantity q_2. Benefits are measured by willingness to pay, and we know that total willingness to pay is measured by areas under the demand curve—in this case the area under the demand curves between quantity q_1 and quantity q_2. So for the lower demand curve the benefits of such an increase in availability are equal to an amount shown by area b, whereas benefits in the case of the higher demand curve are equal to the total area $a + b$.

The logic of this seems reasonable. The people with the higher demand curve must place a greater value on this item; whatever it is, they are will-

Figure 3-5   Willingness to Pay and Benefits

ing to pay more for it than the people whose demand curve is the lower function. This agrees with common sense. The more people value something, the more they benefit by having more of that something made available; or, to say the same thing a different way, you can't damage people by taking away something that they don't value.

This is a fundamental notion underlying natural resource economics. It underlies, for example, questions such as the benefits conferred on people when natural resources are used in production, as compared to the benefits they would provide if preserved. It underlies the question of evaluating the impacts of environmental programs and policies undertaken by local, state, and federal governments. This is its strength—the fact that it is based on a clear notion of the value that people place on different things.

But the idea of benefits also has shortcomings. For one thing, demand and, therefore, benefits are often very hard to measure with regard to natural resources, as we see in later chapters. For another, we have to remember that demand curves are critically affected by the ability to pay for something as well as preferences. In figure 3-5, for example, the lower demand curve could represent a group of people with lower incomes than those with the higher demand curve. The logic of the argument would lead to the conclusion that the increase in quantity of $q_2 - q_1$ would produce fewer benefits among lower-income people than among higher-income people. This may not be a very equitable conclusion, depending on the circumstances. Thus, although the logic of the concept is clear, we have to be careful in using it, especially when we are dealing with groups of people with diverse income levels. To do so, we must find out as clearly as possible how the various natural resource policies and programs, present or proposed, affect people at different income levels. We discuss this at greater length in later chapters.

One other possible problem exists in using conventional demand curves to measure benefits. An individual's demand for something is clearly affected by how much he knows about it; a person would not be willing to pay for a good if, for example, he were ignorant of its very existence. In figure 3-5, the higher demand curve might be the demand for a biodiversity product after it is found to contain a promising pharmaceutical component, while the lower demand curve shows demand before this fact becomes known. This is not especially surprising; people naturally become more knowledgeable about things over time as a matter of education, experience, and the availability of information. But people's views about the importance of particular resources and the relevance of nature in their lives are often blown back and forth almost daily by the media, by the scientific press, and so on. Care must be exercised in taking people's demand curves of the moment, influenced as they are by all kinds of real and imagined factors, as true expressions of the benefits of actions affecting natural resources. They are highly relevant, but they need to be considered with a certain amount of caution.

The term "benefits" implies the existence of beneficiaries, i.e., people to whom the benefits accrue. Any defined group of people can be identified as beneficiaries, depending on the problem being looked at. So we could ask, for example—what benefits accrue to the people of Wyoming from the state's program of wolf restoration? In the widest possible context, we can ask what benefits accrue to all citizens of a country (or the world, for that matter); in cases like this, it is customary to call these **social benefits,** benefits accruing to everyone, without exclusion.

Willingness to Pay Over Time

Problems in natural resource economics are particularly complex because the **time dimension** plays a major role in them. Decisions made today, or this year, will have consequences in future years. Trade-offs are necessary because present and future willingness to pay, and present and future costs, are involved. We talked earlier about willingness to pay as it applied to the consumption of a certain quantity of a good or service. The assumption was that we were working with events in the present. But consumers are usually involved with streams of consumption over a series of time periods. If a person buys a car, for example, the services of the car will be realized both today and in the future over its service life. The consumption of necessities such as food, clothing, and shelter by definition occur over a series of years, not just a single one. Thus consumers can be thought of as having a willingness to pay not just for current consumption, but also for a stream of consumption quantities extending into the future, as pictured in figure 3-6 on the next page. This shows a sequence of willingness to pay, for the current quantity q_0, and for a sequence of future quantities, q_1, q_2, q_3, and so on.

We must then consider the problem of adding up willingness-to-pay amounts over a string of years to find the total willingness to pay for the overall sequence. How can (or should) values of willingness to pay (or of cost, as we see in the next chapter) occurring in different time periods be added together? The standard answer to this is by discounting future values.

■ Discounting

Discounting involves applying a discount factor to future values in order to convert them into **present values.** Most people readily understand **compounding.** If a sum of money equal to \$M is put in a savings account at

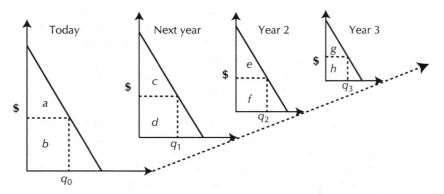

Figure 3-6   Willingness to Pay over Time

an interest rate of r, the value after one period of compounding is given by the formula

$$\$FV = \$M(1 + r)$$

The formula compounds the present value ($\$M$) into the future value (FV). If M is left in the bank account at r percent interest for t periods, then the future value is found by compounding the present value t times, thus:

$$FV_t = M(1 + r)^t$$

As an example, if M = $\$1,000$, $r = 0.04$, and $t = 6$, the future value is

$$FV_6 = \$1,000(1 + 0.04)^6 = \$1,265$$

Discounting is the reverse of compounding. It is a procedure for finding the present value corresponding to some future value. Discounting answers the question—If I expect to receive something of value in the future, what is it worth today? Or, for example, if someone promised you a sum of money next year or a lesser sum of money this year, which is the better deal? Algebraically, the expressions for present values are simply the ones above but rearranged to get present value (which we will now call PV instead of M) on the left side. Thus, for example, the present value of a sum equal to $\$FV$ to be realized one period from now, at a discount rate of r, is

r = discount rate;
n = number of periods

$$\$PV = \frac{\$FV}{(1+r)^n}$$

Suppose somebody gave you an IOU stating that they will pay you $\$100$ one year from now, and that the discount rate is 4 percent. The value of that IOU is the present value of that future $\$100$, and is found with the expression:

$$\$PV = \frac{\$100}{(1+0.04)} = \$96.15$$

This means that $100 one year from now is the same as having $96.15 today, based on a discount rate of 4 percent.

Suppose the IOU was for $100, but to be given to you 5 years from now rather than after just one period. Then the present value of the IOU would be:

$$\$PV = \frac{\$100}{(1+0.04)^5} = \$82.19$$

Discounting translates future values into a single metric, that of present value. So, for example, if we had numerous different future values occurring in various future years, we can convert them all to present values and aggregate them in those terms. For example, suppose the IOU given to you specifies the following payment schedule:

	Year[3]					
	0	1	2	3	4	5
Payment	$100	$100	$150	$150	$50	$50

The present value of this stream of payments[4] is found as follows:

$$PV = \$100 + \frac{\$100}{(1+r)^1} + \frac{\$150}{(1+r)^2} + \frac{\$150}{(1+r)^3} + \frac{\$50}{(1+r)^4} + \frac{\$50}{(1+r)^5}$$

If the discount rate is 4 percent, this present value sum is equal to $552.02.

Now we are able to aggregate the willingness-to-pay amounts shown in figure 3-6. The present value of the stream of total willingness to pay is equal to

$$PV_{(WTP)} = (a+b) + \frac{(c+d)}{1+r} + \frac{(e+f)}{(1+r)^2} + \frac{(g+h)}{(1+r)^3} + \ldots$$

The areas under the curves at each quantity for each year are the values of FV for that year. The same approach is used to find the present value sum of a sequence of costs. Note that if the discount rate is set equal to zero, all the discount factors go to unity, and we are just adding up the annual values without alteration. For progressively higher discount rates the present value aggregate becomes smaller and smaller, because the denominators in the present value formula get progressively larger. At very high discount rates the discounted future values become very small compared to current values.

■ Summary

The primary way of registering value in economics is through willingness to pay. This does not mean that "money is the only thing of value," but only that willingness to sacrifice is the underlying concept, and a monetary index is the most convenient index of making it visible. We introduced marginal and total willingness to pay, for individuals and for groups of individuals (called aggregate measures). Willingness-to-pay curves are more familiarly known as demand curves. We distinguished between two fundamental types of goods: private goods and public goods. The difference lies in the technical nature of the goods and not in the institutional means chosen to supply them. The step from individual to aggregate willingness-to-pay curves has to be carried out differently for the two types of goods. People's willingness to pay for something normally extends over time, and this presents the problem of adding up willingness-to-pay amounts that occur in different time periods. This is done through discounting, which is essentially the reverse of the compound interest process.

Notes

[1] We have to be a little careful here. For a defined group of people the MWTP curve is also a demand curve. We see in chapter 5 that the market demand curve for something may not include the MWTP of all the people who might be affected by transactions involving that good or service.

[2] Remember that total willingness to pay is the area under the MWTP curve of each individual consumer, whereas aggregate willingness to pay is a summation over a number of individuals.

[3] We are assuming that the payments are made at the beginning of each year. Remember the convention that the present period is indexed 0 and is not discounted; next period is indexed 1 and is discounted one period, etc.

[4] A generalized way of writing this is $PV = \sum_{t=0}^{6} \dfrac{FV_t}{(1+r)^t}$

Key Terms

ability to pay

benefits

compounding

demand curves

discounting

marginal willingness
  to pay (MWTP)

present value

private good

public goods

social benefits

total willingness to pay

Questions for Further Discussion

1. We talked about willingness to pay for a good or service. How does the concept apply to an act of strict preservation, in which the flow of traditional goods and services from a natural resource is put at zero?

2. There are ways of expressing value other than willingness to pay. Can you think of some?

3. Calculate the present value of the following sequence of willingness to pay amounts: this year, $100; next year, $150; year 2, $150; year 3, $50. Use a 5 percent discount rate. Recalculate using a discount rate of 8 percent. What is the effect of using a higher discount rate?

4. Is a movie theater a public good? How about a mode of public transportation? A lighthouse? The music you are playing in your apartment?

5. Suppose your house or apartment has become very cluttered and messy and needs to be cleaned. As you proceed through the tasks of cleaning, how does the marginal willingness to pay (sacrifice) for more cleaning change? Which tasks generate the greatest impact or benefit, and which tasks the least?

Useful Websites

Several websites feature introductory text material:

- Saylor Academy offers an online course in microeconomics with numerous links to readings and resources (http://www.saylor.org/courses/econ101/)
- *Cybereconomics: An Analysis of Unintended Consequences*, by Robert E. Schenk (http://ingrimayne.com/econ/TOC.html)
  See the chapter on "The Logic of Choice"
- *Microeconomics*, Khan Academy (www.khanacademy.org/economics-finance-domain/microeconomics)

Some of the most successful commercial websites are based on letting people express their willingness to pay for various items:

- For airline tickets (http://www.priceline.com)
- For almost anything else (http://www.ebay.com)
- For recycled electronic equipment (escrapauctions.com)

Selected Readings

The subjects covered in this and in the next several chapters are treated in all introductory microeconomics textbooks. The best way to proceed, in order to get a more in-depth treatment and deeper understanding of the ideas, is to consult the appropriate chapters of one of these books. Some of the more popular ones are the following:

Baumol, William J., and Alan S. Blinder. *Microeconomics, Principles and Policy*, 12th ed. Mason, OH: South-Western, 2012, chapter 5.

Boyes, William, and Michael Melvin. *Economics*, 9th ed. Mason, OH: South-Western Cengage, 2013, chapter 3.

McConnell, Campbell R., Stanley L. Brue, and Sean M. Flynn. *Economics*, 20th ed. New York: McGraw-Hill, 2015, chapter 3.

Samuelson, Paul A., and William D. Nordhaus. *Economics*, 19th ed. New York: McGraw-Hill, 2009.

Schiller, Bradley R., Cynthia E. Hill, and Sherri L. Wall. *The Microeconomy Today*, 13th ed. New York: McGraw-Hill, 2013, chapter 3.

4

Costs/Supply

It is now time to move to the other side of the picture and consider production costs. Even though some things in life may be free (though it is getting harder and harder to think of any), it is generally true that the production of anything requires the expenditure, or using up, of things that have economic value: To get outputs it is necessary to use inputs. This is clearly true in the case of traditional extractive processes; inputs are required to harvest natural resource commodities. But it is just as true in the case of non-extractive resources. Natural resource preservation is not just "nonuse"; it is in general a more activist activity that requires the expenditure of productive resources to be effective. In addition, strict acts of preservation imply that we are willing to give up alternative values that the preserved resource might have produced.[1]

This chapter covers the fundamentals of cost: important general cost concepts, the depiction of relationships between costs and output levels, and some very important notions of cost that are specifically useful in looking at natural resource issues. It is easy sometimes to concentrate on the benefits that flow from natural resource utilization and preservation, while overlooking the cost factor. But courses of action that are "best" or "optimal" for society clearly cannot be distinguished without taking both costs and benefits into account.

■ Opportunity Cost

The most fundamental notion of costs in microeconomics is **opportunity cost.** Production processes, traditional or otherwise, require the expenditure of inputs to produce outputs. The costs of inputs used to produce a particular output are the values those inputs would have produced had they been devoted instead to their next best production opportunity.

Suppose somebody is engaged in commercial fishing. The operation requires equipment, fuel, materials of various types, crew to operate the boat, and so on. All these inputs could have been devoted to something else: The crew could have worked elsewhere, the supplies could have been used by some other person, the fuel could have been consumed in another operation, the inputs represented by the fishing boat itself could have been devoted to some other type of capital good, and so on.

The opportunity costs of these inputs are the values they would have produced in their next best alternative. Opportunity costs include "out-of-pocket" cash costs but are much wider than this. Suppose that the fisher has a spouse who keeps the books and does the accounting for the fishing operation and that this person receives no monetary compensation for doing the job. Although this input service has no cash cost, there is an opportunity cost, represented by what the spouse could have earned if he had worked in his next best alternative.

Another important kind of opportunity cost that usually does not show up as a monetary cost is the **environmental cost** of a production process. The city of Tampa, Florida, built (or had built) a saltwater desalination plant to provide fresh water for the city. There were traditional costs of labor, machinery, and building materials, but when the plant began operations city officials found that there was an additional cost in the form of marine organisms destroyed by the water intake system. Although the marine organisms did not show up on the revenue/cost report of the plant, their destruction presented a real opportunity cost to society and needed to be accounted for in evaluating the operation.

In a later chapter on water economics (chapter 15) we will discuss, among other things, the costs associated with withdrawing water from a body of water for purposes of irrigation. These costs include both the direct monetary costs of extracting and conveying the water, and the opportunity costs in the form of reduced value to those downstream who use the river for recreational purposes. These instream flow values can be substantial.

The idea of opportunity cost is relevant to many situations. The examples above refer to production of some physical output. For a public agency the opportunity cost of spending resources on one program include the forgone benefits of using them on another program. For a student, the opportunity cost of studying more for one final exam is the lower grade on another exam for which study time is reduced.

■ Cost Curves

In subsequent chapters, our models of natural resource use employ graphical representations of costs. The primary relationship is that between the rate at which something is produced and the costs of that production. Just as in the previous chapter it is useful to distinguish between a marginal concept and a total concept. Here we distinguish between marginal costs and total costs of production.

Marginal cost is defined as the change in total cost resulting from a one-unit change in the quantity of output. Consider the top panel of figure 4-1. It shows a step-shaped marginal cost function. The graph is laid out as those in chapter 3, with quantity on the horizontal axis and a monetary index on the vertical axis. Remember that this quantity variable has a **time dimension,** such as quantity of output per year. The graph shows that it costs $4 to produce the first unit; next it shows that if production were to be increased from 1 to 2 units, total costs would increase by $5. Producing one more unit—the third—would add $8 to total costs, and so on. The height of the rectangles depicts, in other words, the marginal cost of producing additional units of output. Marginal cost works in both directions. It is the added costs, the amount by which total costs increase when output is increased by one unit, and it is also the cost savings if production were to decrease by one unit. Thus, the reduction in output from four to three units would reduce total costs by $11, the marginal cost of the fourth unit.

It is inconvenient to work with step-shaped curves, so we assume

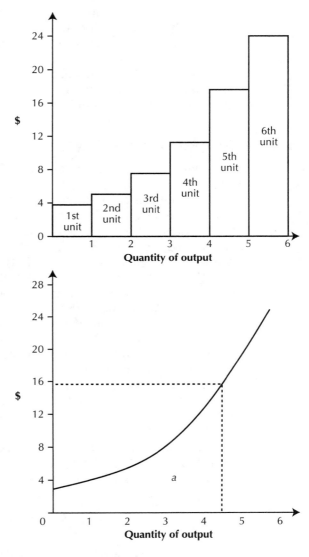

Figure 4-1   Marginal Cost

that the firm can produce intermediate quantities as well as integer values. This gives a smooth marginal cost curve, as shown in the bottom panel of figure 4-1. This curve now shows the marginal cost for any level of output. For example, at an output level of 4.5 units, marginal cost is slightly less than $16.

Marginal cost curves can be used to determine **total production costs.** On the stepped marginal cost curve of figure 4-1, the total cost of producing five units is equal to the cost of the first unit ($4), plus that of the second

($5), the third ($8), the fourth ($11), and the fifth ($18). The total is $46; geometrically this is equal to the total area of the rectangles above the first five units of output. Analogously, in the smoothly shaped version of the marginal cost function, the total cost of producing a given quantity is the dollar amount equal to the area under the marginal cost curve between the origin and the quantity in question. So, for example, the total cost of producing 4.5 units of output is given by the area marked *a* in the figure.

■ The Shapes of Cost Curves

Economics
of
Scale

Marginal cost curves summarize the important technical and economic characteristics of a production process. The height, shape, steepness, etc., show the quantities of inputs required to produce different levels of output. Figure 4-2 depicts several marginal cost curves. Panel (a) shows a very common situation: Initially marginal costs decline as output increases, but then increase at larger output levels. Suppose the production process involved is the generation of electricity. Here quantity refers to kilowatt-hours produced per year. At low levels of output the plant is not being fully utilized; thus, as output increases, marginal costs actually decline. But suppose we are dealing with the **short run,** a time short enough that the size of the plant cannot readily be expanded. At higher output rates, the capacity of the plant is approached. Machinery must be worked longer, additional people must be hired, and so on. Thus marginal cost begins to increase. As the capacity of the operation is neared, these problems become more acute. To continue to increase output, more extraordinary measures are required, which can only be done at a high cost; thus, marginal cost increases even more. A point may come at which it becomes almost impossible to increase output further, which is the same as saying that the marginal costs of production at this point increase without limit. This limit is indicated by the vertical dashed line in panel (a) of figure 4-2.

This marginal cost curve depicts an important generic characteristic of all marginal cost curves, namely, that of **increasing marginal costs.**

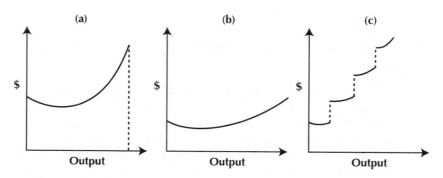

Figure 4-2   Marginal Cost Curves

Although marginal cost may initially decline, it will always increase, eventually, as output becomes large enough. These increases are related to certain underlying factors, such as increased plant utilization, the need to reach farther away for raw materials, and the inevitable higher management costs that accompany larger operations. Virtually all economic studies of particular operations and industries demonstrate increasing marginal production costs, and this fact will be an important shaping element in our later discussions specifically related to natural resource use.

Panel (b) of figure 4-2 shows a marginal cost curve similar in general shape to the one in panel (a), but with less pronounced curvature. In particular, although this marginal cost curve eventually increases, it does so less steeply than the first one. This is more typical of a **long-run marginal cost curve;** that is, one where enough time is available for operators of the firm to adapt fully to an increase in the rate of output. In the short run, the example power plant has a certain capacity that is basically fixed; but in the long run, there is time to expand the size of the plant by adding generating capacity. For larger outputs the marginal costs of this higher capacity plant will be lower than those of the smaller plant. But even in these long-run situations marginal costs will eventually increase, as depicted in panel (b). In later discussions we will assume long-run marginal cost curves unless specified otherwise.

Panel (c) in figure 4-2 shows a more complicated case. Here the marginal cost curve increases, but in a discontinuous, or jumpy, fashion. These jumps might be associated, for example, with the need to shift to newer and larger machines or to hire more individuals as the firm's output gets larger.

■ Social Costs

In this chapter our concern is with costs in the broadest possible context. The marginal cost curves depicted are meant to include all the costs of producing some resource-related good or service. We dub this all-inclusive notion **social costs.**

Consider figure 4-3 on the following page. It shows a marginal cost curve associated with the protection of wildlife species diversity in a given geographical area. The curve is labeled MSC, because it shows the full **marginal social costs** of carrying out this program. These include the out-of-pocket costs of the plan, together with, for example, the opportunity costs of the land used, as well as the damage costs that the species preservation might imply. The quantity in the diagram is the percentage of species protected. It could be some other index relevant for the general goal of species protection (e.g., the probability of a particular species going extinct, starting at the origin at 100 percent and declining as one goes to the right). Thus, at a 50 percent preservation level, the marginal costs of added protection is p, while the total cost of this level of protection is an amount equal to area a. We will often use the terminology of social costs to refer to the complete set of costs, to whomever they accrue, of achieving a given

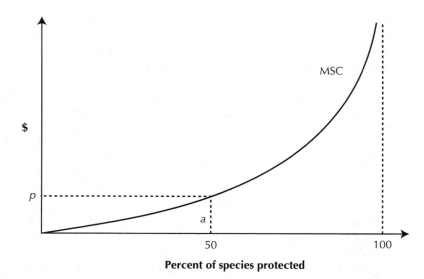

Figure 4-3   An Imagined Marginal Cost Curve of Species Preservation

level of performance. This idea is analogous to social benefits as discussed in the last chapter. Social costs refer to all the costs to society of a particular course of action.

■ Present Value of Cost

In chapter 3 we apply the procedures of present value analysis to time streams of benefits. The same procedure also is useful for evaluating future time streams of costs. Resource development or protection programs normally extend over long periods of time, with costs being incurred each year throughout their life. This is pictured in figure 4-4.

Costs in the current period (C_0) are equal to the area under today's marginal cost curve (MC_0) up to today's rate of output (q_0). Likewise, the expected marginal cost curves of future periods are shown, together with the expected rates of output and total costs that will be incurred in each period. The formula for determining the **present value** of this stream of costs is

$C = MC + q$

$$\text{Present value of costs} = C_0 + \frac{C_1}{1+r} + \frac{C_2}{(1+r)^2} + \frac{C_3}{(1+r)^3} + \dots$$

where r is the rate of discount.

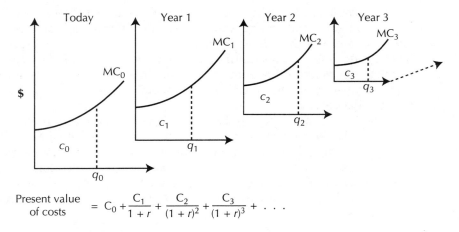

$$\begin{matrix} \text{Present value} \\ \text{of costs} \end{matrix} = C_0 + \frac{C_1}{1 + r} + \frac{C_2}{(1 + r)^2} + \frac{C_3}{(1 + r)^3} + \ldots$$

Figure 4-4   Present Value of a Stream of Costs

■ Costs and Technological Change

One of the major factors impacting natural resource markets is **technical change** in the processes by which resource-related goods and services are produced and distributed. Technical change normally makes production less costly. Graphically this shifts the marginal cost curve downward, as depicted in figure 4-5. This is a marginal cost curve for generating electric-

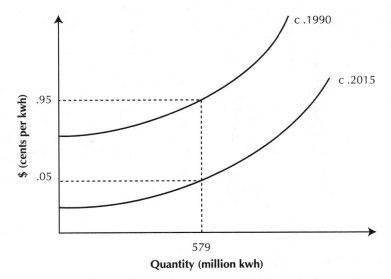

Figure 4-5   Marginal Costs of Electricity Production with Photovoltaic Cells

ity from solar energy with photovoltaic cells. In fact, these costs fluctuate depending on location and weather, so the numbers indicated are only approximate. But they depict a major change that has taken place over the last few decades: a substantial reduction as a result of the research and development that has gone into this technology. The marginal cost of generating electricity in this way today is about one-twentieth of what it was twenty-five years ago.

The costs of wind energy have also been substantially reduced through technical changes in wind turbines. Given these shifts, why hasn't renewable power made bigger inroads into the energy market? The answer is that there have also been major technological developments in conventional fossil-based energy sources. This applies both to coal technology and, even more, to natural gas as exhibit 4.1 discusses, but with a reference to future uncertainty.

Exhibit 4-1   Fracking and Natural Gas Expectations

A decade ago, in the mid-2000s, supplies of natural gas in the United States appeared to be limited. Plans were underway to expand the capacity of natural-gas receiving ports under the assumption that imports would be growing rapidly. Predictions were that domestic natural gas production would remain flat. Then along came "fracking," the technical ability to extract gas from underground shale formations. New drilling techniques made it feasible, and profitable, to tap into a resource once thought to be inaccessible. Gas production soared. Much of it came from the Marcellus shale formation in Pennsylvania and New York. Other significant sources were the Barnett shale deposits in Texas, the Fayetteville in Arkansas, and a deposit on the Louisiana-Texas border. Tens of thousands of wells have been drilled in these locations.

The old predictions of natural-gas scarcity have been replaced with the opposite: expectations of a huge growth in production that will last for the next three or four decades. Some observers have suggested turning natural gas importing facilities into exporting ports. But several recent developments have tempered this enthusiasm. One has been a substantial decline in natural gas prices driven by the higher supply. The other has been a rethinking of the forecast for continued high production.

Researchers have now examined the existing shale gas formations in much more detail. Some have concluded that the amounts of recoverable gas are lower than first predicted, based on a more particularized understanding of the deposits. Thus, they anticipate that production of shale gas will actually peak in the next few years, and then start to decline. This is a good example of how difficult it is to not only predict new technological developments but also how these developments will impact resource availabilities and prices.

For more information see J. David Hughes, *Drilling Deeper: A Reality Check on U.S. Government Forecasts for a Lasting Tight Oil and Shale Gas Boon*, Post Carbon Institute, 2014.

■ Costs and Supply

Having considered the cost changes in solar electricity generation, we need to remind ourselves that these costs are largely costs incurred by the private firms comprising this particular industry. An individual **supply function** shows the quantity of a good or service that a firm will produce and make available at alternative prices. On the assumption that firms have as their goal the maximization of net income, these supply functions are none other than their marginal cost functions. So it is with aggregate supply functions for an industry; it consists of the aggregation of all the individual marginal cost/supply curves of firms in the industry.

■ Summary

The prime topic of this chapter is economic cost. The most important notion of cost is that of opportunity cost. The opportunity cost of producing something is the maximum value that could have been produced of something else if the good or service in question had not been produced. We distinguished among marginal costs, total costs, and aggregate costs, and we discussed the importance of technology in determining costs in any concrete situation. We linked marginal costs with supply functions, the key factor in this case being the profit-maximizing incentives of market-oriented firms. We discussed also the issue of discounting future costs to find the present value of costs.

Notes

1 We will continue to use the word "output" to indicate the quantity of some good or service. It's important to keep in mind that it applies both to physical production, such as tons of some mineral, and to nonphysical "outputs," such as acres of preserved habitat.

Key Terms

marginal cost	supply function
opportunity cost	technical change
present value of cost	total costs
social costs	

Questions for Further Discussion

1. How does the concept of opportunity cost apply to the following situations:
   a. A piece of land that is to be devoted to a public park
   b. An abandoned railroad that is given to a community for constructing a bike path
   c. The costs of diverting water from a river to irrigate nearby farmland
   d. The costs of clear-cutting timberland
2. What might you expect the marginal cost curve to look like for the following operations:
   a. A water-supply system in the short run; that is, with its existing system of reservoirs, pumps, and pipes

b. A public park in terms of the number of visitor days accommodated

c. Wolf restoration in western Wyoming

3. What are the major factors behind shifts in supply functions? Illustrate this with an example from a natural resource–based industry.

4. Determine the present value of costs for the following time profile of costs:

$C_0 = 10$

$C_1 = 8$

$C_2 = 6$

$C_3 = 5$

Do this for discount rates of 4 percent and 6 percent.

Useful Websites

The economics textbook sites listed at the end of the preceding chapter can be consulted for material on costs and supply functions:

- Saylor Academy offers an online course in microeconomics with numerous links to readings and resources: (http://www.saylor.org/courses/econ101/#overview)

- *Cybereconomics: An Analysis of Unintended Consequences*, by Robert E. Schenk (http://ingrimayne.com/econ/TOC.html) See the chapter on "The Logic of Choice."

- *Microeconomics*, Khan Academy (www.khanacademy.org/economics-finance-domain/microeconomics)

Selected Readings

A statement similar to the one at the end of the last chapter is appropriate here. Consult the appropriate chapters (those dealing with cost concepts) of one of the main microeconomics textbooks currently available:

Baumol, William J., and Alan S. Blinder. *Microeconomics, Principles and Policy*, 12th ed. Mason, OH: South-Western, 2012, chapter 7.

Boyes, William, and Michael Melvin. *Economics*, 9th ed. Mason, OH: South-Western, 2013, chapter 21.

McConnell, Campbell R., Stanley L. Brue, and Sean M. Flynn. *Economics*, 20th ed. New York: McGraw-Hill, 2015, chapters 3 and 9.

Samuelson, Paul A., and William D. Nordhaus. *Economics*, 19th ed. New York: McGraw-Hill, 2009.

Schiller, Bradley R., Cynthia E. Hill, and Sherri L. Wall. *The Microeconomy Today*, 13th ed. New York: McGraw-Hill, 2013, chapters 3 and 7.

5

Efficiency and Sustainability

In this chapter we bring together the two main concepts that were introduced earlier: willingness to pay and marginal cost. Combining these two ideas leads to a major concept used throughout economics, that of economic efficiency. The notion of efficiency is used in positive economics to help explain how people behave in the real world. It is also used in normative economics as a criterion for judging outcomes; for example, evaluating in specific instances whether the rate at which individuals are using a natural resource is the best one from the standpoint of society as a whole.

We look at economic efficiency from two angles: static efficiency and dynamic, or intertemporal, efficiency. A state of affairs that is efficient in the static sense is efficient strictly from the perspective of a single time period, in particular the present one. In the spring a farmer plants a crop, later harvesting it and shipping it to market. A timber-harvesting firm cuts down a number of trees this year and ships them to market. A public agency allows a certain number of visitors into a park this year. These decisions are efficient in the static sense if they are undertaken in light of their consequences for this year only.

Dynamic, or intertemporal, efficiency means a situation that is efficient when not only the present year is taken into account, but future years as well. A decision is intertemporally efficient if it takes into account all the consequences flowing from it, those occurring this year and those in the future. If no future consequences stem from today's decision, a static perspective is sufficient to also achieve dynamic efficiency. Consider the farmer. There is essentially no connection between this year's decision as to how many acres to devote to cantaloupes and anything that will happen in future years. This decision can be made, and harvests produced, with essentially no future consequences.[1] In this example a decision made only on static grounds will capture all the consequences that are involved.

But this is not true for the logging company. Cutting down and replanting trees this year means there will be no trees to cut on this parcel until such time as the new trees mature. There are clearly future consequences flowing from today's decisions. Pumping petroleum out of an underground deposit is

61

also a decision of this type; pumping more today means having less to pump out in the future. In these cases, decisions made only on static grounds (considering only current consequences) will be very different from those made on dynamic grounds (considering both current and future consequences).

The next two sections deal, respectively, with static and dynamic economic efficiency. After that we turn to the idea of **sustainability,** which has become widely popular as a possible alternative, or additional, criterion for evaluating the long-run consequences of natural resource decisions.

■ Static Efficiency

To understand the notion of static efficiency we bring together the two major concepts of the last chapter, marginal willingness to pay and marginal cost. Consider figure 5-1. The horizontal axis depicts quantities of the output of a good or service and the vertical axis has a value scale. The MSC curve represents **marginal social costs;** that is, the marginal costs to all of society of producing this good or service. The MSB curve represents **marginal social benefits,** which are measured by the marginal willingness to pay of all members of society for this good or service. Both the MSB and MSC curves are <u>aggregate relationships</u>. They represent the summed marginal willingness to pay and summed marginal cost relationships of all the people and firms in our "society." Since nothing (or no one) is left out, they are called "social." The <u>rate of output that is socially efficient is the one that yields the maximum</u> **net benefits to society.**[2] Net benefits refer to the total benefits of the thing that is produced minus the value of the resources used up to produce it. The total benefits of a quantity of output are given, as we saw earlier, by the area under the social marginal willingness-to-pay curve. At a quantity of q^* in figure 5-1, the total social benefits of output are equal to the area labeled $a + b$.

Total costs are equal to the area under the marginal social cost curve. For the quantity q^* in figure 5-1, this is shown as area b. Thus the **net social benefits** of the output level q^* is $(a + b) - b = a$. In other words, net benefits are equal to the difference between the area under the marginal social willingness-to-pay curve and marginal social cost curve.

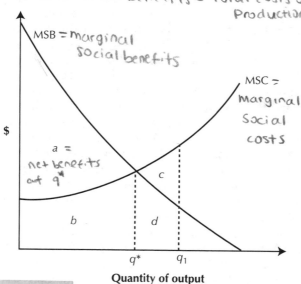

[handwritten: net benefits = total benefits - total costs of Production]

[handwritten labels on figure: MSB = marginal social benefits; MSC = Marginal Social costs; a = net benefits at q^*]

Figure 5-1   Static Social Efficiency

[handwritten: Socially efficient rate => MSB = MSC]

It is straightforward to show that q^* is the rate of output that maximizes the net social benefits associated with the production of this good or service. To do this, take some other output level, such as q_1 in figure 5-1. The net benefits of this output are derived as follows:

Total benefits: $a + b + d$
Total costs: $b + c + d$
Benefits – costs: $a - c$

In other words, net social benefits are equal to what they would have been had output been q^*, minus the quantity c. We can conclude that net social benefits are definitely lower at q_1 than at q^*. In fact this same conclusion can be drawn[3] about any output that is different from q^*.

Of course the condition that identifies output level q^* uniquely is that MSB = MSC at that output. The notion of efficiency involves a trade-off between willingness to pay and production costs. To the left of q^*, an additional unit of output would add more to social benefits than to production costs (i.e., marginal willingness to pay exceeds marginal cost) while to the right of q^* the opposite is true. At q^*, therefore, these two quantities are in balance, marking the socially efficient rate of output.

The reason this is called static efficiency is that it is based on a balance between two contemporaneous, or current period, quantities. Quantity of output, marginal benefits, and marginal costs are all values pertaining to the current year. There is nothing in this simple model that applies to some other time period; for example, some future period's marginal costs as they might be affected by this period's output rate.

■ Dynamic (Intertemporal) Efficiency

By dynamic (intertemporal) efficiency we also refer to a state of affairs in which there is a maximum of net benefits, but now benefits and costs are extended to include not only those of the present period, but also the future consequences flowing from today's decision. Consider figure 5-2 on the following page: It shows a series of marginal benefit and marginal cost curves, one set for each year starting with the current year and stretching into the future. Dynamic efficiency now requires choosing a **time series of output quantities,** not just one. And since time is involved, our criterion for that decision now becomes to choose the one time series of quantities that gives the **maximum present value of net benefits.**

Which particular time series of outputs will maximize the present value of the net benefit stream depends on whether and how the different qs are linked together. Suppose they were not linked. Suppose, for example, that figure 5-2 refers to the farm case mentioned earlier. In this case there is no connection between the time periods. Intertemporal efficiency would be achieved by selecting the statically efficient output rate in each time period, shown in the figure as $q_0, q_1, q_2, \ldots$. But suppose there is a connection. Maybe there are extraction rates for a small mineral deposit, in which case

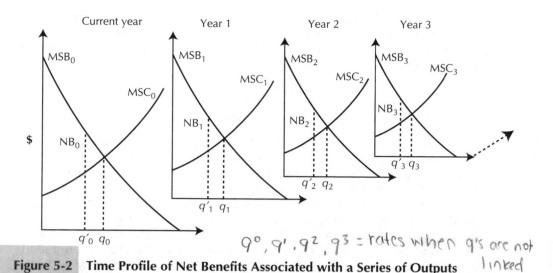

Figure 5-2   Time Profile of Net Benefits Associated with a Series of Outputs

q^0, q', q^2, q^3 = rates when q's are not linked

we can't change output in one year without having to change it in some other year or years. Our intertemporally efficient time series of outputs might now be something like $q_0', q_1', q_2', \ldots$.

Let us look explicitly at the criterion to be maximized in the search for intertemporal efficiency. It can be written as follows:

$$\text{Present value of net benefits} = \text{Net benefits in year 0} + \text{Net benefits in year 1}\,\frac{1}{1+r} + \text{Net benefits in year 2}\,\frac{1}{(1+r)^2} + \cdots$$

or

$$PV = NB_0 + \sum_{x=1}^{n} NB_x \times \frac{1}{(1+r)^x}$$

$$\text{Present value of net benefits} = \text{Net benefits in year 0} + \text{Sum of all discounted future net benefits}$$

The present value of net benefits can be thought of as consisting of a sum; the first term in the sum is the net benefits in the current period, while the second term shows the net benefits of all future periods **discounted** by the appropriate factors. Dynamic efficiency requires that current and future rates of use be chosen that make this sum as large as possible. This means that there is normally a **trade-off;** decisions that increase the net benefits of using a natural resource in the present period often have the effect of decreasing net benefits from the resource in the future. This problem of finding the appropriate balance between present and future characterizes the concept of dynamic efficiency.

Clearly, the discount rate plays a critical role in intertemporal efficiency. In chapter 3 we cover the mechanics of discounting, and here we use it to convert future net benefits into their present values. Our idea of intertemporal efficiency depends, in other words, on the notion that future net benefits of natural resource use are to be discounted in order to determine their present values. Discounting future net benefits to help identify social efficiency is controversial. And controversies rage over what the discount rate actually should be. We take up these issues later in the chapter.

We can take the last expression and convert it into marginal terms. Remember that "marginal" refers to the extent to which something changes. Thus if there is a one-unit change in today's rate of resource use, we have

Change in the present value of net benefits (MNB)	=	Change in benefits of present period (MB)	−	Change in costs of present period (MCC)	+	Change in discounted value of future net benefits (MUC)

which can be rewritten, using the indicated designators, as:

$$MNB = MB - MCC + MUC$$

The designator MCC can be thought of as "marginal current costs"; that is, marginal costs incurred in the current period. MUC stands for **marginal user costs**. User cost, in other words, is the name that will be given to the change in the discounted value of future net benefits. Anything that affects these future net benefits is expressed through what we call user costs.

If the choices of today's output actually have no future consequences, then user costs would be zero; in effect, we would have a static situation. The decision about how many acres of cantaloupes to grow this year on a 100-acre farm is strictly a static decision. There are no future consequences flowing from this decision, only contemporary ones; hence, user costs in this case are zero.[4] Or suppose the decision is how much water to withdraw from a passing river to irrigate some crops. Increasing or decreasing the amount withdrawn is not likely to have an impact on future water availabilities in the river, hence the user costs of the water are zero.

But in cases where user costs are not zero, intertemporal efficiency requires that today's rate of output be set so that today's marginal willingness to pay is equal to the sum of today's marginal costs and marginal user costs. This is depicted in figure 5-3 on the next page. The figure shows the current market for a natural resource good or service—for example, the number of units (tons, barrels) of a resource harvested or extracted, or the number of acres of land devoted to a park or wildlife refuge. MCB (marginal current benefits) shows society's valuation of this resource-based good or service in the present period, while MCC shows the social costs of harvesting or extracting or otherwise making it available this year. To repeat, if this were a static problem, these would be the only relevant relationships and the efficient rate of output would be q_0^1. But assuming there is a user cost of some amount, this has to be added to today's harvest cost, giving the marginal total cost function labeled MTC (= MCC + MUC). The intersection of this curve with MCB gives q_0^* as the intertemporally efficient rate of output in the current period.

User cost is, in effect, the factor that accounts for the future resource-related consequences of today's decisions. Think of user cost as a single term that shows the discounted present value of the sum of all future conse-

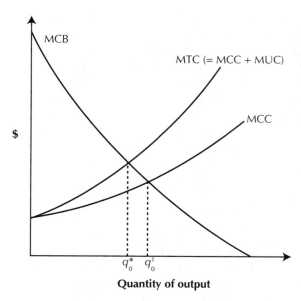

Figure 5-3   Intertemporally (Dynamically) Efficient Rates of Output of a Natural Resource Good or Service

quences stemming from today's decisions. Clearly, the higher the user cost, the more the MTC curve will diverge from the MCC curve, in other words, the bigger the difference between dynamic and static efficiency. The exact form that user cost takes depends on the problem at hand. If the problem is a simple one, say, with just two time periods and a strictly nonrenewable resource, user cost also will be simple; it will be equal to the discounted value of extracting one less unit next year. But complex situations have complex user costs. Suppose the issue is how current output decisions affect future species diversity over the next century. This is a biologically complex, difficult-to-measure, long-run problem. User cost in this case will be very hard to estimate. Conceptually, however, it is clear. It is the present value of all the future consequences arising from today's natural resource use decisions.

Natural Resource Rents

The **in situ price** of a natural resource is its price **as situated in the natural world.** The stumpage price for wood, what it sells for on the stump, is an in situ price, whereas the price of timber delivered to a mill is not, because that price includes the stumpage value plus the cost of harvesting. The landed price of fish is not an in situ price, because that price reflects both the in situ value of the resource and the costs of catching it and getting it to market. The in situ price of copper ore is the price of a ton of copper in the ground, before it is extracted and delivered to a refinery. The price of land to be used for farming, or on which to build houses, is an in situ price.

In natural resource economics the in situ price of a natural resource is commonly called its **resource rent.** In a sense, it is the value of something that the workings of nature itself have made available. Consider figure 5-4, which shows the marginal willingness-to-pay curve for lobsters by people vacationing in New England in a recent year. The intertemporally efficient quantity of lobsters is 1.8 million pounds, and the efficient price is $3.50 per pound. The marginal harvesting cost at this level of catch is $2.80 per pound. At a catch of 1.8 million pounds, the marginal rent of lobsters is the

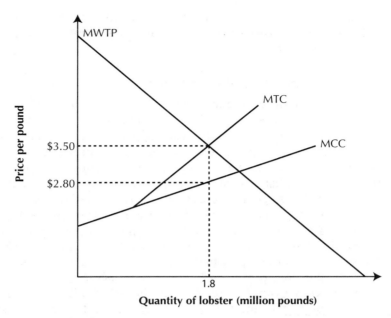

Figure 5-4   The Lobster Market

market price minus marginal harvesting costs, or $3.50 – $2.80 = $0.70. Note that this is a **marginal value;** it applies to the marginal thousand pounds of lobsters when total output is at 1.8 million pounds. If we take the marginal lobster rent of $0.70 and multiply it by 1.8 million pounds, we get a total lobster rent of $1.26 million. In other words, resource rent can be either the rent on the marginal unit of resource, in which case we can call it the **marginal rent;** or the rent on the total harvest, or in some cases the total stock, in which case we can call it the **total rent.** Marginal rent has different names in different situations: In timber economics it is usually called the **stumpage price;** in mineral economics it is often called the **royalty rate.**

Look again at figure 5-4 and compare it to figure 5-3. At 1.8 million pounds of lobster, MTC is equal to $3.50 while marginal harvesting cost (MCC) is $2.80, so marginal user cost is $3.50 – $2.80 = $0.70. At the margin, in other words, resource rent and user cost are exactly the same, at least when we are dealing with an intertemporally efficient situation. But why use two terms to refer to the same thing? The answer is that the terms tend to emphasize two slightly different perspectives: User cost refers to the value of future consequences of today's decisions, whereas rent refers essentially to a price. But it is very informative to realize that these are two different perspectives on exactly the same thing.

We have to be careful when discussing the idea of resource rent. It refers to a price, not necessarily to a social value. A price is a market phenomenon. If there is no market, there can be no rent. If resources produce services that do not pass through markets, then the rent for these resources will not reflect these services. We will have many occasions in later chapters to consider this.

Is It Appropriate to Discount?

Intertemporal efficiency, which maximizes the welfare of the present generation, involves discounting the future values of benefits and costs. This is a controversial issue. Discounting appears to put a lesser value on future net benefits than on net benefits occurring closer in time. Furthermore, discounting reflects the perspective of the current generation. Is this fair to future generations? By discounting are we not giving short shrift to the interests of future generations, who are not around to represent themselves? There are many who feel that discounting is essentially anticonservationist; by putting a higher value on today's output relative to future output, we tilt the production profile toward the present. How valid is this objection? There are several different parts to this question, which we will address in turn.

One question to ask is whether people actually discount in practice, in their everyday lives. The answer here is yes. The fact that there are positive rates of interest in the world is partly a reflection of the fact that people place a higher value on something today than on that same something happening sometime in the future. Direct research has also been done on the discount rates applied by people. In a well-known study a large number of people were queried on the question of trade-offs between public programs that would save a certain number of lives today as compared to other programs that would save some larger number of lives at varying distances in the future. By asking enough people to choose among enough different combinations, it was possible to find out the relative values about which they were indifferent, and therefore their implied discount rate. For example, if a person responded that she was indifferent between a program that would save 10 lives today and one that would save 500 lives 50 years from now, the implied rate of discount that the person is applying to these payoffs is about 8 percent.[5] The results of this research are shown in the following tabulation:[6]

Length of time period (years)	Implied discount (%)
10	12.0
20	9.0
30	7.0
40	6.0
50	5.0
60	4.8
80	4.2
100	3.8

These results show that the farther in the future the event being considered is, the lower the discount that people apply to it. For events that are only 10 years distant, the average rate of discount was about 12 percent; for events that will happen in 50 years, the discount was 5 percent; and for 100 years, the discount was 3.8 percent.

Since people (in both their consumer and producer roles) in fact discount, on average, in their everyday lives, should we not take this as implying that we ought to discount when assessing the social desirability of natural resource use rates? Some observers have taken the position that when individuals use some positive rate of discount to evaluate future benefits and costs, they are demonstrating a defective capacity for weighing the future consequences of their actions; they are being myopic. To believe this, one has to believe that people who discount are somehow less in touch with the benefits and costs that impinge upon them than are certain observers. This is not only condescending, it is also scientifically dubious—especially so when we are looking at the behavior of people at markedly different wealth levels. People with low wealth positions clearly have an incentive to emphasize near-term payoffs over future ones. It is difficult to see how the lives of these people would be improved by asking them in effect to put more weight on distant (in time) values and less on the immediate requirements of making a living and supporting their families.

From the perspective of the **current generation,** therefore, the arguments for discounting future benefits and costs are reasonably compelling. The rub comes when we wish to factor in the welfare of **future generations.** Does discounting put future generations at a disadvantage relative to those people alive today? Or to put it the opposite way, does discounting tend to improve the welfare of today's generation at the expense of future generations? Would we be better off today if our grandparents had used lower discount rates in their decisions? If future generations could somehow have a seat at today's table, would they agree with the discounting practices of today's decision makers? If we could show that future generations will be better off if people alive today discount the future, we could argue that discounting was both efficient and fair to the future. But can we show this?

The first point to be made is that higher discount rates are not invariably anticonservationist; in fact, plausible circumstances exist in which low discount rates work against conservation rather than the reverse. In the 1960s, natural resource policy makers in Washington were wracked by a dispute over the choice of discount rates to be used in water development projects like large-scale dams built for purposes of flood control and irrigation. The major dam-building public agencies—the Army Corps of Engineers (U.S. Department of Defense), the Bureau of Land Reclamation (U.S. Department of the Interior), and the Soil Conservation Service (U.S. Department of Agriculture)—all evaluated their proposals with relatively low discount rates.[7] Using those low rates, they justified many water development projects that had high up-front construction costs and relatively low future annual benefits. The low discount rates led to relatively high aggregate benefits because future benefits were not heavily discounted. Low discount rates in this case led to greater dam building, thus working against the goal of preserving natural habitats, though of course it also worked toward the goal of providing larger amounts of water for traditional extractive uses (see exhibit 5-1).

We also must be aware of the role of the discount rate at the **macroeconomic level.** In general, low discount rates are associated with higher rates of economic growth. This is because low discount rates spur investment, which enhances growth rates. But higher rates of economic growth, by leading to higher rates of economic activity (production and consumption) in the future, thereby cause a greater demand for natural resource inputs than would otherwise have prevailed. The lower discount rate leads to greater future demand for natural resources.[8]

Can a present generation make itself better off by adopting a resource utilization rate that reduces the long-run productivity of the resource base? Think of a single, 52-year-old farmer who plans on retiring at 60 and doing some traveling to see the world.[9] Might this farmer be tempted to work the

---

Exhibit 5-1 Low Discount Rates and Dam Construction

In the 1950s and 1960s, three large federal agencies had very active dam-building programs. The U.S. Army Corps of Engineers (in the Department of Defense) built large mainstem dams primarily for flood control and navigation purposes, the Bureau of Reclamation (in the Department of the Interior) specialized in large western dams whose primary purpose was providing water for irrigation, and the Soil Conservation Service (in the Department of Agriculture) built smaller upstream flood-control dams. Many of these dams were controversial because they massively changed the rivers' functions and substituted flat-water resources for previously free-running water resources. The time profiles of costs and benefits for most of these dams were characterized by very high initial costs followed by many years of relatively low annual benefits. During the heyday of dam construction, the dam-building agencies strove to get congressional authorization for their projects. To do this they had to show essentially that the present value of their benefits exceeded the present value of their costs. But, although most costs were incurred immediately, most benefits accrued only in the future. How to ensure that the present value of estimated future benefits would exceed costs? Use a low discount rate.

Suppose, for example, a planned dam has the following cost and benefit streams (in millions of dollars):

	Year					
	0	1	2	3	. . .	50
Costs	10	0	0	0		0
Benefits	0.5	0.5	0.5	0.5	. . .	0.5

Using a 5 percent discount rate, we get a present value of costs of $10 million and a present value of benefits of $9.1 million; so the benefits are lower than the costs in present value terms. But using a discount rate of only 3 percent gives a present value of benefits of $12.9 million. So the project could be authorized at 3 percent but not at 5 percent, which illustrates why the agencies used relatively low discount rates to evaluate their proposed dams.

Low discount rates do not necessarily mean greater conservation.

farm at too high a rate for the next 8 years to gain somewhat higher incomes in these years that could then be added to the retirement fund? The critical question is—what will he do with the farm at the end of the 8 years? One obvious alternative, since there is a ready market for farmland, is to sell it and add those proceeds to the retirement fund. But running down productivity in the short run to boost temporary earnings will reduce the sale price of the farm, because it means that he will be selling an asset of less long-term value. In other words, he faces a trade-off between temporarily increasing incomes and reducing the sale price at the end of the 8-year period. Note that this is essentially an intergenerational trade-off, because the sale of the farm basically hands it along to the next generation. The procedure that solves this dilemma from the standpoint of the farmer is to calculate the present value of the sum of the incomes over the 8-year temporary period plus the sale price at the end of the period. It is important to see that discounting, at a positive rate of discount, in effect incorporates the regard for future generations, as long as the value of the asset (in this case the farm) can be transferred to future generations. This is, of course, what markets do.

But even granting this argument, could there be cases where the negative consequences of today's natural resource use are so far in the future that people simply are unlikely to take them into account? Even with a very low discount rate, the present values of these very distant consequences may be so low that people of today may be led simply to disregard them.

■ Efficiency and Intergenerational Equity: The Issue of Sustainability

There is another way to think about this problem of balancing the interests of distant future generations with those of people today. The concept of **sustainability** has been increasingly applied to this type of problem. Sustainability was emphasized in a well-known 1987 report issued by a United Nations commission set up to, among other things, "propose long-term environmental strategies for achieving sustainable development."[10] It is worth noting that "sustainable" here is used as an adjective for "development." The commission recognized, in other words, the desirability of future economic development, especially for those parts of the world where per capita wealth levels are currently very low. The objective, however, is to do whatever is necessary to make this development "sustainable."

Sustainability has become a rallying cry and an organizing principle for much of the subsequent public discussion about natural resource and environmental policy. In that arena it has clearly served to encourage a longer-run perspective in policy discussions and decisions. But is it a useful criterion for evaluating resource use decisions? To answer this, it has to be defined more explicitly. According to the commission report, sustainable development is "development that meets the needs of the present without compromising the ability of future generations to meet their own needs."[11]

Without getting into arcane discussions of the meaning of words like "compromise" and "needs," one way of interpreting this operationally might be the following: Any actions on the part of people today that would make future generations worse off than we are today is to be called nonsustainable. Sustainability implies, therefore, that future generations are to be no worse off than today's generation.

But worse off in what respect? Suppose we insist that it be in the sense of the physical supplies and availabilities of natural resources. The condition for sustainability would be that future generations should have no smaller supplies than currently exist. There is no particular conflict between this and intertemporal efficiency when the subject is **renewable resources.** Intertemporal efficiency normally implies constancy of the resource stock through time, which would be in agreement with this particular notion of sustainability. For **nonrenewable resources,** however, there is obviously a problem if sustainability is to be defined in terms of physical availability. In this case any positive rate of extraction today obviously must lead to reduced availabilities at some time in the future.

Sustainability defined in terms of physical quantities might still be a viable idea if it were interpreted as nondiminution of the total of natural resources rather than any particular single resource. In this case drawing down a nonrenewable natural resource could perhaps be compensated for by augmenting supplies of a renewable resource. We might, for example, increase the acreage of preserved ecosystem in one region as quantities of coal or some other mineral are extracted elsewhere.

But the practical usefulness of a procedure like this is open to question. A basic problem is knowing the "exchange" ratios between resources; for example, how many acres of preserved wetlands are worth one ton of extracted coal or other mineral. To make this approach feasible, we switch from a physical-units notion of sustainability to one based on value. This makes it possible to assess different resources in terms of a common metric that allows comparison and aggregation. If natural resources are converted to values, then an injunction to preserve them in terms of their aggregate value is at least operationally feasible, whether or not the rule makes sense in terms of preserving or enhancing human welfare.

Suppose, however, we wish to develop a concept of sustainability that is applicable to any political jurisdiction: countries, states, regions, or communities. Some political areas are well endowed with a range of natural resources, whereas many are not. It may be reasonable to say that sustainability in the United States as a whole requires that the value of the national resource stock be nondiminishing; it is probably not reasonable to require the same of each and every country and community.

Suppose there were a community, or small country, only modestly endowed with some nonrenewable resource. Sustainability in the above sense would require that community to replace the nonrenewable resource with some other resource as the former is drawn down. But there may be no such resource with which to do this. If there is no such resource, this is not a very useful objective. Nor would it be for any community whose resource endowment consists of a preponderance of some nonrenewable resource.

The basic problem here is that sustainability is being defined too narrowly. A better approach is to recognize that human welfare is based on both natural resource capital and other forms of productive capital, in particular human capital and produced capital. **Human capital** refers to the human capacities and capabilities that usually result from experience, training, and education. Human capital should also be defined broadly to include **intellectual capital,** basically ideas and operating procedures, improvements of which are important to advances in human welfare. **Produced capital** refers to such things as machinery and buildings, but also includes investments in physical infrastructure (such as roads and ports) that are so important for the productivity of any economic system.

Sustainability in a broader sense now becomes the following: Use of a nonrenewable natural resource is sustainable if the value of the resource used up is matched by capital investments of equal value in other natural resources or in productive nonresource capital. This concept of sustainability can be used to evaluate decisions in political units of any size, from small communities up to nation-states and the global economy.

To be able to apply this definition of sustainability, we must have a measure of the extent to which the value of nonrenewable resource stocks is reduced as a result of current extraction. To think about this, we can go back to the concept of **user cost.** User cost is a measure of the present value of future net benefits sacrificed as a result of today's extraction. If compensating investments can be made sufficient to offset the user costs of a nonrenewable resource extraction, sustainability will be attained despite the gradual drawing down of the resource.

Remember that we also want to apply the notion of sustainability to the case of a renewable resource. In this case sustainability means the **continued availability** of a renewable resource to present and future generations. Here we need to identify the specific quantity of the resource that is to be maintained for the future. Take the resource **soil fertility,** for example. Sustainability implies that soil fertility is to be maintained for future generations; we need to identify the level of fertility that is intertemporally efficient. This does not rule out the case in which future generations decide to hold fertility at a different level.

■ Summary

In this chapter we dealt with two primary criteria for evaluating performance: efficiency and sustainability. Economic efficiency is a situation in which net benefits to society are at a maximum. We distinguished between static and dynamic, or intertemporal, efficiency. A rate of output that is efficient in the static sense is one that maximizes the net benefits of the current period only. Intertemporal efficiency requires the maximization of the present value of the stream of net benefits, starting today and extending into the future. We defined the concept of user cost as the present value of all future consequences stemming from a small change in today's rate of output. If there are no future consequences, user cost is zero, so static and dynamic efficiency amount to the same thing. We also introduced the concept of natural resource rent, which is basically the price of a natural resource in situ. Intertemporal efficiency implies discounting future benefits and costs, an idea around which there is controversy. The concept of sustainability deals with very long-run, intertemporal, issues. We discussed several possible definitions of this term, and concluded that to be most useful it has to be understood as applying to general measures of welfare, not just to specific resources.

Notes

1 This is not to suggest that all farming decisions are essentially static, of course. Things can be done today that clearly will have an impact on the future, say, through affecting future soil fertility.

2 The difference between "efficiency" and "social efficiency" is the degree of inclusiveness. Efficiency is a condition of maximum net benefits and could apply to a single firm, community, or country. Social efficiency is efficiency pertaining to the full, all-inclusive, society.

3 To see this, pick some output level below q^* and label the resulting areas. Then follow through the arithmetic the same way.

4 As mentioned, however, we could think of a scenario in which this would not be the case; for example, the cantaloupe production might have an impact on future land productivity.

5 To find this we find the r that makes the following equation hold true: $10 = \dfrac{500}{(1+r)^{50}}$

6 The study is reported in Maureen L. Cropper, Sema K. Aydede, and Paul R. Portney, "Rates of Time Preference for Saving Lives," *American Economic Review*, 87(2), May 1992, pp. 469–472.

7 The rates were tied to historical yields on government bonds in such a way that made them much lower than current rates.

8 For a technical discussion of this see Bob Rothorn and Gardner Brown, "Biodiversity, Economic Growth and the Discount Rate," in Timothy M. Swanson (ed.), *The Economics and Ecology of Biodiversity Decline: The Forces Driving Global Change*, Cambridge University Press, Cambridge, UK, 1995, pp. 25–40.

9 This example was inspired by Alan Randall, *Resource Economics*, 2nd ed., John Wiley, New York, 1987, pp. 128–129.

10 The report is titled *Our Common Future*, done by the World Commission on Environment and Development (Oxford University Press, 1987). This Commission was called the Brundtland Commission after its chair, Gro Harlem Brundtland of Norway.

11 *Our Common Future*, p. 43.

Key Terms

dynamic, or intertemporal, efficiency
human capital
in situ price
natural resource rent
  (marginal and total)

net social benefits
static efficiency
sustainability
user cost

Questions for Further Discussion

1. Prove that the rate of output that equates MSB with MSC is efficient in the static sense. Apply this idea to a problem involving the preservation of a natural resource.

2. What happens to the statically efficient rate of output when there is a technical change in the mode of production such as new satellite-based resource exploration techniques? When there is population growth?

3. How would the intertemporally efficient time path of output be affected by a zero discount rate?

4. What are the future costs associated with:

   a. Extracting coal from an open-pit mine?

   b. Harvesting timber in an ecologically sensitive area?

   c. Taking steps to preserve a wetland?

5. A small community has discovered a mineral deposit within its borders. How can the community extract this deposit sustainably?

Useful Websites

Refer to the websites of the economics texts listed after chapters 3 and 4. Sustainability is the new organizing concept, and there are many sites that feature it, at least in the title:

- Center for Sustainable Economy (sustainable-economy.org)
- International Institute for Sustainable Development (http://www.iisd.org)

Selected Readings

For general information on the notion of efficiency look again at an introductory microeconomics textbook, such as one of those listed at the end of chapters 3 and 4. For readings about efficiency as it is applied to natural resource use and sustainability, the following references might be useful.

Goldin, I., and L.A. Winter, eds. *The Economics of Sustainable Development*. Cambridge, England: Cambridge University Press, 1995.

Hackett, Steven C. *Environmental and Natural Resource Economics: Theory, Policy, and the Sustainable Society*, 4th ed. Armonk, NY: M. E. Sharpe, 2001.

Heal, Geoffrey. *Economic Theory and Sustainability*. New York: Columbia University Press, 1998.

Page, Talbot. *Conservation and Economic Efficiency*. Baltimore, MD: Johns Hopkins University Press for Resources for the Future, 1977.

Tietenberg, Tom, and Lynne Lewis. *Environmental and Natural Resource Economics*, 10th ed. Upper Saddle River, NJ: Prentice-Hall, 2015.

SECTION III

GENERAL NATURAL RESOURCE ISSUES

The previous section dealt with some fundamental building blocks that are used in microeconomics. In this section we take a step closer to dealing with important natural resource issues, though we continue to work at the conceptual level for the most part. We live in a market system, and it is important to know how normal markets function in the case of natural resources. This is addressed in chapter 6. Having inquired into the positive question, we then deal (in chapter 7) with the normative question of what steps should be taken to ensure that we move in the direction of managing resources in a socially optimal way.

6

Markets and Efficiency

The last chapter was devoted essentially to definitional matters: what it means for natural resource use, or any economic situation for that matter, to be efficient and/or sustainable. In this chapter we take up the question: Do markets involving natural resources normally function so as to give efficient or sustainable outcomes regarding the rate of use of resources? There are good reasons for pursuing this question. Virtually all developed economies in the world are market economies; that is, the primary social institution relied upon to make decisions about resource use is the private market. And in recent years most of the economies that once operated on the basis of decisions and directives made by central planning authorities have rejected that approach in favor of greater reliance on private markets. So it is vital to understand the basics of how markets operate: when they give efficient results and when not, when public intervention is called for and when not. We are particularly interested, of course, in the operation of markets for natural resource goods and services.[1]

■ Market Demand and Supply

A market is a process where buyers and sellers negotiate transactions among themselves to transfer the ownership or use of a good or service at agreed-upon prices. Markets vary from the most primitive—two people meeting face to face to trade a sack of potatoes in return for two hours' worth of labor, to the most sophisticated—a room full of people in electronic contact with their counterparts around the world buying and selling foreign exchange at prices that vary from second to second. But all markets essentially do the same job; they guide the flow of goods and services among buyers and sellers in terms of quantities and prices.

The basic market model used to summarize these interactions is shown in figure 6-1 on the next page. It shows two price-quantity relationships, one for demanders and one for suppliers. The **demand curve,** labeled D, shows the various quantities of the item that demanders will purchase at alternative prices. We described these types of functions in the previous chapter.

79

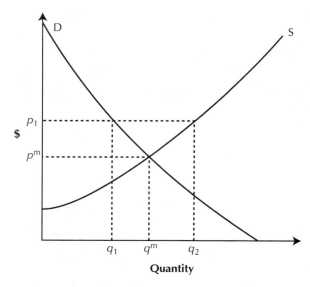

Figure 6-1   Basic Market Model

They are based on the notion of willingness to pay, and their downward slope illustrates the principle of **diminishing marginal willingness to pay**. It is important to see the demand curve as comprising a menu of possibilities. It tells not only what the quantity demanded is at the present price, but also what it would be if the price were higher or lower.

The market demand curve summarizes the behavior of all the people who are in the particular market under consideration, those who have just bought something and those who might buy something if the price were lower. The demand curve is a reflection of their incomes, tastes and preferences, and other relevant economic factors of their circumstances. If any of these underlying factors change, the market demand curve will change.

The supply curve, labeled S, represents the behavior of sellers of this good or service. Its upward slope is a reflection of increasing marginal production costs, and its exact shape—how steep it is, how far to the right or left—is related to input prices used in production and the fundamental technologies employed in the production process. Like the market demand curve, a market supply curve basically consists of a large number of potential output levels, only one of which will be realized during any particular time period.

Market Quantities and Prices

Given the demand and supply curves as shown, there is only one price where the quantity demanded by consumers is the same as that supplied by producers: This is when the price is p^m, the quantity is q^m. At any other price, there is a discrepancy between quantity supplied and quantity demanded. At a price of p_1, for example, suppliers would attempt to supply q_2 units of this item, while demanders would desire only q_1 units. As long as the demand and supply curves remain the same, something has to give. Excess supply normally leads to downward pressure on prices; as prices go down, the quantity demanded increases. So market adjustments in this case move prices and quantities toward the **equilibrium** pair, p^m, q^m.[2] Prices that are temporarily below p^m will lead to excess demand; that is, quantity demanded by consumers in excess of quantity supplied. This puts upward pressure on price and increases in quantity supplied toward the equilibrium levels.

In a dynamic economy we usually don't see prices and quantities that stay constant over a long period of time. That's because the underlying factors that affect the demand and supply functions are regularly changing. Demographic growth shifts demand curves, and technical change shifts supply curves, for example. Shifting expectations affect how demanders and suppliers react on current markets. So over time we often see prices moving upward or downward and not necessarily coming to some resting place as in equilibrium. But the model is still very useful, because it explains how the basic market process operates.

The essence of this process is that the interaction of buyers and sellers, actual and potential, causes prices and quantities to adjust, normally toward some equilibrium level. For the price-quantity combination p^*, q^* to materialize, it is not necessary for some economists first to figure out what those numbers are, or for a politician or public administrator to intervene and enforce them by fiat. It happens as a result of the more or less unrestricted interactions and transactions among buyers and sellers.

■ Markets and Static Social Efficiency

Markets tend toward equilibrium values like p^m and q^m in figure 6-1. But how do we know that these values represent those that are **socially efficient?** Markets tend toward equilibrium values determined by the interaction of demand and supply. But are these values also the ones that maximize the net benefits to society? Consider figure 6-2, which juxtaposes a diagram showing a market outcome (the one on the right) with one showing a socially efficient outcome. Suppose these refer to the U.S. plywood industry. Thus, the plywood market will tend to produce an output of q^m, at a price p^m. But to achieve social efficiency in plywood production we must achieve

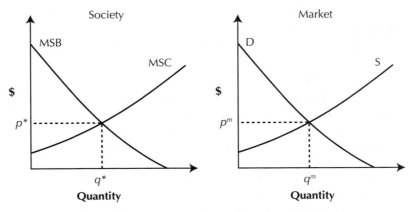

Figure 6-2   Comparison of Social Efficiency and Market Outcome

an output of q^* with MWTP = MSC = p^*. For the market to be socially efficient, we must have $p^* = p^m$ and $q^* = q^m$. It is clear that at least two things have to be true for market outcomes to be socially efficient: The market demand curve and the MSB curve have to be the same, and the market supply curve and the MSC curve have to be the same. If these two conditions are met, markets tend to generate socially efficient outcomes.

Market demand curves register the willingness to pay of the participants in those markets. Thus, to say that the market demand curve must be the same as the MSB curve is to say simply that there are no sources of social value that are not registered by market participants themselves; in effect, nothing is left out. Similarly, market supply curves are based on the costs that impinge on the private parties who make up the supplying entities on the market—business firms, for example. Thus, to say that the supply function and the MSC function are the same is to say simply that there are no sources of cost to members of society that are not registered in those private cost/supply curves.

Our job, then, is to consider the conditions under which these relationships will be consistent, MSB and D, and MSC and S. But before this, one other condition has to be true for markets to be socially efficient: They must be **competitive.** Competition means that buyers and sellers cannot exert influence on the market: suppliers cannot band together and collude to produce a higher price, nor may buyers do anything on the other side of the market to force lower prices. Competition also requires a large number of buyers and sellers in order to foreclose any one of them gaining a controlling position, and a set of rules defining the limits of acceptable behavior (you may outbid a rival, you may not physically trash their goods). Of course in real-world markets, it is always a question of how much competition rather than just the presence or absence of competition. "Acceptable" levels of competition are those that allow a market to achieve efficiency; competition that is either too weak or too strong makes it impossible for markets to do this.

Let us now return to the question of whether market demand curves and market supply curves are equal to, respectively, marginal social benefits and marginal social costs. We will first take up the cost question.

External Costs

To pursue this point we reiterate the distinction between social costs and private costs. Social efficiency is defined according to social costs, while supply curves are based on private costs. Under what circumstances might there be a discrepancy between the two? Consider the costs of harvesting the trees in a forest to get timber that ultimately will be turned into building supplies. Private costs in this case are the costs incurred by the logging companies to get the trees out of the forest: labor, equipment, and fuel costs. These are the costs (which we have called marginal private costs or MPC) that show up on the logging companies' profit-and-loss statements at the end of the year. These private costs are legitimate social costs, because these inputs could have been used elsewhere in the economy to produce something else.

But in this case, the full social costs of logging may include other cost elements as well. The U.S. Forest Service may devote some resources to the operation, for example, by constructing logging roads into the forest. Social costs may also include ecological costs. Certain forests may have unique ecological values that are diminished as a result of the logging. These costs may be very difficult to measure in practice, but they are legitimate social costs nonetheless.

The difference between private costs and social costs is called **external costs.** External costs, in other words, are costs incurred by people who are not party to the decisions that give rise to them. In the forestry example the external costs result from the decisions of the logging companies, but they are incurred in part by others, in particular those people who place value on the ecological characteristics of the forest.[3]

As another example, consider a collection of paper mills located on a river. They produce paper and in the process emit residuals into the river. The water quality of the river is reduced, which leads to damages suffered downstream by recreators and communities using the river as a water-supply source. This situation is illustrated in figure 6-3. The market supply curve (labeled S) depicts the behavior of the supplying firms: the paper mills. The factors determining the shape and height of this supply curve are the costs that impinge directly on the profit-and-loss sheets of these mills—

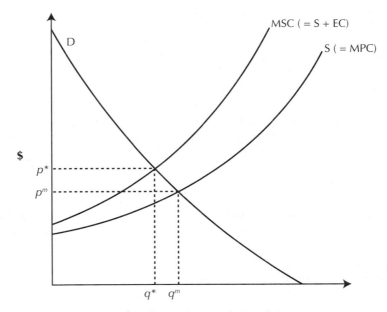

Figure 6-3   Market Performance in the Case of External Costs

such items as labor costs, energy costs, raw materials, and buildings. These costs—and the technology of paper production—determine the quantity of inputs needed to produce various quantities of output, their marginal costs of paper production, and therefore the market supply curve of paper. But the downstream external costs are legitimate social costs that need to be included when determining the socially efficient rate of paper output. The curve labeled MSC is the market supply curve plus the external costs (EC). MSC thus includes all the social costs of producing paper. Assume further that the demand curve D registers accurately the full social benefits of this product. Then the **socially efficient** quantity and price of paper are q^* and p^*, while the market will tend to settle at q^m and p^m. In other words, when environmental external costs are involved, normal market operations tend to lead to quantities that are too high and prices that are too low relative to socially efficient levels.[4] From a policy perspective the question is how to get these external costs **internalized,** so that the paper mills will choose output level q^* rather than q^m. We focus on this in the next chapter.

External Benefits

On the other side of the market, to say that the demand curve must be the same as the social marginal willingness-to-pay curve is to say that the market demand curve must include all the social benefits arising from the consumption of the good or service in question. Nobody is left out; all benefits are included, no matter to whom they accrue. If, on the other hand, significant social benefits accrue to people who are not direct participants in the market in question, then the market results are unlikely to be efficient. They may also be regarded as inequitable.

External benefits can be present in the same direct way that external costs are present. Suppose I consider buying a new lawn mower. I evaluate the different models available and the important characteristics of each, especially their prices. Another important feature is their noise level; in general, I can get a quieter machine if I am willing to pay a somewhat higher price. In making my decision I try to balance these two factors (there are probably more factors involved than just these two, but we disregard them to keep the example simple) in terms of my own tastes, preferences, and budget. But buying a quieter model would also confer benefits on my neighbors in the form of a generally quieter neighborhood. For my purchase to be fully socially efficient, not just efficient from my own perspective, these other benefits need to be included. These are **external benefits;** they accrue to somebody other than the person making the decision that produces them.

Suppose I own a farm that contains, in addition to a certain area of cleared fields, an area of woods. I maintain the woods because I like to produce maple sugar from its maple trees. In deciding how much wooded acreage to maintain, I weigh the benefits in terms of revenues from maple sugar with the costs in terms of not having the land available for pasture or cultivation. But suppose some interesting wild animals live in these woods. They are interesting perhaps because they are endangered or because people like to see them occasionally or simply know that they are there. The benefits produced by the wild animals are largely external benefits; they accrue to people who are not involved in the decision about how much of my land to keep as woods. When external benefits are involved, market outcomes tend to be inefficient, the outputs responsible for the external benefits are too small, and its price is too low.

External benefits are present whenever public goods are involved. We introduced this concept in chapter 3. A **public good** is a good that, once made available to one person, automatically becomes available to others. On Martha's Vineyard Island off the southeast coast of Massachusetts, there are two medium-size lighthouses guarding the entrance to the main harbor. The one on the eastern headland was built privately by Captain Daggett in 1878. The good captain, having built the lighthouse at his own expense, then approached the various companies and owners whose boats regularly came and went in the harbor and asked them for contributions to help cover the costs of the lighthouse. At this point, he ran into the classic problem of private markets and public goods. The lighthouse was (and still is) a public good: Its services can be used by anybody using the harbor, whether or not they have contributed anything to its construction and operation.

When public goods are involved, private markets find it difficult to supply socially efficient levels of output. Table 6-1 contains some numbers from chapter 3. They refer to the willingnesses to pay of three individuals for a program to restore bald eagles in a particular habitat. It also has a column showing the marginal cost of this program, which can be carried out at three different levels: light, moderate, or extensive. Comparing the aggregate marginal willingness to pay with the marginal cost shows that a moderate restoration program would be the one that maximizes net benefits to this society of just three people.

Suppose, then, a private firm were to engage in this restoration program. It puts up the $80 required for a moderate-level program, and then asks the three beneficiaries for contributions, commensurate with their willingnesses to pay, to cover the costs. Because of the nature of the good involved, it now becomes possible for the individuals to **free-ride.** Free-riding means holding back on one's contribution to get the benefits while bearing less of the cost. This is possible because it is a public good; once

Table 6-1 Benefits and Costs of Restoring Bald Eagles

| | Marginal Willingness to Pay | | | | |
	A	B	C	Aggregate WTP	Marginal Cost
Light	50	10	25	85	40
Moderate	30	5	10	45	40
Extensive	10	0	5	15	40

available, it produces benefits for everybody, regardless of how much or little they have contributed.

If everybody tries to free-ride,[5] then the firm doing the restoration is
likely to experience a revenue shortfall relative to its costs. Knowing this
was likely to be the case, they probably would not have undertaken the project in the first place. Thus private markets, in which transactions are concluded voluntarily and without coercion, will be hard put to supply the
efficient levels of this type of good or service. Free-riding tends to reduce
the revenues realized by sellers, thus weakening the incentive to produce
and make them available in efficient amounts. This is why relatively few
lighthouses are privately provided. In Captain Daggett's case, the free-rider
problem led him, after just a few years, to sell his lighthouse to the state of
Massachusetts, which could use tax revenues to maintain it.

Open-Access Resources

We come now to an important class of natural resources, the utilization
of which typically gives rise to external costs, and the effective management of which typically involves public goods and external benefits. For
these reasons they are often overutilized and overdepleted. The resources
in question are called **open-access resources.** An open-access resource is
simply one that is open to unrestricted use by anyone who might wish to utilize it. The classic example has always been the ocean fishery. Until fairly
recently most fisheries, for example the North Atlantic groundfish fishery,
could be fished by anybody who had a boat and the appropriate gear.
Another example is terrestrial wildlife in North America; historically hunters have had unrestricted access to stocks of wild game, such as birds, deer,
buffalo, or elk. Open-access resources need not be extractive resources.
Public parks, where visitors may enter without restriction, are also open-
access resources.

Open access typically leads to overuse. We can illustrate this with a very
simple example, that of a small public beach. Being public, the beach is
open to use by anybody who wishes to visit. This is somewhat artificial, of
course, because today beach access is often restricted in some way, for
example to residents of a particular community. Use restrictions are usually
a response to the problems stemming from open access. Let's consider a
simple numerical example of an open-access resource.

The essential data are shown in table 6-2. This small beach is located a
number of miles from a town center from which all the visitors originate.
The first column shows the potential number of visitors who might make
use of the beach on an average day; it runs from one to ten (it's a small
beach). The next two columns show individual marginal willingness to pay,
and then aggregate WTP. Marginal willingness to pay is the MWTP, given
that the number of visitors is currently at the level indicated. For example,
if today there are two visitors, the marginal willingness to pay of the third is
$20. Note—and this is critical—that MWTP stays constant at $20 until there

Table 6-2   An Open-Access Resource: Public Beach

Number of visitors	Individual marginal willingness to pay	Aggregate willingness to pay (WTP)	Cost per visit	Total costs (TC)	Aggregate WTP minus TC
1	$20	$20	$12	$12	$8
2	20	40	12	24	16
3	20	60	12	36	24
4	20	80	12	48	32
5	18	90	12	60	30
6	16	96	12	72	24
7	14	98	12	84	14
8	12	96	12	96	1
9	10	90	12	108	−18
10	8	80	12	120	-40

are four visitors; after that it begins to fall off. The reason for this is congestion. At higher levels of visitation, the quality of the beach diminishes because of congestion, so the MWTP by additional visitors declines.

On the cost side, we assume that the cost of visiting the beach is the same for every visitor, $12. We are assuming that the travel costs for each of the visitors to get to the beach are basically the same. We assume that there is no entry fee charged at the beach. The fifth column shows total visitation costs.

The efficient level of beach visitation is evidently four people per day. This is the level that maximizes the net benefits of the beach. We will now see, however, that if beach access is uncontrolled, visitation will be higher than this efficient level. Suppose that there are currently four people using the beach and that a fifth is trying to decide whether to visit. The cost to the fifth visitor is $12, her willingness to pay is $18; her visit will apparently lead to net benefits of $6, so she visits. But a sixth person will also realize positive net benefits from a visit, as will a seventh. It is only when we get to the eighth potential visitor that net individual benefits fall to zero, and for the ninth and tenth visitors, they are negative. So we can reason that with open access, total visitation will reach seven visitors and possibly eight (if the MWTP for the eighth were just slightly higher). This is substantially higher than the socially efficient visitation level.

In this case open access leads to a substantial overshoot—excessive use rates relative to efficient levels. The main reasons for this overshoot are called **open-access externalities.** These are externalities that the users of the resource inflict on one another in the form of diminished resource value.[6] In the beach case the diminished value stems from increased congestion. When the fifth prospective visitor is deciding whether to visit, she compares the gain she will have of $18 with the cost of $12 and acts accordingly. But in proceeding with her visit, she reduces the value of the beach to the four already there, from $20 to $18 for each one, a $2 loss times 4 visitors equals a total external cost of $8. This external cost is in fact higher than the individual gain of the fifth visitor and, for the sixth and seventh visitors, the individual gain would be less than the externality losses.[7]

The exact nature of the open-access externalities will differ from one type of resource to another. For the beach it was externalities in the form of beach congestion, which reduces the value of a beach visit. For hunters sharing a territory, including fishers working the same fishery, it is the added cost of harvesting, which stems from two sources: hunters more often intrude on one another and higher catch rates mean lower stocks. We encounter this type of resource problem many times in the following chapters.[8]

Open Access and the Dissipation of Resource Rent

There is another important observation to be made with this simple example. At the efficient visitation level of 4 visitors, aggregate willingness to pay is $80 and total costs are $48, for a net of $32. This $32 is actually a return attributable to the resource itself, in this case the beach. This is actually the **resource rent** being produced by the beach. A way of seeing this is to note that if the town authorities were to sell the beach to a private operator (and this is not a subtle hint for recommending this course of action; it's only to show the basis of the value of the beach), its price in a competitive market would be a reflection of this net valuation, because that would be the income-earning potential of the beach to anyone who happened to own it.

Suppose the open-access visitation level of the beach had in fact risen to eight people (the eighth is right on the margin, but let us assume he or she visits). At this level of use there is no rent; aggregate willingness to pay is $96, as is total cost. Open access has led, in other words, to the **dissipation,** or disappearance, of all natural resource rent. The total value of the visitation is being absorbed by the visitation costs of the recreators; it is as if the natural resource responsible for the benefits, the beach, is essentially of zero value. Note also that at other visitation levels (1, 2, 6, 7, and so on) the implied rent is positive but less than it is at 4 visitors. Another way of saying this is that the efficient use rate is the one that produces the **maximum natural resource rent.**

Overuse and rent dissipation are features of many natural resources: game resources harvested by recreational hunters, ocean fisheries harvested by commercial fishers, groundwater extracted by irrigators or municipalities, and so on. Clearly, the management issue in such cases is how to reduce the rates of resource utilization to something approaching efficient levels. This is the subject of the next chapter.

■ Markets and Intertemporal Efficiency

Compare panels (a) and (b) in figure 6-4. They represent two different versions of the output from, say, a group of timber companies. The output in this case is cubic feet of timber harvested during a particular year from a

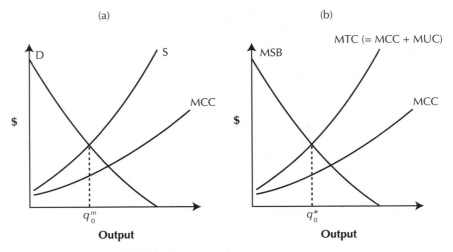

Figure 6-4   Markets and Intertemporal Efficiency

given geographical region. Panel (a) shows the classic market demand and supply curves. Panel (b) shows the socially efficient level of output, given by the balance of marginal social benefits and a function representing the total of marginal current costs and user costs. Will q_0^m and q_0^* be the same? Evidently they will be if all functions in the two panels are the same. Note that now the output has a time index; it is the output of the first period, recognizing that in the dynamic case this is just the first year of a multiple-period production program.

If there are no external benefits, then MSB = D. But on the cost side things are trickier. Panel (a) shows MCC (marginal current costs) and the supply function S. Here we have to recognize that there can be a difference in user costs seen from the private and social points of view. Private user costs incorporate future revenue changes impinging on firms as a result of decisions made today. The market rate of output, labeled q_0^m, is based on private user costs. Will this output level be intertemporally efficient from the social viewpoint?

Panel (b) shows the MTC as the sum of marginal current costs (MCC) and marginal user costs (MUC). In this case user costs are defined as future costs from the **social standpoint.** Evidently the market rate of output (q_0^m in panel a) will equal the socially efficient rate of output (q_0^* in panel b) if and only if the private user costs actually taken into account by suppliers are equal to the user costs considered from the standpoint of society as a whole.

Assume for the moment that there are no classic external costs of the type we discussed in the previous section (like emissions from pulp mills or ecological destruction by timber firms). Then the only way we can get a difference between S and MTC is for **private future costs** to be different from social future costs. For the most part, we are concerned with factors that may make private future costs lower than true social future costs, because when this is the case, the market rates of output will be too high relative to the output that is intertemporally efficient.

Markets and Discounting

There are several reasons why today's markets may function in ways that are not intertemporally efficient. Remember that the future costs of today's actions are in terms of **present value;** in other words, it is a future consequence **discounted** back to the present period. On the market this discounting will occur at discount rates that today's market participants apply according to their own views about the effects of time and its impacts on relative values to themselves. But suppose, in some wider social sense, people typically apply discount rates that are too high. There have been many observers through the years who have thought that the average person is too short-sighted; that individuals do not put sufficient weight on the future effects of their actions. In other words, they use private discount rates that are too high.

If this is true, then future costs affecting decisions of market suppliers will be too low relative to what might be called the socially efficient levels of future costs. And if this is indeed true, then contemporary natural resource markets will produce at levels that are too high and at prices that are too low relative to the levels that are socially efficient. Of course, like a lot of other things, it is easy to say this on a conceptual level. It is harder to figure out if it actually happens in the real world.

Tenure Conditions

Private future costs reflect the present value of future net revenue consequences flowing from today's decisions. By tenure conditions we mean factors that determine whether people today are affected by all the future consequences flowing from their behavior. Consider a logging firm operating on a timber concession given by the government of the region where the forest is located. Suppose the terms of the concession are only that it is non-renewable and lasts for 5 years. The effect of this is to cut off the impact today of any consequences that are more than 5 years in the future. In this extreme case, for example, a logging firm would have no incentive to replant after harvesting the trees, because the benefits from doing this would occur well beyond the time limit of the concession. In fact, the terms of concession would sharply reduce private future costs and lead the timber company to adopt something approaching a completely static viewpoint.

Another way in which private future costs can be attenuated (weakened or reduced) is through a lack of future marketability. Suppose the timber concession mentioned in the previous paragraph is long-run (permanent, in fact), but that it cannot be sold. If and when the current logging company no longer wishes to harvest trees in this area, it must give the concession back to the regional government. This has the same type of impact as the time limit, though it would probably not be as extreme as that case in terms of its impact on private user costs. A market, in this case a market for standing timber and the land on which it stands, is what allows the harvesting firm to profit from actions that maximize the value of that land. Without that possibility the firm would not have the incentive to avoid all actions that diminish the very long-run productivity of the timberland. That is to say, the private future cost would be lower than social future costs of harvesting the timber.

Of course, relaxing the assumption made above on traditional externalities also affects our conclusions. Suppose that one impact stemming from logging a particular piece of land this year is that higher rates of runoff and soil erosion will be experienced in the future. These are in effect future external costs, and would have the effect of making private future user costs from the standpoint of the individual lower than social user costs.

■ Some Additional Caveats

Humans come into contact with natural resources closely and continually, and at many points. So it is useful to have some way of systematizing our understanding of this interaction, and particularly some way of evaluating the relative importance of these points of contact. Market interactions provide a means of doing this.

Traditional markets work on the basis of individual incentives and voluntary participation. "Equilibrium" market prices in effect reveal the marginal value of an item to demanders and the marginal cost of making available an additional unit (or the cost saved by reducing supply by a unit). Traditional markets are "welfare improving," in the sense that they make demanders and suppliers better off than if they had no way of interacting at all. But there are a number of caveats we need to keep in mind.

We have seen a number of situations where private, voluntary markets will not function effectively. These situations involved externalities, public goods, and open-access resources.

One of the most obvious and important caveats about markets is that, for many important natural resources, markets simply may not exist. In which case market prices won't exist, and there is no ready way to discern the marginal value of either demanders or suppliers. Bald eagles exist, and have significant social value for their symbolic role. But there are no organized markets where interested people can exchange the symbolic services of bald eagles. We will deal with this issue in chapter 9.

We must remember also that markets register the value of those with enough purchasing power to participate in them. In other words, they reflect the current distribution of income and wealth; market prices would be different if these distributions were different. Not everyone can afford pricey vacations to those places in the world known as "hot spots" of biological diversity. In exhibit 6-1 on the next page we show a situation in which a subsidy is introduced into a market on grounds that an open-market, "socially efficient" price would be too high for certain low-income consumers. Energy markets in many countries are frequently managed this way, for example.

Exhibit 6-1 Market Subsidies to Promote Equity

Markets work on the basis of willingness to pay and willingness to supply. They provide the incentive for suppliers to produce, and make available, goods and services that are of value to others. But they do not provide incentives to make available goods and services to people who have no, or little, purchasing power. To achieve market results that are seen as more equitable, many governments **subsidize** the supply of particular goods or services. Several common subsidies that are relevant to natural resources, for example, are subsidies of the costs of purchasing more effective fishing equipment, and subsidies to users of groundwater for irrigation.

The figure below depicts how subsidies work. In this case it is assumed that government payments are made to suppliers to offset part of their costs. The unsubsidized supply curve is shown as S. With no government intervention the market price and quantity would be p_1 and q_1. Suppose the subsidy works by compensating producers a certain amount for each item produced. This lowers the effective supply curve to that labelled S_e, which is below S by the amount of the subsidy.

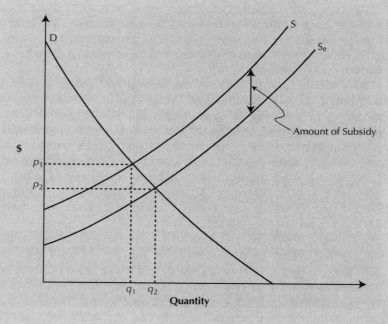

In the presence of the subsidy, the market-derived quantity and price are now p_2 and q_2. Price has gone down, quantity has gone up. On equity grounds the new situation might be regarded as an improvement over the unsubsidized outcome. This would be so if one thought that the original price was unfair to buyers in some respect. Note that with the subsidy in place there is a discrepancy between the marginal willingness to pay of buyers and the marginal cost of suppliers. This is often characterized as a **market distortion**. On a strictly efficiency basis, the most desirable outcome would be p_1 and q_1. But on grounds of equity, or fairness, p_2 and q_2 may be the most desirable outcome. We should mention that in the real world, subsidies are often the result of skillful political action rather than an ethical regard for equity in economic outcomes.

Finally, we must understand that, to function effectively, markets require an appropriate **institutional structure**, particularly a legal structure. This means rules and regulations regarding how they should operate, and how they should not operate, and the enforcement machinery to make sure the rules are followed. In the more developed countries of the world, the presence of this institutional structure is taken for granted. In many parts of the developing world effective market institutions do not exist, which accounts for the frequent cases in which efforts to use markets to guide resource use have ended in failure.

■ Summary

The basic question undertaken in this chapter was—Under what conditions will private markets be socially efficient? Markets operate according to the conditions of private demand and supply; that is, according to the marginal willingness to pay and marginal production costs of the participants in the market. If these conditions include all social benefits and all social costs, then markets will be socially efficient. We looked at some cases where external costs and/or external benefits might be a problem. Environmental costs are important instances of external costs, and social efficiency in the case of these costs requires that they be internalized or subject to direct public regulation. One important source of external costs is the case of open-access resources; we examined the problem of rent dissipation in resources of this type. We also discussed public goods, and saw that private markets in this case will normally lead to suboptimal output levels. Finally, we took up the question of markets and intertemporal efficiency and focused on the question of the conditions under which the future costs facing resource users will be too low relative to socially efficient levels.

Notes

[1] It bears repeating that we are using "market" in a general sense. To a financial trader in New York the "market" refers to the stock or bond market; to a cattle rancher in Nebraska the "market" refers to the Omaha livestock market; to a home builder in North Carolina the "market" refers to the market for new houses in that area, etc.

[2] "Equilibrium" is a somewhat technical term in economics, referring to a situation in which all the various forces that would tend to cause a situation to adjust and change are in balance. An equilibrium is not defined as a state of affairs where everybody is happy in some sense. Consumers would like to see a lower price, suppliers would be happy to have a higher price. Equilibrium is simply a state of affairs where there is a balance between quantity demanded and quantity supplied.

[3] It is, of course, true that many individuals running logging companies also place high values on the ecological services produced by forests.

[4] Note that even at q^* some external cost is present. Efficiency does not require, in other words, that all external costs totally disappear, only that they be properly included in the overall trade-off.

[5] Technically, a "free-rider" is a person who pays nothing toward the public good, while a person who pays something but less than commensurate with their true willingness to pay is an "easy-rider."

[6] There was a famous paper written on open-access problems titled "The Tragedy of the Commons" (Garrett Hardin, *Science*, Vol. 162, 1968, pp. 1243–1248). Commons in this case refers to open-access resources, which are sometimes called commons or common property. Hardin's example was an open-access pasture where individual farmers could graze as many animals as they wished. Here the open-access externality that leads to overuse of the resource is the diminution in the quality of the pasture as more and more animals are put on it.

[7] For the fifth, sixth, and seventh visitors, the situation is:

Visitor	Individual gain	External costs	Net gain
5	18 – 12 = 6	2 × 4 = 8	–2
6	16 – 12 = 4	2 × 5 = 10	–6
7	14 – 12 = 2	2 × 6 = 12	–10

[8] It is not just natural resources that have the open-access problem. Roads that are open to anyone are also open-access assets; the external costs in the case of road congestion are the increased travel times that motorists inflict on one another.

Key Terms

external benefits

external costs

free-riding

market prices and quantities

market supply and demand

markets and intertemporal efficiency

open-access resources

public goods

rent dissipation

subsidies

Questions for Further Discussion

1. Show that when external benefits are involved, market outputs and prices tend to be too low relative to socially efficient levels.

2. What is the impact of a rise in market interest rates on the intertemporally efficient rate of today's output?

3. How does the free-rider problem apply to: (a) radio stations, (b) bus riders, (c) commercial fishers?

4. Refer to the open-access beach problem in the text of this chapter and table 6-2. If the cost per day rose to $15, how many people would maximize the net benefits of the beach? And how many people would visit the beach under open access?

5. Roads (except for toll roads) are typically open access. In what sense are the rents dissipated in this case?

Useful Websites

The U.S. Environmental Protection Agency has a web page for the National Center for Environmental Economics (NCEE); it offers links on topics in environmental economics, which include many of the concepts covered in this chapter:

- (http://yosemite.epa.gov/ee/epa/eed.nsf/webpages/homepage)

For an online lecture on externalities, public goods, and market failure, see Public Economics Lectures, Part 7, by Raj Chetty and Gregory A. Bruich:

- (https://www.youtube.com/watch?v=o0lS2fljH-U)

Selected Readings

Folmer, Henk, H. Landis Gabel, and Hans Opschoor. *Principles of Environmental and Resource Economics*. Aldershot, England: Edward Elgar, 1995, chapter 2.

Hackett, Steven C. *Environmental and Natural Resource Economics: Theory, Policy, and the Sustainable Society*, 4th ed. Armonk, NY: M. E. Sharpe, 2001.

Kahn, James R. *The Economic Approach to Environmental and Natural Resources*, 3rd ed. Mason, OH: Thomas/South-Western, 2005.

Tietenberg, Tom, and Lynne Lewis. *Environmental and Natural Resource Economics*, 10th ed. Upper Saddle River, NJ: Prentice-Hall, 2015.

■■■■■■■■■■■■■■■■■■■■■■■■■■■■■■■■■■■

7

Public Policy for
Natural Resources

When individuals make decisions about resource use they are guided by their own incentives, the medley of actions available to them, and the institutional setting in which they find themselves. Guiding these actions so that they are socially useful and not just individually advantageous is the role of public policy.

Public policy refers to the collective actions that people undertake through governmental institutions. These actions shape the terms under which natural resources are used. Collective action can be pursued at many levels, from the local neighborhood and community to statewide or national efforts, or even at the global level. The public institutions through which policy is pursued differ from level to level, region to region, country to country, and even from time to time.

In this chapter we review some of the major types of policy alternatives that are available in a market economy to manage natural resource conservation and utilization. Although the discussion is conceptual to a large extent, we use natural resource examples to illustrate general cases. We are moving closer to the later chapters, which focus more deeply on issues involving specific natural resources. The objectives are (1) to understand that there are different types of natural resource policies and (2) to assess the applicability of these policies in different circumstances. Policy decisions are not simply technical exercises; they are full of conflict and political controversy. Benefits and costs are involved, and so are political ideologies and strategies. We are not going to deal with the political dimensions of the public policy process in this chapter. The goal is, rather, to clarify the economic/incentive aspects of different natural resource policy approaches so that we can identify which alternatives represent the best course of action for particular circumstances.

■ The Objectives of Public Policy

To say "best course of action" implies that we have a good idea what the **objectives** of public policy should be or, to say it another way, what **criteria** should be used to judge the effectiveness of different resource policies. Controversies over public policy occur for many reasons, one of which is disagreement and/or lack of clarity about policy goals. The most important of these goals are the following: economic efficiency, equity, flexibility, and enforceability.

Economic Efficiency

The attraction of economic efficiency is that it takes into account both the benefits and the costs of taking an action. Efficiency in the use of natural resources implies that the natural assets of society are being utilized in a way that **maximizes their net benefits** to the members of that society. So efficiency would seem to be a reasonable goal for any policy that purports to be in the public interest. A policy that is efficient, or moves toward efficiency, would be preferred over one that is not, other things being equal.

It needs to be said loudly and clearly that efficiency does not presuppose that market values are to be preferred over nonmarket values. Efficiency does not require, in other words, that some strictly monetary aggregate, akin to current gross domestic product (GDP) or gross community product (GCP),[1] be maximized. Many benefits from natural resources, particularly when we consider preservation rather than commercial harvest, are hard to measure. But the very essence of social efficiency is that all benefits, including nonmarket benefits, are to be counted.

Although efficiency as a goal may be fairly noncontroversial in the abstract, its actual realization in any particular resource-using circumstance is likely to be problematic and contentious for several reasons. One is that people differ in terms of the values they place on different outcomes. If what is involved is a private good, this is not a problem. Some people like cantaloupes and some do not, and it is perfectly plausible for some people to eat lots of cantaloupes and for others to eat few of them. But for public goods, production can be only at one level, which by definition is the same for everybody. Thus, conflicts can easily occur as to what that one level should be.

But perhaps the major difficulty leading to conflicts over the achievement of efficiency is the **information problem.** Everyone may agree in the abstract that we want to maximize net social benefits, but how can we be sure that this is being achieved in any particular case? Policies differ in terms of the amount and kinds of information needed in order to achieve outcomes that are reasonably efficient.

Equity

To be equitable means to be fair. Just because a resource-use plan is efficient doesn't mean it is fair. Fairness has to do with how the overall benefits and costs of natural resource use are distributed among subgroups of the overall population. Achieving fairness is very much a matter of getting underlying institutions and rules right. Any law or regulation will tend to advantage some people and disadvantage others; equity requires that these interests be balanced in a way that is regarded as fundamentally just. In natural resource economics there is always the problem of balancing a local interest with a national one.

Suppose a local community has an important deposit of a nonrenewable resource, such as petroleum. From an economy-wide perspective, efficiency might call for extraction of the deposit at a rapid rate; depletion of this one deposit may have relatively little national significance because it is only one of many. From the standpoint of the community, however, it may have great significance. It may represent the primary source of nonhuman wealth in the community. An efficient extraction program at the national level may be regarded as unfair at the local level (see exhibit 7-1).

One of the major issues in contemporary natural resource economics is that of **preservation vs. extraction.** A local community may have an important resource, such as an expanse of standing timber or a large body of water. Overall national efficiency may call for preservation of these resources or for their utilization at relatively low rates. But this might be regarded as unfair to local communities that rely on these resources for an economic base. For example, a town may rely on fees from timber or mineral sales to finance its schools.

Public resource policies (indeed virtually any type of public policy) very often are characterized by a distributional disconnect regarding their benefits and their costs. It is often the case that either (1) benefits are widely spread among the population while costs are localized or (2) benefits are localized and the costs are widely dispersed. These spreads are illustrated numerically in table 7-1 on the following page. The numbers represent benefits and costs from three possible policies as they would accrue to five different individuals. Policy A has benefits and costs that are evenly distributed among the population of five individuals. Policy B has evenly

---

Exhibit 7-1   Fracking for Natural Gas: Local or State Control?

The rush headlong into "fracking" (short for hydraulic fracturing) for natural gas in the United States has left many communities dotted with drilling rigs and wells. The underlying U.S. legal structure is that, as long as energy companies own or lease the required mineral rights, they can drill just about anywhere. In something of a backlash, many affected communities have come to realize that there may be places in town (parks, water supplies, historical sites) where drilling ought not to be permitted. But in most states the rules regarding who may drill, and where, are promulgated at the state level rather than by local governments. Lots of communities are struggling with efforts to change the rules, on grounds that it would be more equitable to give the locals a greater say in drilling practices since they are the ones most directly affected.

Table 7-1   **Alternative Distribution of Benefits and Costs**

		Individuals				
	Total	**1**	**2**	**3**	**4**	**5**
Policy A						
Benefits	100	20	20	20	20	20
Costs	80	16	16	16	16	16
Policy B						
Benefits	100	20	20	20	20	20
Costs	80	40	10	10	10	10
Policy C						
Benefits	100	80	5	5	5	5
Costs	80	16	16	16	16	16

distributed benefits but concentrated costs; costs are proportionately much higher for individual 1 than for the other individuals. Policy C has evenly distributed costs but concentrated benefits.

In the case of policy B, total net benefits are positive. However, individual net benefits are positive for four people and very negative for the remaining one. An example might be the Endangered Species Act (ESA). Overall, the ESA may have positive net benefits. The benefits of this act are presumably widely diffused, in the sense that all citizens enjoy the benefits (especially the "nonuse" benefits). The costs, on the other hand, are very likely to be concentrated, especially on those individuals owning land where endangered species are found.

In the case of policy C, total net benefits are also positive, but there are four individuals for whom net benefits are negative and only one for whom they are strongly positive. The reason for this is that benefits are highly concentrated. An example might be a beach restoration project, which has substantial benefits locally but few beyond the local area and for which the costs are spread in a very diffuse pattern among general taxpayers.[2]

Another important social dimension of the equity issue is how policies treat people who have different amounts of wealth. Markets are clear in at least one major respect; resources tend to flow toward people who have not only the willingness to pay but also the **ability to pay.** The tastes and preferences of people who lack adequate wealth are relatively unrepresented in normal markets. They may or may not be underrepresented in **political markets.** If they are underrepresented, then charitable or humanitarian causes must take over, and that support may or may not be very strong in particular circumstances.

A major equity issue in current resource controversies is the balance to be struck among the generations: that which is here now and those that will be around in the future, even the distant future. This is the major focus of the concept of sustainability, which refers essentially to the idea that current generations should not undertake actions today that will create conditions making it substantially more difficult for future generations to achieve today's living standards.

Flexibility

The primary national statute governing mineral exploration and extraction on public land in the United States was enacted in 1872. Although it has been significantly amended several times since then, many of the central provisions of that early mining law still apply. The price for purchasing, or "patenting," a mineral claim is still $5 an acre, for example, just as it was when the law was passed. This is an example of a seriously inflexible natural resource management policy. Conditions in mineral industries have obviously changed a lot since the 19th century, as have conditions elsewhere in the economy. As a matter of common sense, if the law was appropriate for the conditions of the 19th century, it is unlikely to be appropriate today. Largely for political reasons, however, the law does not change.

This suggests another important criterion for evaluating natural resource policies—namely, how well they adapt to changing circumstances. "Changing circumstances" in economics means essentially two general things: (1) changes on the demand side in terms of social factors and values that affect the willingness to pay for different goods and services and (2) changes on the supply side that affect the availability of resources. As an example on the demand side, major shifts have occurred in recent decades in the value people place on preserving natural resources; at the same time, a very substantial natural resource-based outdoor recreation sector has emerged. Policies that were appropriate in an era when natural resource development and extraction was a prime objective are not likely to be prudent when values shift strongly toward preservation. As an example on the supply side, urban growth, in terms of number of people and their geographical spread, has led to great reductions in the availability of accessible open land in urban and suburban regions. Policies that guided urban growth in times when open space was ample may not be appropriate when it gets increasingly scarce.

Other factors being equal, policies that adjust and evolve more or less automatically to changing resource availabilities and human values are to be desired over policies that do not.

Enforceability

Public policies result from a political process, in which groups and interests collide and compete, striving for support and influence. The maneuvering and coalition building that take place produce political theater as much as substantive actions. One result of this is that laws are frequently enacted without addressing the issue of enforcement. Sometimes they are simply unenforceable at a reasonable cost. Often it is simply assumed that enforcement will be carried out with vigor and with ample resources, but this is never true in the real world. Enforcement resources are always scarce, which is why the **enforceability** of laws and regulations is an important criterion.

■ Types of Public Policies

In a fundamental sense, the policy problem refers to the question of how to bring about a state of affairs in which people's private behavior is also socially appropriate. There are basically only two general ways of doing this. One is to structure the system so that the **incentives** people face will lead them to make decisions that are simultaneously both in their own best interest and in society's best interest. The other way is to institute **direct controls** that limit the actions of people through fiat, or involve direct public production and/or distribution. These options can be further broken down as follows:

I. Incentive-Based Policies

A. Market/property rights policies: Many natural resource problems can be attributed to inadequate or inappropriate property rights governing access to the resources. The most effective way to solve the problem may be to institute a new system of property rights. Essentially this means establishing and enforcing a new set of rules governing property rights and market transactions, and then letting the rate of use of natural resources be established by voluntary interaction among suppliers and demanders.

B. Government-sponsored incentive policies: Public agencies employ such devices as taxes and subsidies to structure the incentives facing resource users.

II. Direct Public Action

A. Command-and-control policies: Public authorities establish direct controls on individual actions, enforcing these controls with standard legal enforcement practices.

B. Direct public production: Public agencies themselves own natural resources and themselves pursue programs of production and distribution.

We can best distinguish among these options by considering a specific natural resource. Barnstable Bay on Cape Cod is a large, relatively shallow embayment that contains extensive areas of productive shellfish flats. For many years these resources were open to harvest by any person who was a bona fide resident of the community and had the minimal equipment necessary for the job. For a long time this sufficed, in the sense that the number of fishers and quantities harvested did not substantially reduce the productivity of the clam beds. Around the middle of the 20th century, however, this began to change, as the number of summer recreators in town began to grow and the commercial shellfish market experienced rapid expansion. This brought added fishers, greater pressure on the fishery, and declining yields in terms of quantity and quality. The problem in this case was one of open access, a concept that was introduced in chapter 6. What are the options for reducing the overfishing and moving toward the efficient utilization of this resource?

Property Rights Policies.   In this case the town would divide the bay into a relatively large number of parcels (the water is shallow so markers can be used, or shore points can be used for reference). It would then lease or sell these parcels to individual fishers, who would be free to make their own harvest decisions on their parcels. The leases would be long-term, so leasees would have time to take advantage of long-run management plans, such as seeding the areas with young clam stock and systematically rotating harvest plots within their overall leaseholds. The leaseholds may be bought and sold among fishers. The job of the town shellfish officer now is to keep a record of who holds each parcel and make sure that trespassers do not encroach on anyone's holding.

Government-Sponsored Incentive Policy.   The town could simply levy a tax per bushel of clams harvested on fishers in the bay. The tax could be different for commercial and recreational diggers, and for different sizes of clams. In effect the tax now becomes a new operating cost for clam diggers. By shifting their cost curves upward, the expectation is that the quantity of clams dug in the bay would decrease, simply as a result of fishers responding to the new financial conditions of harvesting and not because of any direct controls on their operations. The job of the shellfish officer is to get accurate data on the quantity of individual harvests, and then send out and collect the tax bills.

Direct Command and Control.   The town of Barnstable would establish a set of rules governing the harvesting of shellfish in the bay. It already has a rule limiting access to town residents; different rules could be set for year-round residents and for summer residents. Rules could be established for the maximum allowable individual harvest per day or per year. Rules could be set for the type of fishing gear that would be allowed, for the minimum size of clam that could be kept, and so on. In this case the town shellfish officer would be instructed to take whatever steps were necessary to enforce the rules, such as surveillance, monitoring of landings, examination of financial records, and the like.

Direct Public Production.   The town of Barnstable, or some other public agency, might go into direct production itself, asserting ownership of the resource, hiring people to do the fishing, selling or giving away the clams, and distributing revenues in whatever way it chooses. A town shellfish officer would patrol the clam beds to make sure there is no unauthorized clamming.

In the real world, of course, mixtures of policy measures are possible. For example, direct controls on harvest quantities can be combined with a tax; private property rights may be combined with rules on clamming operations; and so on. Mixtures are very common. Private ownership of land resources is a dominant system in most Western countries. But these ownership institutions are usually accompanied by rules that limit the uses to which land may be put, as well as taxes on land. Many public parks and forests in the United States (direct government production) make use of entrance fees (financial incentives) and harvest concessions (property rights) to control resource use. The reason for discussing them separately is to make clear the way each works and, especially, the conditions that have to be met for them to achieve efficient and equitable resource-use rates.

In the rest of the chapter we consider each of these alternatives in more detail. To do this, we work with a simple numerical example. Consider the data in table 7-2, which show the costs and returns of a small clam fishery. The second column is catch per fisher. From 1 to 4 fishers, this is 20 pounds per day. From 5 fishers up, the catch per fisher goes down because of open-access externalities the fishers inflict on one another; more fishers create congestion and greater scarcity, so the catch rates go down. The larger the number of fishers, the more the decline. The third column shows total catch, which, if we assume the clams sell for $1 per unit, is also equal to total revenue. The last four columns show, respectively, costs per fisher (assumed the same for all fishers), total costs, net returns per fisher, and aggregate net returns (total revenue minus total costs).

You will no doubt recognize these numbers. They are the ones we used to illustrate the concept of an open-access resource back in chapter 6, except that there they were used to illustrate the problem of visitors to an open-access beach. The rent-maximizing number of fishers is 4, as we can tell by looking at the last column. But the open-access number of fishers will tend toward 8, because the returns per fisher are positive up to this point. The policy question is—how do we achieve a reduction in fishers to efficient levels?

Table 7-2 Daily Costs and Returns from Clam Fishery

Number of fishers	Catch per fisher (pounds per day)	Total Catch (revenue)*	Cost per fisher	Total Costs	Net returns per fisher	Aggregate net returns
1	20	$20	$12	$12	$8	$8
2	20	40	12	24	8	16
3	20	60	12	36	8	24
4	20	80	12	48	8	32
5	18	90	12	60	6	30
6	16	96	12	72	4	24
7	14	98	12	84	2	14
8	12	96	12	96	0	0
9	10	90	12	108	-2	-18
10	8	80	12	120	-4	-40

*On the assumption that each unit of shellfish has a market value of $1.

[handwritten margin note, left:] If we Privatize the fishery, the owner will want to get to SO point — SO (at 4); PM (at 8)

[handwritten note, bottom:] • if tax $7, then cost per fisher = 19. 8-7 is 1, then net return is 1 and only 4 fishers would enter the market

■ Private Property Rights

The overuse of many natural resources can be attributed to the fact that **property rights** to these resources are either ill-defined or not adequately exercised. By this diagnosis the rent on open-access resources is dissipated, in whole or in part, because the resource does not have an owner, or owners, who will limit its use in order to maximize its value. Consider the following scenario:

> A large expanse of remote land contains areas of forests, natural meadows, sizeable streams, and several rivers. Over the years substantial amounts of the forests have been logged and some of the meadows have been used for grazing cattle. Many people have also pushed into the area, on the logging roads and trails, to pursue a variety of outdoor recreation activities: hunting, backpacking, canoeing, and camping. In fact in recent years, use of the region became so heavy that the natural resources started to sustain damage—for example, by erosion from heavily used lands, water pollution, fires attributable to humans, littering, and a growing scarcity of certain game animals.
>
> There are calls for intervention by the state department of natural resource management. But the land is currently owned by several dozen large private landowners. The landowners themselves are aware of the resource degradation and the public access that is causing it. They decide that they can act together to reduce this damage and, furthermore, provide themselves with a modest but significant flow of income. So they create a number of controlled access points into the area, and then begin charging entry fees to people who want to use the area. The landowners create a small firm to manage the resources of the region and the outdoor recreators who make use of them. One of the first things the firm does, for example, is to establish rules for the logging companies who are allowed access, so that logging practices will not substantially impact the outdoor recreation values of the region.

What we have here is an example of resource management pursued through the use of **private property institutions**.[3] The essence of social efficiency is that natural resources be used in ways that maximize their net value to society. The essence of the property rights approach is to define these rights clearly enough so that private owners, in pursuing their own personal interests in maximizing their own wealth, will simultaneously maximize the net benefits flowing from the resource.

The property rights approach to our clam-bed problem is, therefore, to convert the clam beds to private property. It will then be in the interests of the owners to adopt levels of use that maximize the value of the resource. In the numerical example the owner(s) would have the incentive to limit entry to 4 fishers and to defend the boundary of the resource so that the level of extraction does not exceed that level. In fact, however, incentives would go beyond this. In an open-access situation, nobody would invest in efforts to, for example, seed the clam bed or cultivate it so as to increase long-run yields. If somebody were to do this, others could move in to reap the benefits. But privatizing the resource would change this: By allowing owners to exclude others, there would be an incentive to invest in these long-run improvements.

Privatization could be accomplished in various ways. In many instances resources of this type have been privatized informally through self-organization and management by users without the official sanction of public authorities. Exhibit 7-2 recounts a case of this type, dealing with the harbor gangs of Maine who have sought in effect to privatize portions of the lobster fishery of that state. In some cases, like the example of the forest owners discussed above, boundaries already exist and it is up to the existing owners to agree on joint action to maintain them and manage the resource. In others, new boundaries may be specified and the resource distributed in some way to new owners. In the case of the Barnstable Harbor clam fishery, long-term leaseholds were identified by boundary markers and these were distributed to some of the people who had been in the clam fishery for many years.

Irrespective of how they are initially distributed, property rights must have several important characteristics if they are to lead to socially efficient resource use. They must be:

1. Complete (or reasonably so)
2. Enforceable at reasonable cost

Exhibit 7-2   The Maine Lobster Gangs—Informal Privatization

The coast of Maine is heavily indented and studded with small islands. It is also the locale of a very rich lobster fishery. Lobsters are sea creatures, the legal status of which historically has been an open-access resource. But to avoid the excessive harvests and overfishing that open-access resources normally experience, the lobster fishers of Maine have resorted to informal privatization. They have done this through means of harbor gangs, which are informal groups of fishers in each harbor who establish and enforce boundaries around "their" particular harbors or islands. The boundaries do not have legal status but are enforced anyway, essentially through trashing (or threats thereof) the gear of interlopers—that is, people from outside the harbor. Of course, the ability of any harbor gang to do this effectively varies. Where it is small and close-knit (consisting, for example, of family relatives around a smallish island), a gang may quite effectively exclude outsiders. In bigger harbors with more diverse populations and greater demand for lobsters, exclusion is more difficult to pursue and so is less complete. There are other formal, legal constraints in effect also, for example, on minimum sizes for harvested lobsters.

History reveals many cases like this, where an open-access resource is privatized to a greater or lesser extent by informal user groups. It demonstrates the potential gains that can be obtained by moving in the direction of private property. When there is open access, there will be rent dissipation. When access is limited, rents will become positive and will accrue to the people doing the excluding (unless they are partially taxed away).

Source: The original work on the Maine lobster gangs appeared in James M. Acheson, *The Lobster Gangs of Maine,* University of New Hampshire Press, 1988. Additional information can be found in Jennifer F. Brewer, "Don't Fence Me In: Boundaries, Policy and Deliberation in Maine's Lobster Commons," *Annals of the American Association of Geographers*, 102(2), 2012, pp. 383–402; and James M. Acheson and Roy Gardner, "The Evolution of the Maine Lobster V-Notch Practice, Cooperation in a Prisoner's Dilemma Game," *Ecology and Society*, 16(1), 2011, p. 41 (online), www.ecologyandsociety.org/vol16/iss1/art417.

3. Transferable

4. Combined with a complete set of competitive markets

Complete.   A fancy way of saying this is that the property rights must not be **attenuated** in any way relevant to the use to which they will be put. In other words, they must not be limited in any way that would reduce the incentives of the owners to search out the use level that maximizes their value.

In actual practice, all property rights are attenuated to some extent. For purposes of protecting the public health, owners do not have the right to use their property in a way that would injure others. But the extent of legitimate restrictions is a controversial issue. People digging clams on private lease-holds in the bay presumably do not have the right to drive large pilings down and construct a hotel on stilts in the middle of the harbor. This would seem to be a restriction that is obviously conducive to the public welfare. But in some circumstances restrictions of this type might foreclose value-increasing courses of action on the part of the owners.

Enforceable at Reasonable Cost.   By enforceable we mean two things: (1) that would-be trespassers can be excluded at reasonable cost and (2) that owners can be effectively enjoined from using their property in ways that are illegal. **Exclusion** has two dimensions, technical and legal. The **technical** side is the physical means available for stopping trespassers: the ability to mark boundaries, the use of fences in the case of some land boundaries, the costs of surveillance, and so on. The **legal** side relates to whether boundaries are recognized by legal authorities. Both factors are important. In many cases natural resources that are legally open-access resources have been essentially "privatized" by individuals or groups who take it upon themselves to exclude certain outsiders. The Maine lobster gangs are an instance of this. There have also been many cases where property, which legally is owned by defined individuals or groups, is still subject to open access because the costs of excluding encroachers is simply too high relative to the gains the owners would achieve by doing so.

The other part of enforceability is that it must be possible to stop the owners themselves from using their resources in ways that are illegal. In most countries there are legal requirements that forestry companies are supposed to follow in harvesting timber—for example, limits on clear cutting. If these limits are not enforceable because of, say, the costs of detection, then they obviously cannot be effective.

Transferable.   Suppose I operate a farm on land leased from the community. It is a long-term lease, but it is not transferable. As long as I wish to farm, I can occupy the land. I may even be able to pass it on to my sons and daughters. But I cannot sell it to third parties. Suppose I am thinking of retiring and moving into town. If I had no heirs I would have to relinquish the land at that point in time. This situation effectively reduces to me the **user costs** of mining the fertility of the soil and the productivity of whatever other natural assets exist on the farm (a small groundwater aquifer, for example). It reduces the incentive to maintain the maximum market value of these natural assets, because in effect they are not marketable.

The Presence of Markets. Suppose I own a piece of forestland that I currently use for light timbering and wood pasture for a small herd of cattle. Suppose also that in my region there is some pressure to convert forestland into house lots; some nearby land has already been converted, and the suburban area is expected to continue to spread. Markets for agricultural land and for suburban land are well developed, meaning that there are well-recognized prices for land devoted to these uses; these prices register the social value of these services producible by the land. Suppose my land is also well recognized by biologists as an area of rich biodiversity. In technical terms, the land apparently produces **biodiversity preservation services,** which would be reduced if the forestland is either cultivated more intensively or converted to house lots.

If a market exists such that I could obtain a revenue flow equal to the value of these biodiversity services, this flow would be capitalized into the price of the land, which then would function as an opportunity cost of devoting the land to some other use.[4] But if no such market exists, land prices will not reflect these other ecological services that the land produces. Market prices for land having unique biological attributes will be too low, relative to land that does not. For private property to lead to efficient resource-use patterns, markets must exist so that owners can capture the full value of the services produced by the resource in question. Only then can we be sure that resources will be devoted to the uses that maximize their social value.

Property rights arrangements have efficiency implications; they also have important distributional, or equity, implications. If the clam beds in Barnstable Harbor are allotted to private owners, many people who used to dig clams there may not be able to do so anymore. And what if many of these people do not have good alternative means of supporting themselves? If an open-access woodland is changed to restricted entry (in the sense of entrants now having to pay for use), local people who used to be able to enter the area may find themselves excluded, especially if their incomes are low. These examples point out that property-rights solutions to resource issues normally have important distributional consequences. This has been especially obvious in some ex-socialist countries, such as Russia and Ukraine, where the privatization of natural-resource holdings has enriched a small number of well-connected people.

■ Government-Sponsored Incentive Policies

A **government-sponsored incentive policy** is one in which regulatory authorities try to shift the incentive aspects of a situation so that resource users will be motivated voluntarily to adjust their behavior in the direction of efficiency. These plans normally involve taxes, subsidies, or a combination of the two.

Taxes

Consider again the situation depicted in table 7-2. Suppose authorities now institute a charge of $7 per day per fisher, which acts essentially as an entrance fee that all fishers must pay to gain access to the fishery. This does not change the fundamentals of the fishery in terms of the harvest rates, harvest costs, and the efficient number of fishers. What it does change is the financial incentives facing each fisher. From the standpoint of the fishers, the Cost-per-Fisher column now consists of $19 throughout rather than $12. We know that in an open-access situation entry will increase up to the point where marginal cost (in this case $19) equals average harvest value. This now occurs at a rate of 4 fishers (actually it occurs between 4 and 5 fishers; we are assuming that fishers come only in integer values). The tax, in other words, has shifted the costs of the fishers so that now, even with no direct control over entry, the number of fishers will stop at 4, the socially efficient level. However, from a **distributional standpoint,** the tax approach is quite different from the property rights approach studied earlier. With the $7 tax, the Net Returns column can now be divided as follows:

Number of fishers	Total	Net returns accruing to fishers	Tax receipts
1	$ 8	$ 1	$ 7
2	16	2	14
3	24	3	21
4	32	4	28
5	30	−5	35
6	24	−18	42
7	14	−35	49
8	0	−56	56
9	−18	−81	63
10	−40	−110	70

Distributionally, then, the tax transfers most of the rent of the fishery from the pockets of the fishers to the coffers of the taxing authorities. In the property rights approach the total rent shared by the 4 fishers would be $32; in the tax approach it would be $4, and the authorities would get the other $28. Of course, such distributional consequences reduce the political attractiveness of using taxes to achieve efficient resource utilization rates.

In order for an efficient tax to be applied, authorities must have accurate knowledge of the costs and revenues of the typical fisher. This is a central weakness of the tax approach because the only reasonable place for the authorities to get this knowledge is from the operators themselves. Note that a standard income tax will not have the desired efficiency effects. A normal income tax would take a certain percentage of a fisher's net income. Suppose a 50 percent income tax rate were applied to the fisher example in table 7-2. The Returns-per-Fisher column would change as if those numbers were all multiplied by 0.5. But the open-access number of fishers would still be 8. To have the desired efficiency effect, in other words, the tax has to be levied per unit of effort (i.e., per fisher) or per unit of harvest. This puts more burden on the taxing authorities, in terms of getting accurate enough information to identify the efficient tax level.

Subsidies

It may not seem obvious, but a cleverly designed system of **subsidies** could have the same efficiency effects as a tax, with entirely different distributional consequences. Suppose the clam fishery is currently operating at open-access levels (i.e., there are 8 fishers on the fishery). The authorities now step in and offer a subsidy of $7 to each fisher who will refrain from fishing. Now consider the eighth fisher; this individual is essentially just breaking even: $12 of catch and $12 of cost. He clearly would be better off by taking the subsidy and ceasing operations that year. The same could be said for the seventh fisher (current net gain of $2, as compared to the $7 subsidy), the sixth, and the fifth. But at 4 fishers, no further reduction would occur because the marginal return ($8) is greater than the subsidy.

For this subsidy to have the appropriate efficiency effects, authorities would have to stop people entering the fishery solely for the purpose of obtaining the subsidy by quitting. This means the authorities must have a reasonably accurate knowledge of the open-access level of the fishery, together with the cost and revenue situation of the typical fisher, so that the subsidy could be set at the correct level. It needs to be stressed that this is a very particular type of subsidy. It is essentially a payment to individuals in return for their reduced use of the resource in question; the objective is to affect the rate at which the resource is used. Subsidies in the real world are seldom like this; they usually have a redistribution objective to transfer income, often from the general taxpayer to favored groups or sometimes to individuals. We discuss some of these in later chapters.

■ Direct Controls

The direct approach to controlling natural resource use, often called the **command-and-control approach**, is simply to enact a regulation specifying, for example, maximum use rates, and then using normal means (like monitors and police) to enforce the regulations. In the Barnstable Harbor case the town could establish a regulation saying that only the first 4 fishers to apply would be allowed and after that no further entry would be permitted. Anybody else caught harvesting clams would be arrested and fined. Many different types of controls have been used in different circumstances:

1. An upper limit on the total quantity of fish caught annually from a certain fishery; after the limit is reached the fishery is closed

2. A limit on the specific uses to which a piece of land may be put, for example, zoning regulations

3. A limit on the quantity of water that particular users may withdraw each year from a nearby river

4. A limit on the number of people who are allowed access to a state or national park

5. A limit on the quantity of timber that may be harvested from a given parcel of land

The command-and-control approach to regulation appears to be simple and straightforward, deceptively so. Consider figure 7-1. It shows the market demand (D) and supply (S) of a natural resource; left to itself the market quantity would settle down at q^m. But suppose there are additional costs not being taken into account by the market suppliers—ecological costs associated with producing timber, for example. After having studied the situation, the authorities decide that the true social cost function is MSC and that the socially efficient rate of output is q^*, not q^m. A regulation is therefore promulgated stating that the maximum allowable production is q^*.

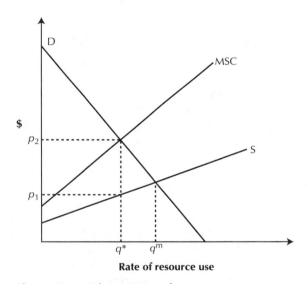

Rather clearly, if a direct regulation like this is to achieve effi-

Figure 7-1   Direct Controls

ciency, the regulators must have good knowledge of the underlying costs and benefits. In order to identify a policy target level like q^* in the figure, they must know not only the nonmarket ecological costs that the market is currently leaving out, they also must have a good idea about private production costs, as well as the market demand curve. Regulation of this type, therefore, places a very substantial **information burden** on the public agencies responsible for regulations. This burden will be higher than is apparent in figure 7-1. If q^* is an **aggregate output limit,** this may have to be broken down into individual output limits for the firms making up the aggregate. To do so effectively requires information about the cost structure of each of these firms. Information on costs of this type usually must come from the regulated community itself, which puts a substantial burden on the agency to get data that is reasonably accurate.

A major issue of the command-and-control approach is the **enforcement** process. Suppose output has been reduced by regulation to q^* in figure 7-1. At that point, the market price is going to be p_2, whereas the marginal costs of production are at p_1. Any producing enterprise that can find a way to produce one more unit of this item will profit by an amount equal to $p_2 - p_1$. We might call this the **incentive to be noncompliant.** The more restrictive the regulation, the larger this incentive will be. This is not to say that regulations of this type are never justified. Historically, direct command-and-control regulations have been the primary way that public policy has been pursued. In many cases, however, the enforcement part of the whole process has been overlooked.

■ Direct Public Production

The last policy approach to be discussed in this chapter is **direct government production.** In the case of Barnstable Harbor, the town in this case would claim title to the clam flats. They would appoint a "clam production committee," which would hire clam diggers, police boundaries, sell the harvested clams on the open market, and deposit the proceeds (the rents) in their own bank account. These funds could then be used by the town for whatever purpose it chooses. In fact, this is analogous to privatization, but in this case the owning and acting organization is a public body rather than a private firm.

In fact, direct public production of this general type appears in many places. Public parks at community, state, and national levels operate in this general way, as do national forests, national monuments, and the like. Much of the original public domain in the United States is still in public ownership. In many other countries whole sectors (electricity production, banking) have been nationalized at various times, although at present the trend seems to be going the other way.

In principle there is nothing to stop a natural resource–owning public organization from using that resource in a socially efficient way. To do this, it would have to function much as a private firm would, with the added proviso that it includes all external costs and benefits, as well as nonmarket costs and benefits, in its deliberations. In actuality, of course, it is difficult for political firms to function in this way. The incentive for private firms to move toward efficiency is that they are residual **claimants**; that is, they get to keep the net revenues or, in the case of natural resources, the resource rents. But public agencies are seldom in this situation. Revenues collected by public firms usually go into general revenues rather than into the specific bank account of the agency itself. Expenditures of the agencies are not constrained by collected revenues but by budgets that are enacted in the context of a political decision process in which outcomes are a result of the interplay of interests and influences by affected individuals and groups. The question is whether public agencies involved in direct production can assess and balance these various interests so as to get close to something that qualifies as a socially efficient outcome. In some cases they may, and in other cases they may not.

In the case of natural resources, public production often takes the form of allowing private firms to have access to public domain resources under controlled conditions. That is, the legal title to the in situ resources remains for the most part with the public, but the extraction is actually done by private firms who harvest and sell the resources. The contractual terms of these arrangements, and therefore the prices paid for the resources, varies from one resource to another. For example:

- The U.S. Forest Service (U.S. Department of Agriculture) auctions the right to harvest timber in national forests.

- The Bureau of Land Management (U.S. Department of the Interior) charges fees to ranchers for grazing animals on publicly owned land.

- The Minerals Management Service (U.S. Department of the Interior) leases through auction offshore areas to private companies for the exploration and production of oil and gas.

Contracts of this type always have been controversial and are destined to become more so. Critics often charge that the prices at which public domain resources are sold are often lower than their fair market values. Users of the resources normally argue the opposite. Managers of the public domain are under increasing pressure to shift resource use away from extractive and toward nonextractive uses. And the environmental impacts stemming from the extraction of public domain resources are becoming a growing concern. In subsequent chapters we revisit this issue as we discuss particular natural resources.

■ Market Failure/Government Failure

In the previous pages we have focused on the many ways in which a society can manage its natural resource endowment. All approaches to resource management involve collective action of one sort or another. In some cases this consists of the collective establishment of a legal system of property rights and markets, after which natural resource use rates are determined through the decentralized interactions of buyers and sellers. At the other extreme is direct public production. And there are many types of policy intervention involving combinations of public and private actions. The usual justification for overt public action of one type or another is that strictly decentralized property rights and markets don't produce results that are socially equitable and efficient. This is called **market failure,** and is linked usually to such problems as the presence of externalities, public goods, and myopia on the part of present generations. When these kinds of problems are present, private markets are incapable of operating efficiently and public policy is called for.

But there is a danger here of evaluating alternative public policy intervention only in terms of what might be called **ideal types**; that is, policy as it would work in theory if it were conducted by totally selfless public servants who always acted in the public interest using good information on possible outcomes. But this is never true. Public policies are normally pursued in a highly politicized environment by public servants who usually mean well but who have their own views of where the public interest lies, and who work with information that is usually incomplete and often biased. So public policies in practice are never likely to give the results that they would appear to promise in theory. A way to describe this is **government failure**. Government failure can happen in many ways:

- Regulations are enacted but **inadequately enforced**.
- Regulations are enacted that create **perverse incentives,** making situations worse instead of better. An example of this is discussed in exhibit 7-3.
- Laws and regulations are enacted in the name of efficiency but in reality are **redistributive**; that is, they are attempts by one group to wrest resources away from another group.
- Laws are enacted in the name of correcting **market failures**, whereas the real objective is to protect the privileged position of an existing group with respect to the use of a natural resource.
- Laws and regulations are pursued that essentially require information that public agencies and private firms do not have and cannot get.

When considering the possibility of public policy, it is not correct to compare the results we are getting from an imperfectly functioning market

Exhibit 7-3   Subsidies to Support the Fishing Industry

In many countries, public subsidies are available to support the income of struggling fishing firms. The perverse aspects of this have been well noted, including this statement by the European Parliament:

Subsidies that reduce the cost of fisheries operations and those that enhance revenues make fishing enterprises more profitable than they would otherwise be. This results directly or indirectly in the build-up of excessive fishing capacity, leading to the over-exploitation of fishery resources. In the 1950s and 1960s, the more subsidies you gave, the more fish you got, but things have changed: the resource base is too diminished for all these fishing boats to turn a profit, and the subsidies, far from having the effect they had earlier, now contribute to overfishing, i.e., more fish being caught than should be according to the biology of the fish stock. The realization of this fact and the current reform of the European Union's Common Fisheries Policy and fisheries subsidies have now put the latter in the spotlight in the EU. In fact, fisheries subsidies have been a matter for policy concern since the early 1990s, when the FAO made an argument, based on economic theory, that such government transfers contribute to excess fishing capacity and over-exploitation.

Source: From U. Rashid Sumaila et al., *Global Fishing Subsidies*, European Parliament Directorate General for Internal Policies, October 2013.

system with what we would get from a perfectly designed and implemented public policy. Instead we have to compare imperfect markets with perhaps equally imperfect public policies. In many cases it may be far more effective to determine why markets are not functioning efficiently and solve that problem, rather than to engage in overt activist public policy. In many cases the opposite will be true.

■ Policy Centralization/Decentralization

The example used earlier in this chapter concerned the management of a local natural resource (a clam bed) by a single community (the town of Barnstable). The resource is local in the sense that it occupies a small part of the territory of the town and in the sense that the question of whether the clam stock is large or small is not a matter of great concern beyond the town's borders. The relevant government body was the town itself, acting through whatever agencies and units were established to deal with the issue. Suppose, however, that the particular species of clam found in the Barnstable clam beds is a unique species found nowhere else, as far as anyone knows at the present time. Now it is reasonable to ask whether the local government is still the appropriate body to solve this management problem. Might it now be desirable to have this resource case addressed at a higher level of government, either the state or perhaps the federal level?

This is the **centralization/decentralization** problem in natural resource policy.[5] What is the appropriate governmental level at which particular natural resource issues should be addressed? In the United States we can distinguish four main levels: local (the single community), county, state, and federal. The importance of county government varies from region to region. We could perhaps also speak of a regional level, encompassing several states. Historically, certain resource issues have been addressed at the federal level (fisheries regulation, managing national parks and forests), whereas others have typically been local (land-use issues).

The general principle for assigning a particular natural resource issue to one or another level of government is fairly clear. It should be addressed at the lowest level of government whose geographic scope encompasses all the relevant benefits and costs of the problem.[6] This makes it easier to compare the benefits and costs of the problem and achieve the balance between them that efficiency requires. Most of the benefits and costs of the original Barnstable case are local. Thus the community forum is the one where people can most directly comprehend them and confront the trade-offs that are involved. Political processes at the state and federal levels cannot do this as effectively.

Real difficulties come up, however, when the geographical spread of benefits and costs are quite different, as they often are in natural resource issues. Consider again the version of the clam-bed case in which the clams are an endangered species. In this case the benefits of preserving them may accrue widely, to all citizens who place a high value on preserving species and encouraging diversity. But the costs of a regulation to limit harvesting below locally efficient levels are concentrated locally. This is a very common pattern in natural resource issues. Widely dispersed benefits argue for a state or federal role; localized costs argue for a local perspective.

The use of markets solves this problem to some extent. When clams are harvested and sold, they presumably go into at least a regional, or perhaps national, market. With established prices for clams, the local clam-managing individuals and groups have an easy way of assessing the benefits produced by digging the clams. But this only works if there are ready markets for the resource. No private market exists for species uniqueness. There is no way for people who value this characteristic of the clams to buy units of it. It might be possible for people to buy the clam bed and preserve the species if public authorities allowed this sort of thing. The public good aspect of this would still have to be solved, of course.

So, how are the clam beds of Barnstable Harbor managed? The harbor is divided into two areas. In one area long-term leases are granted to commercial fishers who manage and harvest clams on their own leaseholds. The other area is fished as an open-access resource by town residents, who must obtain clam-digging permits from the town and the quantity per permit is limited. The leasehold section of the harbor is overseen by the state of Massachusetts, while the permit section is managed by the town of Barnstable.

■ Summary

Public policy involves collective action to influence the rate and manner in which natural resources are used. There are many types of policy approaches, each with strengths and weaknesses. To choose among different policies for a particular situation, one must have in mind some criteria with which they will be evaluated. The criteria discussed were efficiency, equity, enforceability, and flexibility. The four types of policies evaluated for addressing resource issues were the creation of property rights, government-sponsored incentive programs, command-and-control regulations, and direct governmental production. No one policy approach is likely to be the best for all situations; determining the best approach will depend on the characteristics of the problem, the presence of appropriate social institutions and infrastructure, the capabilities and objectives of public officials, and other factors. The chapter also discusses the issues of market failure vs. government failure and the appropriate governmental level for addressing particular public policy problems.

Notes

[1] This is the total monetary output of people living within a given community.

[2] Note that if the three programs were voted on by the five individuals, Policies A and B would be approved by a majority, whereas C would not.

[3] The example is in fact taken from real life. The group of landowners is called North Maine Woods, Inc.

[4] For a discussion of land prices and the capitalization of service flows, see chapter 14.

[5] Of course it's a problem that exists in all types of policy areas, not just natural resource policy.

[6] Robert M. Schwab, "Environmental Federalism," *The RFF Reader in Environmental and Resource Management*, Resources for the Future, Washington, DC, 2006, pp. 109–114.

Key Terms

centralization/decentralization

command-and-control

conditions on property rights
  (complete, enforceable, transferable,
  presence of competitive markets)

direct controls

enforceability

government failure

incentive-based policies

market failure

policy criteria (efficiency, equity,
  enforceability, flexibility)

preservation vs. extraction

property rights

public production

subsidies

Questions for Further Discussion

1. Give an example of a policy that is efficient but not equitable, and of one that is the opposite. Do you think that, in general, efficient policies are likely to be equitable, and vice versa?

2. Suppose, in the clam-fishing example introduced in table 7-2, a tax is applied per pound of clams harvested, rather than per fisher day. This tax, in other words, works to lower revenues rather than raise costs. At what level should the tax be set to bring about the socially efficient use level?

3. Besides income (rich vs. poor) and generations (today vs. future), what other demographic and social factors might be important in assessing the fairness of resource policies?

4. From a political perspective, why do subsidies and property rights policies often get more support than taxes and command-and-control policies?

Useful Websites

For information about federal policy initiatives and developments:

- U.S. Department of the Interior (http://www.doi.gov)
- Natural Resources Defense Council (http://www.nrdc.org)
- League of Conservation Voters (http://www.lcv.org)
- Findlaw (http://smallbusiness.findlaw.com) search environmental law
- Environmental Law Institute (http://www.eli.org)

For news and views of using property rights and free markets:

- Property and Environmental Research Center (http://www.perc.org)

For information on environmental issues at the community level:

- Local Government Environmental Assistance Network
  (http:// www.lgean.org)

A good source on state level issues is the environmental atlas feature of the:

- Resource Renewal Institute (http://www.rri.org)

Selected Readings

Baden, John A., and Douglas S. Noonan, eds. *Managing the Commons*. Bloomington: Indiana University Press, 1998.

Clark, Tim W., et al. *Foundations of Natural Resources Policy and Management*. New Haven, CT: Yale University Press, 2011.

Field, Barry C., and Martha K. Field. *Environmental Economics: An Introduction*, 7th ed. New York: McGraw-Hill, 2017, chapter 9.

Ostrom, Elinor. *Governing the Commons: The Evolution of Institutions for Collective Action*. Cambridge, England: Cambridge University Press, 1990.

Sterner, Thomas. *Policy Instruments for Environmental and Natural Resource Management*, 2nd ed. Baltimore, MD: Johns Hopkins Press, 2012.

SECTION IV

NATURAL RESOURCE ANALYSIS

Many resource development and utilization programs and projects are undertaken by agencies in the public sector. Many are also undertaken by individuals and firms in the private sector. Whatever the case in a particular instance, it is important that society be able to assess in quantitative terms the net benefits flowing to its members. In the next two chapters we look at techniques that economists have developed to do this. In chapter 8 we look at several different types of analysis, devoting most of our time to benefit-cost analysis. In chapter 9 we look at problems of resource valuation, especially problems of measuring resource values in nonmarket situations.

8

Principles of Analysis

Each year federal, state, and local governments pursue all sorts of policies and regulations designed to impact the ways natural resources are used. Controversies swirl around these actions: whether they are effective, whether the trend should be toward more or less public regulation, whether we should have more or less reliance on private markets, and so on. Effective policy, even effective monitoring of markets, requires high-quality information and the presentation of that information in ways that facilitate action. Good analysis does not necessarily produce good decisions. But bad analysis will almost certainly contribute to bad ones.

In this chapter we examine some of the alternative **types of analysis** that are undertaken by policy analysts. Most of the chapter will be devoted to **benefit-cost** analysis, since this is the technique most frequently used. Before examining the basic principles of benefit-cost analysis, however, we look briefly at several other modes of analysis.

■ Impact Analysis

"Impact" is a very general word, meaning the influence that one set of events has on another. In general, impact analysis seeks to measure the impact of a public action, such as a regulation, on a designated sector of the society or economy. Several different types of impact analysis are important in natural resource economics.

Environmental Impact Analysis

An **environmental impact analysis** is essentially an identification and elaboration of all repercussions of a designated activity on all or part of the natural and environmental resource base. Many countries have laws requiring that environmental impact analyses be carried out before a substantial public program or project is undertaken. Analyses also are sometimes required of private actions. In the United States, the relevant law is the **National Environmental Policy Act of 1970** (NEPA). This law requires that agencies of the federal government conduct environmental impact assessments of proposed laws and "of other major federal actions significantly affecting the quality of the human environment." Over the years this has been interpreted to include any actions funded in part or regulated by the federal government, even though the actions may be undertaken by private parties. Many states have analogous laws governing state-funded projects.

The end result of an environmental impact analysis is an **environmental impact assessment** (EIS), sometimes called an environmental impact report (EIR). An EIR is supposed to contain the following information:

- a description of the environmental impact of the proposed action,
- any adverse environmental effects that cannot be avoided should the proposal be implemented,
- alternatives to the proposed action,
- the relationship between short-term uses of the environment and the maintenance and enhancement of long-term productivity, and
- any irreversible and irretrievable commitments of resources that would be involved in the proposed action should it be implemented.[1]

For the most part EIRs are the work of natural scientists, such as biologists, hydrologists, and ecologists. Their main job is to try to clarify the linkages that will spread the impact of a project through an ecosystem and to estimate the qualitative and quantitative repercussions it will have on the various characteristics of that system. These could be impacts on fish and wildlife, the functioning of the water system, or land and plant resources. The objective is to get a clear and comprehensive picture of how these resources are likely to be impacted. The emphasis is not, however, on placing values on these resources—on estimating the worth, for example, of losing 20 nesting pairs of spotted owls, or the value associated with moving certain plant species closer to extinction, or the social costs of losing 50 acres of wetlands.

It would appear that valuation could wait until physical impacts are identified, but this may not be possible. Suppose, for example, a certain forest area is to be preserved for wildlife protection and also to be left open to hikers and backpackers. The extent of the human impact on the region will depend in part on the number of people who visit. This includes not only the direct impact of the recreationists on the site in question, but also related impacts such as those stemming from added automobile traffic in the region. To predict these behavioral factors with reasonable accuracy, it is necessary to have good analytical information on consumer (in this case recreationist) demand for this type of natural resource preservation. Economic analysis is the prime source of studies of this type.

Economic Impact Analysis

When interest centers on how particular public or private actions affect certain dimensions of an economic system, we speak of **economic impact**

analysis. The perspective might be local—for example, how the opening of a community or regional park will affect local employment rates. It might be national—for example, how a new law on harvesting timber in national forests will affect the price of building materials. It could even be global—for example, how a treaty on protecting biodiversity will impact the economic growth rates of certain developing countries.

The range of economic impacts that may be of interest is very wide, including:

- Employment numbers (or unemployment rates), total or in certain industries
- Household incomes
- Rates of technical change in certain resource extraction industries
- Rates of inflation
- Trade balances with other countries

Exhibit 8-1 on the following page discusses an economic impact analysis done by the U.S. Fish and Wildlife Service. The primary concern of the study was to estimate the impact of a wildlife refuge on employment levels and incomes of people living in the vicinity of the refuge. The refuge in this case is located in Idaho.

Any impact analysis can only be as good as the underlying economic data and model used to do the study. The more one knows about how the affected economies normally function, the better one is able to estimate the impacts that can be expected from whatever public or private program is being evaluated. Economic impact analysis also may be incorporated into environmental impact studies. It is also important for evaluating natural resource conservation and preservation initiatives. Many of the target resources have historically been harvested for consumptive uses; forests have been logged, fisheries have been harvested, farmland has been cleared. In most cases these activities have led to the growth of local extractive industries, firms engaged directly in harvesting, transportation, and sometimes a certain amount of processing. Secondary service industries have often appeared to serve the people involved with the direct extractive activities. It is only natural for politicians and policy makers to be concerned with the welfare and status of the people in these firms and the impacts on them of alternative proposals for utilizing the resources in question.

▪ Cost-Effectiveness Analysis

Suppose a community has decided that it needs to increase the capacity of its public water-supply system. Assume that to accommodate future expected population growth, the community has decided it must find an additional 100,000 gallons of water per day. There are, we suppose, a number of ways it could do this: drill several new wells into an aquifer that is currently not being used, hook up to the system of a neighboring town that

Exhibit 8-1   Economic Impacts of Management Alternatives for Deer Flat National Wildlife Refuge

Located southwest of Boise, Idaho, the Deer Flat National Wildlife Refuge has two units, Lake Lowell and the Snake River Islands. The Lake Lowell Unit encompasses more than 10,500 acres, including the almost 9,000-acre Lake Lowell and surrounding lands. The Snake River Islands Unit contains about 1,200 acres and over 100 islands. These islands are distributed along 113 river miles from the Canyon-Ada County Line in Idaho to Farewell Bend in Oregon.

Refuge visitors can enjoy a variety of wildlife-dependent recreational activities, (i.e., wildlife-watching and photography, hunting, fishing, and environmental education and interpretation), as well as nonwildlife-dependent recreational activities, including recreational boating, horseback riding, and dog walking. These recreational opportunities attract outside visitors and bring in dollars to the community.

Because of the way industries interact in an economy, activity in one industry affects levels in several industries. For example, if more visitors come to an area, local businesses will purchase extra labor and supplies to meet the increase in demand for additional services. The income and employment resulting from visitor purchases from local businesses represent the *direct* effects of visitor spending within the economy. The income and employment resulting from these secondary purchases by input suppliers are the *indirect* effects of visitors spending within the economy.

Total spending by nonlocal Refuge visitors was determined by multiplying the average nonlocal visitor daily spending by the number of nonlocal visitor days at the Refuge. The table below shows both the direct and secondary effects for spending by nonlocal visitors for two alternatives. Alternative 1 is for current management and Alternative 2 is for expanded recreational activities. Under Alternative I, nonlocal Refuge visitors would spend approximately $1.95 million in the local economy annually and would generate total economic impacts of 28 jobs, $847,800 in labor income, and $1.4 million in value added.

Average Annual Impacts of Nonlocal Spending by Alternative

	Employment # full & part time jobs		Labor Income, $		Value Added, $	
	Alternative 1	Alternative 2	Alternative 1	Alternative 2	Alternative 1	Alternative 2
Direct effects	19	19	538,200	543,900	877,600	887,100
Secondary effects	9	10	309,600	314,400	546,200	554,600
Total effect	28	29	847,800	858,400	1,423,800	1,441,600

Under Alternative 2, nonlocal Refuge visitors would spend approximately $1.99 million in the local economy annually and would generate total economic impacts of 29 jobs, $858,400 in labor income, and $1.4 million in value added.

On the basis of these estimated economic impacts, Alternative 2 would be the preferred course of action.

Source: Excerpted from Lynne Koontz, C. M. Cullinane Thomas, and E. Larsen, "Regional Economic Impacts of Current and Proposed Management Alternatives for Deer Flat National Wildlife Refuge," *Deer Flat National Wildlife Refuge Final Comprehensive Conservation Planned and Environmental Impact Statement*, Appendix M, U.S. Geological Service, February 2015.

has (at least for now) some excess water, build a new reservoir, plug the leaks in the existing system, find a way to get consumers to reduce their use, and perhaps some others. A **cost-effectiveness analysis** would estimate the costs of these different alternatives to compare them in terms of costs per thousand gallons of water available for use by town residents. A cost-effectiveness analysis, in other words, takes as given the objective of the project—in this case the 100,000 gallons of additional water—and then costs out the different ways of reaching this objective.

Cost effectiveness is particularly useful in cases where there is wide agreement on the objective but not on how to reach it. It does not attempt to measure the objective in the same value terms as costs, but expresses it in terms of some physical target to be obtained. Examples, besides the water supply increase mentioned above, include the preservation of an endangered species; the reduction of fish harvest by, say, 50 percent; the reduction of soil erosion by some percentage; and the reduction of aggregate electricity consumption by some amount. But cost-effectiveness analysis cannot tell us what goals are worth, nor compare the value of resources used up in a program with the value of the objective achieved. For this we must broaden the analysis.

■ Benefit-Cost Analysis

Suppose an energy company was contemplating the construction and operation of a group of electricity-generating windmills. Since the company is bottom-line oriented, it would want to study the **commercial feasibility** of the windmills before it made a commitment to the plan. It would estimate as clearly as possible its costs of production: construction costs, connecting the windmills to the power grid, operating costs, periodic maintenance, and so on. It would also estimate its expected revenues, based on the electricity prices it expected, wind conditions, etc. It would then compare expected revenues with expected costs and come to a decision on the commercial feasibility of the venture.

Benefit-cost analysis is an analogous exercise for projects and programs undertaken in the public sector. Rather than exploring commercial feasibility (though commercial aspects may be relevant), benefit-cost analysis looks at **social feasibility**, in the sense of whether the benefits to society exceed the costs to society of undertaking particular courses of action. One very important difference in practice is that, whereas commercial revenue-cost analysis deals only with inputs and outputs that move across markets, benefit-cost analysis typically involves estimating the value of both market and **nonmarket inputs and outputs**.

Benefit-cost analysis was originally developed in the United States in the 1930s as a tool for studying natural resource decisions in the public sector—specifically to study water resource decisions of federal agencies. The primary applications were the dam-building programs of the U.S. Army Corps of Engineers (Department of the Army), the Bureau of Reclamation (Department of the Interior), and the Soil Conservation Service (Department of Agriculture). At the time, each agency operated under a somewhat different set of purposes and objectives. In the Flood Control Act of 1936 it was stated that federal dam projects would be justified if "the benefits to whomever they accrue are in excess of the estimated costs." The agencies were instructed to develop a common set of principles for studying the benefits and costs of these projects, which were eventually codified in the *Green Book* published in 1950.[2] In recent years benefit-cost analysis has been applied to a wide range of government programs, such as environmental protection measures, health-care programs, and highway construction projects.

Benefit-cost analysis has led two intertwined lives in natural resource policy making. The first has been among its practitioners—economists inside and outside the public sector who have developed the techniques, searched for the needed data, and sought to improve the quality of the results in different types of applications. (The primary goal of the rest of this chapter, in fact, is to consider briefly some of these procedures.) The second has been its political life among the administrators and legislators who have major ideological and political interests in the public programs to which it has been, or might be, applied. In the abstract, few people can be against the idea of having better analysis and more rational decision making in the public sector. But in its concrete application, good analysis can be politically controversial because it can discover results that are contrary to the interests of politicians, agencies, and interest groups.

In 1980 President Reagan issued Executive Order 12291, which required all agencies to conduct benefit-cost analyses of all proposed new regulations issued by federal agencies. His motive was to place a new hurdle in the way of agencies issuing new regulations, since he was committed to a strong antiregulation political agenda. In the 1990s this effort was revived by Republican Congresses, which sought to require benefit-cost analyses of all new federal regulations and programs.[3] Proponents of this effort argued that it would ensure that no public programs would be approved unless their social costs are adequately considered along with their benefits. Opponents frequently argue that since it is usually harder to measure benefits than it is to measure costs, a requirement like this will make it more difficult to pursue socially beneficial public programs.

Natural resource and environmental groups have often been in this latter category, primarily on the grounds that the benefits of public programs to preserve natural resources are often difficult to estimate with accuracy. This may be changing, however, as new analytical techniques are developed. Exhibit 8-2 describes a case where environmental groups are attempting to use benefit-cost analysis as a weapon in their fight to stop coal-mining operations within national forests and other federal lands. The issue here is whether the benefit-cost analysis of a land-leasing operation is incomplete if it does not take into account the social cost of carbon. The social cost of carbon is the estimate of future damages resulting from increased emissions of carbon dioxide.

Exhibit 8-2   Benefit-Cost Analysis and the Social Cost of Carbon

A federal district court in Colorado recently issued a decision faulting federal agencies for failing to calculate the social cost of greenhouse gas (GHG) emissions on the basis that such a calculation was not feasible. The court reasoned that it was arbitrary and capricious for agencies to proclaim the benefits of a project while ignoring the costs. This opinion may impose additional obligations on federal agencies to analyze the cost of GHG emissions in evaluating the impacts of a proposed action on the environment.

In High Country Conservation Advocates v. U.S. Forest Service, No. 13-cv-01723-RBJ (D. Colo. June 27, 2014), a group of plaintiffs brought suit against the Forest Service, Bureau of Land Management, and Department of the Interior challenging the issuance of lease modifications that enabled and expanded coal-mining exploration on federal land in Colorado. The agencies prepared an environmental impact statement (EIS) pursuant to the National Environmental Policy Act (NEPA) to analyze the impacts of a proposed decision to authorize the lease modifications. In the EIS, the agencies stated that there might be impacts from GHGs resulting from mine operations and from combustion of the coal produced. Though the agencies were able to quantify the amount of potential emissions, they did not discuss the impacts of the emissions. Instead, they claimed such an analysis was not feasible. The plaintiffs argued otherwise.

The court held that the agencies were obligated to calculate the cost of the action for two reasons. First, the court concluded that a social cost of carbon protocol was available to the agencies that would allow them to measure the GHG impact of the proposed action. Though the agencies claimed that this was a "controversial" tool, the court believed it was reasonable to use because it was developed with the input of several departments and relied on by the agencies to calculate the benefits of the proposed action. Second, the court held that it was improper for the agencies to quantify the benefits and costs of the lease modifications in a draft EIS but include only the benefits of the action in the final EIS.

Source: Excerpted from blog post by Peter Whitfield, "Federal Agencies Need to Address 'Controversial' Social Cost of Carbon in NEPA Cost Benefit Analysis," July 1, 2014, *Environmental Law Strategy*. © Baker & Hostetler LLP. Used with permission.

In the last chapter we discussed major policy approaches to managing natural resources. One of these was private property and the reliance on private markets to determine how resources will be used. In this case it has been argued that benefit-cost analysis is not needed. If market prices correctly represent all social costs and all social benefits of an activity, then standard commercial feasibility analysis, like the one in our windmill company example, is all that is needed to ensure that resource decisions are in the **public interest.** But this is a fairly extreme position. Although a move in the direction of private markets may be desirable, it can never be a universal policy, good for all circumstances. Such factors as public goods, distributional consequences, intergenerational issues, and externalities will always be with us. Thus, there is always going to be a need for evaluating public programs, as well as private decisions, to assess their social consequences. Benefit-cost analysis is necessary in these cases.

The Basic Framework

As the name implies, benefit-cost analysis involves measuring, adding up, and comparing all the benefits and costs of the public project or program under study. There are essentially five steps in a benefit-cost analysis, each of which has a number of components:

1. Decide the overall perspective of the analysis; which "public" is the relevant one?

2. Specify clearly the project or program under study.

3. Describe quantitatively the inputs and outputs of the program; that is, all the physical consequences that will flow from it.

4. Estimate the social values of all these inputs and outputs; in effect, estimate the benefits and costs.

5. Compare these benefits and costs.

Decide on the Perspective.   Benefit-cost analysis is a tool of public analysis, but there are actually many publics. A benefit-cost analysis of a new town park or a wetlands preservation regulation might be done strictly from the perspective of the local community; that is, the objective may be to estimate the benefits and costs impinging on town residents only. An analysis of a federal regulation would probably be done from the standpoint of all people living in the country, while a global treaty on natural resource use might be undertaken considering the entire population of the earth as the public.

Specify the Project.   This involves a complete (as complete as possible) specification of the project or program, including its location, timing, groups involved, and connections with other programs. In any benefit-cost analysis some assumptions have to be made. Will the economy continue to grow? At what rate? Will population growth continue? Will another public agency continue with a related project? Assumptions such as these have to be made as transparently and as realistically as possible right at the beginning.

There are two basic types of public programs for which benefit-cost analysis may be done:

1. Physical projects that involve some type of direct public production such as irrigation water delivery canals, beach restoration, park trails and visitor centers, logging roads, and habitat improvement projects.

2. Regulatory programs aimed at enforcing laws or practices such as restrictions on certain types of activities in national parks or monuments, land-use regulations, regulations to control commercial or recreational fishing, and regulations covering imports of endangered species. This also includes many financial-type programs like fees charged for grazing cattle on public range, subsidies offered for switching to more energy-efficient equipment, and royalty payments made by miners on public lands.

Measure Inputs and Outputs.   For some projects this is relatively easy. The engineering staff can provide a reasonably complete picture of a water supply system in terms of what it will take to build and operate it over time. The inputs required to lay out a trail system or to carry out a wetland restoration may be fairly easy to estimate. But many types of data outputs are more difficult to measure. How many visitors can be expected in this wilderness area or at this wildlife viewing area? How might fishers who are subject to regulations of one type adjust their operations in an attempt to continue harvesting fish? How fast can we expect industries to grow that would supply essential equipment to backpackers, white-water rafters, or snowmobilers?

A particularly challenging aspect of this analytical element is that virtually all projects and programs extend over time, usually over long periods of time. So the job of specifying inputs and outputs requires making predictions about the future, and these are always going to be subject to some uncertainty, perhaps a lot of uncertainty. How does one predict population growth or rates of technological change in the medium-term future? Long-term ecological relationships are also likely to be highly uncertain. What will wolf restoration do in the long run to elk populations? How much will the survival probabilities of the spotted owl increase if we restrict logging in a defined region?

To answer such questions puts a great premium on being able to draw on diverse sources of expertise and data—like engineers, soil scientists, wildlife biologists, hydrologists, economists, published data, new survey data, and private data collected for other reasons. Benefit-cost analyses are costly in terms of time and expense. It takes money and effort to search for existing data or to conduct surveys to get new data. Furthermore, all benefit-cost analyses are pursued with limited budgets. There is no hard-and-fast rule on how much it costs to do a benefit-cost analysis other than the principle that the bigger the budget, the better chance one has of getting better information and more accurate results.

Value Inputs and Outputs.   This step involves putting values on the items estimated in the previous step, in essence to estimate the benefits and costs of the project or program. We can use any units we wish, but typically this implies measuring benefits and costs in monetary terms. This does not mean in market-value terms because in many cases we deal with effects, especially on the benefit side, that are not directly registered on markets. Nor does it imply that only monetary values count in some fundamental manner. It means that we need a single metric into which to translate all the impacts of a project or program in order to make them comparable among themselves as well as with other types of public activities. Ultimately, certain impacts of a program may be irreducible to monetary terms because we cannot find a way of measuring how much people value these impacts. In this case we must supplement the monetary results of the benefit-cost analysis with estimates and discussions of these intangible impacts.

Compare Benefits and Costs.   Once all benefits and costs have been estimated as accurately as possible, it's time to take the last step, which is to compare them. There are two ways of doing this:

1. **Net benefits:** Total benefits minus total costs gives net benefits.
2. **Benefit-cost ratio:** Total benefits divided by total costs gives the benefit-cost ratio, the value of benefits produced per dollar of cost.

To understand what is involved in very general terms, consider the numbers in table 8-1. They are illustrative but realistic numbers for the construction and operation of a new wildlife refuge. The purpose of the refuge is to provide visitors with opportunities both for wildlife watching and, at certain times of the year, hunting and fishing. Another purpose is to provide continued habitat for several species of threatened wildlife.

The refuge involves three types of costs: the costs of acquiring the land, the costs of constructing the refuge, and the annual costs of operating it. The latter costs include the costs of handling the visitors to the refuge and the costs of maintaining both the constructed facilities and the habitat of the refuge. There are also three types of benefits. **Nonconsumptive benefits** include the benefits accruing to those visitors whose primary purpose is wildlife viewing. Benefits to hunters and fishers are the **consumptive benefits** of the refuge. There are also **species preservation benefits** flowing from the refuge, but since we have not been able to develop a realistic measure of these, they are entered as an amount equal to A. Net benefits and the benefit-cost ratio are shown at the bottom, the first with the indeterminate amount "A" included, and the second with an adjustment factor designated "a."

Table 8-1   Illustrative Results: Benefit-Cost Analysis of a New Wildlife Refuge

	Estimated annual (dollars)
Costs	
Land purchase	153,000*
Construction	
Visitor center	142,000*
Trail system	64,000*
Operation and maintenance	
Personnel	187,000
Other	63,000
Total Costs	609,000
Benefits	
Wildlife watchers	143,000
Hunters and fishers	627,000
Species preservation	A[†]
Total Benefits	770,000
Net benefits: $161,000 + A[†]	
Benefit-cost ratio: 1.26 + a[†]	

*These are the annualized costs of initial one-time outlays. Essentially they are the annual payments necessary to cumulate up, at a given interest rate, to the total initial outlay over the life of the project.
[†] A and a are used to account for the factors that are non-quantifiable in monetary terms.

Scope of the Project

Very often a benefit-cost analyst will be faced with studying a project of predetermined size. That is, the size of the project or program will have been established already, perhaps by engineers (in the case of a structure like a windmill farm), wildlife biologists (in the case of a wildlife refuge or wildlife restoration plan), or ecologists (in the case of a new national or state park). In these cases the size, or scope, of the project has been established on physical grounds, and the benefit-cost analysts must confirm whether this is desirable from a benefit-cost perspective. The example of table 8-1 relates to a wildlife refuge of some given size, but how do we know this is in some sense the optimal size? The same question applies to other types of programs. Should we devote 1,500 acres to a proposed public park, or should it be more or less? Should forest clear cuts be limited to 100 acres, or would 150 acres be better? Should we manage the wolf population at 1,000 individuals, or at some higher or lower level?

A procedure that can shed light on this question is **sensitivity analysis.** This refers to the practice of recalculating benefits and costs for several alternative programs, some that are larger than the one shown in the table and some that are smaller. If the program shown in table 8-1 is indeed appropriately scaled, each of the alternatives will have lower net benefits. Of course computers make it relatively easy to recalculate benefit-cost results with different data or underlying analytical assumptions.

The With/Without Principle

When performing benefit-cost analyses, we must proceed according to the with/without principle: That is, we must compare the situation that would result if the program or project is pursued with the situation that would result if the program is rejected. What is sometimes done instead is to compare anticipated results *with* the program against the situation *before* the program. But this can lead to false conclusions about the efficacy of the program.

Suppose, for example, we are trying to evaluate the benefits and costs of a wildlife restoration project. The population of the target animal is currently quite low, and the program involves, let us say, captive breeding and release. The benefits come from recreational viewing and are directly related to the size of the population. Estimated benefits are the following:

Before the program	$10,000
In the future without the program	$5,000
In the future with the program	$33,000

It would be a mistake to estimate program benefits at $23,000 ($33,000 − $10,000). This is a before/after comparison. But the base level, if the program is not pursued, is $5,000 rather than $10,000. This is because it has been predicted that there will be some attrition of the stock in the absence of the restoration program. Thus, the basis should be taken as $5,000, meaning that the benefits ascribable to the program are $28,000 ($33,000 − $5,000) rather than $23,000. This is not to imply that a with/without perspective will always give higher benefits than a before/after study. Often the opposite holds true. If a certain population of wildlife is expected to increase moderately in the absence of a program, the with/without benefits could be smaller than the before/after results.

Discounting

In chapter 3 we discuss the mechanics of discounting. Discounting is a way of determining the value today (present value) of benefits and costs that will accrue at some future time. Since virtually any public program or project involving natural resources extends beyond a single time period (e.g., year), analysts need a way to add benefits that occur in different time periods, and likewise to subtract costs that occur in different time periods. Consider the following illustrative numbers, showing net benefits for two different projects, each of which extends over 4 years (in actuality, of course, most programs will extend much longer than this, but 4 years is enough to illustrate the general principle involved).

	\multicolumn{4}{c}{Net benefits ($) in year[4]}	Total (undiscounted)
	0	1	2	3	net benefits
Program A	20	20	20	20	80
Program B	50	10	10	10	80

If we simply sum the undiscounted net benefits across the 4 years, we get the same total for each, $80. But the **time profile** of benefits is quite different between the two plans: Program A has an equal distribution of net benefits across the 4 years, while program B has most of its net benefits in the very first year, after which they are substantially lower for the subsequent 3 years. From an intuitive standpoint we might regard program B as somewhat more valuable because a much greater proportion of its net benefits are concentrated nearer in time. What we need is a way of **weighting** the net benefits accruing in different periods to reflect how near or distant in time they are. This is what discounting does. Thus, to compare the net-benefit streams in a way that allows for differences in their time profiles, we calculate the present value of total net benefits for each program. Using a discount rate of 6 percent, we get the following:

$$PV_A = \$20 + \frac{\$20}{1+0.06} + \frac{\$20}{(1+0.06)^2} + \frac{\$20}{(1+0.06)^3} = \$73.45$$

$$PV_B = \$50 + \frac{\$10}{1+0.06} + \frac{\$10}{(1+0.06)^2} + \frac{\$10}{(1+0.06)^3} = \$76.73$$

The Effects of Discounting

Note that in both programs the discounting has lowered total net benefits relative to the undiscounted totals. This is because discounting weights a dollar of net benefits accruing in the future at less than a dollar of net benefits accruing today. But the discounting affects program A more than program B, because a larger proportion of the net benefits of A occur in later periods, whereas the time profile of the net-benefit stream of B is concentrated more toward the present.

Discounting, then, allows us to compare projects or programs that have very **different time profiles of net benefits.** Consider the following net-benefit profiles for two alternative programs.

	Time period			
	0	1	2	3
Plan A				
Benefits	50	50	50	50
Costs	30	30	30	30
Net benefits	20	20	20	20
Plan B				
Benefits	100	50	25	25
Costs	50	40	15	15
Net benefits	50	10	10	10

The undiscounted sums of the net-benefit streams are the same; there are a total of $80 of net benefits in each of the plans. If we had to make a choice between the two plans, and we chose not to discount, we could essentially flip a coin. But suppose we discount net benefits, say, at 5 percent. Then the discounted stream of net benefits for the two projects would be

$$A = \$74.47$$
$$B = \$77.23$$

After the discounting, program B has a higher present value of net benefits than does program A. The discounting has increased the relative value of the plan that produces its net benefits earlier in time. Or, to say the same thing, discounting penalizes projects in which the net benefits occur further into the future.

Discounting and Future Generations

The logic of a discount rate, even a very small one, is inexorable. A thousand dollars, discounted back over a century at 5 percent, has a present value of about $7.60. The logic is even more compelling if we consider a future cost. One of the reasons that environmentalists have looked askance at discounting is that it can have the effect of downgrading future damages that result from today's economic activity. Suppose today's generation is considering a course of action that has certain short-run benefits of $10,000 per year for 50 years, but that, starting 50 years from now, will cost $1 million a year **forever.** This may be somewhat similar to the choice faced by current generations regarding nuclear power or global warming. To people alive today, the present value of that perpetual stream of future cost discounted at 10 percent is only about $85,000. These costs may not weigh particularly heavily on decisions made by the current generation. The present value of the benefits ($10,000 a year for 50 years at 10 percent, or $99,148) exceeds the present value of the future costs. From the standpoint of today, therefore, this might look like a good choice, despite the perpetual cost burden placed on all future generations.

Choice of the Discount Rate

Because discounting aggregates a series of future net benefits into an estimate of present value, the outcome depends importantly on which particular discount rate is used. A low rate implies that a dollar in one year is very similar in value to a dollar in any other year. A high rate implies that a dollar in the near term is much more valuable than one later on. Thus, the higher the discount rate, the more we would be encouraged to put our resources into programs that have relatively high payoffs (i.e., high benefits and/or low costs) in the short run. The lower the discount rate, on the contrary, the more we would be led to select programs that have high net benefits in the more distant future.

The choice of a discount rate has been a controversial topic through the years, and we can only summarize some of the arguments here. First, it is important to keep in mind the difference between real and nominal interest rates. **Nominal rates** are those one actually sees on the market. If you take a nominal rate and adjust it for inflation, you get a **real interest rate**. Suppose you deposit $100 in an account at an interest rate of 4 percent. In 10 years your deposit would have grown to $153, but this is in monetary terms. Suppose over that 10-year period prices increase 2 percent per year on average. Then the real value of your accumulated deposit would be less; in fact, the real interest rate at which your deposit would accumulate would be only 2 percent (4 percent – 2 percent), so in real terms your deposit would be worth only $124 after the 10 years. If the cost estimates are expected real costs, that is, adjusted for expected inflation, a real interest rate is used for discounting purposes. If our cost estimates are nominal figures, a nominal interest rate is used in the discounting analysis.

The discount rate reflects the current generation's views about the relative weight to be given to benefits and costs occurring in different years. Even a brief look, though, will show that there are dozens of different interest rates in use at any one time—rates on normal savings accounts, certificates of deposit, bank loans, government bonds, and so forth. Which rate should be used? There are essentially two schools of thought on this question: the time preference approach and the marginal productivity approach.

According to the **time preference approach**, the discount rate should reflect the way people themselves think about time. Any person normally would prefer a dollar today to a dollar in 10 years; in the language of economics, they have a **positive time preference**. We see people making savings decisions by putting money in bank accounts that pay certain rates of interest. These savings account rates show what interest the banks have to offer in order to get people to forgo current consumption. We might, therefore, take the average bank savings account rate to reflect the average person's rate of time preference.

The problem with this is that there are other ways of determining people's rates of time preference, and they don't necessarily give the same answer. Economists at Resources for the Future[5] completed a large survey in which they asked individuals to choose between receiving $10,000 today and larger amounts in 5 or 10 years. The responses yielded implied rates of discount of 20 percent for a 5-year time horizon and 10 percent for a 10-year horizon. These were substantially higher than bank savings rates at the time of the survey, which simply indicates that the actual discount rates people use may not be reflected well in standard market interest rates.

The second approach to determining the "correct" rate of discount, the **marginal productivity approach**, is based on the notion of the marginal productivity of **investment.** When investments are made in productive enterprises, people anticipate that the value of future returns will offset today's investment costs; otherwise, these investments would not be made. By that thinking, when resources are used in the public sector for natural resource and environmental programs, they ought to yield, on average, rates of return to society equivalent to what they could have earned in the private sector. Private-sector productivity is reflected in the rates of interest banks charge their business borrowers. Thus, by this reasoning, we should use a discount rate reflecting the interest rates that private firms pay when they borrow money for investment purposes. These are typically higher than savings account interest rates.

Distributional Issues

From an efficiency standpoint, the only relevant considerations are total benefits and total costs; efficiency requires maximizing the difference between the two. But in many cases we are interested also in how these benefits and costs are distributed among the people and groups affected by the project or program. We talked about the importance of distributional issues earlier, particularly from a political economic perspective.[6] The political conflicts in which many natural resource issues get embroiled are often related to the fact that the groups who enjoy the benefits are not the same as those who bear the costs.

These are matters of equity, or fairness, which is why they can become so controversial. Another important aspect of distributional fairness in resource programs (or in any program, for that matter) is how they impact people with different income levels. This is a major issue in the **environmental justice** movement, and the same problems exist in natural resource projects. There are essentially two main dimensions of equity: horizontal and vertical. **Horizontal equity** means treating people in similar situations alike. From the standpoint of the income dimension, if all people in the same income class are treated alike, in the sense that they experience the same gain (or loss) in net benefits, then horizontal equity has been achieved. Suppose we have a wildlife restoration program that has the following benefit-and-cost profile for a typical urban resident and a typical rural resident:

	Urban resident	Rural resident
Benefits	80	120
Costs	40	80
Net benefits	40	40

Note that both benefits and costs of the rural resident are higher than for the urban citizen, but net benefits are the same for each. Thus, if these people have similar incomes, we would regard this situation as equitable in the horizontal sense.

On the other hand, suppose they do not have the same income. Suppose the rural dweller has an income half that of the urban person. Then there would be a question of equity in the vertical sense, because **vertical equity** refers to how programs impinge on people who are in different circumstances, in particular people at different income levels. Consider the illustrative numbers of table 8-2. They show monetary benefits and costs of three natural resource projects as they accrue to three different people with, respectively, a low (person A), medium (person B), and high (person C) income. In the adjoining parentheses each number is shown as a percentage of the person's income. Take project 1, for example. Although the net benefits accruing to each person are different, the percentage of income is the same for all three (1 percent). The project in this case has a **proportional impact;** it affects each consumer in the same proportion.

Table 8-2   Vertical Equity*

Income	Person A $5,000		Person B $20,000		Person C $50,000	
Project 1						
Benefits	$150	(3.0)	$300	(1.5)	$600	(1.2)
Costs	100	(2.0)	100	(0.5)	100	(0.2)
Net benefits	$50	(1.0)	$200	(1.0)	$500	(1.0)
Project 2						
Benefits	$150	(3.0)	$1,400	(7.0)	$5,500	(11.0)
Costs	100	(2.0)	800	(4.0)	3,000	(6.0)
Net benefits	$50	(1.0)	$600	(3.0)	$2,500	(5.0)
Project 3						
Benefits	$700	(14.0)	$2,200	(11.0)	$3,000	(6.0)
Costs	200	(4.0)	1,000	(5.0)	1,500	(3.0)
Net benefits	$500	(10.0)	$1,200	(6.0)	$1,500	(3.0)

*Figures in the table show annual monetary values. Numbers in parentheses show the percentage of income these numbers represent.

Project 2, on the other hand, is **regressive;** it provides higher proportional net benefits to high-income people than to low-income people. Project 3 has a **progressive** impact because net benefits represent a higher proportion of the low-income person's income than they do of the person with the highest income. Thus a natural resource project (or any project for that matter) is proportional, regressive, or progressive, according to whether the net effect of that project has proportionally the same, a lower, or a higher impact on low-income people as it does on high-income people.

Note that although the net effects of a project may be distributed in one way, the individual components need not be distributed in the same way. For example, although the overall effects of project 2 are regressive, the costs of that program are in fact distributed progressively (i.e., the cost burden, measured as a percent of income, is greater for high-income people). In this case benefits are distributed so regressively that the overall project is regressive. This is the same in project 3; although the overall program is progressive, costs are distributed regressively.

These definitions of distributional impacts can be misleading. A project that is technically regressive could actually distribute the bulk of its net benefits to poor people. Suppose a policy raised the net income of one rich person by 10 percent, but raised each of the net incomes of 1,000 poor people by 5 percent. This policy is technically regressive, although more than likely the majority of its aggregate net benefits go to poor people.

Although the terminology of horizontal and vertical equity are reasonably clear, it is usually very hard to figure out whether any specific real-world natural resource project or policy has a progressive or regressive impact. To know this, we must know which individuals are impacted and what their income levels are. This may be feasible if the analysis is dealing with a reasonably small group of people (e.g., water rights being transferred from a relatively small group of ranchers to a local community), but it is much less so if benefits and/or costs are widely dispersed (e.g., the benefits accruing to society at large from biodiversity preservation).

Dealing with Uncertainty

In each example used so far in this chapter we have assumed that benefits and costs are known **with certainty.** But reality is not like this, especially since the estimation of benefits and costs actually involves predicting the **future values** of variables going into the analysis—values that will often be quite distant in time. We have to recognize and deal with the fact that we can never know these future values with absolute certainty. How can we do this?

We need to recognize, first, that results like those shown earlier are in reality **point estimates** of uncertain situations. We may regard them as the **most likely outcome** to expect, even though we should not be surprised if actual events turn out otherwise. One possible way to acknowledge uncertainty is to estimate a **range** for net benefits (with sensitivity analysis). If one has only informal information about the likelihood of future events, it may be possible to make qualitative statements such as "we are highly confident that net benefits will fall somewhere within a range between $a and $b." With better data on probabilities, it may be possible to derive statistical conclusions: "We are 90 percent confident that the net benefits will fall within a range between $c and $d."

Many natural resource issues involve **biological uncertainty.** In a study by Richard Bishop and his associates,[7] the objective was to measure the benefits and costs of a fish rehabilitation program in a part of the Great Lakes. The Wisconsin Department of Natural Resources was planning to put restrictions on current fishing activities so that a stock of fish (in this case yellow perch) would recover. But there was much uncertainty about biological relationships and how the stocks would respond to the lower levels of fishing activity. Bishop et al. analyzed the case by looking at six different **scenarios,** each involving a different assumption about how fast and far the fish stock would recover. For each scenario they then estimated the potential benefits. The overall expected benefits were then found by averaging the benefits of the scenarios, with each scenario **weighted by its assumed probability of occurrence,** as in the following example:

Scenario	Benefits ($ million)	Probability of occurrence	Benefits × probabilities ($ million)
I	40	.40	16.0
II	30	.20	6.0
III	20	.10	2.0
IV	10	.20	2.0
V	50	.05	2.5
VI	60	.05	3.0
Total		1.00	31.5

The summed benefits of $31.5 million in this case represent what are called **expected benefits.** Expected benefits (or expected costs, if the technique were used for estimating uncertain costs) may be thought of as **the most likely** outcome, given the uncertainty in the biological processes involved. The uncertainty is represented by the scenario probabilities, which in the case of the Bishop study were established by asking fishery biologists to evaluate the likelihood of each scenario. Note that the sum of the probabilities is unity: The six scenarios represent all possible outcomes.

Another source of uncertainty in benefit-cost analyses is **economic uncertainty.** Benefits and costs are based on assumed prices of inputs and outputs, and we know that relative prices can change through time. Very often the analysis will hinge on a strategic piece of economic information, the future course of which can only be assumed. For example, the benefits of wilderness areas are linked to the rapid rise in demand for outdoor recreation, such as backpacking, that has occurred in the United States over the last several decades. Will this activity continue to grow at the same rate in the future? Some assumption will have to be made about this growth rate if we wish to estimate the benefits of designating new wilderness areas.

Another source of uncertainty is which discount rate to use. Interest rates vary over time according to economic conditions, and there is no way of knowing with certainty what the rate will be 10 or 20 years from now. We may choose to overlook this and simply use today's rate, or perhaps calculate an average over the last, say, 10 years, to use in discounting future benefits and costs.

■ Summary

In this chapter we looked at several ways through which economic analysts assess outcomes of natural resource decisions, especially those within the public sector. We looked at cost-effectiveness analysis and economic impact analysis, but reserved the bulk of our attention for benefit-cost analysis. Benefit-cost analysis is simply a technique of accounting for, and valuing, all outputs and inputs of public projects or programs. We considered the economic factors involved in finding the correct size or scope of the project: discounting, distributional issues, and the question of uncertainty.

Notes

[1] Council of Environmental Quality, "Environmental Quality 1984," Washington, DC, 1985, p. 513.

[2] U.S. Federal Interagency River Basin Committee, Subcommittee on Benefits and Costs, "Proposed Practices for Economic Analysis of River Basin Projects," Washington, DC, 1950.

[3] And the Reagan order was essentially reaffirmed, though in somewhat weaker form, by President Clinton in his Executive Order 12866 of September 1993.

[4] Remember that we are following the convention that the current period is indexed with zero and is not discounted.

[5] Resources for the Future (RFF) is a well-known Washington organization that specializes in natural resource and environmental economics research. It publishes a quarterly newsletter discussing its work. This information comes from RFF, *Resources*, No. 108, Summer 1992, p. 3.

[6] See chapter 7.

[7] Richard C. Bishop, "Benefit-Cost Analysis of Fishery Rehabilitation Projects: A Great Lakes Case Study," *Ocean and Shoreline Management*, Vol. 13, 1990, pp. 253–274.

Key Terms

benefit-cost analysis	expected value
benefit-cost ratio	horizontal equity
biological uncertainty	net benefits
cost-effectiveness analysis	political economy of benefit and
discounting	cost distribution
economic impact analysis	uncertainty
economic uncertainty	vertical equity
environmental impact analysis	with/without principle

Questions for Further Discussion

1. Describe the difference between cost-effectiveness analysis and benefit-cost analysis as they apply to the question of preserving biological diversity.

2. To restore a depleted fish population, it is often necessary to reduce or stop entirely the harvesting of the stock for a certain period of time. If we are evaluating how long the period of reduced harvest should be, what impact would raising the discount rate have on our conclusion?

3. Suppose we are evaluating the benefits and costs of starting an ecotourism project where visitors will be given guided tours of a particularly rich habitat area. What are the main benefits and costs that should be enumerated?

4. Suppose we were doing an economic impact analysis of the project mentioned in question 3. How would this differ from the benefit-cost analysis?

5. Assume you have been asked to do a benefit-cost analysis of a habitat protection program to help preserve a certain endangered species of wildlife. What distributional issues might be important to examine in the course of your analysis?

6. In question 5, what are the sources of uncertainty that this analysis would have to deal with, and how might this be approached?

Useful Websites

For material on resource valuation, discounting, and principles of benefit-cost analysis:

- Resources for the Future (http://www.rff.org)

For general information on benefit-cost analysis:

- United States Environmental Protection Agency (http://www.epa.gov) (search for benefit-cost analysis under the National Center for Environmental Economics)
- Society for Benefit-Cost Analysis (http://benefitcostanalysis.org)
- Benefit-Cost Analysis Center at the University of Washington (http://evans.uw.edu/centers-projects/bcac/benefit-cost-analysis-center)

For information on project analysis and impact analysis:

- Bureau of Reclamation in the U.S. Department of Interior (http://www. usbr.gov) has an economics group handling project analysis and impact analysis

Selected Readings

Arnold, Frank S. *Economic Analysis of Environmental Policy and Regulation*. New York: John Wiley, 1995.

Boardman, N. F. *Cost-Benefit Analysis: Concepts and Practice*, 3rd ed. Upper Saddle River, NJ: Prentice-Hall, 2006.

Graves, Philip E. *A Critique of Benefit-Cost Analysis*. Blue Ridge Summit, PA: Rowman and Littlefield, 2007.

Hanley, Nick, and Clive L. Spash. *Cost-Benefit Analysis and the Environment*. Aldershot, England: Edward Elgar, 1993.

Nas, Tevfik. *Cost-Benefit Analysis: Theory and Application*. Thousand Oaks, CA: Sage, 1996.

9

The Valuation of Natural Resources

Having looked at the general framework of benefit-cost analysis, we now consider the question of how to measure the actual values of input and output flows in any given situation involving natural resource use. It is easy to say "put each resource to the use that maximizes net social value," but how do we measure what these values actually are in concrete situations? Consider the following scenarios:

- An oceanside community is contemplating the purchase of an expanse of shoreline to use as a town beach. It must buy the land from its current owners. What benefits will town residents receive from this public beach, and are the benefits substantial enough to warrant the purchase?

- The fish and wildlife agency of a midwestern state proposes to devote substantial resources to restoring bald eagles in portions of the state. What benefits and costs will accrue to residents of the state, and what benefits will accrue to nonresidents?

- Authorities managing a river in the West are under pressure to regulate its flow so as to provide better habitat for several species of fish downstream from a large impoundment. What social benefits will flow from such a policy?

- A private logging company is being asked to avoid large clear-cuts so that the effectiveness of a forest to control water runoff is not impaired. What are the net social benefits of this practice?

- A ranch owner in the West charges hunters a fee for hunting elk on his property. His annual revenues from this activity are about $200,000. Is this an accurate measure of the wildlife preservation benefits on this parcel of land?

- Congress is considering the establishment of a new national park in a western state. What benefits will accrue to people who visit the park, and what benefits will accrue to people who never visit the park?

- An area of wetlands is being altered to allow housing development to take place without any long-term decrease in the total amount of wetlands. But the change will result in the temporary loss of about 5,000 migratory waterfowl. It's expected that after 5 years the waterfowl stock will recover to its original level. What are the social costs of this temporary loss of waterfowl?

- An agency is considering the designation of a remote part of a forest as a wilderness area. It's expected that few people will actually visit the area because of its location. Are there significant social benefits from establishing this area despite the low visitation?

These diverse questions all call for valuation of resources or the service flows stemming from resource use. We do not have sufficient time and space to take up each one in detail. Thus in this chapter we try to deal with certain principles of valuation that can be adapted to specific circumstances.

■ Measuring Benefits

We first make some distinctions among types of benefits. Perhaps the most important step is to distinguish between active and passive sources of value. **Active resource values,** sometimes called **use values,** are those stemming from situations where people come into direct contact with the resource in question. This can be divided into consumptive and nonconsumptive values. **Consumptive values** arise from what we have termed extractive resources: timber, minerals, recreational and commercial hunting and fishing,[1] and agriculture are examples. **Nonconsumptive values** (nonextractive resources) are resources that are utilized but not removed or diminished in quantity or quality, such as ecotourism, animal watching, boating, hiking, camping, and rock climbing.

Passive natural resource values, sometimes called **nonuse values,** are involved when people place value on a resource independent of their actual use of the resource. Various motives have been suggested as the source of these values. Some of these are:

- **Option value:** People may be willing to pay to preserve a resource or increase the likelihood of its continued existence, because they may wish to utilize the resource at some undetermined future time. Example: Value expressed for maintaining or expanding national parks, with the possibility of later visits.

- **Existence value:** Willingness to pay to maintain the existence of resources even though no future utilization is likely. Example: Preservation of remote wilderness; steps taken to increase the survival probabilities of endangered species.

- **Bequest and gift value:** Willingness to pay to ensure that others, in both current and future generations, will enjoy a world in which the particular resources are present. Example: Willingness to protect open space so one's grandchildren will live in a world with ample amounts of this resource.

In the rest of this chapter we look at techniques that natural resource economists use to measure resource values of these different types.

■ Active (Use) Benefits

Benefits obtained when people actually use the resource in question, consumptively or nonconsumptively, are called active, or use, benefits. Use values can be further subdivided into those which are expressed through markets of one type or another, and nonmarket values. When markets are involved, interactions among buyers and sellers establish prices and quantities of transactions, which can often be analyzed to determine the willingness to pay of demanders and the marginal costs of suppliers. Market prices and quantities can be used to reveal these values in two ways. They can be used directly when the resource being evaluated is actually traded in its own right, and they may be used indirectly when what is being traded is not the resource itself but another good or service that is closely associated with it.

Direct Market Price Analysis

Suppose it is proposed that a dam constructed on a stream many years ago be removed. One impact of that removal is that it would restore a trout fishery on portions of the stream below the dam site. In making the decision, we would like to know, among other things, the net benefits this trout fishery would generate. It clearly has to be an estimate, because the trout fishery does not yet exist. But suppose there does currently exist elsewhere a private market in trout fishing. The suppliers in this case are certain people who control access to several trout streams, perhaps the riparian (or adjoining) property owners. "Production" in this case takes the form of maintaining good water quality and other conditions for a productive fish habitat, fishing access points, and the means of regulating entry. Demanders are the people who are willing to pay for access to this type of fishery. Suppose we look at existing operations and determine that the average price for a privately provided day of trout fishing is $25. May we use this value to estimate the benefits of our new trout fishery?

Figure 9-1 on the following page shows the standard supply and demand functions of a market, which in the present case we suppose is the market for privately provided trout fishing. The price of $25 is the one that brings the quantity supplied into balance with the quantity demanded. On the assumption that there are no externalities on either side of the market and that the market is competitive, this price is an accurate indicator of both **marginal willingness to pay** and **marginal cost** at the number of fisher days represented by the quantity q^*. Therefore if the new fishing area represents only a marginal addition to supply (i.e., if the market price of fishing days is not expected to change as a result of this new area coming online), the $25 tells us what the marginal benefits are, and we can multiply this figure by the expected number of visits to get an estimate of total benefits. This assumes

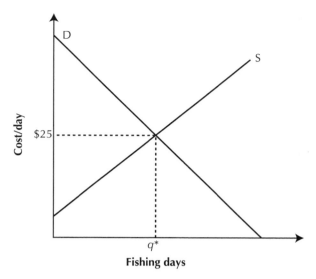

Figure 9-1   Market for Fishing Opportunities

that the new fishery will be reasonably similar to those now operating in terms of the expected quality of the fishing.

When markets are present, they provide a good avenue for estimating resource values because market participants are essentially revealing these values through their interactions. Thus, valuation of timber and minerals is often straightforward because they are traded on markets, both in situ (e.g., markets for trees on the stump) and as commodities after they have been harvested.

Market data may also exist to facilitate some nonextractive resource uses. Valuation of benefits from a public beach might be estimated from data on visitations to private beaches, if enough of the latter exist in the study region. Or suppose there was a public policy conflict over taking steps to protect whales. The benefits produced by having abundant whales (at least some of the benefits) might be estimated by analyzing the whale-watching market. The market suppliers in this case are the whales, together with the private boating firms that conduct whale-watching excursions. The demanders are people who are willing to pay to be taken out to the parts of the ocean where they may eavesdrop on the whales. The prices, quantities, and costs in this market are the data we would analyze to get estimates of net benefits.

There may be many situations, however, where market prices do not give an accurate measure of social benefits. This would be true, for example, when environmental externalities are involved. Figure 9-2 presents the standard externality model introduced in chapter 6, in this case applied to the electricity market. D is the electricity demand curve, assumed to be an accurate representation of social marginal willingness to pay for electricity. MPC is the marginal private cost of producing electricity, and MSC is the marginal social cost of production. The difference is accounted for by the external costs of electricity generation, primarily air pollution. In the absence of anything (e.g., property rights changes or government policy) that causes these external effects to be priced, the private market supply curve for electricity will be MPC, and the market price and quantity of electricity will be, respectively, p_m and q_m.

Suppose, now, that we are interested in building an array of windmills to generate power. It will be a relatively small addition to total electricity gen-

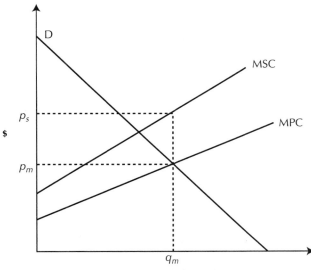

Figure 9-2   Market for Electricity with External Costs

Quantity of electricity

eration, but it will replace a part of the present polluting generating technology. Suppose the private cost of the windmill operation is the same as the conventional capacity. How do we value the power that the windmill project will provide? If we use simply the present market price for electricity p_m, we will be undervaluing the new power. This is because this new technology is valuable for two reasons: It produces power and it allows a reduction in the external costs coming from the electric power industry. The correct value to use in estimating the benefits of a small increase in windmill power is p_s, which is equal to the present price of power plus the current marginal value of external costs.

In many other cases market prices may not adequately represent the true social value of a natural resource-related good or service. This would be true, for example, where government subsidies or taxes lead to market prices that do not reflect true social opportunity costs. The search for correct prices to use in cases like this is a search for what economists call **accounting,** or **shadow** prices, which are simply prices that more correctly represent true economic scarcities than do the current or expected market prices. The use of shadow prices is especially important in cases where governmental policies of one type or another have produced these market distortions. We see in chapter 20 that this is particularly important in developing countries.

Indirect Market Price Analysis

Market prices, even when they have to be adjusted somewhat, are very useful for establishing the value of certain natural resources. But in many cases direct markets simply do not exist, or they exist in such rudimentary form that they do not provide good price data. In some cases the nature of the resource is such that direct markets are difficult to organize (e.g., air quality, which is a strong public good). In other cases government regulations have made it difficult or impossible for a market to form (e.g., wild game harvested within the country, which is illegal to sell on markets in the United States).

There are many such resources. An important natural resource in the United States is suburban wildlife, wildlife that exists in close proximity to areas of intensive human habitation. Issues related to the efficient management of these animals and plants will proliferate as urban sprawl continues at the same time that many people are changing their views about the value of wildlife. But there are no markets where people buy and sell the services of these wildlife. There may be some related markets, such as for hunting or bird watching, but these are likely to give only a very partial answer to the question of the true social value of these biological stocks. Or consider the benefits associated with wilderness backpacking. Much of this activity takes place in remote, publicly owned regions. Relatively little of the activity is arranged through private markets, though there may be related markets; for example, backpacking equipment is bought and sold in private markets, as are the services of wilderness guides.

In some cases activity in related markets can be studied to determine resource values. In such cases the value of the resource may be estimated **indirectly** by examining price, quantity, and quality data of the associated good or service in the related market.[2] As an example, consider the issue of open-space preservation in the suburbs. As suburban development in the United States continues, more thought is being given to preserving some parcels in open space, like parks, visual buffers, and areas of ecological value. The costs of preservation are the value of development that they foreclose. These costs are fairly easily measured. But how can we assess benefits?

Although there is no market where people buy and sell units of open space directly, there is a closely related market in which open space can be expected to have an impact: the **suburban housing market.** The market for new and used houses is very active throughout the country. The price of a house is affected by many factors: the characteristics of the house itself and those of the neighborhood in which it is located. We assume that buyers purchase houses having the most desirable set of characteristics, given their incomes. One important neighborhood characteristic is the proximity of a house to open space or conservation land. These characteristics, if they indeed are valued (positively or negatively) by the average buyer, will be **capitalized** into the market prices of houses.

Since many factors affect house prices in the suburbs, we need a large data set containing, for each house that was sold in a given time period, its transaction price and a description of all the characteristics that could be expected to have a noticeable impact on price. Among these would be, for example, the distance to the nearest significant parcel of open space. Statistical means can then be used to find out how this distance variable affects house prices and eventually to figure out the marginal willingness to pay that homeowners express for living close to preserved open space.

Another type of indirect market-price analysis is the **travel-cost approach.** This method takes advantage of the fact that people incur travel costs when visiting natural resource sites. Many resources, for example, are used by people for outdoor recreational purposes. Shoreline areas are used for picnicking, swimming, and fishing; coastal and interior wetlands are used for hunting and bird watching; forest and mountain areas are used for back-packing, camping, and hunting; streams, rivers, and lakes are used for boating and fishing activities; and so on. The benefits people get from these experiences depend in large part on the qualitative characteristics of the resources: how broad the beach is, how good the fishing is, or how scenic the mountain trail is. However, most (though not all) of this activity takes place outside the market, in the sense that it does not involve direct transactions between recreators and private resource suppliers. So there are few direct market prices that could be used to estimate recreational demands for the resources.

Although recreators often do not pay direct admission charges to these resources, as they would if going to a movie theater for example, they do normally have to spend money to make the visits. The costs of visiting a national forest, or a coastal wetland, or a distant lake, are the costs of traveling to these areas and engaging in the specific recreational activities chosen. Resource economists have developed techniques for deducing demand and benefit estimates by using these **travel costs as proxies** for the normal market prices that are used in market demand studies.

There are essentially two major components of travel costs: direct monetary costs such as fuel and en route lodging, and the value of the time that travelers require to get from home, or some other point of origin, to the recreational site. Both types of cost would be expected to be higher for people living farther from the site in question. The procedure therefore is to survey visitors to recreation sites (and perhaps also nonvisitors in some cases) by asking questions in face-to-face interviews or via mail questionnaires. The surveys provide data on the number of visits (which could be zero), various components of travel costs, and relevant economic and demographic information (such as income level, age, and educational attainment). These data can be analyzed to yield a demand curve for recreational visits.

Nonmarket Techniques

Resource economists have developed a special technique for estimating willingness to pay when direct or indirect market techniques are not available. **Contingent valuation** is a survey technique based on the straightforward idea that people's willingness to pay can be determined by asking them directly. The technique is called "contingent valuation" because it attempts to elicit peoples' valuations of contingent, or hypothetical, situations. In the absence of markets, people are essentially asked to choose as if there were a market for the resource in question.

Contingent valuation (CV) studies have been done for a long list of natural and environmental resources: endangered species, wilderness congestion, fishing experiences, clean air, view-related natural amenities, the recreational quality of beaches, and others. In fact, CV methods have spread into nonenvironmental areas; for example, the value of programs for reducing the risks of heart attacks, the value of supermarket price information, and the value of a seniors' companion program. Over time the method has been developed and refined to give what many regard as reasonably reliable measures of the benefits of a variety of public goods, especially environmental quality.

The steps in a CV analysis are:

1. Identify and describe the environmental quality characteristic to be evaluated.

2. Identify the respondents to be approached, including sampling procedures used to select respondents.

3. Design and administer a survey questionnaire.

4. Analyze the results and aggregate the individual responses to estimate values for the group affected by the environmental change.

The central purpose of the questionnaire is to elicit from respondents their estimate of what the natural resource is worth to them. In economic terms this means getting them to reveal the maximum amount they would be willing to pay rather than go without the resource in question. The most obvious technique to elicit this is to ask people outright to provide the amount with no prompting or probing on the part of the interviewer. Other approaches include using a bidding game, where the interviewer starts with a bid at a low level and progressively increases the value until the user indicates that his or her limit has been reached. Alternatively, the interviewer could start with a high figure and lower it to find the respondent's threshold value. Another method is to give the respondents printed response cards with a range of values, and then ask the respondents to check off their maximum willingness to pay. Exhibit 9-1 shows some examples of questions used in several contingent valuation studies.

■ Passive (Nonuse) Benefits

People may gain benefits from the preservation of the Grand Canyon, or a species of wildlife, or even a regionally significant wetland, even though they never expect to visit the Canyon or the wetland, or to directly observe the wildlife. These are called **nonuse benefits.** The evidence that benefits of this type exist is easy to see. A number of environmental organizations, the most widely known probably being the **Nature Conservancy,** raise money from donations to purchase and preserve important resource areas; it is highly unlikely that the average contributor expects to visit all the preserved sites. Thus a substantial proportion of the benefits obtained must be nonuse benefits.

Exhibit 9-1   Examples of Questions in Contingent Valuation Studies

Study to Estimate Certain Benefits of Better Water Quality in the Connecticut River

1. Have you heard about the Connecticut River salmon restoration program?
2. Did you make any donations for wildlife management or preservation last year?
3. Suppose that a private foundation is formed to take private donations and use them to support salmon restoration. What is the maximum donation you would make to this foundation?
4. What is your age?
5. How much money do you spend on entertainment each month?

Study to Estimate the Benefits of Outdoor Recreation in Northern New England

1. What is your favorite outdoor activity?
2. Please imagine that you have some time to enjoy the outdoor activity you named in Question 1. Assume that the following options are the ONLY ones available. Please rate EACH option by using 5 for the option that you would DEFINITELY CHOOSE and a 1 for any option(s) that you would DEFINITELY NOT CHOOSE. If you are not sure, use 2, 3, or 4 to indicate the likelihood that you would choose each option.

Option 1	Option 2	Option 3	Option 4
Stay Home	Go to state park in Vermont	Go to Green Mt. National Forest	Go to White Mt. National Forest
	No garbage pickup	Full garbage pickup	Full garbage pickup
	Pit toilets	Pit toilets	Flush toilets
	0 increase in wildlife population	25% increase in wildlife population	0 increase in wildlife population
	$1 access fee/visit	$5 access fee/visit	$2 access fee/visit
1 2 3 4 5 would would not definitely do do	1 2 3 4 5 would would not definitely do do	1 2 3 4 5 would would not definitely do do	1 2 3 4 5 would would not definitely do do

3. What is your age? _____ (number of years)
4. Are you: _____ Female? Or _____ Male?
5. Excluding yourself, how many family members live with you? _____(number of people)

We mentioned earlier some of the motives that could lie behind the existence of nonuse values and benefits (see p. 142). Here we address the issue of how they might be measured. This is currently a topic of great controversy. There are those who feel that significant benefits will be missed if no attempt is made to measure nonuse values and include them in the overall evaluation of natural resource benefits. There are others who think that nonuse values are largely insignificant compared to use values and that attempts to include them normally lead to the inflation of total benefit estimates.

One possibility is to interpret the contributions that people make to groups such as the Nature Conservancy as estimates of the social benefits flowing from preservation of important natural resources. Nature Conservancy is a national (in fact international) group; there are others of this scope, and there are many other regional and local groups that pursue essentially the same agenda and activities. Exhibit 9-2 discusses one such group, the Freshwater Trust; among its purposes is the acquisition of water rights. It obtains funds from a variety of sources: individuals, private firms, private foundations, and public agencies. Clearly, these funds are an indication of social benefits coming from instream water flows relative to traditional

Exhibit 9-2   Instream Water Rights

In the western United States, water rights historically have been controversial and something to fight over. One source of the conflict is between those who use water for traditional purposes, such as irrigation, and those who benefit from water left in the relevant water body. These include benefits arising from habitat preservation and instream recreational activities. In 1987 Oregon enacted a law recognizing these instream rights; they are defined for specific locations or sections of streams, and they have the same legal status as traditional rights. On application to appropriate authorities, it is possible to convert traditional rights into instream rights. The existence of transferable instream rights creates the incentive for people to acquire and hold them, thus ensuring higher instream flows than would otherwise occur.

A system such as this creates an opportunity for beneficiaries of instream flows to, in a sense, make manifest these benefits by purchasing instream rights. Through purchasing the rights it is possible to fund:

- water quality improvements that will enhance habitat for fish and other wildlife
- plans for minimum flow assurance, to avoid damaging fluctuations in water levels
- monitoring systems to track important water parameters and guide instream flow management
- new research and development of technical means for improving water conservation measures

In Oregon, the Oregon Water Trust (OWT) was formed in 1993 by a group of agricultural, recreational, environmental, legal, and tribal authorities. Its primary mission was to acquire instream water rights in the rivers of that state through purchase, gift, or lease. The OWT subsequently became part of a larger organization, the Freshwater Trust, which gave it the ability to organize appeals over a wider population for funds to support instream water rights acquisition.

In some sense, contributions made to trusts of this kind—which target conservation of specific resources—can be thought of as registering willingness to pay by beneficiaries for the "outputs" of the rights purchased with the funds, since concrete payments to the trusts are involved. This might be contrasted with systems where beneficiaries are simply asked to state preferences for specific resources, without actual payment. But we have to keep in mind the *public good* aspect of this type of resource. As long as access is not restricted, beneficiaries can enjoy benefits even without making contributions, so voluntary contributions to a trust may substantially understate the true benefits coming from preserving instream flows.

The Freshwater Trust may be accessed through its website: www.thefreshwatertrust.org

water uses. And the fact that this is a somewhat local group helps pinpoint these benefits to a particular set of rivers and streams, primarily in Oregon. On the other hand, a large portion of the benefits from preserving instream flows may be direct use values accruing primarily to recreators; it is unclear how much of the total contributions made to the Trust can be attributable to nonuse benefits produced by these particular streams and rivers.

Another potential problem with using contributions as a measure of willingness to pay for nonuse benefits is that the preserved resources that generate them are essentially public goods. There is no feasible means of excluding would-be beneficiaries when the issue concerns nonuse benefits, based on the simple knowledge that a resource has been preserved. When public goods are involved, private, market-related economic exchanges undersupply the goods in question. Thus, there are conceptual reasons for thinking that private contributions to conservancy-type organizations understate the nonuse values flowing from the resources they seek to preserve.

Since nonuse benefits are, almost by definition, independent of such factors as location or the consumption of other specific goods or services, indirect and travel-cost techniques are of no use in trying to measure them. This means that the only practicable means of assessing their magnitude is with contingent valuation. Contingent valuation studies have been controversial when measuring use values; they have been even more controversial when applied to nonuse values. This is because some of the problems inherent in the CV method become more acute in the case of nonuse benefits. Some of these are the following:

1. In the case of use values, beneficiaries may be presumed to be familiar with the resource whose valuation is being sought, through present or past contact with that resource. In the case of nonuse benefits, direct contact is not necessary, though it may have occurred in the past. Thus, there may be more ambiguity about the natural resource being evaluated, and the CV may be obtaining evidence of a general attitude rather than the valuation of a specific resource.

2. In many cases a person may experience both use and nonuse benefits from a natural resource. The difficulty then becomes how to distinguish between the two sources of value. A person living in proximity to a national park, for example, may get nonuse benefits from the knowledge that the park area is preserved and may also get direct use benefits from hiking or hunting in the area.

3. Where use values are concerned, it may be relatively easy to find out who the prime beneficiaries are. For visitors to a national park, for example, a survey will reveal the demographic characteristic of users. But this is not possible when nonuse benefits are involved. Thus, there is a real question about how wide the survey net should be cast to identify nonuse beneficiaries. If we are dealing with a certain species of wildlife in the Rocky Mountains, for example, should we survey people in the local community, the state, the region, or the country?

These, and other problems, make CV studies of nonuse values difficult, but not impossible. Researchers have investigated the magnitude of many nonuse values, such as the preservation of individual species of wildlife; the preservation of sites that have ecological or historical importance; and the characteristics of specific sites, such as water quality in a particular river or lake. Table 9-1 lists some of these studies.

Table 9-1   Several Study Results Dealing with Willingness to Pay by Nonusers of Resources

Resource:	Protection of land through wilderness designation
Authors:	Walsh, Loomis, and Gillman
Results:	Respondents (expected nonusers) were willing to pay between $14 and $19 just to preserve areas in wilderness states.
Resource:	Humpback whales
Authors:	Samples, Dixon, and Gowen
Results:	Respondents' (nonusers') mean willingness to pay to preserve whales was between $35 and $60.
Resource:	Bald eagles and stripped shiners
Authors:	Boyle and Bishop
Results:	Respondents (expected nonusers) were willing to pay between $4 and $6 for shiner preservation and between $10 and $75 for eagle preservation programs.
Resource:	Whooping cranes
Authors:	Bowker and Stoll
Results:	Nonusers expressed willingness to pay between $21 and $70 for preservation programs.
Resource:	Salmon fishery in the Fraser River Basin of British Columbia and fishing resources in the southeastern United States.
Authors:	Described by Fisher and Raucher
Results:	Nonuse values approximately half of user values.
Resource:	Bald eagles, wild turkeys, Atlantic salmon, coyote
Authors:	Stevens et al.
Results:	Ninety-three percent of total willingness to pay was identified as nonuse value, only seven percent was use value.

Sources: Bowker, J. M., and John R. Stoll, "Use of Dichotomous Choice, Non-Market Methods to Value the Whooping Crane Resource," *American Journal of Agricultural Economics,* 70(2), 1988, pp. 372–381; Boyle, Kevin J., and Richard C. Bishop, "Valuing Wildlife in Benefit-Cost Analyses: A Case Study Involving Endangered Species," *Water Resources Research,* 23(5), 1987, pp. 943–950; Fisher, Ann, and Robert Raucher, "Intrinsic Benefits of Improved Water Quality: Conceptual and Empirical Perspectives," in *Advances in Applied Microeconomics,* V. Kerry Smith and Ann Dryden Witte (eds.), Greenwich, CT, JAI Press, 1984; Samples, Karl C., John A. Dixon, and Marsha M. Gowen, "Information Disclosure, and Endangered Species Valuation," *Land Economics,* 62(3), 1986, pp. 306–312; Stevens, Thomas H., Jaime Echeverria, Ronald J. Glass, Tim Hager, and Thomas A. More, "Measuring the Existence Value of Wildlife: What Do CVM Estimates Really Show?" *Land Economics,* 67(4), November 1991, pp. 390–400; Walsh, Richard G., John B. Loomis, and Richard A. Gillman, "Valuing Option, Existence, and Bequest Demands for Wilderness," *Land Economics,* 60(1), 1984, pp. 14–29.

■ Measuring Costs

We switch now to the cost side of benefit-cost analysis. All actions have cost consequences, whether they are costs of the obvious sort in classical natural resource extraction or costs of a more subtle kind when we consider resource preservation alternatives. It is easy to overlook the cost side, sometimes under the mistaken belief that "costs don't matter," or under the equally mistaken belief that they are easy to estimate. But costs often are difficult to determine accurately, and they do matter. The results of a benefit-cost analysis can be affected equally by over- or underestimating costs, as by over- or underestimating benefits. Furthermore, in the political realm it is almost axiomatic that options will be selected in the heat of political controversy and enthusiasm, without sufficient regard to the true social costs (or benefits) of the alternatives. All the more reason why the cost side of the analysis should be treated with as much importance as the benefit side.

General Issues

Cost analysis can be done on many levels. At its simplest it focuses on the cost to a single community or firm of a natural resource project or regulation, such as a new state park or a new community wetlands preservation plan. Although these cost estimates may still be hard to produce, the task is made relatively easy by the fact that the geographical extent or the physical nature of the programs is limited and well defined. At a higher level there are regulations or programs that affect relatively large groups: all timbering companies in the Northwest, all farmers in California, all consumers in the Northeast, for example. Here the job of collecting cost data is multiplied: Some sampling is usually necessary, and this will be complicated by a substantial amount of heterogeneity among the groups that must be studied. At the highest level are national cost estimates; for example, of the effects on the American economy of an international oil embargo.

There are two avenues through which social costs are incurred: the **opportunity costs** of using resources[3] in certain ways, and the **costs of price changes.** As discussed in chapter 4, the opportunity cost of using resources in a particular way is the highest-valued alternative use to which they might otherwise have been put. This alternative value is what society forgoes in using the resources in the specified fashion. Note the word "society." Costs are incurred by all sorts of individuals, firms, agencies, industries, and groups. Each has its own perspective, and each focuses on those costs that directly impinge upon it. As we stressed earlier, social costs include **private costs** plus all other costs that are incurred as a result of resource use; that is, all **external costs.** Most people have an instinctive feel for the concept of opportunity cost;[4] the problem arises when we try to determine what that cost is in concrete circumstances. When an input has a market price, and the market is reasonably competitive, this price will normally be a good measure of its opportunity cost.

Price changes can create costs to producers and consumers that are somewhat different in concept than costs in the form of real resource expenditures. In order to measure these costs, we need good data on the supply and demand functions for the markets on which prices change. Regulations on clear-cutting, for example, change the costs of timbering and perhaps the price of lumber. Knowledge of the supply and demand factors on the timber market is necessary to predict these effects. It is conceivable that the appropriate statistical studies have been done to analyze these factors. If this is not the case, another approach is to carry out an engineering study to predict the effects of the regulation. We deal with these issues at greater length below.

Costs of Physical Facilities

Perhaps the easiest case to deal with is estimating the costs of a project that involves constructing and operating some type of physical facility like dams (and, in recent years, dam removal), irrigation works, parks with trail systems and visitor centers, animal refuges and restoration activities, or beach restoration activities. Most of the relevant costs here relate to the opportunity costs of the inputs used in the project, the **capital costs** of initial construction, and the annual **operating and maintenance** costs that will extend over the life of the project. The source of data on costs of this type is normally **engineering** or scientific authorities who can specify in detail the inputs needed for various phases of the projects.

Costs of Public Regulation

A great deal of public activity on natural resource issues is not related to physical projects, but to **public regulation** of private actions. Cost estimation in this case is usually more difficult because it requires knowing something about the costs of the private operations that are affected by the regulations. As examples, consider the various regulations that public agencies pursue with private timber companies, including specifications for clear-cutting, the use of chemicals in forest cultivation, and leaving intact certain wildlife habitat areas. These regulations shift the costs of these private companies. This adds a major complication, however, since the cost shifts, by changing supply functions, may lead to output changes. This complicates the task of determining the costs of the regulation.

As an example, consider figure 9-3. This diagram might depict the situation, for example, of a small regional forestry operation where local timbering companies are faced with a new regulation designed to protect the habitat of an endangered animal. Since this is a local impact only, it is not expected to have any influence on the national price of wood. In other words, the demand curve for timber harvested by the collection of local companies is flat, as depicted by the line marked D. Before the regulation their marginal cost curve, equal to their supply curve, was $MC_1 = S_1$. Thus, total output was q_1, total costs were $c + f$.

The regulation increases the costs of harvesting timber, depicted by an upward shift in the marginal cost curve to $MC_2 = S_2$. If output were unchanged, the total increase in costs would be measured by the area $b + e + d$. But the added costs, in the face of a constant price, normally lead to output adjustments. In the depicted case, output would fall to q_2. One way of highlighting the significance of the change is to look at net benefits before and after the

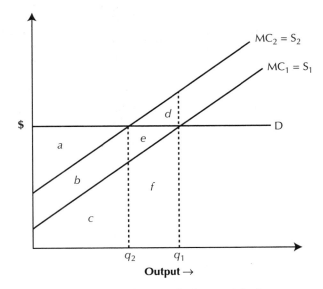

Figure 9-3   Costs of a Regulation on Timber Harvesters

change. Before the regulation they were $a + b + e$, whereas afterward, they are a; thus, there was a reduction in net benefits of $b + e$. Note that this number is smaller than the cost increase for a constant output $b + e + d$. By lowering output, a part of the cost increase that would have been incurred in the absence of output change is avoided.

The information needed to measure the cost implications of the regulation includes (1) the extent to which the marginal cost/supply function will be shifted up by the regulation and (2) the extent of any output adjustments that firms will make as a result of the cost changes. Where does one get the cost data necessary to analyze the cost structure of an industry? Normally, from the industry itself. Much of the data can be generated by **cost surveys,** in which questionnaires are sent to all, or a sample of, the firms in the particular industry. In effect, questionnaires are sent out to these firms asking them to supply information on their numbers of employees, processes used, costs of energy and materials, and so on. With a sufficiently detailed questionnaire and a reasonably high response rate by firms, researchers hope to get a good idea of basic cost conditions in the industry and how they might be affected by regulations on natural resource use. Because the regulated firms themselves are the source of much of the cost data used to develop the regulations, there is clearly a question as to whether these firms will supply accurate data. By overstating the potential costs of adjusting to regulations, firms may hope to convince agencies to promulgate weaker regulations than they would if the agencies had an accurate idea of costs.

Another problem with cost surveys is that they are usually better at getting information on past data than on future costs under new regulations. Firms can probably report past cost data with more reliability than they can estimate future costs. But historical data may not be a good guide to the future, especially because environmental regulations, almost by definition, confront firms with novel situations and because future technological change can impact costs in major ways. In these cases it is common to supplement survey data with technical engineering data that can be better adapted to costing out the new techniques and procedures that firms may adopt.

Note that in figure 9-3 the regulation led to an output reduction from q_1 to q_2. This shows the extent to which resources currently used in this industry will no longer be needed there. Certain inputs, for example energy and various types of material inputs, are easily reduced. But inputs like labor are much more complicated. In a reasonably full employment economy, one could expect labor withdrawn from one industry to switch to another industry; the bigger the economy we are dealing with, the easier this will be. But adjustment problems, some temporary and others longer term, can be quite challenging in cases like this. Not only is direct income from the affected industries reduced, but the secondary effects on support and service industries can be impacted. Adjustment costs of this type have made natural resource management politically sensitive in many cases, such as the reduction of parts of the timbering industry in response to forest regulation and the reduction in a fishing fleet in response to attempts to reduce overfishing.

Regulatory programs often produce other types of costs in the form of **increased prices** paid by consumers. The model of figure 9-3 did not note this because it was assumed that only a segment of a much larger industry was involved, and so the regulation would not be expected to affect output price. But with regulations that affect an entire industry, or a substantial portion thereof, consumers may experience **price effects.** These are costs in a sense different from the notion of opportunity costs. When prices paid by consumers change, there is a gain or loss in welfare: a gain to consumers if prices drop and a loss to consumers if they go up. Figure 9-4 gives the relevant analysis. Here there is a downward-sloping demand function and horizontal marginal cost/supply relationship. The initial price-quantity situation is p_1,

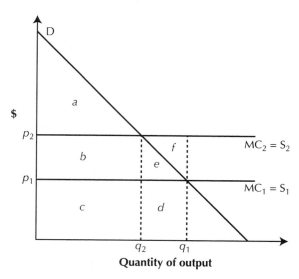

Figure 9-4   Effects of a Regulation on Consumers

q_1. Then a regulation is enacted that lifts the marginal cost curve to $MC_2 = S_2$. Price now rises to p_2, which makes consumers worse off. By how much? If we take the original quantity q_1 and multiply it by the price increase, we get an amount equal to $b + e + f$. But here again, we expect consumers to respond to the price increase. In the figure, quantity drops to q_2. Looking at the change in net benefits brought on by the cost increase, this comes out to $b + e$.[5] The adjustment in quantity reduces the cost to consumers relative to what would have been the case with no quantity change.

To estimate this cost, especially to predict it ex ante, we must know not only what the change in cost will be, but also the **conditions of demand** in the industry. This is an important lesson. To measure the costs of the regulation, we must know both costs and the demand function facing the industry that we are studying.

■ Summary

This chapter is devoted to a discussion of how analysts actually measure the benefits and costs flowing from specific natural resource utilization situations. Benefits can be classified as consumptive vs. nonconsumptive and as use vs. nonuse. Nonuse benefits of natural resources consist of option, existence, and bequest values. In many cases, direct market prices can be used to measure benefits of different types of natural resource use; sometimes these prices must be adjusted to take into account external costs and benefits. Market prices may also be used indirectly, in cases where natural resource use is closely connected to the consumption of a marketed commodity (e.g., the value of open space in the vicinity of houses). Travel cost analysis has frequently been used to estimate the benefits of outdoor recreation. For nonmarket benefits the most commonly used method is contingent valuation, which is essentially a survey technique in which respondents are asked directly about their willingness to pay to use natural resources in certain ways.

Cost measurement often seems easier than benefit measurement, but accurate cost estimates can often be difficult to make. In cases where physical-type projects are involved (e.g., dams, wildlife refuges, irrigation works) the relevant concept is opportunity costs, the value the inputs could have produced in their next best alternative use. For regulatory-type programs (e.g., regulations on clear-cutting, regulations on access to fisheries), there may be both opportunity cost changes as firms respond to the regulations, and costs to consumers stemming from price changes in markets for goods and services.

Notes

[1] But catch-and-release fishing may be regarded as a nonconsumptive activity.

[2] The name given to some of these studies is the hedonic price approach.

[3] Remember that "resources" is a word that can have two meanings; it can be a short way of saying "natural resources," or it can be used as a general reference analogous to the word "inputs." Here it is being used in the second sense.

[4] For example, the opportunity cost of time is the relevant concept when allocating a fixed amount of time among several tasks.

[5] Net benefits before the change are $(a + b + c + d + e) - (c + d) = a + b + e$. After the change they are $(a + b + c) - (b + c) = a$. Thus, the change is $b + e$.

Key Terms

active (use) values
bequest values
consumptive values
contingent valuation
costs of price changes
existence values
market prices as measure of value

nonconsumptive values
opportunity costs
option values
passive (nonuse) values
shadow (accounting) prices
travel cost analysis

Questions for Further Discussion

1. Distinguish between use values and nonuse values in the specific case of preserving the quality of water in an underground aquifer. How might you measure the different types of benefits in this case?

2. A proposal is made to ban the use of a particular type of gear by vessels engaged in a certain saltwater fishery. Indicate conceptually how costs would be measured in this case. How might the necessary data be obtained?

3. What is the conceptual relationship between use values, consumptive values, and market values?

4. A proposal has been put forward to remove a dam on a river, which currently produces hydroelectric power. You have been hired to estimate the costs (not the benefits) of this action. What are the main types of costs in this case, and how might you go about measuring each type?

5. What types of questions might you ask in a contingent valuation study to estimate the benefits of limiting timber harvesting in certain areas so as to preserve habitat for the spotted owl?

6. Select one of the scenarios given at the beginning of the chapter. Propose a way of answering the question posed in the scenario using one (or more) of the techniques discussed in the chapter.

Useful Websites

See the material under nonmarket valuation at

- Resources for the Future (http://www.rff.org)
- Environmental Value Reference Inventory, EVRI (https://www.evri.ca)

Many countries have developed programs in benefits measurement, for example,

- Australian Bureau of Agricultural and Resource Economics and Sciences (http://www.agriculture.gov.au/abares)

For a private firm in the valuation business:

- Environmental Damage Valuation and Cost Benefit News (http://www.envirovaluation.org/)
- Industrial Economics, Inc. (http://www.indecon.com)

Selected Readings

Bateman, Ian, and Ken Willis, eds. *Valuing Environmental Preferences: Theory and Practice of the Contingent Valuation Method in the U.S., EC, and Developing Countries.* Oxford, England: Oxford University Press, 1999.

Champ, Patricia A., Kevin Boyle, and Thomas C. Brown. *A Primer on Nonmarket Valuation.* New York: Springer Science, 2003.

Freeman, A. Myrick. *The Measurement of Environmental and Resource Values: Theory and Methods*, 2nd ed. Washington, DC: Resources for the Future, 2003.

Herriges, Joseph A., and Catherine L. Kling, eds. *Revealed Preference Approaches in Environmental Valuation*, Vols. I and II. Burlington, VT: Ashgate Publishing, 2008.

Jantzen, Jochem. *The Economic Value of Natural and Environmental Resources.* The Netherlands: TME The Institute for Applied Economics, 2006.

Mitchell, R. C., and R. T. Carson. *Using Surveys to Value Public Goods: The Contingent Valuation Method.* Washington, DC: Resources for the Future, 1989.

Smith, V. Kerry. *Estimating Economic Values for Nature: Methods for Non-Market Valuation.* Cheltenham, England: Edward Elgar, 1996.

SECTION V

APPLIED NATURAL RESOURCE PROBLEMS

The remainder of the book is devoted to the analysis of specific resource problems. Volumes could be written about each of these resources simply to describe all the challenging issues that currently exist. The physical, demographic, and economic diversity of the world is so immense that it creates a corresponding diversity in natural resource issues. Even within individual countries diversity is the norm. Within the United States, for example, there are substantial differences between East and West. This is also true of natural resource issues in the North and South. We cannot cover each resource comprehensively in the individual chapters. Rather, we shall survey some of the most important problems and employ simple tools of economic analysis to clarify them and point toward possible solutions.

10

Mineral Economics

"**Mineral**" refers to the wide range of inorganic solid substances that normally are found in or on the ground and are used by humans for a great variety of purposes. We can distinguish between **fuel** and **nonfuel minerals**; the former are covered in the chapter on energy. Nonfuel minerals can be further subdivided into **metals** and **industrial minerals**. The major classes of metals are ores, such as iron, nickel, and bauxite, and **precious metals**. Important classes of industrial minerals are natural aggregates (crushed rock, sand, gravel), cement, fertilizer minerals (phosphate rock, potash), abrasives, and gemstones. Table 10-1 on the next page presents a list of the quantities and values of selected minerals produced in the United States in 2004 and 2011. Of the metals, copper and gold together accounted for two-thirds of the total value of production. Of industrial minerals, cement and natural aggregates represented about 70 percent of the total.

Minerals appear to fit the classic definition of the **nonrenewable resource,** one for which $\Delta S = 0$ in the terminology of chapter 2. For a given deposit, the quantity of material would appear to be strictly nonreplenishable, hence one that can only be drawn down over time. In the next section we see that this state of affairs is somewhat ambiguous because minerals normally exist in different **grades.** The notion of nonrenewability is sufficiently compelling in the case of minerals, however, that our first analytical job is to explore conceptually the simple but classic question: Given a certain quantity of a nonrenewable resource available in a deposit, how fast should it be extracted and used? We then take up the broader question of **exploration, discovery, and development** of mineral deposits, where the question is not only the pace at which known stocks are extracted but also how much to spend on finding new stocks. Finally, since minerals are the major component of materials, we focus on the economics of recycling.

■ Geological Factors and Costs of Extraction

Copper is widely distributed throughout the world. In fact the copper content of a randomly chosen bucket of the earth's crust contains 63 parts

Table 10-1   U.S. Production of Selected Minerals, 2004 and 2011

Metals	2004 Quantity*	2004 Value†	2011 Quantity*	2011 Value†	% Change Quantity*	% Change Value†
Copper	1,160	3,420	1,110	9,960	–4%	191%
Gold	258,000	3,400	234,000	11,800	–9%	247%
Iron ore	54,900	2,080	55,600	5,530	1%	166%
Lead	430,000	523	334,000	895	–22%	71%
Molybdenum	42,000	1,420	63,700	3,830	52%	170%
Palladium	13,700	102	12,400	295	–9%	189%
Silver	1,250,000	268	1,120,000	1,270	–10%	374%
Total		12,500		36,000		
Industrial Minerals						
Cement (Portland)	92,400	7,110	66,100	5,820	–28%	–18%
Clays (common)	24,600	157	11,700	141	–52%	–10%
Lime	20,000	1,370	19,100	2,130	–5%	55%
Phosphate	35,800	955	28,100	2,720	–22%	185%
Salt	45,000	1,270	45,500	1,770	1%	39%
Sand and gravel	1,240,000	6,590	853,700	8,020	–31%	22%
Crushed stone	1,590,000	9,590	1,160,000	11,200	–27%	17%
Total		33,200		38,700		17%

*Thousand metric tons, except gold, silver, and palladium, expressed in kilograms.
† Millions of dollars.

Source: U.S. Geological Survey, *Minerals Yearbook 2004 and 2011*, Washington, DC. Posted July 2013, http://minerals.usgs.gov/minerals/pubs/commodity/statistical_summary.

per million (ppm) of copper. But copper is actually mined in a selected number of spots where the concentration of copper in the ore is substantially high. It is high enough, in other words, that it can be extracted and refined at reasonable cost with current extraction technologies. Thus, although copper (and most other minerals) is a nonrenewable resource in some ultimate physical sense, there is actually a long grade–quantity continuum like that pictured in figure 10-1. Relatively few very high-grade deposits exist, but at progressively lower grades, the potential supply increases. Some very low-grade deposits, indicated by g_1 in the figure, correspond to average crustal abundance of the mineral, at which the potential supply is extremely large. The profile appears to be very definite, but it is actually quite speculative. Under technology presently available, there is some **cutoff grade,** such as that indicated by g_2 in figure 10-1, representing the minimum grade that can be economically extracted and refined. Geological exploration and conjecture may give us a reasonably good idea about how much is currently available at or above this cutoff grade, but the relationship between g_1 and g_2 is much more uncertain. It may rise smoothly and steeply, or it may have bumps at various points. The actual relationship will be revealed only in the fullness of time, as geological theory and exploration progress.

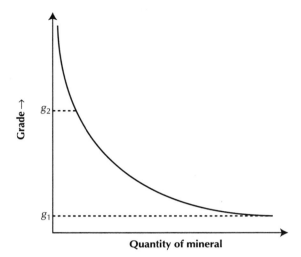

Figure 10-1   Relationship between Grade (Mineral Content per Quantity of Material) and Total Quantity

Thus, as the mineral grade decreases, known and expected quantities increase. Also, as grade decreases, the costs of extraction and refining increase. So when it comes to the economics of extraction and supply for "nonrenewables" like minerals, there are essentially two questions to address:

1. Given a deposit of known quantity and grade, what is the socially efficient rate at which that deposit should be used up?

2. What is the economically efficient rate at which geological exploration should be pursued in order to expand our knowledge of known deposits?

We will direct our attention to these two questions in the following sections.

■ Extraction Economics for a Known Stock

In this section we look at the simple economics of a nonrenewable resource in which the basic question is: Given a known quantity of a nonrenewable resource, how fast should it be extracted and used? To address this in a simple but revealing way, we limit the analysis to just two time periods, this year and next year. A two-period analysis is clearly unrealistic, but the essence of efficiency in this case is the balance achieved between "today" and the "future," and the logic of this trade-off can be explored quite well with this simple model.

Suppose that a community has discovered a mineral deposit within its borders and has decided to extract it for the benefit of the town's citizens. There is a market for the material, and to keep it analytically simple we assume there are no environmental quality issues connected to its extraction. Community output will be small relative to the total size of the market, so it is expected to be able to sell whatever output it chooses at the going market price. Thus, as pictured in figure 10-2, the demand curves for the community output in the two periods labeled D_0 and D_1 are effectively hori-

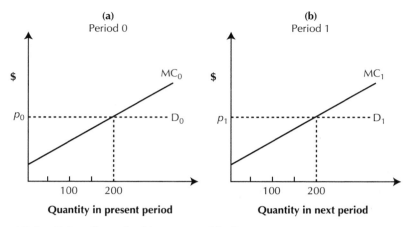

Figure 10-2 **Extraction of a Nonrenewable Resource**

zontal. Furthermore, they are level at the same price; this price is known today, and the assumption is that the price next period will be the same as this period.[1] The marginal extraction cost curves, labeled MC_0 and MC_1, are also expected to be the same; they are linear and sloped upward to the right, as depicted in the figure.

According to the situation depicted in figure 10-2 (a) and (b), statically efficient extraction levels of this resource (identified by the condition $p = MC$) are the same in each period: 200 units.[2] If the total quantity of resource available were greater than 400 units, there would essentially be no problem; the resource could be extracted at its static efficiency level in each period. The efficient multiple-period production plan in this simple case is to produce the same output each year. But suppose the total amount of this resource were less than 400 units, for example 300 units. An extraction rate of 200 units each year for 2 years now would exceed the total availability of the resources; thus **extracting more today means being able to extract less next year, and vice versa.** In order to determine our efficient intertemporal production plan, this overall limit on the amount of the natural resource must be taken into account.

It is easiest to work this problem out with a little algebra. Static efficiency required the choice of a single output rate, but now we must identify, simultaneously, two rates of output, one for the first year and one for the second. We assume that the community wishes to maximize the present value of net benefits; this would allow it to invest these returns in alternative assets of value to the community, perhaps a school or health clinic. The present value of net benefits in the case of the two-period model is given as

$$\text{Present value of net benefits (PVNB)} = \left(\begin{array}{c}\text{Net benefits}\\\text{in year 0}\end{array}\right) + \frac{1}{1+r}\left(\begin{array}{c}\text{Net benefits}\\\text{in year 1}\end{array}\right)$$

Remember that r is the discount rate.

The **trade-off** inherent in this intertemporal problem is depicted in the two terms to the right of the equal sign. Starting from some initial output levels q_0 and q_1, if q_0 is changed, it will change the first of the right-side terms in one direction, and through its impacts on q_1, will change the second term in the **opposite direction.** If output increases in period 0, it must decrease in period 1. The two output rates that give a maximum PVNB are the rates where the change in this year's net benefits and the change in next year's net benefits (discounted) are exactly offsetting. This condition can be written as

$$\frac{\text{Change in net}}{\text{benefits in year 0}} = \frac{1}{1+r}\left(\frac{\text{Change in net}}{\text{benefits in year 1}}\right)$$

If the output in either year is changed a small amount, the change in net benefits is equal to $p - \text{MC}$ for that year. Thus, the last expression can be rewritten as

$$p_0 - \text{MC}_0 = \frac{1}{1+r}\left(p_1 - \text{MC}_1\right)$$

The intertemporally efficient time profile of extraction is the two extraction rates q_0 and q_1 that satisfy this equation.

To draw out the implications of this last expression, consider an initial production profile in which $q_0 = q_1$, as depicted in panel (a) of figure 10-3. Since both demand curves and marginal cost curves are the same in the two periods, this production profile implies that $p_0 - \text{MC}_0 = p_1 - \text{MC}_1$. But if this were true, it would have to be the case that, as long as $r > 0$,

$$p_0 - \text{MC}_0 \neq \frac{1}{1+r}\left(p_1 - \text{MC}_1\right)$$

This means that the equal production profile ($q_0 = q_1$) does not satisfy the condition for intertemporal efficiency. To satisfy that condition, the term on the left of the last expression must be reduced and that on the right must be increased.

The way to accomplish this is to increase q_0 and decrease q_1, because increasing q_0 will decrease $p_0 - \text{MC}_0$, whereas decreasing q_1 will increase $p_1 - \text{MC}_1$. This leads to the conclusion that the dynamically efficient production profile involves a "tilt" toward the present, in the sense that extraction in the first year q_0 exceeds that of the second year q_1. This situation is depicted in panel (b) of figure 10-3 (on the following page), with the efficient values of q_0 and q_1 labeled q_0^* and q_1^*.

Thus, we see that intertemporal efficiency implies $q_0 > q_1$, that is, a production profile that is **tilted toward the present.** What drives this is the presence of the discount rate, the assumption that demand and marginal cost functions are the same in each period, and of course the fact that the community has the objective of maximizing the present value of its chosen extraction path.

In real-world situations the entities doing the extraction are likely to be private firms who own mineral deposits or have contracted for access to publicly owned deposits. We discuss in chapter 6 the conditions under which private markets are socially efficient, and these apply here: competition in the industry and no externalities on either side of the market. Now we must add another factor: the private firms must use a discount rate that is the most appropriate from the standpoint of society. If they use a discount that is too low, for example, they will extract the mineral too soon, as compared to the socially efficient path.

If this happens, does the community have any recourse? Of course it does, as suggested in chapter 7 when we discussed policy options. One is a

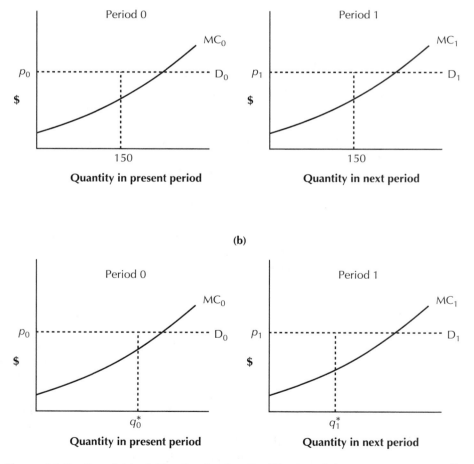

Figure 10-3   Panel (a): A Flat Production Profile; Panel (b): An Intertemporally Efficient Production Profile

direct command and control regulation specifying maximum extraction rates by the private firm. Another is through various monetary charges, such as **severance taxes** and **royalties**. We will discuss these below.

Capital Values

There is another useful way of looking at the efficient extraction profile. Remember the term that we introduced earlier: **resource rent.** Resource rent is the value of a marginal unit of the resource **in situ**—in other words, what it would be worth if somehow an extra unit of the resource could be added to the size of the deposit. The value of the rent in the first period is $p_0 - \text{MC}_0$, whereas the rental value in the second period is $p_1 - \text{MC}_1$. But efficiency requires that

$$p_0 - \text{MC}_0 = \frac{1}{1+r}(p_1 - \text{MC}_1)$$

which can be expressed as

$$\text{Rent}_1 = (1 + r)\,\text{Rent}_0$$

The optimal extraction profile is the one that yields a rent that rises at the rate of discount r.

Suppose the community uses a discount rate (r) that is equal to the rate of return it could get on other types of productive assets (e.g., in the simplest case, the return it could get on money in a savings fund). Then the efficient extraction profile is one that makes the value of the resource asset appreciate at the same rate as these alternative assets. Efficient resource extraction, in other words, becomes a matter of maximizing a **portfolio** of valuable capital assets.

User Costs

Another informative way of analyzing the situation is with **user costs.** In this two-period example, an increase of one unit of extraction today means a decrease of one unit in period 1; the value of the latter is equal to the future marginal willingness to pay p_1 minus the future extraction cost MC_1. The **marginal user cost,** in other words, is $p_1 - \text{MC}_1$, and its present value is

$$\frac{1}{1+r}(p_1 - \text{MC}_1)$$

Let us change the overall scenario somewhat, and think of the discussion as applying to an entire extractive industry, composed of a large number of firms operating in competitive market conditions. So the demand curve for the output of this industry (D_0) is not flat, as it was for the single community above, but downward sloping, as depicted in figure 10-4. The marginal cost curve, labeled MC_0, is an aggregate cost curve of all the firms in the industry. The dotted line that starts at $q_0 = q_0{}^0$ and goes up to the right is the aggregate marginal user cost of extraction in the current period. At

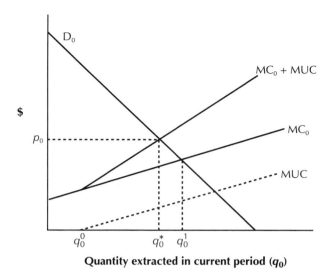

Figure 10-4 Efficient Extraction Rate in Current Period

Quantity extracted in current period (q_0)

rates below $q_0{}^0$, user cost is zero, because at this rate or anything below, this first-period use is so low that it would not detract from availabilities in the next period.[3] The solid line labeled MC_0 + MUC shows the sum of marginal extraction cost and marginal user cost. This curve intersects the D_0 curve at an output level of q_0^*, which is the efficient rate of output in the first period. Compare this to the static efficiency level $q_0{}^1$.

As we discussed earlier, the concept of user cost provides a useful way of thinking about how efficient current and future extraction rates would be affected by changes in some of the factors in the model. Suppose, for example, that we expect the marginal extraction costs in period 1 to be higher than those of period 0 because smaller resource stocks make extraction more costly.[4] There is now another consequence of increasing first-period extraction rates, and this will have the effect of increasing the user cost. Current extraction, in other words, reduces future availabilities and makes future extraction more costly. The increased user cost in period 0 implies that the first-period efficient extraction rate is decreased. So the expectation of future extraction cost increases results in a smaller degree of tilt in the time profile of extraction rates, as compared to the case of no increase in extraction costs.

Another future change that might be expected is population growth. This would have the effect, in our simple model, of pushing out the D curve for the second period. And this would have the effect of increasing the user cost of extraction today. The implication is that the intertemporally efficient rate of extraction in period 0 would decrease. This is true of other factors, such as income growth, that shift out the future demand curve.

The optimality condition above can be rewritten as:

$$p_1 = MC_1 + (p_0 - MC_0)(1 + r)$$

which in words is:

$$\begin{matrix} \text{price in} \\ \text{second year} \end{matrix} = \begin{matrix} \text{production costs} \\ \text{in second year} \end{matrix} + \left(\begin{matrix} \text{rent in} \\ \text{first year} \end{matrix} \right) \left(\begin{matrix} \text{compound} \\ \text{interest} \end{matrix} \right)$$

The calculation is that, if extraction costs are constant, we should see the price of the resource **increase over time**. In other words, increasing scarcity should lead to rising resource prices. However, for few, if any, non-renewable resources do we see this pattern in the historical record. What has actually happened to these prices over the last few decades?

In fact, minerals prices over the last few decades have not shown an upward trend but rather substantial volatility, with a slight downward trend. There was a brief period in the early 1970s when the prices of many minerals shot upward. Many observers at the time talked ominously about how natural resource scarcities were about to threaten the world and bring the developed economies to a grinding halt. It did not happen.[5] In a few years most prices dropped to previous levels. Several prices spiked again in the late 1980s, but this was again followed by a marked drop. In real terms (i.e., after adjusting for the effects of general inflation), mineral prices were lower in the late 1980s than they were in the 1960s. In recent years, starting in 2006, many minerals and metals prices have shown marked increases. It remains to be seen if this is the beginning of a long-term upward trend. Overall, however, the "market" apparently does not see quantitative restrictions in these materials, despite the fact that we are calling them nonrenewable resources.[6]

Minerals markets have historically been very volatile. Price fluctuations are traceable to, among other things, **demand shocks** and **supply shocks**. When we examined the simple analytics of markets in chapter 5, we saw how price and quantity changes could be produced by shifts in underlying demand and supply functions. In resource markets, demand changes can come from new technologies (palladium used in car exhaust filters, for example) or growth in resource-using industries (new resource demands from China's growing economy, for example). Supply shifts can be produced by new resource discoveries (massive iron-ore deposits in Guinea, for example) and new technologies that vastly impact resource extraction and refining operations (natural gas through hydraulic fracturing, for example).

Another source of price instability arises from the fact that resource markets, like many others, are "forward-looking" in the sense that expected future supplies and demands can have a big impact on today's prices. World political events, for example, can affect expectations of future resource availabilities, thus causing prices to shift, sometimes drastically.

■ Resource Exploration and Development

Individual deposits usually contain fixed quantities of a resource, but it is unlikely that all deposits are currently known. In most cases, **exploration**

and development can increase the inventory of known deposits. With continuous exploration effort, the stock of new deposits, or new reserves, may be pushed out more or less continuously. Of course the effectiveness of exploration and development will vary from mineral to mineral. Predictions of substantial reductions in the rate of resource discovery have been made almost continuously for quite some time. But it appears that for many minerals we may expect new deposits to be found and developed with some regularity.

Another important phenomenon is developments in **extraction** technology. Better extraction methods can make it possible to extract resources of lower grades. These new methods will expand the available inventory of extractable deposits, similar to the exploration process discussed above. Suppose that we can summarize these factors with what we will call a **resource discovery function.** As pictured in panel (a) of figure 10-5, this shows the **marginal cost of expanding reserves.** It has a positive and increasing slope. At a reserve level of r_1 the marginal cost of an additional unit of reserves is c_1. Expanding reserves from r_1 to r_2 units takes a total of b dollars, and at r_2, marginal discovery costs are c_2. Remember that we are talking here about the quantity of reserves, not the quantity of material extracted.

Panel (b) of figure 10-5 depicts the supply and demand circumstances for reserves. The supply function is simply the marginal cost function depicted in the top panel. The demand function represents the willingness to pay by a firm or firms for additional quantities of reserve. The intersection of these curves shows the market

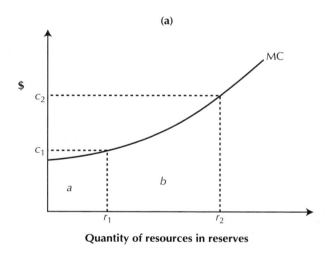

(a)

Quantity of resources in reserves

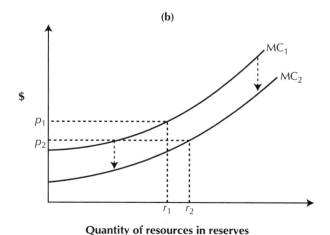

(b)

Quantity of resources in reserves

Figure 10-5   Resource Discovery Function

price that will tend to be established for quantities of materials held in reserve. Furthermore, this price is sensitive to technological changes that take place in the reserve discovery function. These technological changes are represented by a downward shift in the resource discovery function. In the figure the marginal costs of discovery function shifts from MC_1 to MC_2. As it shifts downward because of these technical improvements, the price of reserve quantities goes down, and the quantity of reserves increases.

Consider now a firm that engages in resource extraction and exploration. It has essentially two big decisions to make: (1) how much to extract this year and (2) how much effort to devote to expanding reserves. These two decisions are closely related. A way of understanding this is to see that a firm (or group of firms) in this position has essentially two ways of adding to future stocks: (1) by reducing today's extraction rate and (2) by finding new stocks. If the firm is making efficient decisions, it will adjust so that the marginal costs of these two activities are the same. But the cost of adding to reserves by cutting back today's extraction is simply the rental rate, or in situ price of the resource, while the cost of adding to resource stocks is the marginal cost of discovery. What this chain of reasoning allows us to conclude is that there is another important factor behind the perceived historical drops in mineral prices: historical reductions in exploration and development costs. Of course, we know also that demands have been increasing, which increases mineral prices. Until recently, however, the reductions in extraction costs have occurred even faster than demand increases, driving prices down.

■ Nonrenewable Resources and Sustainability

With renewable resources it is not too hard to envisage long-term, or sustainable, rates of production. But minerals are a different case. Minerals, once used, are gone forever. How, then, can a nonrenewable resource be used in a sustainable fashion? There are two ways of doing this:

1. Consider mineral use, or the use of any particular mineral, as a transition process in which we will eventually shift to a substitute resource of greater abundance.

2. Invest the rents earned from current mineral extraction into other types of assets so as to maintain the overall productivity of the economy even though the supply of minerals diminishes.

Switch to a Substitute

Suppose an essential natural resource experienced a long-term price increase. Eventually, if there were no substitutes, the price would rise high enough to choke off economic growth, a nonsustainable result. But suppose there are high-priced but superabundant substitutes. For petroleum, a nonrenewable resource, there is solar energy, a substitute that is both renewable and available in very large supply (except perhaps in polar regions). At some relatively high price it will presumably be efficient to shift to this new resource, sometimes called a **backstop resource** or **backstop technology**. So in the very long run, the path of price might be expected to look like that depicted in figure 10-6.

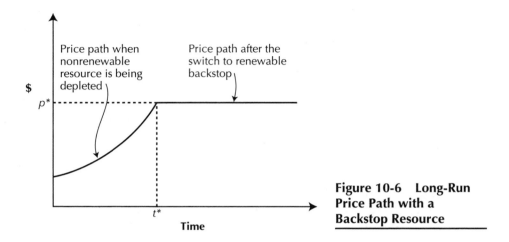

Figure 10-6   Long-Run Price Path with a Backstop Resource

Up until year t^*, which of course may be a very long time in the future, the price rises in accordance with the expression above for the period during which the resource is being depleted. But when the price reaches p^* (at time t^*), the renewable backstop resource kicks in, and the path of price now becomes level, essentially forever. In other words, the nonrenewable resource has been extracted during a transition period; it has been a bridge resource allowing us to eventually reach the renewable one. Of course, several stages of nonrenewables could be depleted before reaching the final backstop (e.g., wood to coal to petroleum to solar). In the diagram this would give several more upward-trending price path segments before reaching the horizontal path.

How plausible is this type of scenario? Perhaps much more so than we might be able to appreciate. We are talking of the extremely long run here, not the next few decades, or even the next half century. The average person finds it quite hard to extrapolate a long way into the future. But the average person might legitimately be a little nervous in assuming that a backstop resource will be available whenever an important nonrenewable gets very scarce, and also about the ability of ordinary humans to adjust to continually elevated rates of technical change. In some cases (solar energy, desalination, industrial diamonds) backstop technologies are sufficiently predictable now that we can believe in their future practicality. In many cases (production of food and clothing), however, future technical backstops are harder to visualize.

Invest Rents

Consider again the efficient extraction path in figure 10-3. One of its implications is that $q_1 < q_0$, that is, the amount extracted in the second period is less than that of the first. Extractive resources of this type are usually not consumed directly by consumers, but are used to produce consumer goods. Suppose that to produce $10 of national income, you need exactly 1 ton of a nonrenewable resource, no more and no less.[7] This declining resource extraction path also implies a diminishing consumption path (with no imports). This is not sustainable because sustainability means, at the very least, nondiminution. How can we convert this to a sustainable outcome? Suppose it is possible to produce the same output with fewer resources, provided that we substitute other forms of capital (say, tractors, fertilizers, better seeds, or better management) for the diminished natural capital. We can do this by investing in these other types of productive capital; in other words, the effects of the reduced resource use can be offset. Where does the money come from for investing in the other capital? It comes from the **resource rents** earned from the extraction of the nonrenewable resources.

The conditions that need to be satisfied in order to have a sustainable (i.e., nondiminishing) consumption path have been worked out. It is essentially that the total stock of productive capital of the economy be **nondiminishing**. The total capital stock is equal to the stock of natural resource capital plus the stock of human-made capital. The latter can include both **machine-type capital** and, most importantly, **human capital.** To maintain this total capital stock, the rents achieved from extracting the nonrenewable resource must be invested in these alternative forms of capital.[8]

This principle means, among other things, that considerable attention attaches to how these rents are mobilized and guided toward these investments. Typically this is a role for public authorities. One way of doing it is for public bodies to share, through **joint ownership** of the extracting enterprise, net incomes coming from the operation. The profit sharing essentially transfers some of the rents to the public, where they may be invested in building up alternative forms of capital. In most cases enterprises would be subject to a **corporate income tax**, or something analogous to it, which could also transfer some of the resource rents to public authorities.

More directly, rents may be captured through a variety of **taxes and royalties** levied by public authorities on extracting firms. Royalties (sometimes called **severance taxes**) are charges levied on extraction operations directly. One type, for example, is simply a direct charge on total production revenues, either on quantity (i.e., tq, where t is the tax rate and q is total output), or value (tqp, where p is the market price of the output). Another type of royalty is a charge specifically on total resource rent, that is $t(pq - C)$.

There has been much study of the various taxes used in the extraction of nonrenewable resources.[9] One important point of interest is whether a specific charge tends to shift the intertemporal path of extraction, or whether it is neutral in this sense. Also important are its potential impacts on investments in resource discovery and development. In some cases charges may be used specifically to tilt the time profile of extraction, in cases, for example, where public authorities think that private operators are extracting a resource faster than is socially optimal (for example, when private operators are using a discount rate that is too high from society's standpoint). In all cases we have to remember that the precise impact of a tax or royalty will be uncertain because of the inherent uncertainties of resource markets.

■ U.S. Mineral Import Dependence and Resource Cartels

A recurrent problem in U.S. mineral use is the heavy dependence on imports to supply domestic demands. Table 10-2 depicts data on U.S. import reliance for a number of important industrial minerals. From time to time data like these are viewed with alarm, as they seem to show how vulnerable the country is to any actions that interrupt the flow of imports. For many years (until very recently) this fear was especially strong with regard to U.S. petroleum imports. The **energy embargoes** of the 1970s, engineered by the Organization of Petroleum Exporting Countries (OPEC), heightened fears that similar cartels of mineral suppliers could form and substantially raise the price of U.S. imports by restricting supplies.[10] How likely is this?

Table 10-2   U.S. Import Dependencies for Selected Minerals, 2010 (Imports as a Percent of Consumption)

Bauxite and Alumina	100
Graphite	100
Barite	76
Potash	83
Zinc	77
Copper	30
Cement	8
Iron and steel	7
Salt	24

Source: U.S. Geological Survey, *Mineral Commodity Summary 2011,* USGS, Washington, DC. (http://minerals.usgs.gov/minerals/pubs/mcs/2011/mcs2011.pdf)

In the 1970s some bauxite-producing countries sought to imitate the actions of OPEC and raise export prices. Similar actions were undertaken by some copper-exporting countries. Neither effort was particularly successful. There is a wider appreciation now of the specific factors that apparently must be present if mineral-producer cartels are going to be successful. A **cartel** is a group of producing countries (or a group of individual firms in the case of a private cartel) that act in concert to restrict supplies and raise prices. To be successful there are essentially two general requirements, one that is strictly economic and another that is more **political-economic.**

1. The demand for the commodity in question must be relatively price-inelastic; buyers will tend to purchase only slightly less even though the price increases.[11] In figure 10-7 there are two demand curves, one steep (D_1) and one much less so (D_2). If quantity is currently at q_1 and the cartel is successful in restricting it to q_2, the price will increase much more in the case of D_1 (to p_3) than in the case of D_2 (to p_2).

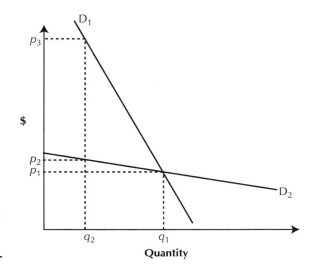

Figure 10-7   Quantity Restrictions and Price Increases

2. Enough countries to account for a substantial proportion of total production must be able to agree on, and enforce, joint action to limit supplies. They have to be collectively strong enough to be able to overcome the temptation each country will have to cheat on the agreement.

Condition 1 is satisfied quite well in practice. Minerals are **intermediate** goods; that is, they are used in the production of other goods rather than consumed directly. Their cost is usually a small fraction of the total cost of producing these goods. In the production of these goods it would normally take some time to develop substitutes for the metals in use. For both reasons, their consumption is unlikely to be particularly responsive to price. But one factor works in the opposite direction: the availability of supplies from countries that stay outside the cartel. Although the overall demand elasticity for a commodity may be low, for the output of countries in the cartel it could be relatively high if noncartel members are ready to make up cartel-sponsored supply reductions.

Condition 2 has several ramifications. Joint action is much more feasible if relatively few countries are involved. This is indeed the case with many minerals; world production is concentrated among a small number of countries. The other major part of this, however, is that the countries must be able to make and to police agreements among themselves. In the past this has been the major weak point of attempts to form minerals cartels. Initial agreement is followed not long afterward by a breakdown in discipline and cohesion among the would-be participants. Even OPEC repeatedly succumbs to this problem, as well as to the problem of increased production by non-OPEC nations.

This phenomenon also needs to be viewed from the standpoint of the supplying countries. Many of these are developing countries and rely on exports of natural resource commodities, including nonfuel minerals, as important sources of income. In a later chapter on natural resources and economic development, we revisit this issue from the perspective of the supplying countries.

■ Price Instability and Boomtowns

As mentioned above, markets for nonrenewable resources have been unstable historically in the sense of experiencing large changes in quantities and prices, monthly and annually. Figure 10-8 shows, for example, the path of international copper prices from 1950 to 2014. Since 2006 these prices have jumped way up owing to the strong entry of China into the market as buyers.

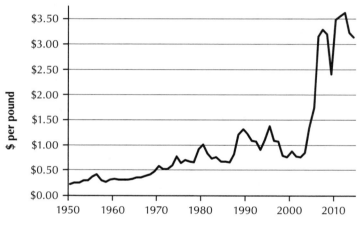

Figure 10-8   Historical Copper Prices, 1850–2014

Source: U.S. Geological Survey, *Metal Prices in the United States through 2010,* USGS Scientific Investigations Report 2012-5188, 2013; *Mineral Commodities Summaries* (Copper), 2015.

Price changes of this frequency and magnitude can lend to major disruptions at the local level, where town economies are dependent on resource deposits which, though small relative to global output, loom large locally. This has produced the **boomtown** phenomenon, where the local economy expands and contracts in response to local pulses in resource extraction. An example is discussed in Exhibit 10-1.

The life cycle of the boomtown is something like this: a resource deposit is discovered, or activated if already known; crews move in to begin operation; workers move in attracted by the new job opportunities; new housing accommodations, temporary or permanent, are made available, roads and other public facilities become more crowded and degraded; now retail businesses open to serve the growing population; demand for public services, such as schools and public security, grows rapidly; new pressures are put on

Exhibit 10-1   Mineral Boomtowns

Morenci, Arizona, is a small (4,000 citizens ±) town in southeastern Arizona, and largely dependent on a single enterprise for its economic livelihood: a company that operates a large copper mine there. The town is a "company town," the company is not only the biggest source of jobs, but also owns most of the property in town. The company could presumably strive to follow an intertemporal production plan based on the theory explained in the text. The reality of it, however, is that the mine's output bounces back and forth according to the booms and busts of the global copper market. People drift into town when the mine is in full operation, and back out when the world price of copper collapses and mine operations are curtailed. The last such drop was in 1996 when copper prices fell below $1.50 per pound. It shot up to a high of about $4.50 a pound in 2011 and has since tapered off somewhat. But mining operations are still strong (as of 2015); enough so that mine operators are facing a challenge to get enough fresh water to expand production in a region of relative water scarcity.

. . . the specter of copper prices dropping haunts the town, littered by rusting cars, abandoned by laid-off workers, and rubble from smelters dismantled a century ago. . . . The expectations were that it was a dying industry. Mines were being closed, smelters were being dismantled, but now the global demand for copper led by China has made resources that weren't thought valuable very valuable.

Source: John W. Miller, "Copper Miners Thirst for Water," *The Wall Street Journal,* May 21, 2014, p. A12.

town authorities to manage the many dimensions of town growth; at some point expansion reaches some upper limit, and for a time may remain at or near this level.

If at some point the local resource is exhausted, or prices drop, the town will face a rapid reduction in its economic base, unless it has managed somehow to develop new export sectors. The whole boom and bust process may repeat according to the episodic fluctuations of the resource price.

There are a number of important economic issues arising in boomtowns:

- What procedures are in place (taxes, royalties, etc.) that will allow the town to capture a portion of the resource rent generated from the operation?

- How will these rents be distributed among landowners, workers, small businesses, town agencies, and others?

- What burdens will be placed on other dimensions of the town's environment? Most extraction procedures require large amounts of water, for example.

- What factors should enter into decisions whether to expand town services, such as schools, public safety, roads, recreational facilities, and water and sewerage?

- What will happen after the bust; for example, is it likely that the pre-boom economy will be reestablished at more-or-less the same level?

■ The Economics of Recycling

Recycling of nonrenewable resources serves both to reduce the draft on virgin supplies and to reduce the discharge of associated residuals back into the natural environment. Many resources change their chemical and physical nature so much during utilization that they cannot be recovered in useful form. This includes, for example, fossil energy resources, fertilizer minerals, and food resources such as fish and game. Other resources, however, finish their useful lives in forms that can be recycled as raw materials back into the production process. This includes many metals, wood and paper, and chemicals derived from petroleum.

The sequence of steps linking the initial removal of the material from the waste stream and its final reincorporation back into a final product can be complex both physically and economically.[12] It starts with the end users of the material in question; either they or some other entity must extract from the waste stream those materials destined for recycling. These materials then often move through a sequence of steps: transporting, sorting, reconcentrating, reprocessing, and finally reuse. Sometimes these functions are accomplished by a single firm, but in most cases the activities of many different firms are coordinated by markets and by the forces of supply and demand that affect them.

There are several important questions when it comes to recycling. Suppose we target a particular material, say, aluminum cans. These can be manufactured from virgin raw material, the cost of which covers mining the bauxite, refining this into alumina and then into aluminum, and finally manufacturing the cans. The cans also can be produced, in whole or in part, from used cans. The cost of the recycling covers retrieving them from the waste stream, reprocessing the aluminum, and then manufacturing the new cans. There are several questions to ask here. What is the economically efficient level of recycling in this case? Will current markets tend to produce this level of recycling, or is there a role for public oversight and perhaps intervention? If the answer to the latter is yes, what kind of policy is appropriate?

Figure 10-9 shows a very simple analysis of the recycling question; we can use it to look at how markets normally function and the conditions under which they are efficient. The demand curve, labeled D, shows the market demand for aluminum cans. It has the standard downward-sloping shape; the higher the price, the fewer the cans demanded, and vice versa. S_V is the supply curve of aluminum cans using virgin raw materials. It's quite flat, based on the assumption that additional quantities of cans can be produced from this source at roughly constant marginal cost. S_R is the supply curve of cans made from recycled aluminum cans; it slopes upward rather steeply, based on the assumption that recycling is subject to increasing marginal costs.

This is an extremely simple model, but it can be used to reveal some interesting conclusions. According to this analysis, the total quantity of cans sold will tend toward q_1, given by the intersection of S_V and D. The price of cans will be p_1, which is the price established by the level of virgin production costs. This bears repeating: The factor governing the market price of cans is the cost of production from virgin sources. The quantity of recycled cans is q_2; if recycled output were pushed beyond this, costs would rise above p_1, which would not be feasible in a competitive world. The quantity of cans produced from virgin material is $q_1 - q_2$, and the recycling ratio, the proportion of total cans that stem from recycled sources, is q_2/q_1.[13]

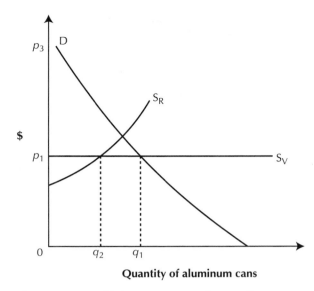

Figure 10-9   Efficient Amount of Recycling

Figure 10-10 on the following page shows the different possible ways to increase recycling. Panel (a) shows the result of a reduction in total demand for aluminum cans. This could come about through, for example, a shift to another type of container (glass, plastic) or an overall reduction in consumption of whatever the cans contain. The demand curve moves back from D_1 to D_2. This reduces total can production from q_1 to q_3, while leaving unchanged the production of recycled cans at q_2, thus increasing the recycling ratio. This is a revealing result. The recycling ratio was increased simply by decreasing total can output, without any direct intervention in the recycling process. This is because of the way the two supply sources (virgin and recycled) relate to one another. When overall production shifts, the adjustment happens entirely on the virgin supply side.

Panel (b) shows the effect of investing in the recycling industry. This lowers the cost of one or more of the recycling functions (collecting, transporting, reprocessing, remanufacturing), and is pictured by a rightward shift in S_R from S^0_R to S^1_R. This lowers the cost of producing any given amount of recycled cans, although the curve still slopes upward. Total can output at q_1 is unaffected, but recycled output increases from q_2 to q_3, and so the recycling ratio increases.

Panel (c) shows the effect of lifting the cost of virgin materials. The primary motivation for increasing recycling is to reduce the use of virgin materials, both because of the environmental benefits this produces directly and because a smaller number of cans will be disposed of in the future. Suppose a tax were put on virgin materials, making them more expensive to the producers of cans. In effect this lifts the S_V line upward by the amount of the tax. This attacks the problem from both sides: Total can production drops from q_1 to q_3, and the output of recycled cans increases from q_2 to q_4.

Which of these approaches is likely to be the most effective? Two factors are involved here: the shape of the functions themselves and the ease with which they can be shifted. Consider the S_R function. Other things equal, the flatter this function, the greater impact there is from a change like a tax on virgin materials; see panel (c). If the capacity of the present recycling sector tends to be fixed and inflexible, the function will be steep. If it is easy for the existing aluminum can recycling sector to expand or contract its output, given its present condition in terms of factors like the number of plants or the technology in use, the S_R function will be relatively flat. A rightward shift of S_R in panel (b) can occur because of investment in additional recycling plants, adoption of better recycling technology, or a combination of both. The development of better recycling technology is, of course, a major pursuit in most modern economies. For aluminum cans and plastic soda bottles, new machines have mechanized the deposit return function.

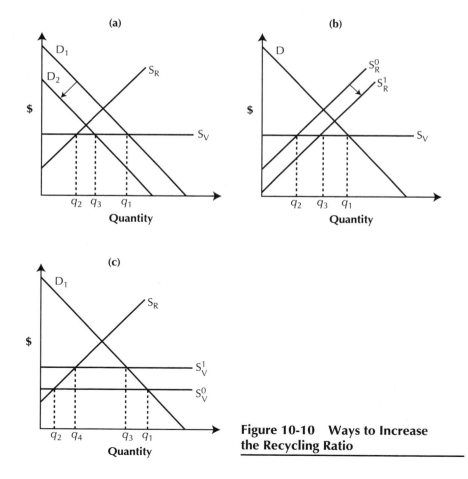

Figure 10-10   Ways to Increase the Recycling Ratio

Although this simple model shows some basic relationships, it cannot show how rapidly situations can change in the real world. Demand can shift because of demographic and economic changes; cost curves can change because technological factors underlying production, especially from recycled sources, evolve, sometimes rapidly. In addition, macroeconomic factors and international trade developments can have substantial effects on resource prices and therefore on markets like the one analyzed in the model.

In the future we can expect to see modest increases in recycling in many sectors of the economy. One factor pushing this, which we have not highlighted above but is important, is the increasing environmental costs of materials disposal. Working against this is the continued decline in the prices of virgin materials. The key to lifting recycling ratios in particular sectors will be in pushing out the S_R function in figure 10-10. This means developing efficient recycling technologies and organizing effective recycling industries to close the loop between suppliers and demanders of recycled materials.

■ Summary

This chapter reviewed some of the economic issues involved in extracting nonfuel minerals. These appear to be classic examples of nonrenewable resources. This is true in some ultimate physical sense, but the processes of exploration and discovery and the technological ability over time to utilize increasingly lower grades of ore give them the characteristics of a renewable resource for the foreseeable future. The first major topic of the chapter was a simple two-period model to explore economic issues involved in extracting a nonrenewable resource from a known deposit. Time profiles of production and prices were featured problems, and the role of user cost was explored. The processes of resource exploration and discovery were examined briefly. Technical change in resource discovery and extraction are the major factors behind the long-run drops in minerals prices. The question of the sustainable extraction of nonrenewable resources was explored, emphasizing the ideas of backstop resources and investing resource rents to achieve sustainable incomes. After focusing briefly on the recent history of minerals prices, we looked at economic issues of import dependence and producer cartels. We considered some of the factors, such as the price elasticity of demand, that determine the probability that cartels will be able to raise prices effectively and increase their incomes. We then discussed briefly the boomtown phenomenon in minerals extraction. Finally, we looked at a simple model of recycling, with special emphasis on the factors that produce changes in the recycling ratio.

Notes

[1] Of course if the next period's demand curve is highly uncertain, this may add some complexity to the problem that we might want to explore, but for now we overlook this issue.

[2] Remember the convention we are using. The present period is indexed with 0, and the next period with 1. Thus, q_0 and q_1 refer, respectively, to current (this year's) output and next year's output.

[3] For example, suppose the total availability is 300 units. We know that extraction in the next period would never exceed 200 units (referring back to figure 10-2) because $MC > p$ beyond 200 units. Thus, if the use rate in year 0 is less than 100 units, there will be no economically relevant restriction on availability in year 1; that is, user cost below 100 units will be zero. Above 100 units, of course, user costs are positive and increasing, as pictured in figure 10-4.

[4] In fact, for many resources, extraction costs have been decreasing for a long time. Technological change has been the dominant factor in this long-run trend.

[5] This was the time of a famous wager between two public personalities on the future of resource prices. Paul Erhlich, an ecologist and strong pessimist about resource scarcity, made a widely publicized bet with Julian Simon, an equally strong optimist. Erhlich was to select five commodities (he chose nickel, tin, copper, chrome, and tungsten). He would hypothetically invest $200 in each commodity as of 1980. In 10 years he would calculate the real prices of the five items. If they had gone up in price from 1980, Simon would pay Erhlich the amount of the aggregate increase; if they went down Erhlich would pay Simon the amount of the aggregate decrease. In 1990 Erhlich sent Simon a check for $576.07.

[6] The "market" is a short-hand way of referring to the thousands of people around the globe who are involved in the various phases of exploration, production, transportation, and use of minerals.

[7] In fact, over time this ratio has increased; that is, changes in the economy have reduced the resource intensity of production. But making this assumption here allows us to make a particular point more clearly.

[8] This is an application of the old idea of a sinking fund. When using a productive asset like a machine, one sets aside each year an amount equal to the depreciation of the machine, so that by the time the machine wears out, there will be just enough in the sinking fund to buy a new machine.

[9] For discussion of the issues see P. Daniel, M. Keen, and C. McPherson, eds., *The Taxation of Petroleum and Minerals: Principles, Problems, and Practice*. London: Routledge, 2010.

[10] High import dependence can lead to paranoid reactions. During the Cold War some were convinced that the Soviet Union was waging a "minerals war" against the United States. These days, similar concerns have been expressed about China.

[11] Price elasticity of demand measures the responsiveness of quantity changes to price changes along a demand function. It is defined as

$$\frac{\left(\text{percentage change in quantity}\right)}{\left(\text{percentage change in price}\right)}$$

Price-inelastic means that price changes do not produce large quantity changes. We deal with this concept in greater detail in chapter 17.

[12] It can also be very simple. Tag sales or garage sales link old users and new users together directly, so the entire recycling process is just a single transaction.

[13] To get some idea of these recycling rates in specific cases, for 2010 the USGS reported the following: aluminum 24 percent, cobalt 24 percent, copper 35 percent, lead 82 percent, and nickel 44 percent. See USGS, *Mineral Commodity Summaries 2011* (http://minerals.usgs.gov/minerals/pubs/mcs/2011/mcs2011.pdf).

Key Terms

backstop technology
capital values
economics of recycling
exploration and development
import dependence
industrial minerals
metals

nonfuel minerals
nonrenewables and sustainability
producer cartels
quantity-grade relationships
recycling ratio
time profiles of extraction and price
user cost

Questions for Further Discussion

1. How is it possible to reconcile the theoretical results we obtained concerning increases in the prices of nonrenewable resources with the declines in actual prices that have occurred in the past and that are still going on?

2. How is user cost affected by the expectation that future demand for a resource will shift outward? What will be the impact of this on today's efficient rate of extraction?

3. What are some of the factors that could make social user costs different from private user costs in the case of mineral resource extraction?

4. Consider a three-period model of nonrenewable resource extraction. Lay out the maximization problem in a way analogous to the two-period model of the chapter, and determine the explicit expression for user cost.

5. Suppose you represented a country that was a heavy producer of cobalt. Several other major cobalt-producing countries have suggested that you form an organization, restrict your exports, and drive the international price of cobalt higher. In considering the desirability of doing this, what are the major economic factors you should take into account?

6. Explain how changes could occur that produce increases in the quantity of materials recycled and, simultaneously, decreases in the recycling ratio.

Useful Websites

The main U.S. government website is:

- U.S. Geological Survey in the Department of the Interior, particularly the material dealing with minerals (http://www.usgs.gov/energy_minerals)

In Canada it is:

- Natural Resources Canada, Mining/Minerals Sector (http://www.nrcan.gc.ca/mining-materials)

Other public agencies and private groups in the United States and abroad that provide information and occasionally some analysis include:

- Congressional Research Service. The CRS has done numerous reports on mining that are available through the National Institute for the Environment (http://cnie.org/NLE/CRS)
- Chamber of Mines of South Africa (http://chamberofmines.org.za)
- American Geosciences Institute (www.americangeosciences.org)
- International Union of Geological Sciences (www.iugs.org)

Some universities have units devoted to minerals studies, for example:

- Bureau of Economic Geology at the University of Texas (http://www.beg.utexas.edu)
- Colorado School of Mines (http://www.mines.edu)

- Penn State College of Earth and Mineral Sciences
  (http://www.ems.psu.edu)

Many minerals companies and associations have websites with useful information, for example:

- LaFarge, a global construction materials company
  (http://www.lafarge.com)
- World Mine Cost Data Exchange (http://www.minecost.com/)

Selected Readings

Cummings, Ron, and Arthur F. Mehr. "Investments for Urban Infrastructure in Boomtowns," *Natural Resource Journal*, 17(2), April 1977, pp. 223–240.

Gaffney, Mason. *Extractive Resources and Taxation*. Madison, WI: University of Wisconsin Press, 1967.

Humphries, Marc. *The 1872 Mining Law: Time for Reform?* U.S. Congressional Research Service, Washington, DC, No. 89130, March 4, 1998.

Krautkraemer, Jeffrey A. "Nonrenewable Resource Scarcity," *Journal of Economic Literature*, 36(4), December 1998, pp. 2065–2107.

Pittel, Karen, Rick van der Ploeg, and Cess Withagen. *Climate Policy and Nonrenewable Resources*. Cambridge, MA: MIT Press, 2014.

Slade, Margaret E. "Trends in Natural Resource Commodity Prices: An Analysis of the Time Domain," *Journal of Environmental Economics and Management*, 9(2), 1982, pp. 122–137.

Smith, V. Kerry, ed. *Scarcity and Growth Reconsidered*. Baltimore, MD: Johns Hopkins University Press for Resources for the Future, 1979.

11

Energy

In the contemporary world, energy has two important dimensions. It is a critical input as a power source. This is especially true of modern, industrialized economies whose service and manufacturing sectors are based on huge systems of nonhuman power supply. It is also true, though perhaps in a different way, of developing countries that are tied more closely to basic sectors such as agriculture. And all people are dependent on incoming solar energy that supports photosynthesis and the production of plant and animal foods.

The other important dimension of energy use is as a source of **pollution.** Energy conversion—for example, the burning of fossil fuels—creates residuals that normally find their way into the environment. Carbon dioxide emissions from fossil fuel burning are implicated in helping to produce major global meteorological changes. Radiation from various parts of the nuclear fuel cycle can impact human health and ecosystems. Discharge of heated water from the cooling systems of power plants has changed local ecosystems. The list goes on.

These two sides of the energy resource are closely connected, of course. If the amount of energy taken into a system for power purposes declines, then the energy-related emissions coming out the end of the system will decline, other things being equal. Underneath the simple aggregate of energy used, however, is the fact that many different forms of the input are in use, each with different environmental implications. So a shift from one type of energy source to another (coal to natural gas or nuclear to solar, for example) also changes the environmental impacts of energy.

In this chapter we focus on the power supply aspects of energy resources. This is by no means meant to imply that the emissions end of the process is unimportant, only that it accords with the idea that this book is meant to concentrate on issues of natural resource supplies.

■ World Energy Use

A quick look at historical data on global energy use shows the massive change that has taken place, especially over the last century (see figure 11-1).

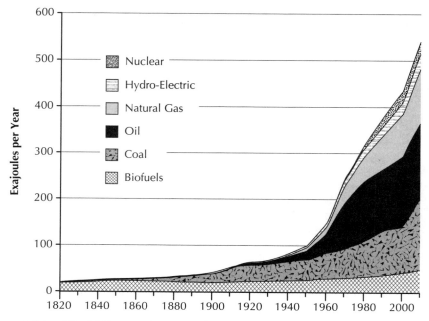

Figure 11-1   World Energy Consumption

Source: Gail Tverberg, originally published in *The Oil Drum* online, March 16, 2012.
http://www.resilience.org/stories/2012-03-16/world-energy-consumption-1820-charts

From 1800 to 1900 global energy consumption increased by about 100 percent. In the last century it increased by about 1,300 percent. Furthermore, the energy mix has drastically changed; 150 years ago the main fuel type was "biofuels," essentially wood for heating and cooking. Today it is largely fossil fuels: coal, oil, and natural gas, which are used to power a heavily industrialized world economy, at least in the "developed" or "emergent" portion of it. With the emphasis placed today on global economic growth and development, it is hard to think of anything that could put a significant brake on this upward trajectory in global energy consumption. And with the upward momentum in global energy use, it is clear that a supreme global effort will be required to shift substantially the global energy mix.

■ Energy in the United States: Consumption and Prices

The total consumption of primary energy of all forms in the United States was about 44 percent higher in 2013 than in 1970. Table 11-1 shows consumption amounts, in quadrillion Btus[1] ("quads") for selected years during this period, while figure 11-2 graphs U.S. energy consumption by source since 1949. Energy use increased rapidly up to the end of the 20th century, but since then it has grown more slowly. The table also shows the

Table 11-1   Energy Consumption by Source in U.S. (quadrillion Btus)

Source	1970	1980	1990	2000	2005	2013
Fossil						
Coal	12.3	15.4	19.2	22.6	22.8	18.1
Petroleum	29.5 (25)*	34.2 (43)	33.6 (51)	38.4 (64)	40.7 (71)	35.1 (40)
Gas	21.8 (<.1)	20.4 (5)	19.7 (8)	23.9 (16)	22.9 (19)	26.6 (12)
Nuclear	0.3	2.7	6.1	7.9	8.2	8.3
Renewable						
Hydro	2.6	2.9	3.0	2.8	2.7	2.6
Biomass	1.1	2.5	2.7	2.8	3.0	4.6
Other**	na	0.1	0.4	0.4	0.6	2.2
Total	67.8	78.3	84.7	99.0	100.6	97.5

*Number in parentheses is the percent of consumption that was imported for petroleum and gas.
**Primarily solar, wind, and geothermal.

Source: U.S. Energy Information Administration, *Annual Energy Outlook 2014*, DOE/EIA-0383, April 2014.

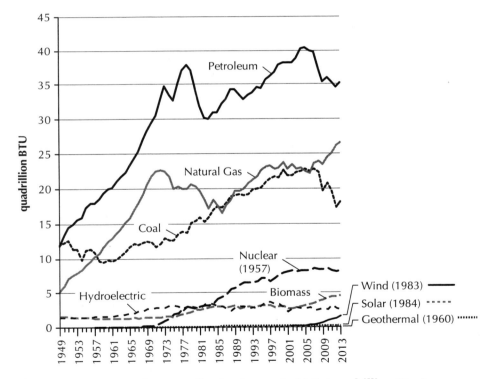

Figure 11-2   Energy Consumption by Source in U.S. (quadrillion Btus)

Note: Dates in parentheses indicate year of first available data.

Source: U.S. Energy Information Administration, *Annual Energy Review 2013*.

breakdown of total energy consumption into its different forms. Although nuclear energy increased rapidly until about 2000, and renewable forms (other than hydro) have increased rapidly in recent years, the system is essentially **fossil-based;** coal, natural gas, and petroleum accounted for slightly more than 80 percent of the total.

Energy markets are extremely complex. They are global, volatile, politicized,[2] and ever changing. Major interest, of course, centers on energy prices. Figure 11-3 shows the real price of coal, gasoline, and electricity in the United States from 1976 to 2012.[3] The gasoline price spike of the late 1970s and early 1980s is clearly visible. These were the years of the "energy crisis," a petroleum shortage produced by trade embargo against the United States by OPEC. Although many people at the time thought of this as an incipient real resource shortage, it was largely a short-run political phenomenon that was soon followed by gasoline price declines.[4] Since the early 2000s, coal and gasoline prices have risen again, and it is hard to sort out the extent to which this has been caused by real shortages, increased demand from such fast-growing countries as China, and market manipulation by its various participants. More recently, petroleum prices have dropped because of the huge increase in U.S. petroleum production.

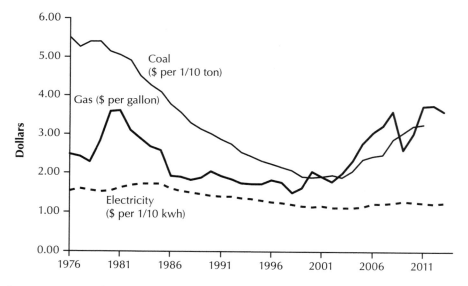

Figure 11-3   Real Price of Coal, Gasoline, and Electricity in U.S., 1976–2012

Source: For gasoline and electricity: U.S. Energy Information Administration, *Short-Term Energy Outlook,* July 2014. For coal: U.S. Energy Information Administration, *Annual Energy Review,* Table 7.9, September 2012.

■ Energy Demand

In a market driven economy such as the United States, the performance of markets for energy are directly related to the factors affecting demand and supply in those markets. The underlying complexity of these factors means that they can be characterized in a number of ways. We will deal with some of those here.

Energy Intensity

Economic growth in the developed world has been accompanied by the copious consumption of energy. Consider the following expression as a way of breaking down the total energy consumption of an economy:

$$\frac{\text{Total energy}}{\text{consumed}} = \frac{\text{Total number}}{\text{of people}} \times \frac{\text{GDP}}{\text{per person}} \times \frac{\text{Energy consumption}}{\text{per dollar of GDP}}$$

Note that the product of the last two terms equals energy consumption per person.

Total energy use is clearly tied to total population. But for a given population, energy use is also related to income. Wealthier societies consume more energy; not only do consumers use larger amounts of energy as their incomes rise, but greater industrial and commercial energy consumption is what produces the higher incomes in the first place. The last term in the expression is **energy intensity**. In 2013 the GDP of the U.S. was approximately $15.7 trillion, and total energy consumption was about 97 quads. Thus the energy intensity of the U.S. economy was about 6,200 Btu per dollar of GDP.

Figure 11-4 on the following page shows energy intensity for the United States and four other countries over the last 30 years. In the United States and Sweden we can see a steady decline in energy intensity over the last three decades. Of particular interest is the experience of the two most populous countries of the world. In China there was a very substantial reduction in energy intensity until the 2000s. In India, on the other hand, where energy intensity started much lower than that of China, there has been hardly any change over this time period; the same is true of France.

Improvements in the energy intensity of a national economy can happen in several ways. One is sectoral change, quite apart from improved efficiencies within any individual sector. Fifty years ago the U.S. economy was much more heavily devoted to manufacturing than it is today; since then the service sector has grown while the manufacturing sector has declined. The average manufacturing operation uses much more energy than the average service operation. Thus, even if these firms themselves used no less energy to produce their outputs, a gradual shift to a proportionately smaller manufacturing sector and a larger service sector produces an economy that uses less energy per dollar of aggregate output.

But explicit improvements in efficiency happen when firms and households find ways to use less energy in their operations, for any given level of output.

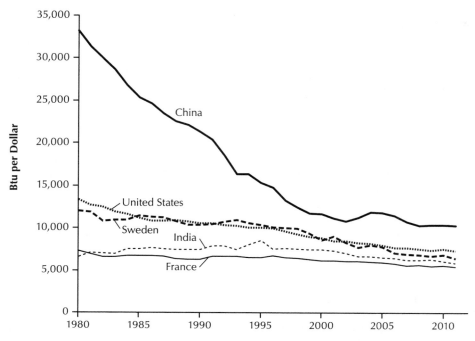

Figure 11-4 Energy Intensity per Dollar of GDP, Selected Countries, 1980–2011 (Btu per 2005 U.S. Dollars, using purchasing power parities)

Source: Energy Information Administration, *International Energy Statistics,* July 2014.

Energy Efficiency

Consider the following expression:

$$\begin{array}{c}\text{Total energy}\\ \text{used in}\\ \text{automobiles}\end{array} = \begin{array}{c}\text{Number}\\ \text{of people}\end{array} \times \begin{array}{c}\text{Cars owned}\\ \text{per person}\end{array} \times \begin{array}{c}\text{Miles driven}\\ \text{per car}\end{array} \times \begin{array}{c}\text{Fuel used}\\ \text{per mile}\end{array}$$

Note that the product of the last three terms equals energy consumption in automobiles per person.

The last term in this expression is often called **energy efficiency**. It comes closest to what engineers think of as technical efficiency, or the energy consumed per unit of some useful effort—in this case, a mile driven in a car. You could apply the same metric to characterize other types of effort, for example the energy used to dry clothes, in which energy efficiency would be measured in terms of energy used per dryer load.

We note that the total energy used in cars is affected not only by energy efficiency in this sense, but also by prior factors: number of cars per capita and miles driven per car. These latter are what can be called **behavioral fac-**

tors, because they depend on personal decisions, not on strictly technical efficiency factors.

The Energy Demand Function

The prime incentive that motivates these behavioral decisions is the price of fuel (as well as the price of cars, new or used). Consider figure 11-5. The line D shows a standard **aggregate demand curve** for energy in the U.S. economy. Suppose the current energy price is equal to p_1. If this price persists, then the quantity of energy demanded in our target year will be q_1. But if we have an increase in price for some reason (to p_2), the quantity of energy demanded in that period will be only q_2 units. In this case, the reduction in energy use consists of a price-induced movement up along a given energy demand function.

To some extent this is what happened in the 1970s in response to increases in the price of petroleum. In the very early days of the oil embargo in the fall of 1973, many observers took the position that this type of energy conservation was essentially impossible—the economy used and required large amounts of energy, without which it could come to a grinding halt. Events proved otherwise. Paradoxically, it might seem, conservation may be easier the higher the initial level of consumption. When energy use is very high, it is fairly easy to find ways to cut back consumption. Consumers in 1973 found numerous ways to conserve energy in response to the price increases of the time (like turning off lights, running air conditioners less often, and going to the grocery store fewer times per week; these changes did not occur without a lot of grumbling, of course).

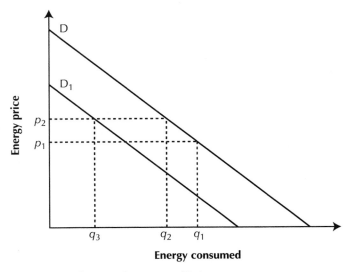

Figure 11-5   Energy Prices and Energy Efficiency

How much consumption decreases when price increases, or increases with price declines, depends on the **price elasticity of demand**, defined as

$$\frac{\text{Percent change in quantity}}{\text{Percent change in price}}$$

Pictorially, this is related to the slope of the demand curve as pictured in figure 11-5. For a given price and quantity, the steeper the slope the lower the price elasticity of demand; that is, the less responsive consumption will be to price changes; and vice versa. Economic studies suggest that the short-run price elasticity of demand for many energy forms is between -0.1 and -0.4; that is, increases in energy prices of 10 percent would produce decreases in consumption of between 1 and 4 percent. This analysis also alerts us to the notion that not all reductions in energy consumption qualify as improvements in energy efficiency. The reduction in energy demand that results from an economic recession and falling incomes, although it reduces energy consumption, is not the same as an increase in energy efficiency, because consumption will increase again as soon as economic growth is reestablished.

In the long run, higher energy prices provide the incentive for research and development devoted to finding technologies that use less energy: cars that get better gas mileage, machines that use less energy, consumer appliances that are more energy-efficient, and so on. Widespread adoption of these new technologies results in a backward shift in the demand function, from D to D_1 in figure 11-5. At the higher price consumption is now reduced to q_3. Should prices drop back to their original level, consumption would increase relative to q_3, but not all the way back to the original level. In order to achieve this effect, two things must occur: (1) R&D (research and development) has to be pursued to develop more energy-efficient technologies and practices, and (2) the new techniques have to be widely adopted throughout the economy. The importance of energy prices here is that they are the primary **incentive** for the R&D and the widespread adoption rates. What we saw in the 1980s and 1990s is the long-run impacts of the structural changes induced by the higher energy prices of the 1970s.

The Demand for Energy Conservation

For economists a major challenge is to understand the factors that affect energy demand. One contemporary issue, which remains perplexing, is consumer demand for energy conservation; that is, consumer willingness to buy new energy-saving devices and products. These involve investments, in the sense that there is usually an up-front cost that is recovered over a period of years through reduced energy consumption. Studies have shown that there is often a general hesitancy on the part of consumers to make these investments, even though engineering-type studies show that substantial savings in energy costs would result. This is sometimes called the **energy-efficiency gap**.

What is it about consumer behavior that leads to this phenomenon? Why aren't consumers willing to buy more energy-saving devices when it appears that in the long run, and not too long at that, they would save more money than the devices cost? Some possible answers to the conundrum are the following:

- Consumers may use higher discount rates than we believe they do for the future savings in energy costs (for discussion of discount rate see chapter 3).

- Although technical data seem to show potential for future cost savings, consumers may be responding to the uncertainty inherent in making any decision about the future; they may hold back until these uncertainties are resolved.

- Consumers may lack convenient access to credit (liquidity) required for up-front purchases of energy efficient goods.

- New work in psychology and economics, called **behavioral economics**, has documented many cases where consumers do not necessarily behave as fully informed, rational decision makers. Rather, consumers may be normally subject to biased beliefs, inattention, and self-control issues that lead them to make decisions that appear to be suboptimal in the classic sense.

In a world facing big energy problems, it is perhaps disheartening to conclude that more research is needed before we can design effective energy policy. Rather than thinking of this as a problem, we should think of it as an opportunity to conduct research that could have a direct and significant impact on energy use.[5]

The CAFE Program

In the discussion above, a long-term backward shift in the energy demand function is understood as a response to higher energy prices. In the case of petroleum, for example, reductions in demand over the last four decades are discernible in the residential, commercial, and industrial sectors. But in transportation, demand continues to advance in a major way, as shown in figure 11-6 on the next page. The uniform drop in consumption among all sectors in 2008 is a reflection of the recession of that period.

Among politicians and policy makers belief is widespread that we can achieve the demand shift without the price increase. We do this, so the belief goes, by either subsidizing the development and adoption of more energy-efficient technology or by simply mandating it through public law and regulations. This thinking led the U.S. Congress to institute the CAFE program in the 1970s. CAFE stands for **corporate average fuel economy**; it is a program that requires manufacturers of cars and light trucks to produce and sell vehicles that achieve, on average, a minimum mileage (miles per gallon) target. The CAFE standards were raised during the 1980s, were constant from then to about 2010, and were raised slightly in 2011. The current administration has announced plans for the standards to increase substantially over the next ten years, to about 55 mpg for cars in 2030 and to about 44 mpg for light trucks.

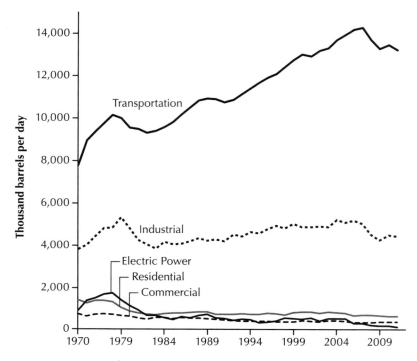

Figure 11-6   U.S. Petroleum Consumption by Sector, 1970–2011

Source: U.S. Energy Information Administration, *Annual Energy Review 2011*, Tables 5-13a, b, c, and d, September 2012.

The CAFE standards appear to offer a direct way of getting a more fuel efficient vehicle fleet on the road. But there are incentives inherent in the programs that actually work against its objectives. It is a general rule that when the price of something goes down, consumers will buy more of it. So a reduction in driving costs per mile will lead people to drive their vehicles more miles per year. This will lead to more fuel consumed, and the effect can offset to a large extent the impact of the improved gas mileage.

In addition, the CAFE program initially included another feature that has helped to undermine its effectiveness. The CAFE standards are substantially less restrictive for light trucks than for automobiles. The thought at the time was that pickup trucks are used largely by farmers, building contractors, and other small-business owners and that this group should not be burdened with the same CAFE standards that applied to cars. We now know what happened. Car makers found that they could make substantially more money on light trucks than on cars, and so developed and advertised new personal vehicles that qualified for the lower CAFE standards. This resulted in a massive proliferation of minivans, SUVs, and pickups designed for personal use, all of which were classified for regulatory purposes as light trucks. Thus the average mileage of the aggregate personal vehicle fleet actually decreased slightly until around 2008. Since then it has started to increase as the result of increasingly stringent mileage requirements under CAFE.

The CAFE program, in its new version, is extremely complex; so much so that it is difficult to predict how it will actually impact total fuel use in the transportation sector. A better approach would be to establish a higher gas tax, which would motivate drivers not only to buy more fuel-efficient vehicles, but also to modify driving habits to reduce their fuel demand.[6]

■ Energy Supply

When we start to look in detail at the entire energy system, its full complexity begins to reveal itself. Obviously, a huge physical system—wells and mines, pipelines, tankers, trains, refineries, transmission lines—is required to move energy resources and products from start to finish. There is also a large and complex institutional system—small and large private firms, markets, governmental bodies of all types, domestic and foreign entities, and consumers—that essentially manages the system.

Structure of the Industry

A large though declining portion of the petroleum that America consumes is imported (see table 11-1), so foreign countries and firms have historically played an important role in this market. The U.S. petroleum industry consists of a relatively small number of large firms. In the crude oil stage, roughly 20 firms control 80 to 90 percent of the activity in the United States, including ownership of petroleum reserves, extraction, and pipeline transportation. The largest companies involved here are household names: Chevron Texaco and ExxonMobil. These companies not only dominate domestic crude oil activity, they are active on a worldwide scale. In fact for many of these companies, global activity—excluding that in the United States—is larger than that within the United States. It's also true that some U.S. subsidiaries of foreign companies are major players in the U.S. petroleum market; this includes such companies as British Petroleum, Royal Dutch Shell, and Phillips. In many developing countries, on the other hand, public firms dominate petroleum production; for example, Petróleos de Venezuela, S.A.

Petroleum refining and distribution are similarly dominated by a relatively small number of very large firms. What is more, these are essentially the same large companies that dominate the production side; in other words, these companies are **vertically integrated** within the petroleum industry. Many of these companies are also **horizontally integrated;** they operate, often through subsidiaries or companies they have purchased, in other industries. In some cases petroleum companies have acquired nonenergy companies or have been acquired themselves by firms in other industries. Change continues to characterize the petroleum industry. The recent expansion of "fracking" (see below) has been carried out by an industry consisting of a small number of large firms, and a large number of small firms, many of which specialize in one or another of the technical steps making up the entire process.

The U.S. **coal industry** is somewhat less **concentrated**; that is, it contains a larger number of smaller firms than the petroleum industry. But most coal companies are actually owned by other firms, either other energy firms or firms in other basic industries such as power generation, steel production, and railroads. **Natural gas** is somewhat different. Gas production is to a large extent carried out by the large petroleum companies, since the technology is similar and much of the gas is located in or near petroleum deposits. Domestic transportation of gas, however, is almost entirely by pipeline, and the interstate gas pipeline network is owned and operated by pipeline companies. Although these companies are highly concentrated, they are to a large extent independent of the major gas and petroleum companies. On the consumption end, most natural gas distribution to industrial, commercial, and residential consumers is handled by gas utilities, which typically are companies that do not have major outside interests.

In addition to direct energy consumption, conversion of primary energy into electricity is a huge sector. The main fuels here are coal (35 percent), natural gas (26 percent), nuclear (21 percent), and renewables (17 percent). The natural gas sector consists of thousands of firms (with a few dozen very large ones) involved in producing, transporting, and distributing the product. The nonfossils sector, including solar and wind plants, consists of large numbers of relatively small firms. The nuclear power industry currently (2015) consists of 99 licensed, operating reactors at 61 plant sites. These reactors are owned by about 35 separate companies, many of which are active also in other energy markets.

Given the central role that energy plays in the modern economy and the globalized nature of most energy markets, it is easy to see why political and public authorities historically have focused so much attention on energy markets. This has tended to politicize energy markets in a major way over the last five decades, with numerous policy enactments, thousands of regulations, and the creation of a cabinet-level Department of Energy in Washington around which pivots the political economy of U.S. energy markets.

Energy Subsidies

A major feature of this political/policy activity is the many public **subsidies** that have been put in place throughout the energy sector. The subsidies are of many types:

- Direct payments to producers or consumers who adopt certain energy-using technology; e.g., cash rebates for using energy-efficient appliances.
- Reduction of tax liabilities for energy producers or users who take specified actions; e.g., reduced federal taxes for producers of ethanol.

- Publicly supported research and development; e.g., public support for coal gasification, CO_2 capture, and many other technologies.
- Indirect subsidies through public provision of below-cost services; e.g., public insurance provided to the nuclear power industry.
- Regulations that alter the market advantage of certain energy types; e.g., requirements for using certain minimal amounts of renewable energy.
- Regulations that allow certain energy producers to avoid some social costs of their actions; e.g., allowing coal-fired power plants to avoid the downwind costs of air pollution stemming from the plants.[7]

All of these subsidies are justified by their advocates as ways of encouraging certain desirable energy technologies or practices. Their end result, however, is major distortions of energy markets. Thus, we can be sure that in most of these markets the price of the energy does not represent the true marginal social costs of producing it. Though it is difficult to tell how large the discrepancy is in particular cases, we can be sure that actual market prices are too low as compared to prices that would be socially efficient. One of the main results of this is that energy consumption is too high, by the efficiency criterion. The likelihood that any of these subsidies will be eliminated is fairly small, given the way federal energy policy is carried out.

Beyond Energy Independence?

Given its enormous coal reserves, the United States is essentially self-sufficient in this fuel; in fact in recent years coal exports have grown, especially to China. Domestic production of natural gas has historically been supplemented by relatively small quantities of imports, in the form of liquefied natural gas. Petroleum consumption, on the other hand, has been supported largely by imports; until recent years imports accounted for 70-80 percent of consumption. Historical patterns have been disrupted by the rise of **hydraulic fracturing** ("fracking") technologies.[8] These are able to tap into the natural gas and petroleum supplies that are held within the small interstices of subsurface shale deposits. U.S. domestic production of petroleum had dropped to about 5 million barrels per day by 2010, but has increased rapidly since then; some predictions are that it will reach nearly 15 million barrels per day by 2030 before beginning again to decline.

We can analyze this situation with the same type of model that we use in the previous chapter to analyze recycling.[9] There, the two sources for materials supply are virgin and recycled; here the two sources of petroleum production are domestic and foreign. Consider figure 11-7 on the next page; the overall national aggregate demand for petroleum is labeled D. We will initially discuss the case where a country is an energy importer. The domestic supply curve in this case is $S_D{}^1$, and import supply is labeled S_I. Note that domestic supply is upward-sloping, while import supply is flat. Domestically, most petroleum deposits have been developed, and additional national production can be produced only at higher prices. On the import side, the

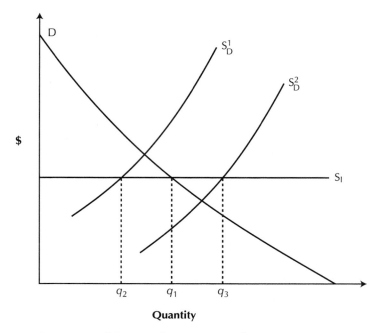

Figure 11-7   Imports and Exports in Energy Markets

assumption is that there is an established world price and that additional supplies could in fact be obtained at this price. This assumption may not be strictly accurate, but making it here allows us to set up and explore a reasonably uncomplicated model and derive clear conclusions. Total quantity consumed is q_1, while q_2 is the quantity produced from domestic sources. Thus imports are equal to $q_1 - q_2$, and the **import dependency ratio** (the proportion of total consumption imported) is $(q_1 - q_2)/q_1$. Note that the world price establishes the domestic price. If demand were to shift right or left, the changes in quantity would occur in imports, not in domestic production.

In this simple model there are only three ways of decreasing the import dependency ratio.

1. Increase the world price. Since this is a world price and not one set domestically, it can only be changed by other means such as an import duty that effectively increases the price to importers. Diagrammatically this would shift S_I upward, which would attack the import dependency ratio from two directions, lowering total consumption and increasing domestic output.

2. Increase domestic supply, in effect shifting the S_D^1 curve to the right to S_D^2. This leaves total consumption unchanged at q_1 but would increase domestic production (q_2 moves to the right), thus cutting the import ratio.

3. Shift demand backward, for example, by pursuing a strategy of energy conservation. This would reduce total consumption (q_1) but not domestic production, thus lowering the import ratio.[10]

What has happened in recent years, particularly for natural gas and especially for petroleum, is a substantial shift to the right in the domestic supply function, which in figure 11-7 we represent as a shift from $S_D{}^1$ to $S_D{}^2$. In this case the total quantity produced is q_3, and q_3-q_1 is **exported**. The international price, in other words, now becomes a demand function governing exports, rather than a supply function for imports.

We note that, with exports, the price paid domestically is higher than if no exports were made. In that case q and p would settle down to those indicated by the intersection of D and $S_D{}^2$. It is this prospect that has led some in the U.S. to favor a ban on exports, in an effort to keep domestic prices lower. As in most cases involving energy markets, local and global, the situation is more complicated than this simple analysis can handle.[11]

■ Reducing Fossil Energy Use

Global climate change, otherwise known as the global **greenhouse effect**, is now an issue of critical importance. Global warming is caused by a buildup of greenhouse gases in the atmosphere. The most important of these is carbon dioxide (CO_2), which accounts for about 75 percent of greenhouse gas emissions worldwide.

Table 11-2 on the following page shows CO_2 emissions by fuel type and by sector for the United States in 1990, 2005, and 2012. Note first that total emissions increased by about 21 percent from 1990 to 2005 then decreased by 12% from 2005 until 2012. The biggest sources of CO_2 emissions in the United States are electricity generation, industrial energy use, and transportation; together these account for about 90 percent of total emissions. A variety of means have been proposed for further reducing emissions from these sectors. A brief catalog is the following:

1. Taking various steps to reduce electricity consumption of household and industrial units.

2. In transportation, encouraging the production and use of more fuel-efficient cars, trucks, and other modes of transit.

3. Shifting among fossil plants, especially replacing coal with natural gas plants since the latter produce fewer emissions than the former per quantity of electricity produced.

4. Shifting electricity production from plants based on fossil fuels to renewable energy forms such as wind, solar, and geothermal facilities.

5. Developing ways of burning coal without the standard emissions, especially through CO_2 recapture and sequestration underground.

The first two of these refer to using energy with greater efficiency. As we earlier discussed, this is a matter both of shifting to devices that are

Table 11-2   Emissions of Carbon Dioxide by Fuel Type and Sector, U.S., 1990, 2005, and 2012 (measured as Tg CO_2 Equivalents^)

Fuel/Sector	1990	2005	2012
Coal	1,718.4	2,112.3	1,593.0
Residential	3.0	0.8	+
Commercial	12.0	9.3	4.1
Industrial	155.3	115.3	74.3
Transportation	NE	NE	NE
Electricity generation	1,547.6	1,983.8	1,511.2
U.S. territories	0.6	3.0	3.4
Natural Gas	1,000.3	1,166.7	1,351.2
Residential	238.0	262.2	224.8
Commercial	142.1	162.9	156.9
Industrial	408.9	388.5	434.7
Transportation	36.0	33.1	41.2
Electricity generation	175.3	318.8	492.2
U.S. territories	NO	1.3	1.4
Petroleum	2,025.9	2,473.5	2,127.6
Residential	97.4	94.9	64.1
Commercial	64.9	51.3	36.4
Industrial	280.9	323.8	265.2
Transportation	1,457.9	1,858.7	1,698.3
Electricity generation	97.5	99.2	18.8
U.S. territories	27.2	45.7	44.7
Geothermal*	0.4	0.4	0.4
Total	4,745.1	5,752.9	5,072.3

^ Tg = 1 teragram = 1 million metric ton
+ Does not exceed 0.05 Tg CO_2 Eq.
NE (Not estimated)
NO (Not occurring)
*Not technically a fossil fuel
Note: Totals may not sum due to independent rounding.

Source: U.S. EPA, *Inventory of Greenhouse Gas Emissions and Sinks 1990–2012*, USEPA Report #430-R-14-003, Table 3-5, Washington, DC, April 2014.

technically more efficient (which includes things like refrigerators that use less electricity and cars that use electricity rather than gas); and to new behavioral patterns that reduce energy use (e.g., driving slower, increased carpooling, or setting air conditioning slightly higher). And the key to both of these is to use the incentive effects inherent in energy prices, by getting rid of subsidies that make energy prices lower than would otherwise be the case, and instituting something like a carbon tax.

Item 3 above refers to shifts within the fossil-fuel sector itself, away from coal and toward natural gas. Natural gas produces less CO_2 per million Btus of power than coal (117 pounds of CO_2 versus 205–229 pounds for coal depending on the type of coal). Shifting from coal-burning power plants to gas-using plants would thus reduce CO_2 emissions—by a large amount if the changeover was extensive enough. The advantage of this strategy is that it could be done relatively quickly; the disadvantage is that it still leaves us with a fossil-based system.

A substantial reduction in greenhouse gases could be achieved with a widespread switch to renewable energy technology. Under this heading comes hydroelectric, solar energy, and wind technology. Hydropower is limited by the availability of sufficient geological sites; the others are less affected by this factor but must be structured to allow for the intermittency of wind and sun. The history of nuclear power has been one of initial enthusiasm but later disappointment, arising from fears of radiation pollution. But many people still see nuclear as an important part of a long-run solution.

Estimates of the future costs of energy sources are controversial, with advocates of particular technologies making very different predictions. For many observers renewable forms of energy are the only alternatives that are sustainable, meaning feasible, in the long run. But in the short run their adoption is hindered by an unwillingness of people to accept the cost implications of a large-scale shift in that direction. Table 11-3 contains cost data for electricity generation by different technologies, as developed in a recent study. It shows the cost penalty, over fossil sources, of current renewable technologies.[12]

Several things will have to change before renewables are embraced widely enough to make a difference. One is large-scale climate change, sufficient to drive home the need to make a thorough conversion in the minds of consumers. The other is continued technical work to lower the costs of solar and wind power,

Table 11-3   Electricity Generation Costs: Lifetime Costs by Generation Type ($/megawatt hours)

Generation Type	Cost Midpoint*
Wind, onshore	68
Solar, photovoltaic	192
Small hydro	108
Nuclear	31
Coal	32
Gas	55

*Cost midpoints of ranges, based on estimate of lifetime costs of capital, operating, maintenance and fuel, discounted at 5 percent.

Source: Extracted from G. Cornelis van Kooten, *Climate Change, Climate Science and Economics.* New York: Springer, 2013, p. 390.

including methods of large-scale electricity storage. Even a monumental effort to stimulate renewable energy use will still leave a substantial portion of future (e.g., 30–40 years) energy supply dependent on nuclear and/or fossil sources. Given the relentlessness of climate change, a good interim strategy might be to move rapidly away from coal toward gas and nuclear. This is already happening to a certain extent due to changes in relative prices, with gas becoming substantially cheaper than coal.

■ Economic Issues in Electricity Deregulation

The energy sector is so important that it has always attracted public attention and political oversight. Major parts of the sector have at times been subject to public regulation, but just as in many other important sectors (airlines, trucking), the contemporary move is toward **deregulation.** Many years ago the **natural gas** sector was tightly regulated, especially through controls on prices. This has since been abandoned. The **electric power** industry also has been closely regulated historically, but here too contemporary events are pushing toward deregulation and vast structural change. In this section we take a very brief look at this phenomenon, especially at some of the changes that may occur in the industry.

The electric power system is extremely complicated, both technically and organizationally. Electricity is **generated** in a wide variety of **power plants:** large base-load plants fired by nuclear, coal, or petroleum; middle-sized fossil-fueled plants; hydro facilities; thousands of small plants using diesel engines, gas turbines, or other technologies; and new sources based on wind or solar power, geothermal resources, and so on. Electricity is transported long distances over a network of high-voltage **transmission lines.** The current system is highly integrated among states and internationally into Canada and Mexico. **Local distribution** networks, covering communities or relatively small regions, take the power from the transmission grid and transport it in usable form to the millions of retail customers in the urban and rural areas of the country.

Organizationally, the system is highly integrated vertically. We can depict the dominant business form, the one that deregulation is designed to change, as in figure 11-8. The functions of electricity generation, transmission, and distribution are combined in a single, **integrated company,** which is granted monopoly rights to supply power to all consumers within a given region. Historically, a large, integrated form of business was considered necessary in the electricity sector to take advantage of the large **economies of scale** in the industry.[13] To achieve low generating costs, power plants had to be large. But it was not feasible to crisscross the land with competing sets of transmission and distribution lines. Hence an integrated system, in the hands of a single large company, was thought to be the best business form. And since this did not involve competition in any significant way, **public utility commissions** (PUCs) would provide public oversight and attempt basically to mandate the results that would have occurred in a competitive system if that had been possible.

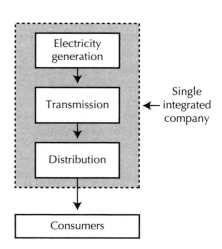

Figure 11-8   Electricity Generation: Structure of the Large, Integrated, Public Utility

The system as it exists incorporates many exceptions to this single integrated form of power company. Some communities own their own distribution systems and contract with outside power companies to provide them with power. Some communities even have their own generating facilities, as do some large industrial operations. The overall systems owned by a single power company are highly coordinated with those of other companies. Company A may use the transmission lines of Company B to reach some of its customers. One company may augment its own generation capacity by purchasing power temporarily from another company, and so on. Nevertheless, the dominant single form is the integrated company as depicted.

Several things have happened in the last few decades to upset this pattern. In the 1970s the **Public Utilities Regulatory Policies Act of 1978 (PURPA)** created a new type of power source, called **qualifying facilities**, consisting largely of cogenerators[14] and small power producers that used renewable energy sources. PURPA required the large electric utilities to connect these qualifying facilities to the grid and purchase their power. Then in 1992 Congress enacted the Energy Policy Act, which required that utilities open up the grid to a large number of alternative energy sources, not just those covered by the earlier law. Technological developments in electricity generation have helped push the system toward more competition. New combined-cycle gas turbine plants based on jet engine technology have permitted the construction of small power plants with very low costs. Also, there has been an increase in homeowner photovoltaic installations and photovoltaic farms. Taken together, these changes have moved substantially in the direction of opening up the system to the forces of competition.

Competition is not desired for its own sake, but for the positive economic effects it is expected to have:

1. Competing firms are motivated to produce at the lowest possible cost and sell their electricity at the lowest possible price; if they do not do so, other competitors may take their markets.

2. Competing firms have the incentive to search for new, cost-reducing technological improvements in electricity generation and transportation.

3. Consumers have wider choices to pursue to satisfy their own preferences. If a consumer wishes to buy "green power" (power from companies that use windmills, solar, or other renewables), for example, they can do this by searching for the appropriate supplier.

Alternative Structures in the Electricity Market

Figure 11-9 on the following page shows several possible deregulated structures for the electricity market. Panel (a) shows a structure in which there is competition at the wholesale level but not at the retail level. The solid lines depict the contractual delivery route of electricity, and the dashed lines show the routes over which financial contracts are concluded. With wholesale competition only, consumers at the retail level are still supplied by monopoly local distribution companies. But the latter are free to contract with alternative power generators according to price and whatever other factors are deemed important. In the pictured case, the local company contracts with generator C for power. It must also pay a grid company for transmission services. Since the aim of this is to foster competition among generators, the presumption is that the grid company will be independent of any of the generating firms.

ISO stands for **independent system operator.** With a multiplicity of generators all supplying the grid and a multiplicity of local distribution compa-

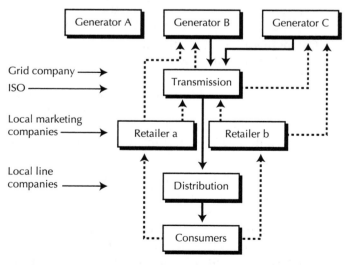

Figure 11-9   Alternative Structures for the Electricity Market

nies taking power from the grid, there are clearly serious problems in achieving physical balance in the entire system. These are further complicated by day-to-day exigencies like power plants breaking down or storm-related damage to the system. Thus there is a role for a company whose primary job is operating the system. This might be the grid company itself, or perhaps a separate entity.

Panel (b) of figure 11-9 shows a system that incorporates both wholesale and retail competition. In addition to alternative power-generating sources, there are now alternative local marketing companies from which consumers may choose. The local distribution lines are owned by a line company, whose job is simply to maintain the physical system and distribute whatever power is contracted for among consumers and local marketing companies. Local marketing companies could take a wide variety of forms: private firms that sign up individual consumers in a community; all consumers in a particular part of town who decide to buy power together; a group of commercial users acting together; communities as a whole working through a cooperative, or perhaps through the normal town government. The local marketing companies, having brought together a number of local consumers, would contract for power with one or more of the generating sources. It might be a source actually owned by the local companies or by any other source with which appropriate contractual terms can be concluded.

Economic Issues

A huge number of problems must be worked out to make a reasonably smooth transition from the current system to a deregulated one. A considerable amount of public regulation will still be necessary, because there will still be only one set of transmission and distribution lines. These will continue to be monopoly operations, and so public oversight will be required to make sure these positions are not abused. One issue that has been very sensitive is that of cost recovery by the large utilities that have to pay for the systems built up under the previous regulated system. This is the problem of **stranded costs.** Public utility commissions historically had allowed the large utilities to set electricity prices high enough to cover the costs of the large generating plants they constructed. If electricity prices fall because of competition, how do these utility companies continue to generate sufficient revenues to pay off the costs of these facilities?

Electricity deregulation also has implications for environmental matters. The overall impact of deregulation is supposed to be a substantial reduction in energy prices to consumers. This will lead to increases in the quantity of electricity consumed, other things being equal. This implies either developing new generating capacity or using the existing system at a higher rate. If the latter, we will have larger emissions from existing power plants, such as large coal-fired power plants in the Midwest that currently have excess capacity. If the former, emissions may not increase as much, for example, if the system shifts markedly toward natural gas as a generating fuel. On the other hand, electricity consumption in the eastern United States may use more hydropower imported from Canada, and there is controversy over the environmental and resource impacts of this power.

■ Summary

After briefly summarizing the current world and national situation with respect to energy consumption, we divided the chapter into analytical sections on energy demand and supply. On the demand side we covered the related concepts of energy intensity and energy efficiency. The discussion then focused on the energy demand function and its characteristics, especially the price elasticity of demand for energy. This led into a discussion of the demand for energy conservation, and we featured one example from the transportation sector: the national CAFE program.

On the energy supply side we summarized briefly the current structure of the energy sector, the question of energy subsidies, issues related to energy independence, and prospects for reducing fossil energy use. The need to address global warming has led us to consider ways of shifting the energy system so that it produces less greenhouse gases. While renewable energy sources should be encouraged, attention also has to be directed at improving energy efficiency and changes within the fossil-fuel sector itself.

The chapter concluded with a discussion of basic issues behind deregulation of the electricity sector.

Notes

1 A Btu is a measure of energy. One Btu is the amount of heat required to raise the temperature of a pound of water by one degree Fahrenheit.

2 By "politicized" we mean subject to major intervention and distortion by political/policy authorities as consumers, producers, importers, environmentalists, and others attempt to shift the operation of energy markets to better serve their interests or their interpretation of the public interest.

3 Real prices are actual, or nominal, prices adjusted for inflation.

4 Although it was of political origin it had real economic implications around the world. GDP growth in the United States was slowed and, because of the globalized nature of energy markets, many developing countries were severely impacted by the higher energy prices.

5 For further discussion, see Kenneth Gillingham and Karen Palmer, *Bridging the Energy Efficiency Gap, Policy Insights from Economic Theory and Empirical Evidence*, Resources for the Future, Discussion Paper DP13-02-REV, October 2013.

6 For a good discussion of the economics of the CAFE program see Virginia McConnell, *The New CAFE Standards: Are They Enough on Their Own?* Resources for the Future, Discussion Paper 13-14, May 2013.

7 For further information see U.S. Energy Information Administration, *Federal Financial Interventions and Subsidies in Energy 2010*, Washington, DC, July 2011. (http://www.eia.gov/analysis/requests/subsidy/pdf/subsidy.pdf)

8 For a good discussion of this technology see Union of Concerned Scientists, *Towards an Evidence Based Fracking Debate*, October 2013.

9 See figures 10-9 and 10-10.

10 There is another way to limit imports, which is to do it quantitatively by establishing a quota on imports. This is a somewhat more complicated case to analyze, and we do not undertake it here.

[11] See, for example, Stephen P. A. Brown, Charles Mason, Alan Krupnick, and Jan Mares, *Crude Behavior: How Lifting the Export Ban Reduces Gas Prices in the United States*, Resources for the Future, Issue Brief 14-03-REV, February 2014.

[12] For similar results see Charles R. Frank, Jr., *The New Benefits of Low and No-Carbon Electricity Technologies*, Brookings Institute, Working Paper 73, May 2014.

[13] Economies of scale mean essentially that the long-run marginal production cost continues to decline with increasing output until plant size becomes very large.

[14] Cogeneration means plants that produce both useful heat and electricity from the same fuel source (also called "combined cycle" generation).

Key Terms

CAFE standards
economies of scale
elasticity of miles driven
  with respect to driving cost
electricity deregulation
energy conservation
energy efficiency
energy efficiency gap
energy independence
energy intensity
Energy Policy Act of 1992 and 2005

horizontal and vertical industry integration
import dependency ratio
independent system operator (ISO)
perverse incentives
price elasticity of demand for energy
Public Utilities Regulatory
  Policies Act of 1978
retail electricity competition
stranded costs
wholesale electricity competition

Questions for Further Discussion

1. Suppose gas costs $3 a gallon and the average car gets 28 miles per gallon. If Congress mandates that cars have to get 36 miles per gallon, by what percentage will this lower the costs of driving? If the elasticity of total miles driven (per year) with respect to the cost of driving is –1, by how much will total miles driven per year increase, assuming it is 10,000 miles at the beginning? How much will total annual gas consumption of the average car change as a result of the mandated program?

2. What has the history of energy consumption in the United States been over the last four decades, in terms of energy consumption per dollar of GDP (gross domestic product)? What political or economic factors account for this history?

3. Who are the winners and losers if a country changes from being a petroleum importer to a petroleum exporter?

4. When we analyze energy demand we find that people tend to undervalue energy savings they would get from devices that are more energy efficient. What are the possible explanations for this?

5. Discuss the factors affecting the trade-off between the costs of shifting to renewable energy forms and the speed with which the shift is made.

6. If electric power companies make their profits by selling electricity, why do these companies actively promote electricity conservation by consumers, which would tend to reduce the amount of electricity they sell?

Useful Websites

For information on energy use:

In the United States:

- U.S. Energy Information Administration of the U.S. Department of Energy (www.eia.gov)
- United States Association for Energy Economics (www.usaee.org)

Internationally:

- Center on Global Energy Policy, Columbia University (www.energypolicy.columbia.edu)
- International Energy Agency (www.iea.org)
- International Association for Energy Economics (www.iaee.org)
- Organization of the Petroleum Exporting Countries (www.opec.org)

For information on renewable energy:

- National Renewable Energy Laboratory (www.nrel.gov)
- Renewable Energy Association/UK (www.r-e-a.net)
- American Solar Energy Society (www.ases.org)
- American Wind Energy Association (www.awea.org)

Studies on energy use:

- Resources for the Future (www.rff.org)
- Tellus Institute (www.tellus.org)
- Center for Energy Economics (www.beg.utexas.edu/energyecon)

For information on Energy Policy Acts of 1992 and 2005:

- Congressional Research Service (http://www2.epa.gov/laws-regulations/summary-energy-policy-act)

Selected Readings

Bhattacharyya, Subhes C. *Energy Economics: Concepts, Issues, Markets and Governance.* New York: Springer Publishing Company, 2011.

Bjoorndal, Endre, et al. *Energy, Natural Resources and Environmental Economics.* New York: Springer, 2010.

Bosselman, Fred, Joel B. Eisen, Jim Possi, David B. Spence, and Jacqueline Weaver. *Energy, Economics and the Environment,* 3rd ed. St. Paul, MN: Foundation Press, 2010.

Nersesian, Roy L. *Energy for the 21st Century: A Comprehensive Guide to Conventional and Alternative Sources.* Armonk, NY: M.E. Sharpe, 2007.

Simon, Christopher A. *Alternative Energy: Political, Economic, and Social Feasibility.* Blue Ridge Summit, PA: Rowman and Littlefield, 2007.

van Kooten, G. Cornelis. *Climate Change, Climate Science and Economics.* New York: Springer, 2013.

12

Forest Economics

Forests cover about 30 percent of the land surface of the earth.[1] These forest resources are a heterogeneous collection ecologically, socially, institutionally, and economically. Ecologically it's customary to distinguish between tropical forests (up to about 35° north and south latitude), temperate forests (35° to between 50° and 55° north and south latitude), and boreal forests (higher latitudes). Within the tropical band there are rain forests, moist deciduous forests, and dryland forests. There are hardwood and softwood forests. There are expanses of natural forests (sometimes called "old-growth" forests), forests modified by humans through use of various types, and human-made forests (sometimes called forest "plantations"). There are public forests and private forests, open-access forests and controlled-access forests. More than 60 percent of the world's forests are in seven countries (Brazil, Canada, China, the Democratic Republic of the Congo, Indonesia, Russia, and the United States). Twenty-nine countries have more than half their land area in forests; forty-nine countries have less than 10 percent of their land area in forests.

There is a wide array of issues in connection with the use, and abuse, of the world's forests:

- Maintaining and increasing the productivity of forests in keeping with expanding populations and economies. Traditional forest products include wood for individual use, building materials, and paper. Non-timber products include honey, nuts, pharmaceutical products, and cork. In many developing countries wood is still the primary source for fuel.

- Managing the creation and development of forest "plantations," industrial forests devoted solely to the cultivation and harvesting of valuable wood species.

- Reducing deforestation and conversion of forestland to agricultural and urban uses; this implies that the management of forestlands must be coordinated with other features of economic and social development.

- Expanding the management of forests to recognize nontraditional values, such as ecosystem services (e.g., flood control) and, especially, the value of forests in providing carbon sequestration services.

- Reducing illegal logging and harvesting. Rough estimates are that 10 percent of world forest harvest consists of illegal logging. The majority of forests around the world are publically owned, making it difficult and costly to monitor and control illegal encroachments.

All of these problems have technical aspects connected to the biological and technological factors affecting the growth of forests and their utilization. They also have important institutional and economic dimensions connected to the valuation and use of forest resources and the incentives facing those whose decisions impact the quantity and quality of forest resources. We deal in this chapter with some basic analytical issues with respect to the economic decisions regarding the use, or non-use, of forest resources.

■ Institutional Arrangements for Forestry

In the U.S., forested land accounts for about 30 percent of the total land area (750 million acres out of a total of 2.5 billion acres). About 70 percent of this is classified as timberland, of which 22 percent is in private hands, and the rest is owned by federal, state, or local government.

Most commercial U.S. forest production is from private lands. A large part of this is from **industrial forestland,** consisting of relatively large parcels of land used primarily for harvesting timber. On these lands decisions are generally made with the objective of maximizing long-run net revenues. The extent to which these decisions also maximize social efficiency depends on whether unpriced outputs, on- or off-site, are taken into account by the decision makers. Some of these clearly are, because we know that private timberlands are often made available to hunters and hikers. Systematic data on these matters are not readily available, however.

Timbering is also carried out on nonindustrial timberlands. This is land held by owners who may produce some forest products, but for which timber output is not necessarily the primary goal. We can expect decisions in this case to be partially motivated by revenue considerations, but also to a large extent by the personal objectives of the landowners. Finally, some timbering is done on public lands, in which case decisions on harvesting are made by public agencies. This is particularly the case in the developing world.

■ Industrial (Plantation) Forests

Over the last few decades there has been a major shift to the use of "plantation forests" to produce wood for industrial uses, especially paper production. It's anticipated that by the middle of the 21st century at least half of the world's wood harvest will be from plantation operations.

Harvest Decisions

Intentionally planted industrial forest normally consists of single-species, same-age stands. In this they are analogous to any crop cultivation/harvest process, except for the fact that the growth of the crop in this case is a multi-year phenomenon.

We begin with what sounds like a very innocuous problem, but one that actually contains a perspective that can be used to analyze many of the issues involved in decisions about using forest resources. It's the problem of deciding **when to cut a tree.** Suppose we have a 1,000-acre plantation forest. Our objective is to manage this forest so as to maximize the sustainable value of the timber harvest. Suppose, for the moment, that there are no nontimber values involved. Whenever we harvest a portion of its territory, we immediately replant that acreage. Assume also that our timber output is small relative to the total market, so our harvest decisions do not affect the selling price of timber. How much of its acreage should we harvest each year?

One way to derive an answer to this is to focus on one representative acre of forest, which we assume to be covered with trees of roughly the same age. When should this acre be harvested? The solution lies in the combined effects of the biology and the economics of the situation. The biology in this case is wrapped up in the growth pattern of the trees. Many things affect how fast trees grow, but we will consider a generalized relationship like that shown in the numbers of table 12-1, which are pictured in figure 12-1 on the following page. Growth rate is here related to the age of the tree. The total quantity of wood on the acre of trees grows modestly for the first several decades. In the third through fifth decades the growth rate is rela-

Table 12-1   Total Volume, Average Volume, and Annual Increase in Volume of Wood, by Decades, of One Acre of Forest

Age of trees (years)	Total volume of wood (cu ft)	Average volume (cu ft/yr)	Annual increase in volume (cu ft/yr)
0	0	0.0	0.0
10	80	8.0	8.0
20	200	10.0	12.0
30	400	13.3	20.0
40	720	18.0	32.0
50	1,360	27.2	44.0
60	1,660	27.7	30.0
70	1,840	26.3	18.0
80	1,960	24.5	12.0
90	2,040	22.7	8.0
100	2,090	20.9	5.0
110	2,090	19.0	0.0
120	2,090	17.4	0.0
140	2,090	14.9	0.0

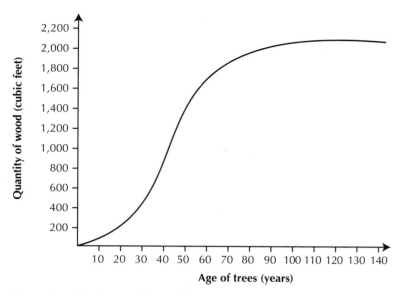

Figure 12-1   Total Volume of Wood by Age of Forest

tively rapid. In the sixth and later decades the rate slows down and eventually, at an age of about 100 years, becomes zero. The columns of table 12-1 show total and average volume of wood, and the yearly growth rate, in successive decades of the forest's life.[2] The average volume is simply the total volume in the forest divided by its age.

It is possible to undertake various **silvicultural** steps to shift this growth function. For example, periodic thinning or fertilizing can increase the production of wood from a given acre of forest. It's also true that plant breeding can produce trees that grow faster. There has been enormous change through the years in the yield of timber that can be obtained from an acre of forest, in effect an increase in the volume figures shown in table 12-1.

It is possible to make harvest decisions referencing only the biological growth function. We might plan simply to maximize the amount of wood obtained at the time of harvest. This implies delaying harvest until the forest achieves its maximum volume, around year 100. The problem is that we have to wait quite a long time to realize this harvest. Might it not be better to have a somewhat smaller harvest, in return for having it earlier?

One might think that it would make sense to cut at perhaps 60 years—when the average yield is the highest. Over, say, 1,000 years, this would yield about 27,666 cubic feet, as compared to a 100-year cycle, which would yield only 20,900 cubic feet in 1,000 years. In fact the 60-year cycle would yield the largest volume of any cycle, so it could perhaps be thought of as the **maximum sustained yield** for this forest. The question remains, however: Is this the harvest age that maximizes the net benefits of the forest to society?[3] Cutting at 50 years would produce less wood, but it would be available sooner. Thus there is a trade-off, and the solution depends as much on the values that society places on time as it does on the value of wood.

But the decision is somewhat more complicated. Cutting the trees results in an acre of cleared ground. The optimal harvest time depends in part on what that land will be devoted to. We will assume, in keeping with the logic of the overall situation, that the land will be replanted with trees as soon as it is harvested and that this will be done each time the trees are cut into the indefinite future. So what we are actually asking is: What is the optimal length of **timber harvest rotation** for our community? A "rotation" is a recurrent length of time, in years, between successive harvests of the same piece of land. A 40-year rotation, in other words, means that the typical acre of timber is harvested every 40 years. If we were to find, for example, that 40 years was the optimal rotation period, we would conclude that we should harvest one-fortieth of the thousand acres, or 25 acres, each year. A rotation pattern is pictured in figure 12-2. The first harvest is made at t years from the beginning. Harvests are subsequently done at $2t$, $3t$, $4t$, and so on. Each harvest yields q cubic feet of timber. The question is: What is the socially efficient value of t?

To visualize this problem, imagine that we are presently at the beginning of some year in the life of the trees on our acre. It doesn't matter which particular year it is. We ask whether we should cut the trees and send them to market this year, or wait and do it next year. This is really just a simple two-period problem, but it allows us to identify the efficient rotation period. If we decide not to harvest this year, then next year the community will be faced with the same two-part comparison. So the community is essentially faced with a sequence of benefit-cost decisions. It compares the benefits of cutting this year with the costs, which are the returns they forgo because they won't have the trees to cut next year. In the early years of the trees' lives, the benefits of cutting are presumably less than those of waiting, because in these years the trees are growing rapidly. On the other hand, in later years when the growth rate is very low, the benefits of waiting would be very small compared to those of cutting today. At some point there will occur

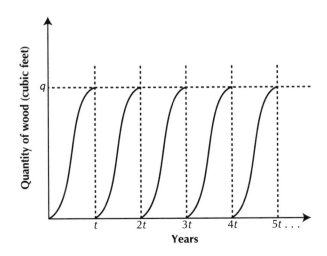

Figure 12-2   Typical Forest Rotation Pattern

a tipping point, at which time the benefits of cutting are equal to, or slightly in excess of, those of waiting. This is the time to harvest the forest.

It's easier to look at this question with a little algebra. First we define some variables:

V_0 = The monetary value of the wood that would result if the forest were harvested this year

V_1 = The monetary value of the wood that would be produced if the harvest is delayed 1 year

$\Delta V = V_1 - V_0$ = The value of the 1-year growth increment

C = Harvest costs, the monetary costs of felling the trees and getting them to market

r = Discount rate

S = The present value of the vacant site after the trees have been harvested

The last term needs some explaining. There are obviously many uses to which the cleared land might be put: intensive agriculture, housing development, and so on. But when we focus on identifying the optimal rotation interval, S is the value of the land when it is devoted in perpetuity to raising trees. To understand this, pretend that after harvesting the cleared land is going to be sold to somebody who plans to replant and then harvest forever at the optimal rotation period. The price the land would sell for is equal to the present value of the future stream of net benefits from following this course of action.

If the forest is harvested this year, the proceeds will be $(V_0 - C) + S$. This is the sum of $(V_0 - C)$, the net benefits of harvesting the timber, and S, the selling price of the land. If the harvest is delayed until next year, the present value of the proceeds will reflect the added growth, ΔV, and the revenue from selling the land next year. These must be discounted, giving

$$\frac{V_0 + \Delta V - C + S}{1 + r}$$

In this case both the realized yield next year and the selling price S must be discounted back one period. When the forest is young and ΔV is relatively large, the following inequality holds:

$$\frac{(V_0 + \Delta V) - C + S}{1 + r} > (V_0 - C) + S$$

In other words, the net proceeds of waiting to harvest until next year will be greater than those of harvesting this year. But as the forest gets older, ΔV eventually declines, and the net proceeds of harvesting this year eventually become equal to those of waiting until next year. Thus the condition

$$\frac{(V_0 + \Delta V) - C + S}{1 + r} = (V_0 - C) + S$$

tells when to harvest the forest.

The last expression can be reduced to the following[4]

$$\Delta V = (V_0 - C)r + Sr$$

What this amounts to is a benefit-cost type of expression. ΔV is the benefit received by waiting one more year for harvest, and $(V_0 - C)r + Sr$ is the cost of waiting. As long as the benefits of waiting exceed the costs, we put off harvest; when the benefits fall to the level of costs, it is time to harvest the trees.

This solution is shown in figure 12-3. The curve labeled ΔV shows annual growth increments at varying ages. Growth is low at the beginning, increases to a maximum (which corresponds to the point on the graph of figure 12-1 where it reaches its steepest slope), then declines to zero again when the forest reaches its maximum biomass. The other

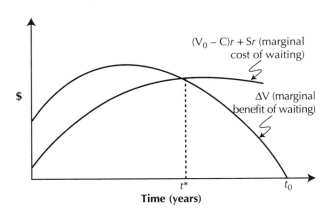

Figure 12-3   Depiction of the Optimal Rotation

curve in figure 12-3 shows the right side of the last equation. As the volume of wood in the forest (V_0) increases, this function also increases, up to some maximum. The optimal rotation is identified by the intersection of these two functions, labeled as t^* on the horizontal axis. This can be interpreted in benefit-cost terms. $(V_0 - C)r + Sr$ is the benefit of harvesting this year, while ΔV is growth forgone, or the cost, if harvesting is done this year.

Portfolio Choice

We can also interpret this as a portfolio choice; that is, as a choice about the form in which the community should hold its assets. Solving the last expression for r gives

$$r = \frac{\Delta V}{S + (V_0 - C)}$$

which we can interpret as an asset portfolio statement. The left side is r, which can be interpreted as the rate of return obtainable on general productive assets in the community. The right side is the rate of return we expect if we let the trees stand for another year. The solution for the optimal rotation gives us a rule that says: Maintain the trees as long as the rate of return from doing so exceeds the rate of return on alternative assets. When the rate of return on the growing trees falls to that of alternative assets, harvest the trees and replant.

Factors Affecting Efficient Rotation

We can further our understanding by looking at some of the factors facing the forest manager that, if they change, will change the efficient length of rotation. For example, suppose that **harvesting costs** increased substantially when a nearby logging mill closed and made it necessary to transport the logs a further distance. Note that harvest costs appear in one of the functions shown in figure 12-3 with a minus sign. The impact of the increase in C is to shift the $(V_0 - C)r + Sr$ function downward, thereby lengthening the optimal rotation period. In fact, if harvesting costs become expensive enough, it may be efficient to refrain from harvest altogether; that is, the efficient rotation period might get pushed right out to t_0 in figure 12-3. One way in which the social costs of harvest could increase is through **externalities** associated with timber cutting. If flooding or soil erosion is increased as a result of harvesting the timber, as has happened in many of the world's watersheds, this essentially increases the social costs of harvesting. The effect, as we have seen, is to lengthen the optimal rotation.

Consider what happens to the length of the efficient rotation when the **interest rate** changes. For example, if the interest rate were to fall in the long run, this would tend to shift down the marginal cost function, that is, $(V_0 - C)r + Sr$. The intersection of the marginal benefit and cost curves would shift to the right, indicating that the efficient rotation would get longer. Note that if the interest rate were actually zero, the marginal cost curve would essentially disappear, moving t^* all the way to the right where $\Delta V = 0$. A zero interest rate implies that the return on alternative assets is zero, and so it is efficient to let the forest continue to grow until the natural growth rate falls to zero.

Suppose that timber became relatively more scarce, leading to an increase in the harvested price of timber. In this case the outcome on the efficient rotation period is ambiguous, because higher timber prices increase ΔV, V_0, and S, though not necessarily all in the same proportion. So the interaction of the marginal benefit and marginal cost curves could shift either to the right or to the left.

Forests and Carbon

A nontimber value provided by forests is **carbon sequestration**. The main factor behind global climate change is the buildup of carbon dioxide (CO_2) in the atmosphere. Trees carry out photosynthesis to produce the glucose necessary for tissue growth and maintenance. The inputs into photosynthesis are atmospheric CO_2 and water. Thus growing trees absorb CO_2 from the air and thus help ameliorate the buildup of CO_2 in the atmosphere. To sequester more carbon, there are two courses of action: (1) convert land currently in other uses (e.g., agriculture) into forestland and (2) manage existing forestland so as to increase the amount of carbon sequestered. If a forest is left standing, it eventually reaches and maintains a maximum biomass. At that point the carbon contained in the forest is at a maximum, and this amount of carbon can be sequestered permanently by leaving the trees standing.[5] Intuitively, this appears to support a conclusion that counting the value of carbon sequestration would make standing trees relatively more valuable; in other words, it would tend to lengthen then the optimal rotation period.

But this may not be true if we account for what happens to the wood after the trees are harvested. If trees are immediately burned or destroyed after harvesting (as in clearing land for agriculture, for example), the carbon is immediately released back into the atmosphere. But if the timber is harvested and converted into building materials, the carbon stays sequestered until the materials decay. Suppose these building materials did not decay at all. Then by cutting trees and converting them to building materials, we are permanently sequestering the carbon. If there were a market for carbon-sequestration services, the market values of timber would reflect both its value as building material and its value for carbon storage. In effect, the addition of the carbon-sequestration function simply adds to the value of the timber in proportion to the amount of wood it contains, which is essentially the same as if there were an increase in the price of building materials. In this situation we arrive at the same conclusion as we had earlier in thinking about the impact of the price of timber on the length of the efficient rotation: It could push the efficient rotation in either direction.

But building materials do not exist forever; rather they decay at fairly rapid rates, depending on their form and use. A large proportion of the lumber market is used in the construction of buildings, particularly houses. The rate at which the housing stock decays determines the rate at which the carbon in the building materials is released into the environment. The critical factor is whether this rate is faster or slower than the growth rate of trees. If it is slower, then harvesting trees for building materials will increase the amount of carbon sequestered relative to the quantity sequestered by leaving forests unharvested. If the decay rate is higher than the tree growth rate, the opposite conclusion holds.

One could envisage how a **carbon market** might work to motivate changes in silviculture practices and forest establishment practices that would lead to increased carbon sequestration. The market would allow forest owners to capture the value of stored carbon, thereby providing incentives for the appropriate decisions and trade-offs that would lead to efficiency in carbon sequestration. It would have to be a sophisticated market—for example, adjusting for the particular forest products into which trees are transformed if harvested. The benefits of carbon sequestering are a massive public good. To generate demand, there has developed a market whereby industrial sources of greenhouse gases may purchase forest **carbon offsets**, in effect sequestrating a quantity of carbon sufficient to "offset" an equivalent quantity of their industrial emissions. See exhibit 12-1.

Exhibit 12-1   Demand for Carbon Offsets Provides Incentive for Maintaining Forests

Carbon finance supported the management of forests spanning 26.5 million hectares worldwide as businesses in 2012 injected a near-record $216 million into projects that plant trees, avoid deforestation, improve forest management, and support low-carbon agriculture.

These projects, a key defense against the ecological and socioeconomic impacts of climate change, were financed by the sale of 28 million tonnes of carbon offsets, according to *Covering New Ground: State of the Forest Carbon Markets 2013 Report,* prepared by researchers with the nonprofit Forest Trends and its Ecosystem Marketplace initiative.

Representing 162 projects in 58 countries, the report tracks forest carbon management over a land area larger than Ecuador. While market size grew 9%, the global average price for forestry offsets was $7.8/tonne—down from $9.2/tonne in 2011, but still higher than prices paid by voluntary buyers for other offset types ($5.9/tonne).

Multinational corporations driven by responsible business ethics and a desire to show leadership on climate change bought two out of every three forestry offsets sold. The top buyer sectors—energy, agriculture/forestry, and transportation—depend on forests' ecosystem services (e.g., clean water) for their business, and some view investments in forest carbon offsets as a kind of insurance against direct exposure to climate risks.

Overall, this year's report findings illustrate growing corporate interest in incentive payments to protect forests as a climate response, despite political and economic challenges to carbon price mechanisms more broadly.

Source: Ecosystem Marketplace: A Forest Trends Initiative, November 5, 2013. (www.ecosystemmarketplace.com)

Natural (Native) Forests

Although the global acreage in forest plantations is increasing rapidly, most of the world's forests are native, or natural, forests. Some of these are remote wilderness forests, little impacted by humans, while others are subject—to a greater or lesser degree—to human decisions regarding impacts management and utilization.

Optimal Clear-Cutting

Clear-cutting is the practice of harvesting all the trees in a particular area, as opposed to **selective cutting,** which means harvesting only those trees meeting certain criteria, such as species, size, or age. Clear-cutting is widely practiced in commercial forestry, and is controversial. Proponents point to harvesting cost savings and the advantages of promoting commercial forests that have trees of uniform characteristics. Opponents cite damages in terms of aesthetics, ecological integrity, watershed destruction, and reduced values for outdoor recreation.

It is relatively easy to frame the problem in conceptual terms. Suppose a company has a large forest from which it harvests timber on a 60-year rotation. Also assume that it wishes to have a constant annual yield (in order to plan its workforce and so on), and plans to harvest one-sixtieth of the forest each year. If the total forest contained 6,000 acres, they would thus harvest 100 acres each year. The harvesting pattern to be followed, in terms of clear-cutting, can vary over a wide continuum. On the one hand, it could be harvested as one large 100-acre clear-cut. At the other extreme, it could be harvested in 100 scattered 1-acre clear-cuts.[6] Or it could be harvested in any pattern between these two extremes: two 50-acre cuts, ten 10-acre cuts, and so on. Define n as the number of separate areas harvested in a year; thus $1 \leq n \leq 100$. The question is: What is the socially efficient value of n?

In general we can identify two types of cost factors that vary with n. Harvest costs are one. As n increases, presumably the costs of harvesting timber increase, owing to the need for the logging operation to visit an ever increasing number of scattered sites.[7] We may lump all other costs under one category, called ecological costs. We expect these costs to decrease as n increases, although once n gets relatively large, the costs may increase owing to the forest disruption on nonharvested acres when harvesters must visit many widely scattered cutting areas.

These relationships are pictured in figure 12-4. The number of harvested plots (designated as n) is plotted along the horizontal axis, varying from 1 up to some large number, say N.[8] The curve labeled H represents timber harvest costs, whereas the one labeled E shows ecological costs. The curve marked T shows total costs and is the vertical summation of H and E. If harvesting were done simply to minimize harvesting costs, one large clear-cut would be called for, whereas if it were done in such a way as to minimize ecological costs, clear-cuts of n_0 acres would be called for. The socially efficient number of acres lies between these two, at a value of n^*, where total costs are minimized.

Although it is relatively easy to discuss this on a conceptual basis, it obviously is much harder to determine the actual value of n for a specific situation. To do so, we have to know the two cost functions H and E. It may not be too difficult to determine the former—timber harvest companies presumably have good knowledge of their cost

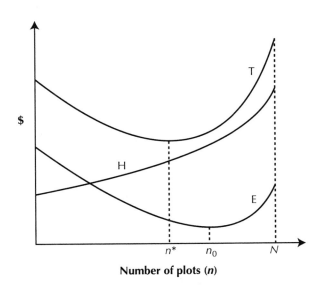

Figure 12-4   Efficient Clear-Cutting

factors—but it is clearly a difficult problem to measure ecological costs with a high degree of accuracy. Even without detailed knowledge of E, however, we can say that, as long as ecological costs are positive, the optimal clear-cut is greater than one, the number that maximizes private profits.

Ecological and Amenity Values in Forestry

In addition to wood products and carbon sequestration, forests produce many other valuable outputs.

One major service provided by forests is **animal habitat.** Obviously, many different animal species rely on forest resources, from tiny insects to large carnivores, and animals that are ground-dwelling, tree-dwelling, flying, and so on. Consider a situation involving only a single species. This is approximately true in the famous case of the northern spotted owl, which lives in old-growth forests of the northwestern United States. Its required habitat, in other words, is forest that consists of relatively old trees. Suppose we had a way of valuing our acre of forest in terms of contribution to spotted owl habitat and expressing this in monetary terms. The function relating this value to forest age might look like that in figure 12-5. The value is essentially zero until the forest is at least 60 years old; it then increases rapidly and reaches a maximum at around 100 years, and is constant thereafter. Let us assume also that the price of timber, and of forestland, is unaffected by its owl habitat value.

To examine this further we will look at it in the context of the optimal rotation problem discussed above. It is fairly easy to see how adding this value to the forest management decision affects the choice of efficient rotation. The habitat value function, if added to the overall timber value function shown in figure 12-1, would give a total value function like the earlier one but now with value for the older years increased somewhat. This would push out the ΔV function in figure 12-3. Since the owls do not have a commercial value (this would change if, for example, there was an ecotourism market that sold owl-spotting tours in the forest) and the market value of the land is unaffected by the owls, the marginal cost function, $(V_0 - C)r + Sr$, of figure 12-3 would be unchanged. This would give a new model as in figure 12-6. The new marginal benefit function is shown as $\Delta V + H$. The ΔV term is the same as before; it is the increment in value of timber from another year's growth. The term H is annual value of the forest as owl habitat. Adding H to the

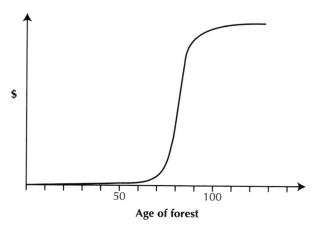

Figure 12-5   Value of Forest as Spotted Owl Habitat, Related to Forest Age

model increases the optimal rotation. Several new marginal benefit functions are shown (the dotted lines), corresponding to higher values of H. The higher the value, the more the optimal rotation is lengthened. The first dotted curve has an optimal rotation of t_2 years; if H is somewhat higher the rotation increases to t_3, and so on. In fact, if H becomes large enough, there will be no intersection with the mar-

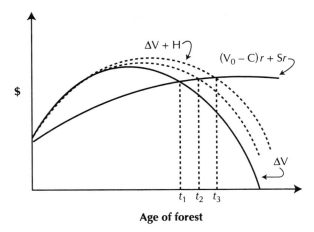

Figure 12-6   Optimal Rotation When Habitat for Spotted Owl Is Included

ginal cost curve, indicating that the optimal rotation is essentially infinite; that is, social efficiency implies that the trees are never to be harvested.

While it may seem easy, at least conceptually, to factor a single species like the spotted owl into the situation, it is likely to be much more difficult to do this when a number of animal species are involved and where the ecological factors affecting them differ. Deer, for example, may be advantaged in relatively young forests, where the amount of available browse is relatively high. Certain insects may be advantaged in fully mature forests where there is an abundance of decaying wood. If the full habitat value of a forest is to be added to the timber value, some way would have to be found to develop some aggregate measure of habitat value from these conflicting elements.

Illegal Logging

In the publicly owned forests of the developing world there are several major problems: (1) the shaping of the **commercial agreements** (called "concessions") entered into with private companies to extract timber from the public forests, (2) the continued use of forest resources by local groups who rely on the resource even though they do not technically own it, and (3) the terms under which the forestland may be converted to private ownership, which determines the incentives that prospective owners have to use the land in various ways.[9]

In many forests of the world—particularly, but not exclusively, those in the tropics—illegal logging is widespread.

> The vast majority of deforestation and illegal logging takes place in the tropical forests of the Amazon basin, Central Africa and Southeast Asia. Recent studies into the extent of illegal logging estimate that illegal log-

ging accounts for 50–90 percent of the volume of all forestry in key producer tropical countries and 15–30 percent globally. Meanwhile, the economic value of global illegal logging, including processing, is estimated to be worth between US $30 and US $100 billion, or 10–30 percent of global wood trade.[10]

This takes several forms:

- Excessive harvesting: harvesting in excess of quantities specified in contracts and agreements between loggers and owners, public or private.
- Encroachment: unlawful entry on public or private land to harvest valuable trees, when revenue and cost conditions provide the incentive and legal means of forestalling the activity are insufficient.

The key to reducing illegal logging is to put sanctions in place sufficient to make the practice unprofitable. Easier said than done. In remote areas, simply monitoring and detecting illegal activity is costly. Nor is it adequate simply to put in place a fine, or other penalty, to be levied on illegal activity. In many of the countries where there is a problem, the salaries of monitors and inspectors are relatively low, so corruption in the form of bribery is common. The **effective monetary sanction** in any situation is the lower of:

1. relevant financial penalty and
2. the costs of bribing officials to avoid or reduce the imposition of the penalty.

It is possible that increasing the stated penalty may reduce the effective penalty if it generates greater efforts at bribery.[11]

Deforestation

The importance of forests for global respiration is well understood. Aggregate world forest cover is a result of both efforts to restore old forests and the continuing forces of deforestation. In the last decade, annual deforestation has amounted to roughly 0.8 percent of global forest cover. In some cases illegal logging has been the cause. For the most part, however, deforestation has involved a conversion of land from one use to another. In South America it has been largely a shift to large-scale cattle grazing or soybean cultivation. In Asia the main shift has been to forest plantations, whereas in other parts of the world it is not industrial agriculture but rather small-scale subsistence farming that has replaced forestland.

If we define R_F as private returns from an acre of forest, and R_A as private returns from an alternative nonforest use, then conversion results from a situation where $R_F < R_A$. From society's perspective, however, conversion is socially efficient if and only if $R_F + P_F < R_A + P_A$, where P_F and P_A are, respectively, the public (nonprivate) returns from an acre of forest and the public returns in an alternative nonforest use. Efforts to forestall deforestation are called for when these two conditions hold simultaneously.

One way of trying to forestall conversion is to prohibit it through regulatory action. Another is to levy a penalty, T, such that $R_A - T < R_F$.

In recent years a new initiative has developed in which public authorities offer payments to landowners, based on the social value of preserved forest, sufficient to reduce the incentive for owners to convert the land. These are called **payment for environmental services**. In our notation, we note that if a payment Y is made by the public to the landowner, such that

$$R_A - R_F < Y < P_F - P_A$$

both the public and the landowner will gain; that is, the payment will exceed the private landowner's gains from conversion, and be less than the public's loss from conversion of the forest.

This is another case, common in economics, where the conceptual nature of the phenomenon is reasonably clear, but the exact, or approximate, values of the factors involved are hard to determine. This is why the valuation techniques discussed in chapter 9 are so important.

■ Timber Harvesting from National Forests

The national forest system of the United States was begun in the late 19th century and now consists of about 190 million acres of land in 155 different sites around the country. When an agency such as the U.S. Forest Service makes decisions about harvesting timber from national forests, its objectives and procedures are presumably dictated by its political mandate and the extent of the political and administrative conflicts in which it finds itself embroiled.

During the first half of the 20th century relatively little wood was harvested from national forests, but this changed after World War II. Timber sales from national forests rose steeply to a peak of about 12 billion board-feet in the early 1970s. After a second peak in 1992 timber sales from the national forests have dropped by about 75 percent (see figure 12-7 on the next page).

The reason for the dramatic drop in these timber sales is the perceived shift in relative valuations of the goods and services produced by national forests, in particular an increase in the demand for services such as outdoor recreation and ecosystem protection relative to the demand for harvested timber of the traditional sort. The situation is depicted in figure 12-8 (on the following page). The horizontal axis indexes the annual quantity of timber produced from national forests; the demand curve labeled D represents the marginal willingness to pay for that timber, and MPC represents the costs of harvesting it. If these were the only two values involved, the efficient harvest level would be q_1. However, there are other services produced by national forests, which for the most part are competitive with timber production. These are such services as opportunities for various types of outdoor recreation, protection of biodiversity resources, scenic values, and such ecosystem protection services as flood control and soil erosion control. To a large extent these are use values, but nonuse values (e.g., existence value) are also important. On the assumption that the nontimber services diminish as the harvested timber quantity increases, they can be treated as an additional cost of timber harvesting. The curve labeled MTC in figure

12-8 represents the total of marginal timber harvesting costs and marginal costs in the form of lost nontimber services. The difference between MTC and MPC, in other words, represents the marginal value of nontimber services being lost. According to this, full social efficiency requires that the timber harvest be reduced to q_2.

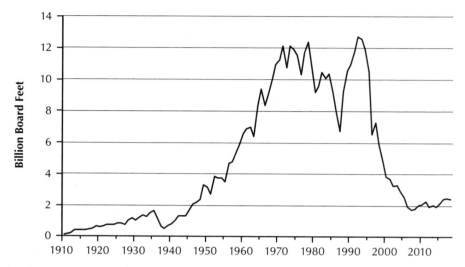

Figure 12-7   Timber Harvest in U.S. National Forests, 1910–2013

Source: Data from U.S. Forest Service, FY 1905–2013 National Summary Cut and Sold Data and Graphs, Nov. 24, 2013.

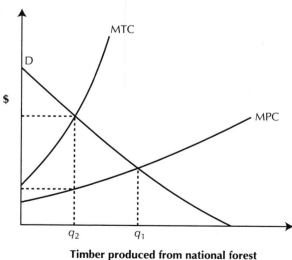

Timber produced from national forest

Figure 12-8   Efficiency with Nontimber Values

■ Summary

This chapter first focused on the classic problem of when to harvest a tree. The decision involves a trade-off between the benefits one would receive immediately if it were harvested today and the benefits of waiting, which are related to the rate at which the tree will grow in the next year. This basic model can also be used to look at cases where trees have value other than for timber, for example, for the provision of animal and plant habitat, a locale for outdoor recreation (e.g., hiking and hunting), and carbon sequestration. In all these cases, the optimal rotation is affected by benefit and cost values and the discount rate. We looked at a simple model that captured the major dimensions of the clear-cutting decision and the reasons for the recent precipitous drop in sales of timber from national forests in the United States.

Notes

[1] Eight thousand years ago this percentage was about 50.

[2] Clearly growth rates and volumes vary each year, but a table showing annual data would be too big and we can get what we need with a table based on decades.

[3] Remember that for now we are assuming that the only thing of value is the trees for wood; we relax this assumption later.

[4] Multiplying both sides of the first expression by $1 + r$ gives: $(V_0 - C + S)(1 + r) = V_0 + \Delta V - C + S$. Isolating ΔV on the right gives $(V_0 - C + S)(1 + r) - (V_0 - C + S) = \Delta V$. Factoring gives $(V_0 - C + S)(1 + r - 1) = \Delta V$, which gives the result above.

[5] Of course natural events like fires and hurricanes can affect this conclusion.

[6] We are assuming that one acre is the smallest possible harvest area.

[7] The spirit of this analysis is, of course, that the n areas are noncontiguous.

[8] N is the number of one-acre plots required to make up the total desired annual harvest area.

[9] For a discussion of some of these issues see chapter 21.

[10] C. Nellemann, ed., *Green Carbon, Black Trade, Illegal Logging, Tax Fraud and Laundering in the World's Tropical Forests*, INTERPOL Environmental Crime Programme, United Nations Environmental Program, GRID-Anrendal, 2012, p. 6.

[11] For a good discussion of the problems involved in combating illegal logging see Marilyne Pereira Goncalves, et al., *Improving Criminal Justice Efforts to Combat Illegal Logging*, World Bank, 2012.

Key Terms

biological growth function

carbon market

carbon sequestration

habitat values

illegal logging

national forests

optimal clear-cutting

optimal rotation

payment for environmental services

portfolio choice

timber concessions

Questions for Further Discussion

1. Derive the condition for the optimal rotation when a forest also provides species habitat services.

2. How would the optimal rotation be affected when a forest is an important supplier of outdoor recreation services, such as backpacking and hunting? How do these factors affect the size of the optimal clear-cut?

3. How would decisions about managing forests for carbon sequestration be affected by the speed at which wood building materials decay?

4. Are privately owned or publicly owned forests likely to result in the most efficient management of forest resources?

5. Describe what is meant by the "portfolio choice" approach to managing renewable resource stocks like forests.

6. What types of benefits and costs are involved when forests that were previously open to commercial forestry are now placed in preservation status?

Useful Websites

The primary federal forest agency in the United States:

- U.S. Forest Service (http://www.fs.fed.us)

Forestry programs are pursued by a number of public and private agencies:

- World Resources Institute, program on forests (http://www.wri.org)
- Food and Agriculture Organization of the United Nations (http://www.fao.org)
- United Nations Forum on Forests (http://www.un.org/esa/forests/)
- American Forests (http://www.americanforests.org)
- European Forest Institute (http://www.efi.int)

Most other countries have public forest agencies:

- Canadian Forest Service (http://www.nrcan.gc.ca/forests)
- Japan Ministry of Agriculture, Forestry and Fisheries (http://www.maff.go.jp/e/)

Many universities have schools of forestry and forest resources:

- University of Florida, School of Forest Resources and Conservation (http://www.sfrc.ufl.edu)
- Yale University, School of Forestry and Environmental Studies (http://environment.yale.edu)
- University of California at Berkeley (https://cnr.berkeley.edu/site/fnr.php)

Selected Readings

Amacher, Gregory S., Markku Ollikainen, and Erkki Koskela. *Economics of Forest Resources*. Boston, MA: MIT Press, 2009.

Helles, F., N. Strange, and L. Wichmann, eds. *Recent Accomplishments in Applied Forest Economics Research*. Boston, MA: Kluwer Academic, 2003.

Kant, Shashi, and R. Albert Berry, eds. *Economics, Sustainability, and Natural Resources: Economics of Sustainable Forest Management.* New York: Springer, 2006.

Klemperer, W. David. *Forest Resource Economics and Finance.* Self-published, 2003.

Lorenz, Klaus, and Rattan Lal. *Carbon Sequestration in Forest Ecosystems.* New York: Springer, 2010.

Whiteman, Adrian. *An Economic Framework to Analyze Illegal Activities in the Forest Sector.* World Forestry Congress, 2003.

13

Marine Resources

Oceans and inland waters cover more than two-thirds of the surface of Earth. This aquatic ecosystem is the source of numerous products and services of value to humans and to the ecological health of the globe. Major ones include: commercial fishing, recreational fishing (including aquarium fish), transportation services, shore-based and offshore recreation activities, atmospheric and climate control, and mineral supplies.

In this chapter we focus on the first of these: the exploitation of fish resources by commercially oriented harvesters. On a global basis, about two-thirds of commercial fishing is to provide food for humans. The rest is fish for industrial purposes, such as producing fish meal to use as animal feed. Figure 13-1 on the next page shows the trend over the last few decades of the total commercial fish harvest in the world. The overall trend clearly has been up. The fish resource looms larger in some parts of the world than in others. In North America only about 7 percent of animal protein intake comes from fish, but in Africa this proportion is 21 percent and in Southeast Asia it is almost 30 percent.[1] Of total global commercial landings, about 90 percent (by weight) comes from saltwater fisheries and the rest from inland waters. About 50 percent of the total is from "wild" fisheries and 50 percent is through aquaculture. The latter is a fast-growing segment of the total world harvest. World totals mask many changes that have taken place regionally and among different species of fish. Much of the growth in total harvest of recent years has been accounted for by lesser-valued species (sardines, pilchard) to which fishers have shifted their attention as some of the higher-valued species (cod, halibut) have become more scarce.

Within the United States, commercial landings in 2012 totaled about 9.6 billion pounds, of which about 5 percent derived from aquaculture. Total harvest (by weight) has been fairly flat for the last ten years. In 2012 the total value of commercial landings was slightly more than $5 billion. Table 13-1 shows the top ten finfish and shellfish fisheries of the United States by value. For many years the Pacific Coast/Alaska has been the largest U.S. regional fishery.

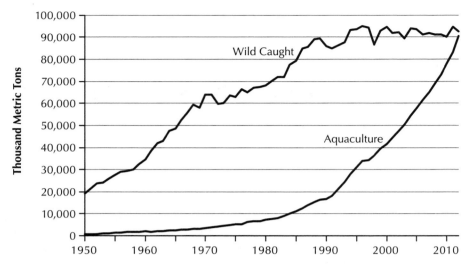

Figure 13-1   World Total Wild Catch and Aquaculture Production, 1950–2012

Source: Fishery and Aquaculture Statistics, *FAO Yearbook 2012.* (ftp://ftp.fao.org/FI/CDrom/
CD_yearbook_2012/navigation/index_content_aquaculture)

Table 13-1   Top Ten U.S. Finfish and Shellfish Fisheries, 2012

Finfish	Landings ($ millions)	Shellfish	Landings ($ millions)
Salmon	489.1	Sea scallops	559.2
Alaska Pollock (Walleye)	343.3	Lobsters (American)	429.3
Pacific cod	186.6	Shrimp	490.1
Tuna	163.9	Clams	193.1
Menhaden	127.7	Blue crab	189.7
Goosefish (Monkfish)	27.1	Oysters	155.1
Grouper	28.1	Dungeness crab	180.5
Pacific whiting (Hake)	47.1	King crab	90.8
Yellowfin sole	48.2	Squid	105.6
Atlantic cod	22.2	South Atlantic shrimp	55.0

Source: National Marine Fisheries Service, *Fisheries of the United States, 2012.*
(http://www.st.nmfs.noaa.gov/commercial-fisheries/commercial-landings/annual-landings/index)

■ Current Problems in Marine Fisheries

Major contemporary marine fisheries problems include:

- Overfishing, resulting in substantially diminished stocks of some species
- Overcapitalization; that is, excessive investments in national fishing fleets

- Water pollution that threatens spawning areas vital to the health of many marine species

- Conflicts over fishing rights, both inter-country (e.g., United States and Canada), and intra-country (Native American fishing rights within the United States or Canada)

- The rapid growth in aquaculture; that is, fish (and other aquatic organisms) farming

In this chapter we deal primarily with overfishing and overcapitalization. They are, of course, closely related: too many fishers catching too many fish relative to what is known about the current size of the various fisheries. This situation is largely the result of the **open-access** nature of marine fisheries. Until recently, anyone who wanted to buy a boat and commence fishing could do so, resulting in too many boats and a commensurate driving down of fish stocks. Historically, opening up new fisheries leads to a rapid influx of boats, overfishing, and, ultimately, depletion of the stocks. Figure 13-2 shows the landings profile of five historical fisheries of the United States from 1837 to 1993. The profiles are remarkably similar and are probably representative of many other fisheries around the world.

Many countries have sought to regulate fishing to protect fish stocks, with mixed success. A major part of the problem is that public agencies

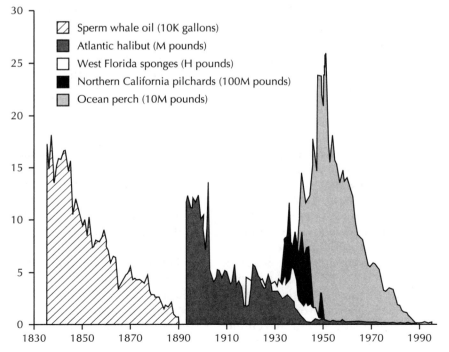

Figure 13-2   Profile of Landings for Five Historic U.S. Fisheries, 1837–1993

have typically relied on command-and-control measures that have not adequately accounted for the incentives facing fishers. Governments also have usually been very much conflicted between the desire to avoid overfishing and the even stronger desire to protect the economic livelihoods of fishing communities.

■ U.S. Fisheries Management Institutions

The primary authority for fishery management in the United States is the **Magnuson Fishery Conservation and Management Act (MFCMA) of 1976.** This law established eight **Regional Fishery Management Councils** to pursue fishery management goals in their particular regions. The councils prepare **Fishery Management Plans** (FMPs) for the fisheries in their region that are in need of regulation. The councils, the states and other territories they include, and important species in each region, are shown in table 13-2.

The councils are composed of public officials from the states and territories in the region, and from the federal government, as well as "interested and knowledgeable members of the public," who have been, for the most part, representatives of the fish harvesting, processing, and distributing sectors. The FMPs prepared by the councils attempt to establish limits on total catches and regulations on such items as fishing gear, harvesting practices, and closure times as necessary for managing the fisheries.

The deliberations and decisions of the Regional Fishery Management Councils have been contentious and ongoing, both because of the scientific difficulties of understanding the biology and ecology of fisheries, and because of the socioeconomic implications of reducing allowable fish catch levels.

Continuing problems with developing effective fisheries management plans led to the passage of the **Sustainable Fisheries Act of 1996.** This law is meant to give the regional councils more authority, as well as responsibility, to develop plans to rehabilitate fisheries deemed to be overfished. The law put a temporary moratorium on incentive-based management systems. In 2006, however, Congress passed the **Magnuson-Stevens Fishery Conservation and Management Reauthorization Act**, which authorizes the establishment of these types of programs. According to 2013 information from the National Oceanic and Atmospheric Administration, about 20 percent of U.S. fisheries that have been assessed are overfished.[2] The 2006 reauthorization of the Magnuson Act requires that when stocks drop to an overfished level (defined as 50 percent of "maximum sustained yield"), fisheries managers put in place a plan that will rebuild stocks in ten years. According to a recent National Academy of Sciences Report, recent efforts have been reasonably successful at rebuilding stocks.[3] To understand the full ramifications of this, we must focus on the bioeconomics of fisheries management.

Table 13-2   Regional Fishery Management Councils

Council	States and other territories	Species in the Fishery Management Plans
New England	Maine New Hampshire Massachusetts Rhode Island Connecticut	groundfish, sea scallop, monkfish, herring, skates, whiting (hake), red crab, dogfish atlantic salmon
Mid-Atlantic	New York New Jersey Pennsylvania Delaware Maryland Virginia	summer flounder, scup, black sea bass, mackerel, squid, butterfish, surf clams, ocean quahogs, bluefish, tilefish, spiny dogfish, monkfish
South Atlantic	North Carolina South Carolina Georgia Florida	coastal migratory pelagics, coral and live bottom habitat, dolphin and wahoo, golden crab, shrimp, snapper grouper, spiny lobster, and sargassum
Caribbean	Virgin Islands Puerto Rico	reef fish, spiny lobster, queen conch, corals and reef associated plants
Gulf of Mexico	Texas Louisiana Mississippi Alabama Florida	reef fish, shrimp, spiny lobster, corals, migratory pelagics, red drum
Pacific	California Oregon Washington Idaho	ground fish, salmon, pacific halibut, highly migratory species, coastal pelagic species
North Pacific	Alaska Washington Oregon	halibut, ground fish, crab, scallop, salmon, arctic species
Western Pacific	Hawaii American Samoa Guam	albacore tuna, spiny lobster, bottomfish, crustacean, precious coral and coral reef, pacific pelagics

Source: National Oceanic and Atmospheric Administration (NOAA), U.S. Regional Fishery Management Councils, 2014 (http://www.fisherycouncils.org).

■ Modeling a Fishery

In this section we develop a simple **bioeconomic model** for analyzing both positive and normative questions about exploiting a fishery. A bioeconomic approach combines two elements: the **biology** of fisheries growth and decline and the behavioral consequences that flow from **economic decisions** made by humans.

The Biological Growth Function

Consider a single fishery. By **fishery** we mean a collection of fish that inhabit a reasonably well delimited section of marine habitat. It might be fish of a single species (e.g., oysters in Chesapeake Bay) or fish of multiple, but related, species (e.g., all groundfish on Georges Bank off Cape Cod). At any given time the fishery consists of many individuals of different ages and sizes. To simplify this, we measure the total size of the fish stock in terms of **biomass,** essentially the aggregate weight of all the individuals of which the fishery is composed. The size of a fishery biomass is determined by many factors, not just the amount of fishing effort that is expended on it. Predator and prey factors, annual fecundity, ocean currents, food supply, water qualities, disease, and other factors play a role. There are few fisheries in the world where these factors are clearly understood. Fisheries biologists continue to research the complicated population dynamics of these situations.

For the moment, however, we set aside all these complex factors and focus on the all-important relationship between the **size** of the fishery biomass and the **growth** of that biomass. There are two major natural growth factors: increases in the number of individuals through processes of reproduction, and increases in the sizes (weights) of individuals through maturation. There are also two major forces working in the opposite direction: losses from predation and food scarcities and losses from natural mortality, especially old age.

At relatively small biomass levels the forces of reproduction and growth may be expected to dominate: With ecosystem abundance, high rates of reproduction are associated with rapid rates of growth of the biomass. But this obviously cannot continue indefinitely. As the size of the biomass gets relatively large, food scarcities start to take their toll. So at some point we can expect a natural equilibrium to assert itself between the factors of growth and reduction. In this way a natural population size is established.

This reasoning has given rise to the famous **logistic model** of population growth, first proposed by P. F. Verhulst in 1938[4] and pictured in figure 13-3. The size of the biomass is indexed on the horizontal axis, and the increment, or change, in that biomass during a period of time such as a year is shown on the vertical axis. The inverted U-shaped function starts at the origin—no fish, no increment. At higher stocks the increment is larger, reaching a maximum at a stock size of s_1. At larger stock sizes the increment is still positive but less than the maximum primarily because of the increased scarcities of food and space that the larger stocks imply. At a stock size of s_0, the different factors affecting stock size are all in balance, so there is no increment. Stock size s_0 is thus a natural equilibrium, in the sense that this is the stock that would result if the population was left to itself and ecological factors were constant. At stock sizes above s_0, biological forces work to actually lead to negative increments—that is, to reductions in the size of the fishery biomass.

The logistic curve can be interpreted as a type of **sustained yield** curve, where by "yield" we mean a certain amount of the biomass harvested and there-fore removed each year. For example, at a biomass size of s_2, the growth increment is equal to y_2 pounds. Thus if, at this stock size, y_2 pounds of fish were harvested each year, the yield would exactly match the growth increment and the size of the stock

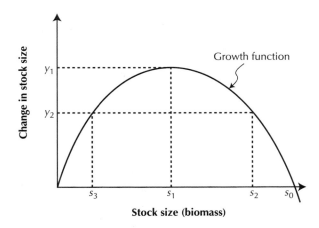

Figure 13-3   The Logistic Model of Population Growth for a Fishery

would be unchanged. This underlines an important point: There is not just one sustainable stock size in this situation. Any stock size is sustainable if the yield exactly matches the natural increment in the biomass. Note that the yield y_2 is also consistent with a stock size of s_3. But this pair, s_3 and y_2, is an unstable pair in the following sense. Suppose, with the yield kept at y_2, the stock size temporarily increased above s_3. Then the natural increment would exceed the yield, and the stock would be larger next year. So if the yield was held at y_2, the stock would slowly grow to size s_2, which is a stable situation in the sense that short-run deviations of the stock above or below s_2 would be self-correcting.

But note another possible outcome. Suppose, with a stock of s_3 and a yield of y_2, there was a short-run diminution in the size of the biomass because of, say, temporary food shortages. If the yield or total catch is held at y_2, it will exceed the natural increment, driving the stock lower. If the yield continues at y_2, the biomass will eventually be driven to zero; the fish-ery will be wiped out.

From this analysis we can conclude that any yield equal to or less than y_1 is sustainable—that is, it can be continued indefinitely with a stable, sus-tainable stock size lying between s_1 and s_0. Any total catch over y_1 cannot be sustainable because this would be greater than the maximum growth incre-ment of which the fishery is capable.

The Effort-Yield Function

Now we bring human behavior into the model. The "yield" referred to in the last section is actually a quantity of fish assumed to be harvested from the fishery, but this yield can come about only when human effort is given to the task. **Harvesting effort** refers to the economic resources devoted to catching fish; this includes capital goods (e.g., boats and gear), labor (captains and deckhands), and materials and energy. To simplify the graphics, we want to convert these resources to a single dimension. Perhaps the easiest way to do this is to think in terms of a standardized fishing boat of a certain size, with a certain size crew, and using a certain complement of fishing gear. Then we can speak of larger or smaller amounts of human effort in terms of the number of days spent fishing by boats of the standard type. We make this assumption in order to proceed with our simple model. In the real world, of course, there can be substantial differences among boats on a fishery in terms of size, equipment, the skills of people on them, and so on. We abstract from these differences here.

With this simplification, a typical **effort-yield curve** is depicted in figure 13-4. It is important to keep in mind that this is a **sustained-yield** relationship. For example, an effort level of e_2 is associated with a sustained yield of y_2. This means that if effort level e_2 is applied each year on a permanent basis, the permanent (i.e., sustained) yield that will result is y_2. Yields may be different in the short run as adjustments occur, but eventually they will settle down to y_2.

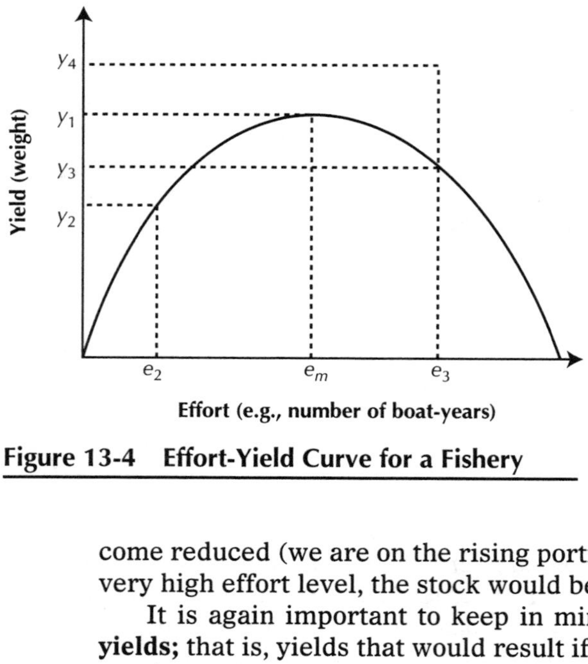

The reasoning behind the inverted U-shape of the effort-yield relationship is because of the linkage between effort levels and the size of the stock. At a zero level of effort, the fishery will adjust to its natural size (level s_0 in figure 13-3). As effort increases, the higher yields taken from the fishery result in the maintenance of small stock sizes; at an effort level of e_m, the sustained yield reaches its maximum point. At still higher effort levels, stock levels become reduced (we are on the rising portion of the graph in figure 13-3). At a very high effort level, the stock would be driven to zero.

Figure 13-4   Effort-Yield Curve for a Fishery

It is again important to keep in mind that the model shows **sustained yields;** that is, yields that would result if the indicated effort level is applied **continuously** and the stock has had time to adjust to these effort levels. It is possible, in the short run, to have yields that are not on the effort-yield curve, for example a yield of y_4 at effort level e_3. But this is not sustainable. A high short-term yield like this will drive the stock down, and the yield obtainable with this effort level will fall, in the long run, to y_3.

Maximum Sustained Yield

All the yields traced out by the effort-yield curve are biologically sustainable. An effort level of e_m produces the **maximum sustained yield** (MSY) from this fishery. This is the maximum quantity of harvest that can be realized in the long run—that is, on a sustainable basis. Maximum sustained yield is often regarded as the best target to aim for in exploiting renewable resources such as a fishery. Its appeal is based on the fact that this is the maximum biological yield that the fishery is capable of producing. When humans are brought in, however, this conclusion does not necessarily follow because social efficiency, the effort level that maximizes the net benefits of the fishery, requires that the consequences of alternative effort levels be expressed in value terms.

■ Efficient Rates of Effort

To explore efficient effort levels, we must establish values for both the harvested fish and the effort that goes into catching them. Let us assume that the harvested fish are sold on a market, at a given and constant price, and that this price represents the full social value of the fish. We also assume that each unit of effort has a given, constant, opportunity cost. These assumptions allow us to construct the revenue and cost functions depicted in figure 13-5. The total revenue curve is the effort yield curve of figure 13-4 multiplied by the unit price of the harvested fish. Thus it preserves the inverted U shape of that relationship. The total cost curve is simply a straight line starting at the origin and rising to the right at a slope that represents the opportunity costs of a unit of effort. The higher this opportunity cost, the steeper the total cost relationship. The **net income** corresponding to any effort level, which equals

net social benefits in this simple model, is given by the distance between total revenue and total cost. The effort level at which this distance is maximized is e^*, and net benefits at this point are equal to $(r_1 - r_2)$.[5] It is easy to see that at any other effort level net benefits—the distance between the two curves—is smaller than at e^*.

In particular, the net benefits produced

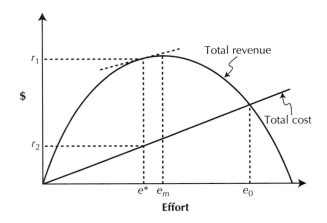

Figure 13-5   Efficient Harvest Level for a Fishery

at the point of maximum sustained yield (effort level e_m) are lower than at e^*. The reason is that, although the yields are indeed higher at e_m than at e^*, the extra costs of harvest are even greater, so the net revenues are lower. This shows that the point of maximum sustained yield in a physical or biological sense is not necessarily the point of maximum net social benefits in an economic sense. In fact, economic efficiency implies a lower effort level, and therefore a higher permanent stock level, than does maximum sustained yield.

To explain an important point about the value of the fishery, suppose this fishery had a single owner. The annual net income of this person would be an amount equal to $r_1 - r_2$ in figure 13-5. This value is in effect produced by the fishery; if this owner were to sell the fishery to another person, this annual net income would determine the price at which the fishery would sell. The annual return realized in this fashion is called the **annual resource rent** produced by the fishery. As we learned earlier, a **natural resource rent** is the net value of a resource prior to extraction—that is, its value **in situ.** Efficiency in natural resource use, therefore, implies using resources in such a way as to maximize their in situ value, or rent. In the case of our fishery the rent-maximizing level of effort is e^*.

■ The Problem of Open Access

Next we ask whether effort levels on fisheries in the real world tend to points like e^* in figure 13-5. To answer this question we have to consider the incentive aspects of the situation, for which we need to understand how the property rights to the resource are held. In the real world, rights to ocean fisheries are typically not held by single owners or even, at least until recently, by defined groups of individuals. Rather, fisheries have historically been subject to **open-access** rules: Anybody who has wanted to buy or build a boat and go fishing essentially had the "right" to do so. To consider the incentive implications of this, suppose there is an open-access fishery in which the harvesting effort level is currently at e^* (figure 13-5). Consider the logic of one more fisher who is contemplating whether to get a boat and start harvesting from this fishery. Open access means that she need not get permission from anybody to do this, nor must she pay anybody for the right to engage in fishing. The only cost is the cost of buying the boat and gear, which are the standard costs reflected in the total cost curve of the model. Since effort is currently at e^*, she could be expected to compare this cost with anticipated revenues. At e^*, average revenues per unit of effort (per boat, for example) exceed average cost. Thus there are apparently profits to be made by any individual entering the fishery. Despite the fact that e^* is the efficient level of effort from the standpoint of society, there are still incentives for additional fishers to devote greater effort to harvesting from the fishery.

In fact this incentive in the open-access situation continues to exist as long as total revenue exceeds total cost (because average revenue exceeds average cost in this situation). The upshot is that entry will continue to occur until total effort has grown to e_0 in figure 13-5. At this point total revenue equals total costs, and so the incentive for further entry has disappeared. Note also that all **resource rent** has disappeared at effort level e_0. At this level of effort the fishery is not producing positive net benefits. The resource rents have in effect been **dissipated** by excess entry and effort levels applied to the fishery.

The open-access condition of the fishery has produced substantially higher effort levels (and therefore substantially smaller stock levels) than is socially efficient. This situation is made much worse if **technological change** reduces the unit costs of harvesting effort. Diagrammatically, this implies a less steep total cost curve in the figure, which makes open-access levels of effort go even higher.

This is the basic incentive situation that historically has characterized most saltwater fisheries and many freshwater resources. It is accurate to say that most approaches to public fisheries management have been attempts to rectify the overharvesting implications of open access. Until recently, these management efforts were based for the most part on trying to directly regulate the performance of people harvesting particular fisheries. More recently attention has focused on changing the property rights aspects of these situations so as to alter the basic incentives facing harvesters.

■ Approaches to Fisheries Management

Throughout the world countries have been struggling in the last few decades to overcome the problems caused by open access in marine fisheries. Some of these efforts have already been successful, while many are still evolving in ways that may lead both to the restoration of depleted fish stocks and their efficient harvesting. A major factor has been a gradual change in attitudes away from the long-standing notion that the ocean was a resource of unlimited abundance that ought to be freely available and toward one that recognizes the need for restraint if fisheries are to be preserved.

Fisheries regulations have, in general, progressed through a series of stages, starting first with modest regulatory moves and finally ending up, more recently, with more fundamental shifts in the property rights systems applicable to fisheries.

Restricting Access—First Steps

Open access means, very simply and in practical terms, that there are too many fishers exploiting a fishery. The natural tendency for people faced with this type of situation is to try to identify some means by which entry to the fisheries can be limited. Anthropologists and historians have found that for centuries localized groups of people have sought to define and defend territorial rights to fisheries, essentially by excluding outsiders from the resource. Informal territorial use rights in fisheries (**TURFs**) have been organized around particular geographical areas that make it possible to set boundaries and exclude would-be encroachers.[6] Sedentary species (clams, oysters, mussels) lend themselves relatively well to this approach because particular bays, lagoons, or coral reefs can be defended. A well-known example in a semi-sedentary species is the harbor gangs of Maine. These are groups of lobster fishers centered on particular bays who have pursued well-organized, but extralegal, efforts to exclude outsiders from fishing in the areas they control (see chapter 7).

But under some conditions TURFs may also be useful for migratory species. A TURF is not resource-specific as much as it is site-specific. So a species that migrates along a shoreline could be exploited by a TURF that controlled access for a certain distance along the shoreline. This might not be effective in controlling overfishing of the species because it doesn't offer control of access to the stock elsewhere in its migratory journey.

The essential logic of the TURF (i.e., exclusion of outsiders) has recently been pursued worldwide at the level of the nation. As of the 1950s, most countries were claiming national jurisdiction over waters and resources within 3 miles (in a few cases 12 miles) from shore based on the long history of maritime custom. This meant that the majority of the productive fisheries of the world were situated on the "high seas," beyond effective political and management control. Large foreign fleets could exploit fisheries that many countries regarded as being essentially in their home waters. Attempts were made to deal with the problem through international negotiations and agreements. The International Fisheries Convention of 1946 targeted the northeastern Atlantic. The International Commission for North-West Atlantic Fisheries was established in 1949. During the 1960s a number of new regulatory bodies and conventions were formed, covering more than 80 countries and most of the world's oceans. But these international efforts were relatively ineffective at stopping overfishing, primarily because of marked differences among countries in terms of fishing technology and costs, opinions about fish stocks, and so on.

Thus the 1960s and early 1970s saw a push toward **extended jurisdiction,** essentially a state of affairs in which countries claimed and enforced offshore limits of 200 miles. This effectively nationalized, or put under the jurisdiction of national authorities of coastal countries, about 95 percent of the world's productive fisheries. In effect this might be thought of as a move toward national TURFs. But TURF will be successful only to the extent that it develops the institutional capacities with which to regulate or manage the affected fisheries within the TURF. In fact, in large countries such as the United States, the 200-mile zone is still subject to problems of open access and overfishing because of ineffective management institutions. In smaller countries, such as Iceland, authorities have been more successful at instituting effective fisheries management programs within their 200-mile exclusion zone.

Regulating Fishing Practices

The dominant approach in fishery regulation has been command-and-control types of restrictions on fishing practices, in the hope that they could be made less productive and therefore less devastating on stocks of fish. These restraints included such measures as closing certain areas, limiting the number of days of fishing, prohibiting fine-mesh nets in order to target larger fish, and restricting the size and horsepower of fishing boats.

Figure 13-6 shows a way of analyzing this approach. What regulations of this type do, essentially, is raise the cost of fishing. Restricting certain inputs, say, the type of net that may be used, makes it more costly to catch a given quantity of fish. In our standard fisheries model, this rotates the total cost curve upward, giving it a steeper slope. If TC_1 is the original total cost curve, the new curve resulting from a regulation of this type would be something like TC_2. Now open access, instead of leading to e_0 units of effort on the fishery, produces only e_m units of effort. This is approximately equal to the maximum sustained yield level of effort. A somewhat larger increase in costs, produced by somewhat more restrictive regulations, would shift up total costs even more, say, to TC_3, moving the open-access level of effort to e_3, which is close to the original efficient effort level.

There are a couple of major problems with this type of approach. First and foremost is that, although it is possible to reduce effort levels and therefore increase stocks, and ultimately yields, in this way, it makes fishing much more costly than it needs to be. Economic efficiency requires more than just arriving at the optimal yield and fish stock, it also requires that this yield be achieved with the minimum expenditure of scarce resources; that is, at minimum opportunity cost.

The second disadvantage of this type of direct control on fishing practices is that it can never be complete. When some parts of the fishing enterprise are constrained, fishers attempt to expand in uncontrolled directions. Suppose, for example, authorities place a limit on the number of boats that may be used on a fishery. Fishers now have the incentive to build larger boats to increase their harvests. Suppose authorities

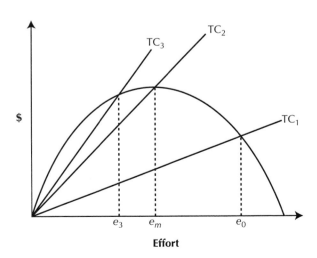

Figure 13-6   Effects of Fishing Regulations

step in and place an upper limit on boat length. Fishers now may shift to boats with larger engines. A limitation on horsepower may lead them to increase the number of trips they make each year. And so on.[7]

Catch Limits

Another common regulatory approach is for authorities to establish upper limits on the quantity of fish that may be taken from particular fisheries. These are usually called TACs, for **total allowable catch** (or sometimes **total catch quotas**). TACs appear to give authorities a means of closely controlling yields. They simply establish a TAC, monitor incoming catches, and when the limit is reached, close the fishery. Apart from the difficulties in monitoring and enforcing this kind of limit, the major problem with it is shown in figure 13-7. The open-access level of effort is e_1, which authorities regard as leading to diminished stocks. They therefore establish an upper limit on catch of y_1 (although there is a monetary scale on the vertical axis, it can readily be translated into quantity of fish by dividing by the unit price of fish). The y_1 level is below the efficient yield, but perhaps it will be set at this level for some time to allow stocks to rejuvenate.

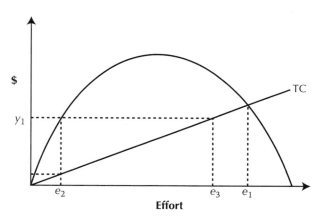

Figure 13-7   Catch Limits

The minimum effort to harvest a yield of y_1 is e_2. Suppose this effort level was somehow temporarily established. At that point, rents are being earned by fishers, which attracts additional resources into the fishery. A common phenomenon that illustrates this is the **derby fishery.** Although the TAC has been set, no quotas have been set for individual fishers. Thus individuals have the incentive to increase their **share** of the TAC. The advantage goes to the fishers who can get out on the fishery first with the greatest fishing power. So the effort level is pushed to the right as fishers do whatever it takes—bigger boats, engines, crews, and nets—to get bigger shares of the TAC before the fishery is closed down. In fact if the TAC is set permanently at y_1, the effort level will eventually increase to e_3, close to the open-access situation.

While setting catch quotas seems to be a very specific and effective way to halt overfishing, the process is normally very complex. Historically, setting TACs for a particular fishery has been a struggle for authorities. This is related to:

- the uncertain biological state of the fishery
- the employment and income consequences of catch limits
- the mix of technologies among the fleet
- the relationships between the target species and related ones
- the uncertain technologies of enforcement and other factors[8]

Individual Transferable Quotas (ITQs)

The problem with these regulatory approaches is that they do not address the fundamental problem—the value represented by the fishery resource is left open to capture by anybody who feels like trying. If rents are temporarily positive in a fishery, nothing stops new entrants from trying to appropriate some of them. This process drives the effort level upward, eventually to e_2, and the rent to zero. Setting TACs and then dividing them up into quotas for individual fishers partly solves the problem, as it reduces the incentive for a "race to fish." But individual catch quotas can lock in inefficiencies and inequities stemming from the way they are originally determined. The last all-important step is to make the quotas transferable, hence the name **individual transferable quotas,** or ITQs. The approach has caught on in many fisheries around the world, as regulatory authorities seek to achieve fish-harvesting levels and methods that are both efficient and sustainable.

To establish an effective ITQ, authorities must follow these steps:

1. Establish TACs that are both economically and biologically meaningful.
2. Divide the TAC into a number of individual catch limits, or catch quotas, to be allocated to participants in the fishery.
3. Allow these individual quotas to be bought and sold, and keep track of who owns how many.
4. Enforce the catch quotas, so that fishers cannot harvest and sell quantities of fish in excess of their quota holdings.
5. Monitor the performance of the ITQ market to spot and manage problems related to concentrated ownership, community impacts, and biological uncertainties.

Step 1 is easy to understand, but may be a lot harder to implement than might first be thought. Clearly some limitation on total catch is necessary if open-access conditions have led to economic and/or biological overfishing. But setting a TAC reasonably accurately requires both biological and economic information that may not be available. This is especially true if, as is normally the case, stocks fluctuate from year to year because of factors not related to fishing pressure. We discuss below some issues related to fisheries management in cases of great uncertainty.

The division of the total quota into individual quotas is the next step, and obviously is one that will be controversial in most cases. The quotas will eventually be valuable property rights. Every participant will prefer to have more rather than less, so some acceptable means must be found for their distribution. They might be auctioned off, or given away on some criterion, for example, past production (measured on some basis) or number of boats.

Step 3 is inherent in the quota system itself. But monitoring all quota transactions requires a good accounting system, especially if the number of present participants is large. In a smoothly functioning market, quotas will not only be bought and sold outright, but leased, or perhaps loaned, in varying amounts for varying periods of time. Step 4 calls on the same type of monitoring and enforcing efforts that any kind of TAC and quota system requires. As mentioned earlier, enforcement is not something that just happens automatically when a regulation is promulgated. Enforcement activities have to be designed and funded with enough resources to achieve acceptable levels of compliance. Enforcing fishery regulations is difficult because fishing is done in places away from easy scrutiny, and in many cases it is fairly easy for fishers to off-load "hot" fish in ways that escape surveillance. One of the major advantages of ITQs is that the kinds of detailed gear and performance restrictions that are inherently hard to monitor and enforce become unnecessary.

Step 5 is sometimes not given adequate attention. The ITQ system works by creating a new property right and a market on which that property right may be traded. It is virtually impossible to predict all of the important problems that novel institutions like this will encounter. Clear and accurate data on their operation is essential. This is especially so because one of the implications of establishing tradable quotas in a fishery is that the natural resource rent will no longer be dissipated. This value, which is squandered under open-access conditions, will accrue, at least initially, to those who possess the fishing rights. There are many who feel that private appropriation of these values is in conflict with the fact that its source is a resource essentially supplied by nature herself. And so the issue of who ends up with the resource rents can become an important point of conflict.[9]

■ Uncertainty and Fisheries Management

In the analyses of the previous section we implicitly assumed that the population biology of the affected fisheries was reasonably clear; regulators were assumed to have accurate knowledge of the stock-yield and effort-yield curves. A major problem with fisheries management in the real world, however, is that knowledge of these relationships is highly uncertain. One source of uncertainty is lack of complete biological and yield data, both current and historical, on the fishery, including landings and factors that affect the stock size. Important economic information may also be missing, such as accurate data on fishing costs and likely future changes in fishing technology. Biological variability is a major problem. Natural variability in ecological variables (e.g., ocean temperature, predators) make it difficult to identify the fish stocks accurately, not to mention the fact that the underlying biological models used for the purpose may not be accurate.

Fisheries management authorities may want to adopt rules that reflect large uncertainties. Consider figure 13-8. Suppose that biologists believe the most likely effort-yield curve is Y_1, but because of uncertainties in their knowledge of the fishery, there is a fairly strong probability that it could be as high as Y_2 or as low as Y_3.

Suppose the authorities establish a TAC of y_1, setting up an ITQ system so that the effort level is e_1. If the actual effort-yield curve is equal to Y_2, or anywhere else above Y_1,

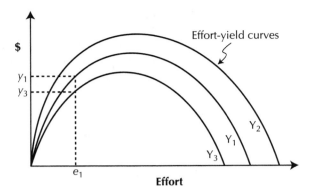

Figure 13-8 A Precautionary Approach in the Face of Uncertainty

the fish stock will either maintain its size or even grow. But suppose the actual effort-yield curve is Y_3. In this case the harvest level y_1 is not sustainable; at effort level e_1 the sustainable harvest rate is y_3. With effort at e_1 and harvests (temporarily) at y_1 something has to give. If the effort level is maintained, stocks will decline and harvest levels will gradually diminish to the sustainable level y_3. But a more likely scenario, perhaps, is that fishers will increase effort levels as they try to maintain the permitted harvest level of y_1. If this were to happen, stocks could be driven to a precariously low level. The way out of this dilemma is for authorities to establish a lower quota level in the first place, commensurate with their uncertainty about the true bioeconomic relationships of the fishery.

■ Aquaculture

The discussion so far in this chapter is applicable to wild catch (capture) fisheries; that is, fisheries in which the target organisms are fugitive and subject to the biological parameters of unconfined populations. As a quick glance at figure 13-1 shows, however, a growing percentage of fish consumption in the world comes from cultivated fisheries, in which the populations are confined and managed in ways analogous to conventional animal and plant agriculture. Hence its name: aquaculture. It is widely expected that **aquaculture** harvest will substantially outrank wild harvest in the future.

Aquaculture covers a wide variety of activities. **Inland aquaculture** refers to activities within several miles of shore, usually in protected waters. This includes the culture and harvest of shellfish, finfish, and plants (e.g., seaweed). **Offshore aquaculture** includes activities extending into open water, within a country's extended economic zone (EEZ), which normally runs out to 200 miles.

Aquaculture involves many husbandry activities analogous to terrestrial animal agriculture: selection of organism, size of initial stock, feeding practices, confinement technology, health maintenance, harvesting and marketing. So the enterprise economics of these activities are reasonably standard. But in some areas, especially in the United States, aquaculture is controversial, especially because of potential external, ecological costs. These include:

- Possible escape of farmed fish, with detrimental impacts on native, wild fish
- Spread of parasites and disease
- Nutrient and chemical discharge from fish farms
- Overharvesting of fish species used for food

The prospect of these types of environmental spillovers has led some to conclude that aquaculture fisheries need to be substantially separated from normal ocean ecosystems. But there is also ongoing interest in developing confined fisheries in offshore settings.

A problem of some uniqueness to offshore aquaculture is that it is being pursued in a resource that is in the public domain. Land agriculture takes place within a well-defined system of private property rights and land markets. Aquaculture uses a marine resource: surface areas, underlying water columns, and sea beds that normally are in public ownership. In the United States, substantial amounts of near-shore aquaculture has developed under a system of state-level regulation, often involving permitting, and **resource leasing**. Leases specify the terms under which operators may access and use specified portions of the resource, to the exclusion of other potential users. Monetary aspects of the lease determine the way the fishery rents are divided by lessor and lessee, and thus the incentives facing the latter with regard to decisions on managing and marketing the capture stock.

In the United States and many other countries, there is a long history of offshore oil and gas leasing. Leases for defined areas are subject to bidding by prospective producers. Minimal acceptable bids are established by the U.S. Department of the Interior, based on the probabilities of finding quantities of oil and gas in the designated areas, and the expected production costs. Naturally these are controversial, as they determine how the resource rents in this case are divided between the private producer and the public, in the form of the overseeing public agency.

At this writing (2015) steps have not been completed in the United States to put in place a leasing system for offshore aquaculture. A bill has been submitted to Congress[10] which would establish terms for aquaculture leasing of offshore areas, including a "resource rental fee" that would recover from permittees ". . . a reasonable portion of value of the use under the permits of ocean resources held in public trust." What would qualify as "reasonable" is not defined.

■ Summary

Ocean (and freshwater) fisheries are renewable resources that require bioeconomic models for understanding and effective management. Such models combine both the biology of the resource and the economics of human behavior. The fish biomass growth function shows the increment to the stock of fish as a function of the size of that stock. After converting this into an effort-yield curve, we can analyze the effects of open access on rent dissipation in the fishery and the effectiveness of different types of fishery regulation. In many historical situations, TURFs (territorial use rights in fisheries) have been developed in an attempt to limit access to certain individuals, but these may be ineffective in the face of rising demand and technological change in fishing. Most fishery regulations historically have been based on command-and-control approaches, especially gear restrictions and catch quotas (total allowable catch, or TACs). These regulations do nothing to solve the rent dissipation problem of the fishery. In more recent years some countries have moved in the direction of incentive-based regulations, especially individual transferable quotas. There is also a strong trend toward aquaculture, the production of fish in captive stocks.

Notes

1 The data in this section come largely from Food and Agriculture Organization of the United Nations, *The State of World Fisheries and Aquaculture 2012*, p. 82.

2 www.nmfs.noaa.gov/sta/fisheries_eco/status_of_fisheries/

3 National Research Council, *Evaluating the Effectiveness of Fish Stock Rebuilding Plans in the United States*, Washington, DC, 2013.

4 P. F. Verhulst, "Notice sur la loi que la population suit dans son accroissement," *Correspondance Mathématique et Physique*, Vol. 10, 1938, pp. 113–121.

5 This is found by drawing a line tangent to the total revenue curve with the same slope as the total cost curve. In the figure it is shown as a dotted line. The tangency point occurs at an effort level of e^*.

6 See Francis T. Christy, Jr., "Territorial Use Rights in Marine Fisheries: Definitions and Conditions," Technical Paper No. 227, Food and Agriculture Organization, Rome, 1982.

7 Another potential problem, which our simple model does not illustrate, is tighter regulations in one fishery leading fishers to shift, thus putting added pressure on different fisheries.

8 For a good depiction of these problems see Lee Anderson, "Marine Fisheries," in Paul R. Portney, ed., *Current Issues in Natural Resource Policy*, Johns Hopkins University Press for Resources for the Future, Baltimore, MD, 1982.

9 In Iceland there is pressure on public authorities to tax away some of the resource rents from the rights holders: to have them pay, in a sense, for the right to fish. For the most part, this is a distributional issue, not an efficiency issue. If the efficient level of effort is being applied to the fishery, the resource rent could be taxed away, in part at least, without inducing a change in this effort level.

10 The "National Sustainable Offshore Aquaculture Bill of 2011," HR2373, 112th Congress, 2011–2013.

Key Terms

aquaculture
bioeconomic model
derby fishery
effort-yield curve
extended jurisdiction
ITQs (individual transferable quotas)
Magnuson Act

maximum sustained yield
natural resource rents
open access
rent dissipation
TAC (total allowable catch)
TURFs (territorial use rights in fisheries)

Questions for Further Discussion

1. What would the biological growth curve look like if a critical stock size exists below which growth rates become negative and the stock evolves to zero?

2. What would be the efficiency and equity implications of granting a fishery to one individual as a sole owner?

3. By decreasing effort, fishers can often catch more fish. Explain how this might sometimes be true.

4. Why is there a difference between the maximum sustained yield and the economically efficient sustained yield?

5. What other natural resources are like a fishery in the sense that there are many different possible levels of steady-state stock among which one may be identified as economically efficient? (A steady state is simply one that persists over a long period of time. The optimal stock is a steady-state stock, but, as the question implies, not all steady-state stocks are efficient.)

6. What are some of the problems that might be anticipated in moving from a temporary, short-run yield to a long-run, sustainable yield?

Useful Websites

The National Oceanic and Atmospheric Administration (NOAA) maintains a number of relevant sites:

- National Marine Fisheries Service (http://www.nmfs.noaa.gov)
- The Sea Grant program (http://seagrant.noaa.gov)
- Regional fisheries management councils, for example, the North Pacific Fishery Management Council (http://www.npfmc.org) and the Mid-Atlantic Fishery Management Council (http://www.mafmc.org)

Various internationally oriented agencies have fisheries programs:

- Fish Net (http://fishnet.ning.com), part of the International Institute for Environment and Development
- Food and Agriculture Organization of the United Nations (http://www.fao.org)

Numerous public interest groups focus on fisheries:

- American Fisheries Society (http://www.fisheries.org)
- Center for Sustainable Fisheries (http://centerforsustainablefisheries.org)
- Sustainable Fisheries Foundation (http://sustainablefisheriesfoundation.org)

Selected Readings

Anderson, Lee G., ed. *Fisheries Economics*, Volumes I and II. Hampshire, UK: Ashgate Publishing, 2002.

Christy, Francis T., Jr., and Anthony Scott. *The Common Wealth in Ocean Fisheries: Some Problems of Growth and Economic Allocation.* Baltimore, MD: Johns Hopkins University Press, 1965.

Crutchfield, James A., and Arnold Zellner, eds. *The Economics of Marine Resources and Conservation Policy: The Pacific Halibut Case Study with Commentary.* Chicago: University of Chicago Press, 2002.

Hallwood, Paul. *Economics of the Oceans: Rights, Rents and Resources.* New York: Routledge, 2014.

Hannesson, Rognvaldur. *The Privatization of the Oceans.* Cambridge, MA: MIT Press, 2006.

Leal, Donald R., ed. *Evolving Property Rights in Marine Fisheries.* Lanham, MD: Rowman and Littlefield, 2004.

National Oceanic and Atmospheric Administration (NOAA). *Offshore Aquaculture in the United States: Economic Considerations, Implications and Opportunities*, Aquaculture Program, July 2008.

14

Land Economics

Land is the ubiquitous natural resource. Human beings are land-dwelling creatures; for them land is both a spatial resource, providing space to live, work, travel, and play, and a productive resource from which they draw their sustenance of food, fiber, and other materials. This chapter focuses on basic land economics, which draws on economic principles to examine and understand human decisions about land use.

Table 14-1 shows some of the major land-use categories and how the amounts of land devoted to these uses in the contiguous United States have changed over the last six decades. Urban land has quadrupled during this time, but still only accounts for about 3 percent of the total. Farmland has declined modestly during this time, as has forestland. Miscellaneous nonurban land use increased from 9 percent to about 13 percent of the total during this time.

Within some of these broad categories and trends there have been some very substantial changes. In forestlands, for example, especially publicly

Table 14-1   Major Uses of Land in the Contiguous 48 States (millions of acres, with percentage of total in parentheses)

	1945		1974		2002		2007	
Farmland								
Cropland	451	(23.7)	465	(24.5)	441	(23.3)	407	(21.5)
Pasture and grazing	660	(34.6)	595	(31.4)	584	(30.8)	612	(32.3)
Forestland	602	(31.6)	599	(31.5)	559	(29.5)	576	(30.4)
Urban land	15	(0.8)	35	(1.8)	59	(3.1)	60	(3.2)
Miscellaneous other*	178	(9.3)	204	(10.7)	250	(13.2)	238	(12.6)
Total	1,906		1,898		1,893		1,893	

* Includes various public installations, rural transportation areas, and land used primarily for recreation and wildlife purposes.

Source: USDA Economic Research Service, *Agricultural Resources and Environmental Indicators,* 2006 (EIB-16) 1996–97 (AH-712) and 2012 (EIB98). (www.ers.usda.gov/publications/arei)

owned forestland, there has been a very substantial drop-off recently in timbering and grazing activity and a rapid rise in recreational use. The growth in land area devoted to urban uses testifies to the trend in **urban decentralization** (sprawl), but in recent decades the nature of this trend has also changed. Decentralized **employment subcenters** and **edge cities** have appeared, which will impact the nature of sprawl and its implications for land-use changes in the future.

The rest of the chapter takes two directions. First, we introduce some conceptual ideas about land values, efficient land use, and the workings of the land market. Then we discuss a number of specific problems in land use applying, insofar as we can, the principles of land-use economics to these issues. A list of important contemporary land-use problems would include the following:

1. **Urban sprawl.**   There is widespread concern in the United States, and much commentary, about the spread of suburban areas out into areas that were once farmland and forest. Is this loose, decentralized, spread-out pattern of urban/suburban growth the best? Should it be discouraged or encouraged?

2. **Resource preservation.**   Some of the land subject to strong development pressure has unique ecological values. Wetlands, for example, are tied into basic hydrological systems; scenic lands are well suited to public parks. How are the values of these lands to be recognized, and what steps are appropriate for their protection?

3. **Implications of land-use regulations.**   Public regulations to control land use are common throughout the country, and pressure is strong to tighten these regulations to ensure certain land-use patterns. But the benefits and costs of these regulations often fall on different people. What is the efficient and fair action for society to take in cases like this?

4. **New types of regulations.**   Traditional land-use control regulations have been based on the police power that the U.S. Constitution gives communities to make decisions. Might other types of land-use policies give better results?

▪ Social Efficiency in Land Use

The first question to consider is what do we mean by a pattern of land use that is **socially efficient**? A given region, such as a community or river basin, has a large number of "parcels" of land. For example, if we define a parcel as one acre, then the number of parcels is equal to total acreage. Any acre can be put to many purposes: agriculture, residential, industrial, commercial, recreational, and so forth. And within each broad category there are many subcategories: single-family vs. multiple-family homes, small office buildings, light vs. heavy industry, and so on. Any particular use, located on any given acre of land, will produce a stream of net benefits extending into the future. The net social benefit produced by an acre of land is usually called rent or, more appropriately, **land rent**. The rent on a piece of land devoted to any use represents the benefits produced by that use minus all the other nonland costs of producing these benefits. Suppose an acre of land, if used to grow potatoes, could produce $1,000 of potatoes annually at a cost (fertilizer, seed, labor, etc.) of $600. The annual rent this acre would produce in potato production is $400. Suppose that if a single-family dwelling were built on the acre, it would produce annual housing services of $4,800, at a cost (operating plus annualized capital costs) of $3,900. Then the rent the acre would produce is $900 per year.

A socially efficient land-use pattern in a region is one in which each acre of land in the region is devoted to the one use that yields the maximum land rent on that acre. Since each acre is producing its maximum rent, social efficiency obviously implies that aggregate land rent in the whole region is at a maximum.

If all parcels of land were exactly the same, it would not matter what uses were made of each one. The interesting thing about land, however, is that each land parcel is by definition unique. In any real-world setting, land differs according to geological and hydrological characteristics. Certain acreage may be capable of producing greater agricultural rents, some acres may have a scenic view, some acreage may have topographical features that make any sort of structures very costly to build, and so on. **Productivity** differences such as these produce differences in land rents according to the different types of uses to which the land is put. All land parcels must also be unique in terms of **location**, since no two acres can occupy the same spot. This is important because the benefits produced by a piece of land will normally depend on its location with respect to land that has complementary, or competitive, uses. The rents produced by land devoted to housing depend on how close the land is to employment opportunities; the value of land devoted to commercial purposes depends on the geographical location of the land in relation to other enterprises that provide essential inputs; and so on.

Compounding the problem of identifying the distribution of land uses that maximizes overall land rents is the abundant network of environmental and natural resource interrelationships that affect net benefits of nearby parcels of land. A factory built next to a group of houses may produce effects (smoke, scenic disruption) that reduce the value of the housing services, and therefore of the land rents, of these neighboring lots. Land devoted to a highway will often have impacts (noise, dust) that affect the rents of nearby land. Agricultural practices can affect neighboring land both negatively (dust, smells, contamination of groundwater) and positively (scenic values). These impacts are often what we think of as external costs and benefits, though whether they are really external depends on ownership factors—how property rights are distributed.

How much rent a piece of land in a particular use produces and how this rent is **distributed** among different parties are two different issues. Suppose I own a small factory and my net profits, after deducting all **nonland costs** (including the opportunity cost of my own skills and time) are $5,000. Suppose the town in which I am located charges me $1,000 per year to lease the land on which the factory sits. Then the land rent of $5,000 ends up partly ($4,000 of it) in my pocket and partly ($1,000 of it) in the coffers of the community. Besides taxes, the distribution of land rent depends also on the state of **competition** in the various markets in which parcels of land are traded.

■ Land Markets and Prices

Even in a relatively small region, the number and heterogeneity of parcels and the number of different uses to which each parcel could be put mean that the number of different ways of distributing these uses among the parcels will be extraordinarily high. How should we (i.e., society) seek to find the one land-use pattern that maximizes land rents? In the United States, as in most other countries, we rely on a **private land market** to do most of the work of determining what uses of land are located on which parcels of land. The private land market works the way all markets do: Buyers and sellers agree on the terms by which land, or sometimes just the services of land, will be transferred between them. The most important aspect of the transaction is the price, because it is the price that reflects all the thousands of factors that go into determining the usefulness and desirability of using a particular piece of land for a particular purpose.

Consider a parcel of land devoted in perpetuity (or at least for a very long time) to a particular use, say, a house, or a small office building, or a public park. The use in question generates a stream of **annual net benefits,** or annual land rents. The present value of this stream of annual rents can be written explicitly as

$$PV_R = R_0 + \frac{R_1}{1+r} + \frac{R_2}{(1+r)^2} + \frac{R_3}{(1+r)^3} + \ldots$$

where R stands for annual rent and r is the discount rate. If the Rs in the numerators are all the same, this sum equals

$$R_0 + \frac{R}{r}$$

Each different use of the land generates a different PV_R. In a completely free, competitive land market, the market price of a parcel of land equals the highest of all the different possible PV_Rs associated with the different ways that the land could be used.

The reason for this is that in the bids and offers of buyers and sellers in the land market, all the potential net benefits associated with owning a piece of land will be **capitalized** into its price. Suppose, for example, a piece of land is currently used for farming, and in this use it has a value of $5,000 per acre (i.e., the present value of rents when the land is used for agriculture is $5,000). Now suppose that, because of the growth of a nearby town, the land could potentially produce a stream of rents (as house lots) with a present value of $12,000. If there is a competitive land market, the market price for this (and similarly situated) land will increase to $12,000, even though it is still used for farming. This is because the price will be bid upward to reflect the potential rents the land could produce, not what they happen to be producing in the short run.

Thus, all changes in the net benefits producible by a parcel of land, as long as these accrue to the owner of that land, will get capitalized into its price. For example, suppose in an urban area steps are taken by pollution control authorities to reduce the level of air pollution. There is no direct market for clean air; people do not literally buy and sell quantities of clean air. But if cleaning up the air in the community adds $85 per year to the net benefits of living in a house there, the prices of land on which to build houses, or of land on which houses already exist, will increase to reflect the capitalized value of these new net benefits. The land prices, in other words, will increase by an amount[1] equal to

$$85 + \frac{85}{1+r} + \frac{85}{\left(1+r\right)^2} + \frac{85}{\left(1+r\right)^3} + \ldots = 85 + \frac{85}{r}$$

There are several provisos to the idea that land prices reflect land rents. One has to do with **land taxes**. Virtually every community in the country raises a portion of its revenues through land taxes; in many cases this is by far the largest source of funds. The part of land rents that is paid in taxes is not capitalized into its price since these rents do not end up in the pockets of the buyers and sellers in the private land market. Thus, communities have sometimes attempted to use differential tax rates to affect land rents and the uses to which land is put within their borders.

Another proviso is that land prices do not necessarily reflect all the net benefits associated with the use of the land. Land prices adjust to reflect (i.e., "capitalize") all net benefits that accrue to the user of the land. But if some net benefits accrue to others, they are not so capitalized. The best example of this is certain environmental impacts that particular land uses may have. Suppose, for example, that a certain large parcel of land is expected to be used for building a number of single-family dwellings. The price of land in this parcel will reflect all the benefits and costs that will accrue to those who end up living in the houses: amenity values (perhaps the land is close to a public park), value of time in commuting (perhaps it is near a rail commuting line), value of time to the nearest grocery store, and so on. But suppose the land is also a strategic component of watershed and building houses on it will impact negatively (i.e., inflict costs) on others who live downstream from the new development. These are external costs. Were they to be capitalized into the prices of the land in question, these prices would be lower (because net benefits are lowered). But because they are external costs, they will not be so capitalized. In cases like this, normal market prices of land will not accurately reflect all the social benefits and costs arising from the uses creating the externalities. By the same token, the prices of land in the proposed development may be affected by external costs and/or benefits flowing in from elsewhere. If a factory is built next to this land, for example, land prices will be pushed down because of the external costs stemming from this source.

A third factor to remember is that land prices reflect **future** net benefits, which in the real world will always be uncertain to some extent, and subject to the ebb and flow of expectations. These can be volatile, especially in areas undergoing, or expected to undergo, shifts in land use.

■ Public Policies and Land Use

Land markets work through the private interactions of individual buyers and sellers. Groups of people, especially groups working through their governmental institutions, can affect the way land is used. We provide first a brief catalog of these means and then set up a simple example to illustrate each one:

1. **Working through land markets.** Both public and private groups (as well as individuals, for that matter) can simply work through the **private land market,** buying, selling, exchanging, or otherwise engaging in voluntary transactions that affect the way land is used.

2. **Eminent domain.** The power of **eminent domain** essentially means the power that recognized political authorities have to condemn property for a public purpose. Condemnation involves the forced appropriation of property and must be accompanied by **fair compensation.** This is a power possessed by federal and state governments and usually delegated by them to local governments and to some quasi-governmental organizations, such as electric companies.

3. **Police power.** The **police power** means the power that governmental authorities have to regulate the behavior of citizens so as to ensure the health, welfare, safety, and morals of the public. This is a power of local governments, not the federal government. Police power regulations include **zoning regulations, subdivision controls** (e.g., minimum lot-size requirements), **building codes,** and **environmental regulations** (e.g., wetlands protection regulations). Whenever these police power tools are applied, the ongoing question in particular circumstances is whether they represent valid exercises of a community's right to govern itself, or "takings" of private property that are forbidden by the U.S. Constitution unless compensation is paid.

4. **Taxes.** Governments have the power to tax, and **property taxes** are an important source of tax revenues. But beyond their revenue-raising capacity, they may also be applied in such a way as to encourage or discourage certain types of land use.

The easiest way to illustrate the strengths and weaknesses of these policy approaches is to apply them to a simple example. Suppose there is a parcel of land that is currently owned by a farmer and used to raise crops. Suppose, however, that suburban growth is encroaching into the region and that the land is also valuable as a site for a housing development. Suppose, further, that if the land is used for farming purposes, it produces substantial net benefits from two other sources besides the crop production: scenic values and wildlife protection values. These last two types of net benefits accrue to members of the broader community, however, not simply to the farmer herself.

The numbers are illustrated in table 14-2. It shows annual flows of net benefits per acre together with the price per acre of land if these net benefits are fully capitalized, in this case at 5 percent. Actual land prices, however, represent only those parts of land rents that accrue to the user of the land in question. The scenic and wildlife benefits are external to the land user.[2] These two types of resource services are also **public goods.** Thus, land prices do not reflect these sources of value produced by the land when it is used for agricultural purposes. The farmer can maximize her wealth by converting the land from agriculture to house lots. Since land prices reflect private rent flow in these two uses, the farmer can do this simply by selling the land to a developer. Assuming competition in this market, the selling price would be $8,000 per acre, which is twice what the land would sell for if it were to be used as a farm.[3]

Table 14-2   Land Rents and Prices for Alternative Land Uses

Land Use	Farmer	Society
	Annual land rents per acre ($)	
Agricultural	200	600
House lots	400	400
	Land price per acre ($)*	
Agricultural	4,000	12,000
House lots	8,000	8,000

*The present value of a perpetual stream of rents is equal to $PV = R/r$, where R is the rent and r is the discount rate. The numbers in the table were discounted at 5 percent.

From the community's standpoint the maximum net benefits, or land rents, are achieved if the land is kept in agricultural uses. We are assuming, of course, that these scenic and wildlife values are known. Net benefits accruing as incomes to land users are relatively easy to measure because they are capitalized into land prices. But the external values are not, so other means have to be found for estimating them. Suppose, now, that the community wishes to take steps to make sure that the land remains in agricultural use. We now consider the different ways it has of trying to achieve this.

Working through the Market

The first apparent option is for the community simply to purchase land. The advantage of this approach is that the price the community is willing to pay probably would bear some relation to the net benefits accruing to the community members from the scenic and wildlife preservation functions. On the other hand, there are the public good, free-rider problems, mentioned above.

If the community does not purchase the land, it perhaps could be purchased by a private group. In the United States and many other countries, there are many private **conservancy groups** whose objective is to operate in the land market to preserve ecologically sensitive land. Deriving the bulk of their funds from members' contributions, these groups then seek to purchase land areas that, in our terminology, produce substantial values in the form of ecological services.

Land preservation through purchase can often be achieved if communities or other groups purchase only partial rights from the landowner. They might purchase from the farmer only the right to develop the land, not the entire **fee simple** ownership of the land.[4] In our example, the **development right** alone is worth $4,000 per acre to the farmer. The land without this right attached to it is still worth $4,000 for agricultural purposes. So the community could forestall development by purchasing the development rights for $4,000 an acre rather than the entire fee simple right for $8,000 per acre.[5] Purchasing development rights is similar to purchasing a **conservation easement,** a legal instrument that creates an enforceable agreement between a landowner and public agency or private group. It restricts development and certain other activities that may be inconsistent with conserving the ecological values of the land. For an example of a private initiative of this type see exhibit 14-1.

There is another way that the private market might provide a solution to this land-use problem. If a market existed, or could be brought into being, that would allow the farmer to receive some or all of the scenic/wildlife values as revenue, then her own private wealth-maximizing decisions could lead her voluntarily to maintain the land in agriculture. Perhaps the wildlife situation is such that hunters, fishers, or wildlife watchers would be willing to pay to have access to the wildlife resources of the farm.[6] Perhaps tourists would be willing to pay to be close to, or to participate in, actual farm operations. In some cases there may be substantial potential for market revenues of this type.

Eminent Domain

The right of **eminent domain** means the right to condemn property and acquire it for a public purpose. The legal rules of eminent domain require that the landowner be paid "just compensation" for the land. Eminent domain is used primarily to obtain land to be devoted to a specific and concrete public purpose, such as a highway, a power line right of way, or a reservoir. These are essentially public facilities required for the production of what most people would regard as essential services in the modern world. Eminent domain might also be used to acquire land for a public park; in this case amenity services are being produced. In our example, questions would

Exhibit 14-1   Using the Market to Protect Land from Development

Cooperative Conservation—Ranchers Unite to Save the Land for Cattle, Wildlife, Way of Life
The image of the lone rancher punching cows and cursing environmentalists has gone by the wayside—at least for the Malpai Borderlands Group.

With Malpai, ranchers run a nonprofit cooperative dedicated to conserving rangeland and preserving a ranching way of life. They work with scientists, an assortment of government agencies, and even environmental groups. They don't see cattle in competition with wildlife.

Malpai area ranches cover 800,000 acres of rangeland stretching from the San Bernardino Valley in southeastern Arizona across the state line into New Mexico's Peloncillo Mountains. To date, 13 ranchers have signed on with the group.

Ranchers in the area can sell conservation easements to the Malpai group, instead of whole chunks of ranchland to developers. The property stays with the ranch, but it cannot be subdivided and built upon. Grazing is still allowed. The push for easements came on the heels of an ongoing drought, which has cut into ranching incomes as drier ranges make for fewer cows to sell.

So far, the Malpai group has bought conservation easements from 12 ranches. "We've protected 77,000 acres of private land from ever being developed," according to the executive director of the Malpai group.

What's open space for cattle is open space for wildlife and native plants as well. So, perhaps, it's not too surprising Malpai ranchers would find themselves allied with the likes of The Nature Conservancy, a high-profile environmental group.

In 1990, The Nature Conservancy purchased the 300,000 acre Gray Ranch in the heart of the Borderlands to preserve the biological uniqueness of this ecologically rich area. After a period of inventory and planning, the Conservancy sought a buyer who shared its vision for the ranch. A nonprofit corporation, the Animas Foundation, was created for the purpose of buying and operating the Gray. They purchased the ranch, with certain conservation easements held by The Nature Conservancy. The objective of the Animas Foundation is to demonstrate sustainable agriculture in harmony with the environment—a goal that is completely compatible with the Malpai Group goals. The foundation is particularly important to the group in that they own more than a third of the planning area.

Source: USDA, Natural Resources Conservation Service, *NRCS This Week* (www.nrcs.usda.govinews/thisweek/2005/110205/coopcon.html); accessed 3/7/07; and R. Randall Schumann, *The Malpai Borderlands Project: A Stewardship Approach to Rangeland Management* (www.geochange.er.usgs.gov/sw/responses/malpai); August 2013.

come up as to whether amenity and wildlife values represent public purposes that would justify land condemnation.

Although condemnation might not be legal in our case, we can use the example to illustrate a major problem in eminent domain cases: the problem of what is **just compensation**. Courts usually define this to mean **fair market value**. This sounds quite specific, but problems can easily appear when trying to apply the idea. Which market is appropriate? The market governing the land's current use? In our example the price of agricultural land is $4,000 an acre. Or should the price be the market for a different use? In our case the market price of the land as a housing development is $8,000 an acre. Or should it be a market price adjusted for amenity values that may exist even though they don't show up in standard market prices? In this case the fair price might be something approaching $12,000 an acre.

Another issue in determining just compensation is that current owners may attach personal values to a property that exceed its current market price. Suppose the farmer in our case is one of a long line of mothers and daughters who have been born, have lived, and have died on this farm, and who have an attachment to it in excess of its current market price. The market price is, after all, a number applying to average sale prices of similar properties over some recent time period. The current owner may value it more highly than this, for any number of personal reasons. Is the market price fair in this case?[7]

Police Power

Communities have the constitutional right to exercise the **police power** to ensure conditions that promote public health, welfare, and morals. For example, they can establish speed limits, require homeowners to fence swimming pools and keep their property picked up, or mandate local factories to avoid conditions that damage public health. They also have certain powers to regulate the way land is used. The most basic right that communities have under the police power is the power to designate the types of uses to which specific parcels of land may be put. This is done through **zoning ordinances**. A typical zoning ordinance divides a community into zones or districts, and designates the types of uses that are permitted in each zone. A typical zoning plan, for example, would designate zones for single-family dwellings, multiple-family dwellings, light commercial, industrial, and so on.

The basic principle behind zoning is to regulate externalities. Certain uses, if located next to other types of uses, are likely to create external costs that would devalue the affected properties. Thus, a factory constructed in a residential area would be expected to inflict external costs in the form of noise, unsightliness, and congestion.

The biggest problem with zoning plans is that they do not address the underlying economic incentives of the situation. Suppose that the farm in our example is placed in an agricultural zone. This does nothing to change the fact that the farmer could realize a substantial increase in wealth if she could get permission to sell the farm to a developer. She could perhaps take the town to court over the zoning plan. More likely she would appeal the zoning designation, asking the local **zoning board of appeals** for a **variance** that would allow the sale to proceed despite the zoning plan. Even though the potential gain from getting a variance might be modest today, in a number of years it could be much greater if the demand for houses continues to grow.

Communities may also use the police power to make specific regulations governing the use of land within their boundaries. Many communities in the United States, for example, have laws that allow a local **conservation commission** to deny a building permit for any structure that would adversely affect wetlands or other ecologically sensitive lands. Most communities also have **planning boards**, which can legally enforce subdivision regulations, such as requirements for streets, sidewalks, and sewers. The regulatory approach to land-use control involves an ongoing struggle between two ideas: the rights and responsibilities of communities to encourage conditions that are conducive to the public welfare, and the rights and freedoms of private individuals to use and enjoy their property in ways they see fit without hindrance from political authorities. The struggle has seen a long series of court battles and legal pronouncements that have evolved over time as people have changed and as the problems faced by communities have changed. The conflict centers on the **takings clause** of the U.S. Constitution, and it is of sufficient importance that we devote a section to it later in this chapter.

For now, however, we return to our simple land-use example and consider the last type of policy approach that a community might take to affect land use.

Land Taxation

Communities typically levy **property taxes** to raise government revenues. Taxes affect the flows of the net benefits landowners receive from land in particular uses, so taxes also affect the incentive landowners have to choose one use over another. Property taxes are usually set at some proportion of the **appraised value** of a property. The appraised value, in turn, is usually based on the supposed market value of the properties. It is "supposed" because for properties not on the market, which includes most of them, a market value has to be estimated by comparing them with properties that have recently been traded.

Property taxation strategies are often used on the rural/urban fringe, where land is frequently converted, usually from agricultural uses to domestic uses. One technique employed by many communities is "use-value taxation." Suppose the community in our example is seeking to keep the farm in agriculture use. If the farmland is taxed at its market value, the tax should be based on what it would expect to sell for if it were devoted to a housing development. In the example this is $8,000 per acre. A way of reducing the tax burden of the farmer, and thus supposedly making it easier for her to continue the farm, is to base the tax on its value in current use, or use value. This would be $4,000 per acre, a tax bill only half as large than if the tax were based on market value.

If land prices are rising rapidly on the rural/urban frontier, the modest effect on farm net income implied by use-value taxation may not be sufficient to outweigh the potential wealth gain that land sale and conversion to houses would produce. Another drawback of some use-value taxation programs has been that by reducing the costs of holding land prior to actually developing it, it can increase the incentive for developers to purchase agricultural land and target it for eventual development. The tax program essentially reduces the developer's cost of holding the land. To reduce this incentive many use-value tax programs require land developers to repay back taxes that were saved by holding the land in agriculture. But the financial penalty of this type of procedure, especially in the face of briskly rising land prices, may not be strong enough to reduce the overall incentives of the practice.

■ Land-Use Economics and the "Takings" Issue

The Fifth Amendment to the U.S. Constitution dictates: "No person shall be . . . deprived of life, liberty, or property, without due process of law; nor shall private property be taken for a public use, without just compensation." This language clearly authorizes governments to take title to private property, provided that it is for a **public purpose** and that it is accompanied by just compensation. Eminent domain cases of this type usually involve physical takings, where land is taken for the construction of a school, road, or reservoir. We discussed earlier the issue of defining just compensation. In a number of recent instances of communities exercising their police powers, however, landowners have argued that the resulting **regulations** have had the effect of taking their property, even without physical invasion of the property. If these cases are in fact takings, then the Constitution requires a clear public purpose and that the landowners be compensated. In the absence of compensation, the regulations would be regarded as an unconstitutional taking of private property.

The "takings" issue raises the following question: Under what conditions does a local land-use regulation amount, in effect, to an unconstitutional taking of private property and require, as a result, either just compensation for the effects of the regulation or a rescinding of the regulation by the authority that issued it? Property rights proponents, who interpret the language strictly, take the position that any regulation that reduces the value of a property right ought to be considered a taking. Advocates of more active public regulation take the position that communities ought to have leeway to enforce a wide range of regulations for the public good without having to face the financial burden of paying compensation to affected landowners.

Thoughts and opinions on the interpretation of the takings clause have gone back and forth over the decades and centuries. The final arbiter is the U.S. Supreme Court, which over the years has rendered many decisions on takings cases. The content of these decisions has reflected both the nature of the cases and the jurisprudential views of changing members of the Court. A recent case on the takings issue was the **Lucas decision** relative to a conflict in a coastal region of South Carolina.[8] Going into the case, there was reasonably widespread agreement with the view that public regulation via the police power is warranted as long as it does not go "too far," but if a regulation does go beyond some point, it constitutes a taking. The question is, where is that point?

Mr. Lucas purchased two beachfront lots in 1986 for $975,000. Nearby lots had already been developed with condominiums, and he fully expected to be able to build similar structures on his lots. The lots were not in any publicly recognized critical area, and therefore a permit to develop was not required. Two years later, however, the South Carolina legislature passed the Beachfront Management Act, which effectively prohibited the construction of any occupiable improvements on the lots in question. Lucas sued on grounds that the regulations effectively denied him all economically valuable use of the lots. The trial court in South Carolina agreed, but the South Carolina Supreme Court reversed on the grounds that no compensation was required for regulations meant to prevent serious harm to the public.

The U.S. Supreme Court, however, reversed the decision, taking the position that the regulation did in fact constitute a taking. The Court based this decision on several grounds:

1. The regulation essentially deprived Lucas of the entire economic value of the property; that is, it rendered the land essentially valueless to Lucas.

2. When Lucas purchased the property there was no prohibition in place, and while normal land transactions must be concluded in the light of some possible future regulatory constraints on the land, Lucas had no good reason in this case to expect that the subsequent regulation would render the land totally valueless to him.

3. The Beachfront Management Act was overly vague in terms of the specific social harms it was attempting to avoid and the general types of land-use prohibitions that were necessary to accomplish this.

The takings issue will continue to be politically and jurisprudentially controversial in the future. It is a major line of collision between the rights of individuals to be free of outside political interference and the rights of communities to constrain individual behavior in the name of the public good.

■ The Economics of Urban Sprawl

We have discussed how the prices of land are ultimately determined by the maximum potential land rents flowing from parcels of land devoted to particular uses. This also implies that the uses to which land is put in practice are related to land prices. So by looking at spatial patterns of land rents and land prices, we can (usually) understand land-use patterns as they actually have developed or as they are likely to develop in the future. One common application of this idea is to look at the typical ways that cities develop spatially. Figure 14-1 on the next page shows two **rent gradients**. A rent gradient is a curve showing how land values diminish with distance from "downtown." One shows the gradient of land devoted to houses. This type of graph has to be understood as a stylized relationship; in the real world there are many local details that affect its shape. But in general it starts high and diminishes with distance, reflecting the higher costs of commuting as distance increases.[9] The agricultural rent gradient is also declining, but it starts lower and is more gradual. The gradients cross at point d_1; this is the **urban/rural fringe**.

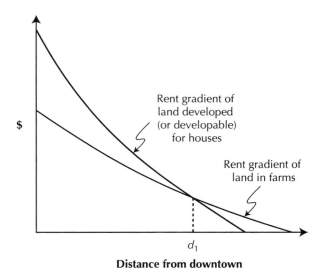

Figure 14-1   Rent Gradient, Showing Land Rates for Developed (or Developable) Land and Agriculture

Of course, the boundaries between land-use types are seldom as sharp and clear as that depicted at d_1. Geographical factors such as hills and bodies of water intervene, highway configurations create irregular patterns of travel cost, and so on. Yet the basic pattern is accurate. By considering how changes in the underlying factors give rent gradients their basic shapes, we can understand how they affect overall land-use patterns in and around urban areas.

We can use some of these insights to investigate the phenomenon of **urban sprawl**. "Sprawl" is usually used negatively. From the previous discussion we have seen that there is a natural tendency in any urban area to progress from high-price, high-density commercial use in the city center to low-density, lower-priced lands in the suburbs, with a transition to agriculture on the urban/rural fringe. Sprawl refers essentially to a situation in which the housing rental/land-price gradient has an overly shallow slope such that the entire urban area spreads over a very large region and the rural fringe extends a long way into agricultural areas. This leads to the conversion of large amounts of increasingly remote agricultural and forestland, with the natural resource consequences this implies.

The visual manifestation of urban sprawl is the construction of low-density suburban housing developments on the fringe. Sometimes there is **leapfrogging**, as developers go out somewhat past the current fringe to build houses, with the land areas over which they have vaulted being left to fill in later with additional developments. Very often, open land outside the current fringe is purchased and held for future development well in advance of planned construction times. This can induce pronounced changes in the ways these close-in rural lands are used. Land in the "holding mode" may not be devoted to particularly productive land uses, so that when the time comes to convert the land to houses, there is no especially strong sense of losing any important natural resource values.

In many places, sprawl has been accentuated in recent years in the development of edge centers—secondary centers of high-density commercial development that have materialized some distance out from the center of the large, parent urban district. These edge developments can push out new higher land-price gradients into the underdeveloped lands lying beyond the old urban/rural fringe, thus increasing the development pressure on these lands.

What is the efficient level of sprawl? Clearly, sprawl can be managed with vigorous public policies. In Great Britain, for example, sprawl has been closely controlled with public regulation; so many towns have relatively high-density development right up to the rural fringe, which tends to be much more sharply defined as compared to the typical case in the United States.

Sprawl, however, represents a trade-off. On the one hand are the lost natural resource values of the land that comes under urban pressure, as well as the added costs (e.g., transportation costs) of living and working in a geographically dispersed urban/suburban pattern. On the other hand are the benefits accruing to people who are able to live in a way that the majority of them apparently want, which is in a single-family house with a reasonably sized lot around it. Of course, if people did not wish to live in this fashion, but preferred living in higher-density areas near city centers, sprawl might not be a problem. The qualifier "might" is necessary because land-use patterns are a direct reflection of housing preferences only if the prices they face are competitively determined, are not affected by unpriced external costs or benefits, and are not subsidized. In urban and suburban regions of the United States, and in many other parts of the world, externalities and subsidies are rampant. The net effect of these may be to encourage urban growth that spreads too rapidly.

A major factor behind sprawl is transportation costs, especially the costs of automobile commuting. Road access is typically unpriced in the United States. While there are some toll roads, most are not, so the cost of driving an extra mile includes only car operating costs and the cost of the time of the people in the car. Because of this, the marginal cost of commuting—that is, the cost of commuting the marginal mile—are below social marginal costs. The effect is to encourage people to commute longer distances than are socially efficient. It is possible that subsidies to home buyers have the same effect. Because of the way that federal and state tax laws are written, tax liabilities may be lowered for those people who have home mortgages. The effect of this may be to lower the effective price of homes in the suburbs, thereby increasing the quantity demanded and encouraging suburban sprawl.

■ Land Management Issues on the Urban/Rural Fringe

Nowhere is there a more complex and vigorous struggle about the way a natural resource is to be used than on the expanding fringe areas that mark the advance of urban/suburban settlement into surrounding rural/agricultural areas. Colliding interests are the norm: developers, homeowners, farmers and other landowners, environmental interests, economic development interests, transportation groups, community groups, and diverse public agencies are regularly involved, each with its own views about how land in general, and certain parcels in particular, should be used.

Over the years, communities and groups have developed a substantial arsenal of means to control land conversion. The main ones are listed in exhibit 14-2. They vary from classic zoning ordinances to individual contracts between towns and developers to third-party actions (e.g., actions by nonprofit environmental groups). The political, demographic, and economic complexity of these cases makes it hard to clearly see the major cause-and-effect relationships that are involved. From our standpoint perhaps our biggest interest is to understand how these various development practices and regulations affect the natural resource and environmental endowments of the urban/rural fringe.

One way in which zoning regulations are used in **edge communities** is establishing **density limits** for development. This can be done through **large-lot zoning**, requiring that all house lots must have a minimum total acreage. Or it might be through establishing explicit limits on development in terms of the number of housing units allowed on developed parcels. The

---

Exhibit 14-2   Methods Used By Communities to Control Land Development

Throughout the United States and in other countries, communities have many ways of controlling and shaping the quantity and quality of land development within their boundaries. Some of these are the following:

- **Zoning regulations**: This is the most common approach, usually supplemented with other means. Zoning can be used to restrict the amount and density of development by specifying minimum lot sizes, maximum structure sizes, and other development features.

- **Tax relief or public grants**: Monies for nonprofit organizations that purchase ecologically sensitive fringe lands and manage them in ways that preserve environmental values. The generic name for this type of organization is conservation trust.

- **Impact fees**: Fees must be paid by developers to proceed with a project. These fees are usually justified by the added costs the community will experience (such as schools and roads) as a result of the development. Impact fees have gained greater importance in some states where traditional property taxes have been limited by law.

- **Contract zoning**: In return for rezoning a development tract, developers are required to proceed in specified ways regarding number and layout of units, road and sewer construction, and so on.

- **Public/private contracts**: These contracts are concluded between public authorities and landowners in fringe areas whereby the latter, in return for annual payments, agree to adopt environmentally sensitive land management practices.

- **Outright land acquisition by public agencies**: Acquisition conserves sensitive natural resources. Acquisition can be the full transfer of fee simple ownership or a partial rights transfer such as purchase of development rights in cases where some private use is compatible with ecological preservation.

- **Land-use covenants**: Groups of propinquitous landowners agree to rewrite their land deeds so that they, and any future owners of the affected properties, are enjoined from engaging in certain types of land uses or management practices.

normal justification given for density limitations is to ensure that overall population growth is kept at a moderate pace, that new homes are of the sort that will maintain or lift average property values in the community, and that it will preserve a substantial amount of natural coverage of the land, such as woodlands, wetlands, and open areas.

The problem that immediately suggests itself is the potential perverse impacts of this approach. Consider the total fringe area of a specific community. The following simple relationship holds:

$$
\begin{array}{ccc}
\text{Total acres} & \text{Number of} & \text{Acres used} \\
\text{developed} = & \text{new houses} \times & \text{per new house} \\
(A) & (NH) & (A/NH)
\end{array}
$$

Rules that establish maximum densities in particular communities are, in effect, increasing A/NH. For a given NH, therefore, this works so as to increase A, the term on the left. When individual communities seek to limit development densities within their borders, it tends to work in the direction of increasing the total amount of land that is converted on the fringe; that is, it tends to encourage suburban sprawl.

Most of the development and density control measures undertaken on the suburban fringe in the past have been aimed at supporting property values. In essence, communities have sought to control the development process so as to ensure that **property values** have been maximized. Some conflicts have involved **natural resource preservation** issues, for example, making sure that development does not impinge on watersheds that nourish important surface or groundwater resources.

In recent years a new motive has been added to the mix, that of **preserving the habitats** of important species of plants and animals. Austin, Texas, has experienced phenomenal growth and suburban expansion. In the early 1980s, the U.S. Fish and Wildlife Service placed on the official list of endangered species the black-capped vireo, a small bird that was once fairly extensive in the western United States but now is confined to a few small areas in Oklahoma and Texas. Plans for new, large housing developments in Austin had the potential to encroach on vireo habitat situated on the (then) outskirts of the city. After a great deal of conflict and political struggle, a plan was adopted to alter normal development processes to preserve some portions of vireo habitat. This and similar cases led the U.S. Congress in 1982 to alter the Endangered Species Act to provide for a mechanism with which to reconcile the incentives of developers and the desire for habitat preservation to protect endangered species.[10] The law calls for the development of **habitat conservation plans**, which basically are a vehicle for creating specific development plans that provide some degree of protection for affected species at a moderate cost.

Another prominent land-use issue in the last few decades is the **protection of wetlands**. Wetlands, in a variety of forms, are found throughout the country. Locally, they may be called swamps, bogs, potholes, marshes, fens, or some other name. They provide a number of valuable hydrological and biological services, the exact nature and extent of which varies according to their location, size, and relationship to adjacent land and water areas.

■ Land Use in Uncertain Environments

In the example discussed earlier, we assumed that there were two alternative land uses (farming and housing development) and that the annual rents flowing from each were **known with certainty**. In the real world, this is usually not the case. Not only do economic variables cause land rents to vary from year to year (e.g., the fluctuating price of agricultural crops), but nature itself can cause rents to vary. Homes built in floodplains or along seashores are subject to storms and flooding; land in seismically active regions is subject to earthquake damage; droughts, hurricanes, and wildfires have their impacts. The main questions here are: (1) How do uncertainties of this type affect efficient land-use patterns, and (2) Do normal private markets function efficiently when uncertainties of this type are important?

Suppose there is a parcel of land on which one might build a house. In an average year, the benefits of living in this house in this particular location would be, say, $1,400, and the costs (including capital costs[11] plus operating costs) would be $600. Net benefits would be $800, which, capitalized at 5 percent, would yield a value of $16,000. In a competitive market, the price of this parcel would be equal to these capitalized rents.

Now suppose this were beachfront property. This kind of property is frequently subject to storm damage, such as from the high winds and waves kicked up by hurricanes along the eastern coast of the United States. Let us assume that in this situation there is a 10 percent chance that the house will be completely destroyed. Thus, we have the following situation:

	No storm (90% chance)	Storm (10% chance)
Benefits	$1,400	$0
Costs (operating)	600	600
Net benefits	800	−600

Now we can calculate the expected value of net benefits, which is the average of net benefits over a very long string of years, 10 percent of which have storms. The expected value of net benefits equals:

$$800 \times 0.9 + (-600) \times 0.1 = \$660$$

and the capitalized value of this at 5 percent is $13,200.

If market participants react to risk in a straightforward fashion, we would expect the market price of this property to be reduced because of the likelihood of periodic storm damage. Suppose an insurance company now steps in and offers storm insurance at **actuarially accurate rates**; that is, at premium rates that accurately reflect annual expected losses. The insurance covers the lost benefits in the case of destruction of the house by a storm. Thus, the insurance company's losses will be $1,400 × 0.1 = $140. Suppose this much is charged as an insurance premium to the homeowner. Their situation is now:

	Annual
Benefits	$1,400
Costs (operating plus insurance premium)	740
Net benefits	660

which, again, capitalizes to a value of $13,200. The presence of the insurance, in other words, does not change land prices, but only the distribution of net benefits flowing from the use of the land.

Why, then, do people build houses right next to the San Andreas fault in California,[12] or on low-lying coastal lands in the East, or on floodplains? A major reason is simply that the benefits associated with living in these locations outweigh the costs, even when the costs include risks associated with natural events. Another reason is that special public programs reduce the effective costs of these events, thereby leading people to make riskier decisions. A good example of this is the program of **federally subsidized flood insurance**. For people living in areas prone to flood damage, this program provides insurance against such losses at relatively modest premium rates, rates below those that would apply if they were set on the basis of real expected damages. In other words, they are sold at rates below cost, with the general taxpayer covering the difference. The impact of this is that net benefits, or land rents, rise by an amount equal to the value of the subsidy.

Suppose, in the example above, federal flood insurance were available at a cost of only one-quarter of the actuarially sound price. Since the latter is $140, the government price is assumed to be $35 per year. Now the net benefits to the homeowner for a typical year are:

	Annual
Benefits	$1,400
Costs	635
Net benefits	765

and the capitalized value of a net benefit stream of this amount is $15,300. The subsidized insurance, in other words, lifts land prices and will lead people to use land in a socially inefficient way.

This type of problem is an ongoing feature of publicly provided flood insurance. Of course, it is a characteristic of any public program that lowers the cost of **foreseeable risk**. Federal disaster relief is often used to lower people's burdens after natural disasters. There are powerful humanitarian motives behind this program. If the relief serves basically to lower the cost to people of predictable disasters, it may actually lead to higher losses in the future, as people persist in making overly risky decisions. Only if disaster relief is forthcoming for truly unpredictable natural events will it tend not to produce these perverse results.

■ Managing Public Lands

So far this chapter has focused on private land markets, how they operate, and how they might be managed to move toward socially efficient land-use patterns. Another important set of land-use issues in the United States, as well as many other countries, revolves around how publicly owned land should be used. In the United States, 29 percent of the total land area is owned by the federal government. State and local governments also own a substantial amount of land. These land areas vary from spectacular natural wonders to barren wasteland, but many of them are under demand for their natural resources. Because they are publicly owned lands, however, these demands are normally not mediated through the private market, but rather are managed through the decisions of various public agencies. Thus the expression of the demands and the decisions about the uses to which public lands are put are part of a lively political process in which groups contend for influence and try to shift the uses of the public lands in directions that are congenial to their own interests.

The number of different activities pursued by visitors to public lands is very long: hiking and camping (day, overnight, and wilderness), animal watching and sightseeing, hunting (big game, small game) and fishing, timbering, mining, snowmobiling and use of all-terrain vehicles, boating of all types, livestock grazing, scientific study, and others. Conflicts arise because these activities often are not compatible with one another. Cutting timber may interfere with sightseeing and camping, white-water boating may conflict with fishing, wilderness hiking is not compatible with use of all-terrain vehicles, and so on. Public agencies typically deal with these conflicts by specifying a list of permitted activities for the areas under their management. This is usually part of their legislative and administrative "charter," with a certain amount of local variation tailored to the features of particular sites. Exhibit 14-3 presents information on the range of permitted activities in the areas managed by the four major federal land management agencies: the National Park Service (NPS), National Forest Service (NFS), Bureau of Land Management (BLM), and Fish and Wildlife Service (FWS). Material relevant to the activities managed by these agencies is located in other chapters: chapters 18 and 19 for the FWS, chapter 17 for the NPS, and chapter 12 for the NFS. We discuss some simple conceptual issues here.

When a range of permitted activities is specified in general enabling laws, local managers' decisions are already constrained to some extent. Significant problems can still exist, however, in terms of whether the activities that are permitted should be pursued together throughout an area or whether managers should identify separate nonintersecting portions of the land for the pursuit of each activity by itself.[13] Suppose two activities might be pursued on a given land area. Should both be allowed over the whole area, or should it be divided, with one activity allowed on one part and the other on the other part? The relevant comparison would seem to be straightforward: the sum of the net benefits of the separate areas compared to the

Exhibit 14-3   Public Lands Managed by Federal Agencies in the United States

Four federal agencies administer most of the 640 million acres of federal land (28% of the land in the United States): the National Park Service (NPS), the Fish and Wildlife Service (FWS), and the Bureau of Land Management (BLM) in the Department of the Interior, and the Forest Service (FS) in the Department of Agriculture. The majority of the federal lands (92%) are in 12 western states, and the federal government owns more than half of the land in those states (54%, ranging from 27% in Washington to 83% in Nevada).

The National Park System

The National Park Service (NPS) manages 85 million acres in the 401 units of the National Park System (also NPS). NPS has many diverse categories for its units, with 20 different designations. The largest units are the national parks, preserves, and monuments.

National Parks. Fishing is allowed in most national parks, but hunting and resource development activities (e.g., mineral extraction and timber harvesting) generally are prohibited unless grandfathered or expressly permitted in the park's authorizing legislation.

National Preserves. Management of national preserves is generally similar to that of national parks, but typically allows fishing and other recreation allowed in the parks, along with hunting and mineral extraction, as long as the natural values for which the preserve was established are not jeopardized.

National Monuments. Permitted and prohibited uses in national monuments are largely the same as in the national parks: many recreation uses are allowed, although hunting may be restricted or forbidden. Wood cutting and most commercial activities are usually curtailed but mineral extraction may be allowed.

In addition to these categories, the NPS has numerous other designations, including national battlefields, historic sites, national seashores and lakeshores, and more. The NPS also administers 19 national recreation areas (NRAs), while 19 are administered by the FS, one by the BLM, and one by the Tennessee Valley Authority. Recreation is the dominant use, but other uses may be allowed in NRAs including recovery of timber or mineral resources, livestock grazing, watershed protection, and resource preservation as long as these uses are compatible with the primary purpose for which the area was set aside.

The National Wildlife Refuge System

The Fish and Wildlife Service (FWS) manages 89 million acres in 512 national wildlife refuges, 198 waterfowl production areas, 50 wildlife coordination areas, and 114 other sites.

The National Wildlife Refuge System Administration Act of 1966 and the National Wildlife Refuge System Improvement Act of 1997 direct the FWS to administer the system primarily to conserve and enhance fish and wildlife and their habitats. Only uses compatible with these general purposes, and with any specific individual purposes set out for each refuge, are permitted. For example, grazing and mineral activities are permitted in certain refuges and under certain circumstances; hunting, fishing, and other recreational uses generally are permitted in wildlife refuges.

The Public Lands [Bureau of Land Management]

The BLM administers 247 million acres concentrated in 12 western states: Alaska, Arizona, California, Colorado, Idaho, Montana, Nevada, New Mexico, Oregon, Utah, Washington, and Wyoming.

BLM manages the public lands for sustained yields of multiple uses: livestock grazing, outdoor recreation, wood production, water supply, wildlife and fish habitats, and wilderness; mineral extraction also is allowed.

(continued)

The National Forest System

The Forest Service (FS) manages the 193 million-acre National Forest System (NFS), consisting of 155 national forests, 20 national grasslands, and 112 other areas. NFS lands are concentrated in the West, and the FS manages more than half of all federal land in the East.

Congress has provided uniform, general management guidance for most NFS lands. As with the public lands, NFS lands generally are administered for sustained yields of multiple uses.

Special Systems

Three special management systems have been created to protect particular features or characteristics of the natural environment, namely wilderness areas, trails, and wild and scenic rivers.

National Wilderness Preservation System. The Wilderness Act defines the purpose of wilderness as "devoted to the public purposes of recreational, scenic, scientific, educational, conservation, and historical use." The Act generally prohibits commercial activities (e.g., timber harvesting), motorized access or mechanical transport, and permanent roads, structures, and facilities in wilderness areas.

National Trails System. National trails are administered by the FS, NPS, and BLM, many in cooperation with appropriate state and local authorities. Most recreation uses are permitted, as are other uses or facilities that do not substantially interfere with the nature and purposes of the trail. Motorized vehicles generally are prohibited on system trails.

National Wild and Scenic Rivers System. As of 2014, 203 rivers totaling 12,602 miles have been included in the National Wild and Scenic Rivers System. The principal protection of the wild and scenic river designation is the prohibition of water resource projects which may divert or hinder the flow of the river. Management of permitted use varies with the class of the designated river.

Source: Excerpted from Ross W. Gorte, *Federal Land and Resource Management: A Primer,* Congressional Research Service, RS 20002, December 22, 1998, Washington, DC; and Katie Hoover, *Federal Lands and Natural Resources: Overview and Selected Issues for the 113th Congress,* Congressional Research Services, R43429, December 8, 2014.

net benefits of the two activities when they are pursued together over the larger area. Two primary factors determine the outcome of this comparison: (1) the nature of the interaction between the activities and (2) the variation in the quality of the area that makes some parts of it more suitable to one activity than to the other.

The activities could vary from compatible to antagonistic. Limited clear-cutting of timber may be quite compatible with small-game hunting (because it creates animal-attracting edges) and not at all with big-game hunting. All-terrain vehicles may be incompatible with most other activities (except perhaps forestry and mining), so separate areas for this type of activity may be called for. Snowmobiling and cross-country skiing are likely to be antagonistic, while fishing and day or overnight camping are much less so. We are speaking here essentially of the nature and extent of external costs that different activities inflict on one another. Separate facilities are called for when the external costs of combined usage outweigh the direct benefits of the activities arising from allowing them over a wider area.

Research is required to estimate these externalities and benefits with any degree of accuracy.

The other important factor affecting the desirability of mixing or separating activities is variation in the qualitative characteristics of the land itself. Some portions of a national park may clearly be better suited to sightseeing, and some to remote hiking and camping. Certain areas may lend themselves to forestry or livestock grazing, whereas others do not. As with most other variables, the adaptability of an area to specific activities is not a yes-no situation but rather a more or less. This puts a premium on knowledge about the relationships between site characteristics and the benefits that accrue to people using them for different activities.

■ Summary

Land is the ultimate resource in the sense that it is the surface of the earth on which the activities of humans and of nonhuman organisms are concentrated. Land is an important resource in two senses: in terms of its physical properties and the ecosystem functions it supplies and in terms of its role in the spatial distribution of human activities. Efficient patterns of land use are those that maximize the net benefits of the activities distributed over its surface. Land prices are the capitalized values of net benefits, or land rents. Land prices are affected both by physical and locational aspects of land parcels and by taxes and external benefits and costs that flow among the uses to which different parcels may be put. The land rent/price gradient is a way of showing the structure of land prices in and around an urban area; it is useful in studying decisions involving open-space preservation and the impacts of land-use controls. Public methods to control land-use patterns include outright purchase, eminent domain, and the police power; the latter includes such approaches as zoning, subdivision controls, and environmental regulations. A major ongoing issue in the exercise of the police power to shape land use has been the takings issue. Public policy can also have an impact on land use by affecting the probabilities of loss and the degree of risk from such things as floods, earthquakes, and storms. The chapter concluded with a brief discussion of management issues on public lands.

Notes

[1] This is based on the standard relationship for equal annual payoffs over an indefinitely long period of time:

$$\sum_{t=1}^{\infty} \frac{M_t}{(1+r)^t} = \frac{M}{r}$$

[2] In actual situations, of course, the farmer would also likely accrue a small portion of these benefits. In Florida, for example, some ranchers receive satisfaction knowing that the Florida panther inhabits their ranches. The vast bulk of the benefits, however, are external.

[3] Of course, the market may not be competitive. There may be relatively few developers to compete with one another; for example, the farmer may not have a good idea of what house

lots are being sold for. This simply means that the price agreed upon by farmer and developer will lie somewhere between $4,000 and $8,000. Some of the stream of discounted rents, in other words, will end up in the bank accounts of the developer. The $8,000 is assumed to reflect the costs it would take to convert the land and build the houses; in other words, it is based on the net returns from houses.

[4] Fee simple is a legal term meaning the entire set of use rights of a piece of land.

[5] There is a substantial caveat here. The community's ultimate objective is to preserve agriculture. Buying the development right will forestall development, but this is not the same as preserving agriculture. If at some future time the net income from farming becomes too low, the land may be abandoned rather than farmed. Of course it may still produce some benefits as abandoned land.

[6] In the western United States, and in some European countries, private landowners in some cases generate revenues by selling rights to fish in streams and rivers passing through their lands or hunting rights for game animals on these lands.

[7] If the farmer attached such a high value to the farm she might not be tempted to sell it to a developer. But the community may not have a very good idea about the strength of these values. Many farms that have been in families for generations have ended up in houses.

[8] *Lucas v. South Carolina Coastal Council*, 505 U.S. 1003, 1992.

[9] In fact land at or close to downtown would presumably be more valuable in commercial use, but to keep things simple we have not drawn a commercial rent gradient in the figure.

[10] For a discussion of this case see Charles C. Mann and Mark L. Plummer, *Noah's Choice*, Knopf, New York, 1995, pp. 175–211.

[11] Annual capital costs are the annualized amount of construction costs.

[12] The San Andreas fault runs near San Francisco, and is the source of the great San Francisco earthquake and fire early in the twentieth century. Seismologists have been predicting, for a number of years now, that a new major earthquake is likely to occur in the vicinity of this fault.

[13] In the policy world, the doctrine of mixing uses is called *multiple use*. The idea is set out in the Multiple-Use Sustained Yield Act of 1960.

Key Terms

development rights	land taxes
eminent domain	leapfrogging
externalities	police power
fee simple	rent/price gradient
just compensation	takings
land market	uncertainty and land prices
land prices	urban sprawl
land rent	zoning

Questions for Further Discussion

1. Suppose a town allows me to operate a small ferry from a point of land in the town to a small island not far away. My operating costs are $50,000 per year, and my total revenue is $62,000 per year on average. Is the $12,000 difference a land rent? The land in question is the site where the ferry dock is located.

2. A piece of land has a market value of $4,000 if used for agricultural purposes. A land "speculator" buys some of the land, paying $6,000 an acre. Five years later she sells it to a house builder for $14,000 an acre. The builder builds a house for $100,000 and sells it (and the land on which it

sits) to a homeowner two years later for $136,000. Assuming the land market and housing market are both competitive and that there was no inflation during all of this, what is the total land rent in houses, and how was that rent distributed among farmer, speculator, builder, and homeowner?

3. A community enacts a regulation that keeps people from building houses within 500 yards of the top of any hill in town. The stated purpose of the law is to protect the scenic quality of the town. Do you think this regulation amounts to an unconstitutional taking of private property?

4. How would the rent gradient of a city change if a new four-lane expressway were built from the middle of the city out to the next city, which is 100 miles away?

5. How do interest rate changes affect land prices?

Useful Websites

Maps on land use, land resources, and characteristics:

- Earth Resources Observation System (EROS) of the U.S. Geological Survey (http://www.eros.usgs.gov)

Land-use and natural resource problems in North America and around the globe focusing on sustainability, social conflict, and political economy:

- University of Wisconsin Land Tenure Center (http://www.nelson.wisc.edu/ltc)

Using the market to accomplish land preservation:

- Nature Conservancy (http://www.nature.org)

Public interest groups focusing especially on the use and abuse of public lands:

- Sierra Club (http://www.sierraclub.org)
- Wilderness Society (http://www.wilderness.org)
- Friends of the Earth (http://www.foe.org)

The U.S. Center of Excellence for Sustainable Development, with a lot of attention focused on land-use issues and the consequences of sprawl:

- (http://www.sustainable.doe.gov)

For wetlands laws, check out the publications by the Congressional Research Service, available through the National Library for the Environment:

- (http://www.thecre.com/fedlaw/legal34b/84171448.htm)

Selected Readings

Barlowe, Raleigh. *Land Resource Economics: The Economics of Real Estate,* 4th ed. Englewood Cliffs, NJ: Prentice-Hall, 1986.

Duke, Josh, and JunJie Wu, eds. *The Oxford Handbook of Land Economics.* Oxford, England: Oxford University Press, 2009.

Goetz, Stephan J., James S. Shortie, and John C. Bergstrom, eds. *Land Use Problems and Conflicts: Causes, Consequences, and Solutions.* New York: Routledge, 2004.

Harvey, Jack, and Ernie Jowsey. *Urban Land Economics*, 6th ed. New York: Palgrave Macmillan, 2003.

Johnston, Robert J., and Stephen K. Swallow, eds. *Economics and Contemporary Land Use Policy.* Washington, DC: Resources for the Future, 2006.

Levine, Jonathan. *Zoned Out: Regulation, Markets and Choices in Transportation and Metropolitan Land Use.* Washington, DC: Resources for the Future, 2006.

15

Water Resources

Water resources are critical to human development. Water is a biological necessity for human existence, like air. But the importance of water resources extends far beyond this—to public health, economic development, and the health of ecosystems.

Most of the water on earth is salty. Throughout history this has not been available for human consumption, but recent developments in desalination technology and increases in the scarcity of freshwater have turned many communities toward the ocean for freshwater supplies. Much of the global supply of freshwater is more or less locked up in glaciers, ice caps, and elsewhere. This means that freshwater supplies for humans and ecosystems must come from the relatively small amounts that run off as **surface water** or are contained in accessible **groundwater** aquifers.

If all freshwater supplies were spread perfectly evenly about the globe, there would be few water shortages. But, of course, they are not. Some regions enjoy a plentiful supply, whereas others face extreme scarcity. In the United States there is great variation in natural freshwater supplies. In general, the eastern half of the country is humid and reasonably well watered, while the western half is arid or semiarid where rainfall and runoff are restricted.

■ Water Use in the United States

Table 15-1 details how water is used across the United States and how this has changed since 1960. Total withdrawals were increasing for many years, but recently have been decreasing, as have withdrawals per capita, which in 2010 were 40% below that of 1980. Agriculture and industrial uses account for the biggest withdrawals; withdrawals for domestic use amount to only 13 percent of the total in 2010. There is a great deal of regional variation in water withdrawal practices. Irrigation is largely a western phenomenon, which increases the per capita withdrawals for those regions. In addition, the states with more industries obviously have larger water-use quantities.

279

It is interesting to look at per capita **domestic** water use; this can be determined by taking the sum of public supply and domestic self-supply in relation to population. Thus, domestic use amounted to 128 gallons per person per day in 1960, 163 gallons per person per day in 1980, and 145 gallons per person per day in 2010.

The data in table 15-1 also show that about 20 percent of water withdrawals come from groundwater aquifers and 80 percent from surface waters. For coastal states a substantial portion of surface water withdrawals are saltwater used primarily as cooling water in power plants and industrial cooling.

Table 15-1   Estimated Water Use in the United States

	1960	1980	2005	2010
Total withdrawals				
(billions of gallons/day)	270	440	410	355
Population (millions)	179.3	229.6	296	313
Withdrawals per capita (gallons/day)	1,506	1,916	1,385	1,134
Withdrawals				
Public supply	21	34	44.2	42.0
Rural domestic self-supply	2	3.4	3.8	3.6
Irrigation	110	150	128	115
Livestock and aquaculture	1.6	2.2	10.9	11.4
Industrial				
Power plants	100	210	201	161
Other	35.4	40.4	22.2	22.0
Source of water				
Groundwater	50.4	83.9	82.6	79.3
Surface water	253	361	328	275

Source: Barber, N. L., 2014, *Summary of Estimated Water Use in the United States in 2010. U.S. Geological Survey Fact Sheet 2014–3109.*

It needs to be emphasized that these are **water withdrawals;** that is, water taken out of the lakes and streams that make up the natural water system. A substantial amount of this water is returned through runoff or wastewater. Amounts that are not directly returned are called **water consumption.**

These aggregate withdrawal data do not immediately reveal the extent of water resource problems in the United States. For the public at large, the perception of water problems probably tends to wax and wane according to hydrological factors. In the East, the last major drought was several decades ago, so today perhaps a somewhat relaxed attitude prevails about water supply issues. In the arid West, where urban population growth has led to the construction of massive water supply systems[1] and where a major drought has occurred in the last few years, water problems are always higher up on the public agenda.

Important contemporary water resource problems in the United States include the following:

1. In the East, there is a continuing need for the effective management of large water systems, public, and private, to adapt to the demands of growing urban and suburban populations.

2. In the U.S., as well as in many other countries, growing urban areas have put stress on water-supply systems. In many cities water-supply infrastructure is in need of expansion and modernization, at the same time that public budgets have tightened.

3. There are growing scarcities of water from many **groundwater aquifers** used heavily for freshwater supplies. In the East, many aquifers have been contaminated from chemicals or from saltwater intrusion. In the West, many large aquifers have been exploited at rates far exceeding recharge rates. In these cases, municipalities and water-supply organizations have been forced to turn to alternative freshwater supplies.

4. In the West, urban areas are searching for new sources of water to support their rapidly growing populations. One possible source is to **transfer water** that would normally go to agricultural irrigation. Water transfers of this type and magnitude have enormous legal, economic, and social ramifications.

5. Throughout the country, demands are growing for **instream water services,** like boating, fishing, ecosystem protection, and scenic values. These must be balanced with traditional demands for water withdrawals.

In this chapter we examine some of the economic analytics that can advance our understanding of these problems.

■ Water Law in the United States

We have stressed many times the importance of **natural resource law** in shaping the way resources are utilized and developed. **Water law** is a prime example. Water is given by nature in certain quantities at certain locations and at certain times. How it is ultimately developed and used is critically affected by the status of the law regarding who has the legal right of ownership or of utilization. Water law has evolved and changed in extent and complexity in response to the demographic, technological, and geographical changes that have occurred over the last 350 years in the United States.

Surface Water

When the first European settlers organized their farms and communities along the northeastern U.S. coast in the 17th century, they found hydrological patterns quite similar to those with which they were familiar. The lands were well watered in general, with an abundance of streams, lakes, and rivers. Being at the time subjects of the English Crown, they naturally applied English legal doctrine to these water resources. By this doctrine, the rights to the use of water (other than for irrigation, which was a right reserved to the government) belonged to those people who owned the banks of the streams or lakes in question. This was known as **riparian water rights,** a word stemming from the Latin word *riparius,* meaning "situated on the banks of a natural watercourse or body of water." Only riparian landowners have a right to the water; non-riparian landowners, and any others who might be interested in how the water is used, do not have legal rights to the water. Each riparian landowner has rights to a "reasonable" use of the water; no one of them may use water in such a way as to damage other riparian landowners.

When settlers ventured into the western part of what was to become the United States, they found that climate and hydrology were very different from the East. In particular, water was much more scarce and consequently the climate much more arid. At first some of the new western states tried to adopt riparian water law, but it quickly became clear that a legal doctrine suited for humid, water-abundant regions would not work in cases of relative water scarcity.

If riparian law were applied to multiple landowners along a low-flowing river in an arid environment, it would be difficult for any one of them to have water sufficient to support an efficient-sized operation. Because of this general kind of problem, a new type of water law developed in many parts of the western United States—the law of **prior appropriation.**

Prior appropriation essentially gives water rights to the first person who appropriates it and makes beneficial use of it. It is sometimes called "first in time, first in right." While riparian water law tends to see water rights holders as equal in status, prior appropriation creates priorities such that first users have rights that take precedence over those coming later. So the first to divert water for irrigation would have the **senior** water right in this case; that is, the absolute right to all the water needed. Those coming later would have **junior** rights, meaning that they could gain rights over that portion of the water not used by senior appropriators. Appropriation water rights are also "use it or lose it" rights. The right exists only so long as the water is actually used; if use stops, the right is lost.

Most of the small- and medium-sized rivers in the West were fully appropriated by the end of the 19th century. The result was a widespread system of privately built diversion ditches, small impoundments, irrigation works, and the like. During the first two-thirds of the 20th century, the federal government sponsored a massive construction program of large dams and canals, primarily for irrigation purposes. This action thoroughly involved the federal government with western water issues. In recent years the huge growth of urban population centers in parts of the West has led most states to get actively involved in managing their water systems. Thus some areas trend toward **administered systems,** in which public agencies are more actively involved in regulating surface water use and in making the trade-off decisions this implies.[2] And with increasing emphasis on maintaining maximum instream flows, the trend is toward a kind of riparian approach in which rivers must be managed so as to balance competing interests.

Groundwater

The law of groundwater resources is different from, but related to, surface water rights. Groundwater is extracted from underground **aquifers,** the geohydrological characteristics of which vary widely. They range enormously in size, some being small and local and others very large interstate formations. Some aquifers have very slow **recharge rates,** whereas others have more rapid rates; some recharge rates are steady, others vary greatly from year to year. In many cases they are hydrologically interconnected to surface water resources, recharging from, and discharging to, water in streams and lakes.

Early English groundwater law, which provided the foundation for early U.S. law, conferred the rights of absolute ownership to those who held surface rights over an aquifer. Essentially this allowed any landowner to pump as much as he wished out of the aquifer without regard to any impact this might have on other landowners who might be extracting water from the same aquifer. Assuming a limited size and a small recharge rate, this puts groundwater resources in the category of **open-access resources,** which we discuss from a conceptual standpoint in chapter 6. We explore there how open-access resources tend to get overexploited because of the "use it or lose it" incentives facing those who utilize the resources. Or, more technically, because of the **open-access externalities** those individual resource users inflict upon one another. In effect, when one person or group of people pumps water without restriction from a groundwater aquifer, it can adversely affect the water supply available to others using the same aquifer. In the West, groundwater law developed in a way consistent with **prior appropriation.** Senior rights to specific quantities could be claimed by the first to exploit the resource, and, subject to limitation, these could be defended against subsequent claimants.

The conflicts these doctrines have produced in situations of ever-increasing demand have led to change. In the eastern United States the idea of **reasonable use** is important. Any overlying landowner is allowed to make reasonable use of water from the aquifer. This rules out uses that might be regarded as wasteful or excessive, as well as transfers to non-overlying landowners. More recently some eastern states have moved toward outright systems of **withdrawal permits.** These involve public agencies issuing permits to water withdrawers that specify maximum quantities of water that may be withdrawn. Many western states have also moved toward more administered groundwater systems. Through the specification of groundwater management areas, a state or regional agency may be empowered to set and enforce rules, such as permit requirements, well spacing requirements, well construction standards, allocation preferences, limited pumping rates, restrictions on place of use, and water use monitoring and reporting.[3]

Alternatively, an aquifer (or surface source) may be regulated by formal or informal private groups who take it upon themselves to impose restrictions on their members. These are sometimes voluntary and more-or-less spontaneous or organized in the light of **enabling rules** set by a state of regional governmental body.

■ Water Pricing

Fundamental to the delivery of any good or service and its distribution among users is the way its price is determined. In a market economy, buyers and sellers interact and trade, and out of this comes the prices of the items traded, which shift up or down through time as supply and demand factors change. If there are reasonable levels of competition among buyers and among sellers, well-defined property rights, and few important externalities, the established prices are efficient and the quantities traded are socially efficient. That is how it works in principle and sometimes in practice. But in the real world any number of factors can upset this process. Some are technical, such as the way users are jointly related when they are hooked up to a single water system. Others are political in nature, brought on by public authorities intervening in markets for one reason or another.

Water is a good example of the latter. Water is usually thought of as something special, with qualities that make it different from "normal" commodities. One can get along without many goods, but one cannot get along without water for very long. In urban areas people have few alternatives when it comes to water; they either hook up to the same system everybody else is on or go without. Nor is it possible to run a modern public sanitation system without copious amounts of water.[4] All of these tend to give water a special status in the eyes of consumers and political authorities. One implication of this is that, over the years, politicians and other public authorities have had a lot to say about how water has been priced. This obviously has had enormous implications for the way water has been used and for the demand for expansion of water supply systems.

Average-Cost Pricing

Most domestic water in the United States is supplied by **public water supply companies.** These entities essentially function as public utilities, holding monopoly positions within communities and subject to the oversight of public advisory boards or commissions. The pricing ideas of these groups have usually determined the actual prices that water supply companies have set. Among the general public, and especially among public administrators, the widespread belief is that the basic reason for having prices at all is to cover the costs of production. For those in charge of water and other public utilities this leads to a **cost-based pricing rule:** Set prices so that revenues cover costs. Revenues should not fall short of costs because if they do, losses presumably have to be made up some other way, for example, from general tax revenues. Nor should revenues exceed costs, because this implies profits, which are thought to be inappropriate for public enterprises. This type of reasoning has historically led to what is called **average-cost pricing.** The total costs of delivering water are divided by the total quantity of water delivered, and the unit water price set accordingly.

The efficiency implications of average-cost pricing are easy to see. Figure 15-1 shows a supply and demand curve for water for a community water supply system. MB is the marginal benefits function, while MC is the long-run marginal cost function based on the costs of delivering water. Note that the demand curve for water is drawn as downward-sloping to the right, just like any other good or service. Water is necessary for life, in particular the biological requirement of two of three gallons per day. But considering the large quantities consumed by the average person in the developed world, it is in fact an economic good. The water consumption of an average U.S. household is several hundred gallons per day, which means that, at the margin, it is being used for many purposes well beyond the biological maintenance of life. Thus, in the normal range of prices, water may be regarded as a normal economic good.

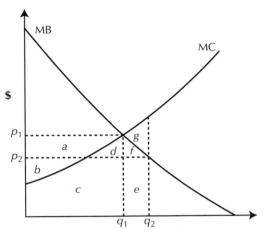

Figure 15-1   Marginal and Average-Cost Pricing

Given the basic relationships of figure 15-1 the efficient quantity of water is q_1 gallons per year, and the market-clearing price for this is p_1 per gallon. Suppose the water company charges this price. Total costs of water supply are equal to the area $c + d$. But total revenue is equal to price times quantity, or the rectangle $a + b + c + d$, which clearly exceeds the amount $c + d$. So if the utility sets its price this way, it will run a profit, in both appearance and fact. To avoid profits, therefore, utilities usually price below marginal cost, for example, something like p_2 in the figure. By setting the price this way, it can find the point where total cost ($c + d + e + f + g$) is equal to total revenue ($b + c + e$). But a price like p_2 is not efficient. The amount of water demanded at that price is q_2, and if the utility produces at this level there will be a discrepancy between marginal cost and marginal benefits; the latter will be below the former. The utility will produce some water for which the marginal valuation of consumers is lower than the marginal costs of production.[5]

Pricing with Diminishing Marginal Costs

Figure 15-1 is drawn with an increasing marginal cost curve, analogous to all of those shown in previous chapters dealing with other resources. The costs of a water system include the costs of conveyance systems and the costs of procuring the supplies of water, surface or ground,[6] that are delivered to consumers. As systems are expanded, the need to reach out farther for additional supplies often implies a rising marginal cost curve.

There may be circumstances, however, where marginal costs actually go down. This may be the case, for example, in cases of ample supplies and where relatively modest additions to the conveyance system are sufficient to provide substantially more capacity. This situation is depicted in figure 15-2. Suppose price is established where MB = MC, a condition of efficiency. Then the water supply company will have revenues (equal to the area labeled b) insufficient to cover costs (area $a + b$).

How do we establish efficient pricing (p = MC) in conditions of declining marginal costs? One possibility is to institute declining block pricing—a higher price (that is, higher than p^* in the figure) for the first quantity of water (some quantity less than q^*), and then a price of p^* at far higher consumption levels. While this solves the efficiency problem in the short run, it has the unfortunate implication that lower prices lead to higher consumption levels, which runs against notions of the desirability of water conservation.

Another pricing approach for conditions of declining marginal costs is a **fixed connection charge** coupled with a per gallon water consumption price. The per gallon price, assuming it is set at p^* as in figure 15-2, is suffi-

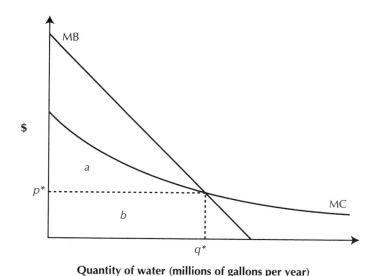

Quantity of water (millions of gallons per year)

Figure 15-2   Declining Marginal Costs

cient to assure efficiency at the margin, while the connection charges cover the cost overage that would otherwise occur.

Investing in Water Supply Systems

The discussion of how **existing water supplies** are allocated—especially how water is priced—can provide some very interesting insights into the ways water is used and misused and into the efficiency and equity implications of changing water utilization practices. Throughout the country, however, communities and water supply companies are faced with a whole range of investment decisions related to the overall **size or capacities** of their systems. These situations might include, for example:

1. Investments to protect existing water supplies (e.g., a community has to decide whether to buy land in the watershed area around its reservoirs so that development on these lands will not threaten water qualities and quantities in the reservoir).

2. Shifts from one type of water supply source to another (e.g., a coastal community faced with saltwater intrusion into its groundwater supply considers whether to switch to a desalination plan).

3. Investments in the existing system that increase system capacity (e.g., a community may decide to replace some of the existing water mains to reduce leakage).

4. Expansions of the existing system (e.g., a community has to decide whether to build an additional reservoir or new water canals to another surface water source in order to increase the total capacity of its water supply system).

All these situations call for **investment-type decisions;** that is, decisions in which most of the costs occur today or in the near future whereas most of the benefits are in terms of future consumption values—often very distant ones. Cases like this require techniques that we discussed earlier for making decisions that have future consequences: some way of predicting accurately what future costs and benefits will be, and the discounting of future values so that all investment costs and benefits are in terms of **present values.**

But in reality it is not really possible to separate the water-pricing problem from the water system investment problem. Investments affect future supplies, and prices affect future demands and thus the balance between demand and supply. Consider figure 15-3 on the following page. Suppose that at the present time the water demand curve for the community in question is D_1 and the price of water is currently p_1. This means that the quantity of water demanded is q_1. Suppose that this quantity q_1 is also equal to the present capacity of the water system. Thus there is a balanced situation, with neither excess demand nor excess supply in the system.

Suppose also that the community believes that because of anticipated economic and demographic growth, future water demand will also grow. For purposes of illustration, suppose that in 10 years the water demand curve is

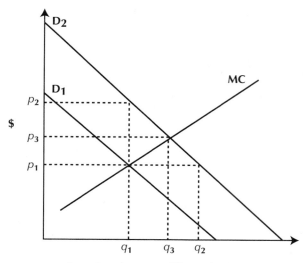

Figure 15-3 **Pricing and the Addition of Capacity to a Water Supply System**

expected to be D_2. The community must now give thought to its water supply system. If it does nothing and the new population materializes anyway, there will be excess demand at the old water price of p_1. At that price, with demand curve D_2, the quantity of water demanded is q_2, which is substantially in excess of the capacity of the current system at q_1. The excess demand could be wiped out if the price were raised to p_2, because even with the expanded demand, the quantity demanded at this higher price would not exceed the capacity of the current system.

It's unlikely that water planners would countenance such an increase in water price, however. Not only would consumers have to pay much higher prices, but the water utility or company would probably make sizable profits in that situation. More than likely, the planners would think in terms of adding capacity to the system by investing in additional water supplies (enlarging a reservoir, adding a new reservoir, or perhaps drilling additional wells). Here is where price comes in. If the planners seek to maintain the current price of water, they need an increment to capacity of $q_2 - q_1$ million gallons per day; because at a price of p_1, quantity demanded with the higher demand curve is q_2 million gallons per day. If future prices are somewhere above p_1 but below p_2, then the increment in capacity could be somewhere greater than zero but less than $q_2 - q_1$. What's the right course of action?

There are several ways to answer this question. From the standpoint of economic efficiency, however, the answer depends on how much it costs to increase the capacity of the system. In technical terms, it depends on the shape of the long-run marginal cost curve (i.e., the supply curve) for water. Suppose this is horizontal, in other words the system can be expanded in such a way that the costs (capital costs plus operating costs) of delivering the water are constant. Then, indeed, the efficient system increment is equal to $q_2 - q_1$, and the efficient price of water remains at p_1.

But suppose the long-run marginal costs of added capacity are upward-sloping, such as depicted in the curve labeled MC that goes through the original price-quantity combination p_1, q_1. This would be the case, for example, if adding capacity becomes increasingly costly. We would probably expect this to be the case, especially in arid or semiarid conditions. Cities may find that they have to reach out farther to get additional water supplies, or they may have to bid additional water supplies away from other users at higher prices than they are currently paying. Even in relatively humid areas, marginal costs may increase if people have to turn to increasingly costly sources of water. With rising marginal costs, the efficient course of action is some combination of higher price and added quantity. With the MC curve as depicted in figure 15-3, the efficient course of action is to increase system capacity to q_3 and raise the price of water to users to p_3.

Conflicts over the price of water have been common, and pressures on these public companies have been to keep prices reasonably low. These considerations do not directly address the political-economic aspects of pricing and capacity. Since most water supply systems have been owned by public organizations, they have normally been open to local political pressures. But this makes it more difficult to accumulate funds for necessary expansions and maintenance of the systems. This has led many municipalities to consider privatizing their systems, thinking that private companies would have fewer constraints on pricing and raising the money needed for the system. But this tends to run against many peoples' view that water is a special commodity and its provision ought not to be operated strictly as a private "bottom-line" firm.

▪ Water Rights Transfers and Markets

Recently the city of San Diego offered to pay $225 per acre-foot[7] for water for which farmers in the nearby Imperial Valley were paying $15.50 per acre-foot.[8] The cost of getting an acre-foot of water from the Imperial Valley to San Diego is substantially lower than the price difference, since they are connected to the same system of large water transport canals in southern California. The reason for the discrepancy is that the farmers of the Imperial Valley have been successful historically at acquiring water rights, largely rights to water from the Colorado River.[9] Cities in southern California, on the other hand, have struggled through the years to obtain additional water supplies to keep up with their exploding population. They have had to reach into northern California and elsewhere to obtain these supplies, which has made them very expensive.

Figure 15-4 on the next page depicts this situation graphically. There are two demand curves: D_c is the demand for water in the city, and D_i is the demand for water by agricultural irrigators. Due to the historical development of water rights, q_i is the quantity of water available to irrigators and q_c is the total quantity available to people in the city. The market clearing prices for these two quantities, given the demand curves, are, respectively, p_i and p_c. The price for irrigation water is far below that for urban uses. In a smoothly adjusting **market economy,** this condition would be something of an anomaly. In principle, the presence of potential **gains from trade** would lead to adjustments where resources shift out of the relatively low-valued

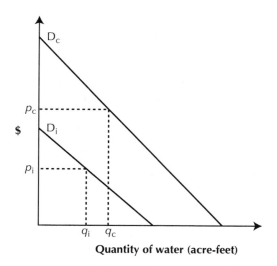

$

p_c

p_i

D_c

D_i

q_i q_c

Quantity of water (acre-feet)

Figure 15-4   Water Rights and Water Prices

uses and into the higher-valued uses. Economic markets are supposed to facilitate this process, with the result that the overall social value of the resources is maximized.

Water Transfers

In the world of water resources, large differences in water prices among users provides fairly strong evidence that this normal adjustment process has not worked. Figure 15-5 shows two water demand functions. The one on the left is for municipal and industrial (M&I) water used in an urban area. The one on the right is for water used in irrigation in the nearby farming area. Suppose that the cost per acre-foot of delivering water to the two uses is exactly the same. Because of the way water rights have been allocated in the past, the city is currently consuming q_1 acre-feet of water while irrigators are applying q_4 acre-feet of water to farms.[10] The marginal value of water for M&I purposes is p_1, whereas that for irrigation water is p_3. These are clearly very different. If we reallocated just 1 acre-foot of water from agriculture to M&I, we would have a gain of p_1 in the latter and a loss of p_3 in the former, hence an overall net gain of $p_1 - p_3$. In this figure some illustrative dollar numbers have been put on the vertical axis to help in understanding the problem. The marginal value of water for M&I is currently $80 per acre-foot. That for agriculture is $15. Gains from trade clearly exist. If an acre-foot of water is reallocated from agriculture to M&I, the net gain is $65 (the $80 gain in M&I minus the $15 loss in agriculture). As long as these marginal valuations differ, reallocations will continue to have positive net benefits. Thus, the total gain is maximized by reallocating to the point where the marginal valuations are equal, which is at a price of $30 in the figure. At that point, q_2 acre-feet go to M&I and q_3 to irrigation. The total net gain from the reallocation is $(a + b) - (c + d)$.

Suppose we have a situation like this in the real world. Should the water transfer be allowed, in whole or in part? Should it be facilitated somehow through public action? If so, how? If the commodity we were talking about were potatoes, we probably wouldn't spend much time worrying about it, because we would expect the flow of potatoes around the market to adjust to price discrepancies like this. But water may be different. Or is it? Historically, nobody has worried about potato rights, but water rights have long been fought over. If water is reallocated among users, and perhaps shipped from one location to another, the potential economic impacts could be far

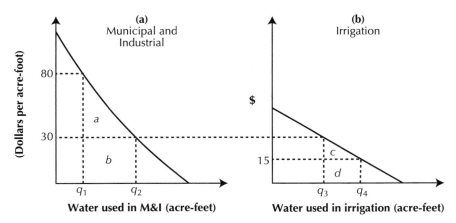

Figure 15-5   Mutual Gains from Trading Water Rights

reaching. Consider the question of how the transfer is to be made. In keeping with the earlier distinctions we made between different types of policy approaches (see chapter 7), there are two basic ways of doing this: an **administrative action** by a public regulatory agency or **transactions on a market for water rights.**

An administered shift in water rights would be carried out by a public agency, such as a state department of water resources, wherein one party's water rights are reduced and these rights are conferred on another party. This would be done by fiat, after ascertaining that the shift is in the **public interest** and using standard **regulatory enforcement procedures** to make sure that the change goes through. Changes of this type, especially large-scale shifts among different types of users (e.g., farmers vs. urban dwellers), usually spark energetic legal and political struggles. The outcome would probably depend as much or more on the political strengths and abilities of the participants as on the economic values (benefits and costs) of the proposed transfer.

The other way to effect the transfer is through transactions on a market for water rights. Market transactions occur because willing sellers meet willing buyers and trade something of value at a price agreed to by both participants. The buyers gain an amount $(a + b)$ from purchasing $q_2 - q_1$ of additional water in figure 15-5. The sellers lose an amount equal to $(c + d)$. It's possible to find a price per acre-foot that, when multiplied by $q_2 - q_1$, the quantity traded, allows both participants to gain from the trade. It will be lower than the gain experienced by the buyer and higher than the loss of the seller.

Water Markets

In the arid western United States, urban populations continue to grow, state and regional economies are increasingly moving away from agriculture, and the ability to meet new water demands by developing new sources of supply continues to diminish—hence the interest in transferring existing water supplies among users to foster its efficient utilization. But as these economies become more and more complex, it becomes increasingly difficult for a public water management agency to be aware of all the efficiency-enhancing transfers that might be concluded or to be able to carry out these transfers without continuous political conflict and turmoil. In recent years, interest has grown in moving away from administered transfers of water rights and toward greater reliance on water rights markets to foster the kinds of transfers depicted in figure 15-5. A water market would function analogously to markets in other types of goods and services: Willing sellers and buyers, individuals or groups, would be able to conclude private agreements to transfer given quantities of water at agreed-upon prices. As with any market, there would have to be rules and regulations covering these transactions. And this is a point of great controversy: Should the rules be set so that there are few limits on permissible water transactions? Or should public water agencies have direct oversight and control over all transactions? We return to this issue below.

Local water markets, for example neighboring irrigators trading small amounts of water among themselves, have existed for a long time. Even some large-scale transactions were carried out many years ago. The notorious Owens Valley case, where the city of Los Angeles secretly bought up agricultural land in the Owens Valley so that the attached water rights could be transferred to the city, took place in the 1920s.[11] But the 1980s saw a very substantial increase in transactions involving large amounts of water, transported longer distances, between different types of users.

In Colorado, cities along the Front Range (Denver, Colorado Springs, and Fort Collins) purchased agricultural water rights to satisfy increasing urban demands. Prices in the 1980s ranged from $1,000 to $5,000 per acre-foot of water (see exhibit 15-1). In Arizona, the cities of Tucson and Phoenix purchased "water ranches," agricultural lands that came with attached water rights. These sold for more than $1,500 per acre-foot in the 1980s. Albuquerque paid over $1,000 per acre-foot for agricultural water rights. In Nevada, developers and municipal water providers bought irrigation water rights in the 1980s for between $2,000 and $3,000 an acre-foot. During that decade Salt Lake City paid between $160 to $250 per acre-foot for irrigation water rights. These lower prices reflect the more water-abundant conditions of that area compared to the very arid southwestern states.[12]

Interest is still strong in expanding the scope for water markets in the future. In California, where huge state and federal water projects have historically made it difficult to transfer water rights, a federal law facilitates the development of water markets. The Central Valley Improvement Act of 1992 allows individuals or districts who receive water from the Central Valley Project (CVP) to sell some or all of their allocations to any beneficial use within or outside the CVP area.[13]

Exhibit 15-1   Functioning Water Markets

The Colorado Front Range consists of an area about 30–40 miles wide and stretching north to south just east of the Rocky Mountains. It contains the large cities of Denver and Colorado Springs and their surrounding suburban developments. Very large-scale water supply systems have been built so that people living in this area could import supplies of water to support economic and demographic growth. In the northern part of the area the Northern Colorado Water Conservancy District integrates the activities of dozens of different water service organizations operating canals, storage reservoirs, pumping facilities, and water treatment plants. One of these organizations is the North Poudre Irrigation Company (NPIC). This company issued 10,000 original shares of stock, each share of which entitled the owner to 6 acre-feet of water per year. There is a well-developed market for these shares, and they may easily be bought and sold. Shareholders may divide their shares into quarter shares, each representing about 1.5 acre-feet of water, in order to buy and sell smaller quantities of water. The rights are rather widely distributed among a variety of municipal/industrial, rural domestic, and agricultural water users. Prices of the shares (per acre-foot of water) were around $200 in the early 1960s, gradually rose to well over $1,000 in the late 1970s, and have since declined somewhat as alternative water sources have come online. Although NPIC water rights are highly marketable, there is a limit on the service area in which trades can be freely made. Sales of rights out of the service area may only occur after satisfying certain legal requirements.

For further information, see Zachary Marchlik, *The Effects of Climate Change on Water Markets in Colorado*. Honors thesis, University of Colorado at Boulder, Environmental Studies, 2014.

Another perspective on markets for water pertains to water shortages in urban areas, in which markets allow users to adjust their use in response to regulatory calls for reduction in water use due to droughts (see exhibit 15-2 on the following page).

Conditions for Social Efficiency in Water Markets

Although many people advocate increasing the role of markets in allocating water resources, many also remain skeptical about the ability of unfettered water markets to attain economic efficiency in the full social sense. And there are also many in the middle who think that water markets will be an improvement over past practices but that these markets will have to be carefully guided by responsible public agencies. We must first look at the requirements that have to be met if markets are to function in a socially efficient way. We can then consider whether these factors are likely to hold in the real world. There are two types of requirements: (1) the nature of the water rights themselves, and (2) the structure of the markets on which these rights are traded.[14]

For markets to perform well, property rights in water have to be **clearly defined, reasonably complete, secure, and transferable**. Transferability, of course, goes to the heart of the matter, because the willing transfer of the water right from one person or entity to another is what produces the **gains from trade**.

Exhibit 15-2   Water Restrictions with Water Trading

   A common response to temporary water shortages in urban areas is to institute mandatory, proportionate reductions in water use. This has the appearance of being fair, in that it requires the same reduction by each user. By some criteria it might be, by others it isn't. Consider the figure. There are two families, family A and family B, whose water demand functions are as shown. The current price of water is p_1, and for convenience we show initial consumption for each family as the same, q_1. Suppose that in a water shortage regime each household is required to reduce its consumption by the same amount, to q_2. We note that their valuation of water is different. Household B, perhaps because it is larger and because it has a greater number of teenagers, has a less elastic demand; household A has a demand curve with greater elasticity; perhaps much of the water it uses is for outside use, which can more easily be reduced. After the reduction, however, household A has a marginal valuation of water of p_A; that of household B is p_B. Whenever there are discrepancies, such as here, between the marginal valuations of the items in question, there are potential gains from trade. In this case both families would be better off by trading water between them, shifting water from A to B, at a price somewhere between p_A and p_B. A device for facilitating such an exchange, and similar exchanges between other families experiencing the shortage, is a water market. We note that a market in effect implies a different standard of equity: equity here implies the same marginal valuation of water, not equal quantities consumed.

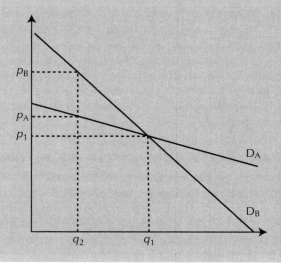

- **Clearly defined** means that there is no ambiguity about the nature of the right that is transferred. Many water management authorities, for example, appropriate a portion of an owner's water under certain circumstances.[15]

- **Secure** means defendable at reasonable cost. This requires that encroachers can be stopped, and that buyers and sellers can identify quantities of water that are actually transferred.

- **Reasonably complete** means a number of things: first that there are not unreasonable limits on the use to which owners may put their water. It also means that all affected parties have the right to participate in the market, and that all impacts forthcoming from a water transfer are tradable on the market.

Suppose I am a farmer who irrigates crops by withdrawing water from a nearby stream. Some of this water runs off and back into the stream; this return flow is used downstream by another farmer. Suppose now a nearby city comes to me and offers to buy my entitlement. They want to build a canal from my property to the city water treatment plant, through which the water will enter the city water mains. Suppose the water is worth $25 per acre-foot to me, and the city will pay me $50 per acre-foot for it. Can we conclude that such a transaction is socially efficient?

The obvious potential problem with this is the impact on the downstream farmer who uses the return flow. If the return flow is disrupted, that person loses something of value. The only way we can be assured that the original transaction is socially efficient is if the downstream farmer has the legal right to the return flow and has no restrictions on his participation in the market. In that case the city also has to conclude an agreement with him, buying, for an agreed-upon price, the rights to the return flow. In water market discussions, impacts like this are often called **third-party effects.** A third party is a party other than the buyer and seller who is affected directly by the water rights transfer concluded by the buyer and seller. A third party is essentially a nonparticipant. If the rules of the market permit participation by people in this case, they are no longer third parties.

Another criterion for market completeness is that all the impacts of a water rights transfer be potentially tradable on a market. Suppose that the return flow, in the above example, supports ecosystem values in the stream below the farmer-irrigator. These values are in terms of, say, habitat protection for certain plants and animals. Without the irrigation return flow, a number of these biological populations would be damaged and perhaps destroyed. The difference between this and a downstream irrigator with rights to the return flow is that there is no well-developed market on which these particular third parties, namely endangered animal and plant species, can be represented. The main problem is that ecosystem protection like this is a **public good,**[16] and private markets are not particularly effective at representing the values of goods of this type.

The other type of requirements for efficient water rights markets is in the **structure of the markets** themselves. Markets work on the basis of **price signals.** If prices go up, it signals that demand is increasing relative to supply (or supply has decreased relative to demand); if prices go down, the opposite is true. For markets to function well, knowledge of prices must be widespread (i.e., no secret deals), and there must be **competition** among and between buyers and sellers. To have competition there must be a relatively large number of participants on both sides of the market. What "relatively large" means varies from case to case, but it's clear that at the present time many, if not most, water rights transactions are being worked out among a small number of participants. The current battle to buy and sell water rights from the Colorado River, for example, is not occurring in a competitive water market but rather through negotiations among the small number of states who have the basic rights to the water of the Colorado River.

Conditions in the real world never match the conditions of economics textbooks. Such problems as competitive "thinness" (i.e., too few participants to foster brisk competition), and third-party representation will be around for a long time. The real question is not whether markets do a perfect job of allocating water efficiently, but whether they are capable of doing a better job than has been done over the years by traditional water-managing institutions. Many people think the markets can do a better job, provided that we strike the right balance between letting the inherent power of markets work its influence and exercising some degree of public control over how the markets function.

■ Instream Flow Protection

Historically most conflicts about water rights and utilization have centered on water withdrawals, where water was physically removed from a stream or lake for irrigation, mining operations, manufacturing needs, and so on. Many rivers, especially in the West but even in the East as well, have reached points where most of the water is fully used or appropriated, leaving very low instream flows, especially in the drier seasons of the year. In recent decades, however, the values produced by water that is left in its natural location have become much more obvious and important. Thus there has been a growing demand for the protection of **instream flows.** Instream flows protect the estuarine environment and its ecological and aesthetic values. They are also the basis for a large and growing segment of the outdoor recreation market: fishing, white-water and flat-water sports, hiking and camping, bird watching, and so on.

The legal status of instream flow water rights varies from state to state. In most cases the major players in protecting instream flows are public water management agencies, and so groups and individuals who seek to increase instream flow have to work within the political process in which these agencies are embedded. A natural extension of the water rights marketing concept would be to allow individuals or groups to buy instream water rights. Naturally, traditional water withdrawers are quite reluctant to move in this direction, as it could lead to major shifts in the way water is managed.

Optimal Instream Flows

How much water should be left in a stream? It is easy to think about this conceptually, though difficult to determine very precisely in practice. Figure 15-6 shows the benefits and costs of instream water flows and how these benefits and costs change as flows change. The curve labeled B shows benefits, starting to the right of the origin. Some minimal amount of water is necessary before any benefits appear at all. The function increases, reaches a maximum at a_1, and then declines, because larger flows actually reduce most instream values. This shape is only illustrative; the actual shape of the benefits function would of course vary from one real-world situation to another.

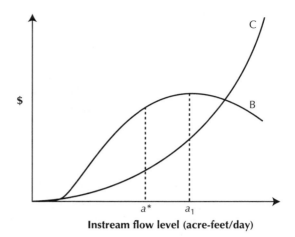

Figure 15-6   Benefits and Costs of Instream Water Flows

The cost relationship is labeled C; it rises to the right and becomes increasingly steep. The primary costs of instream flows are the values of forgone water withdrawals. Since the values of different types of withdrawals (e.g., agriculture vs. urban) differ, the cost curve is drawn under the assumption that it captures the most valuable forgone alternative use. The instream flow that maximizes total benefits is not the one that maximizes net benefits; the former is a_1 and the latter is a^*. The reason for the discrepancy is that costs are taken into account in one case but not in the other. Note that at a^*, marginal benefits (the slope of the B curve) are equal to marginal costs (the slope of the C curve).

There is a certain amount of ambiguity in this model, since it is so simple. The horizontal axis indexes quantity of water per day. But most rivers and streams, unless they can be completely controlled through upstream impoundments, have flows that fluctuate from day to day and season to season. So we might think of the horizontal axis as measuring the mean value of instream flow over a year's time. On any single day the flow might be somewhat, or perhaps substantially, below the average. This would affect the benefits and costs produced by the river over the course of the year. In other words, two rivers could each have the same average instream flow but with very different variation about the mean. In this case benefits and costs are likely to differ between the two.

How sensitive are net benefits to changes in stream flow? If flow is not at a^* but a certain amount above or below it, does this substantially affect net benefits? This is reflected in the shapes, especially the curvature, of the benefit and cost curves. If the curvature is low in both cases, then any flow rate around a^* will be almost as good as any other. If the relationships are very curved, then the opposite is true—a flow of exactly a^* is required to ensure maximum net benefits.

While the logic of figure 15-6 is straightforward and clear, its application in any particular real-world case is going to be difficult. One problem is just getting the necessary data to determine the relationships; data are required on both benefits and costs. Another major problem is that very often there is more than just one type of instream benefit, and the best flow rates may very well differ among the benefit types. The best flow rate for maintaining a trout fishery, for example, may be very different from the best flow rate for maintaining white-water rafting activity. Exhibit 15-3 discusses a problem of this type for a river in New Mexico.

■ International Water Issues

There are 276 recognized international rivers in the world, whose watersheds include more than 45 percent of the earth's surface. Many of the biggest are very well known (Congo, Nile, Amazon, Danube, Brahmaputra), but there are hundreds of smaller ones that run between two or more countries. Issues of navigation on these rivers have been the subject of international attention for a long time. Non-navigational uses, however, have been addressed comparatively recently. These include such activities as water diversion (for irrigation, municipal use, etc.), impoundments, energy generation, and flood control. The most relevant international agreement covering these rivers is the U.N. Convention on the Law of the Non-Navigational Uses of International Water Courses, adopted by the U.N. General Assembly in 1997. It required ratification by 35 individual countries in order to go into force, which was finally achieved in 2014 with ratification by Vietnam. Non-ratifiers currently include India, China, and most other countries of Southeast Asia. The Convention "... spells out basic substantive and procedural principles in the use of international watercourses and thus reflects customary norms in the use of international watercourses."[17]

In most of these river situations we have what we can call a non-reciprocal externality: activities of the upstream country (call it country A) can impact a downstream country (country B), but not vice-versa.

We can explore the nature of the relationship between upstream and downstream countries with the aid of a simple diagram such as figure 15-7 (on p. 300). Country A is the upstream country, and the curve so marked shows its marginal net benefits as a function of the amount of water it withdraws from the river during its run through A. Behind this curve is of course the marginal benefits and marginal costs of A, diminishing and increasing, respectively. The curve marked B shows marginal net loss to residents of B as a function of withdrawals in A, derived of course from B's marginal benefits and cost functions.

We note that as long as withdrawals in A are below w_0 there are no costs to residents of B downriver. If A acts unilaterally it would withdraw water at rate w_1, while if B had veto power over A it could push them back to w_0.

Exhibit 15-3   Managing Instream Flows: The Rio Chama

The Rio Chama is in northern New Mexico. It is a tributary of the Rio Grande, and is heavily used for agricultural and municipal purposes. It is also heavily used for recreational purposes. In managing the flow of the river, priority has to be given to certain downstream water rights holders. But it is also possible to vary somewhat the releases of water from the El Vado Reservoir upstream. This brings up the thorny question of how much water should be released in relation to the various services supplied by the instream flows.

A study team examined the situation carefully, identifying the major instream purposes and stream flows that were conducive to these purposes. These are shown in the accompanying tabulation. Note that there are a number of potential conflicts. Most clearly, white-water boating calls for substantially greater releases (800–1,000 cubic feet per second, or cfs) than any other use. Some of these other uses, like aesthetic values, would be compatible with these large releases while others, such as scenic (essentially flat-water) boating would not. The optimal releases for fishing (400 cfs during the winter) are in conflict with bald eagle habitat, and so on.

Since there can be only one release schedule, how are these conflicts to be resolved? One way might be to try to estimate the economic values of these alternative river services, in terms of willingness to pay. This would be relatively easy for, say, white-water boating and fishing, but very difficult for such services as general habitat maintenance and the protection of bald eagles in this region.

Flow Necessary to Support Designated Resource Values in the Rio Chama

	Flow Cubic feet per second (cfs)	Time Period
Wildlife		
Fish habitat (brown trout)	150–170 (400 optimum)	October 15–March 31
	150–300 (200 optimum)	April 1–August 31
	75–300 (200 optimum)	September–October 15
Bald Eagles	150–250	December 1–March 1
Macro-invertebrates	185 minimum	
Activity		
Scenic/aesthetic	40 minimum	
White-water rafting	800–1,000	
Scenic boating	500–600	
Fishing	150–300	
Riparian:		
Maintenance flow	185	April 1–September 30
Regeneration flow	5,000 at least one day every 5 – 10 years	May 15–June 15

Source: This example is taken from David M. Gillilan and Thomas C. Brown, *Instream Flow Protection,* Island Press, Washington, DC, 1997, pp. 87–94.

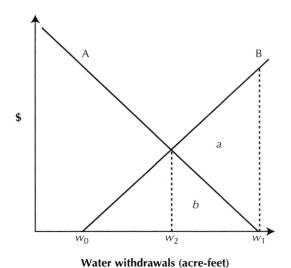

Figure 15-7 Issues on an International River

If we imagined a **river-basin authority** with sufficient power to enforce a withdrawal level that maximized joint benefits of the two countries, it would specify level w_2, where the net benefits to A from higher withdrawals are exactly offset by additional costs to B downstream.

Without an authority with this type of power, resolution of water issues will fall back on the bargaining strengths of the two countries, which will be related to the use of the river but also to other issues and interactions in which the countries are involved. A possibility perhaps is for country B to offer **side payments** to A to achieve some amount of reduction in upstream withdrawals. For example, if withdrawals were reduced from w_1 to w_2, the gain to B would be equal to the area $a + b$.[18] So there is enough for B to compensate, in whole or in part, the upstream country for its reduction in withdrawals.

■ Summary

In the United States, water is relatively abundant in the East and scarce in the West. The historical laws covering the right to make water withdrawals have differed between the two regions, with riparian law in the East and the prior appropriations doctrine predominating in the West. Both systems are giving way in modern times to more administered systems, in which public agencies are responsible for managing water systems and adopt rules to do so. Most water supply-systems are handled by publicly owned companies or private companies subject to public oversight. A fundamental decision to be made by these companies is how water is to be priced. Pricing decisions are usually undertaken with the objective of covering costs, which frequently leads agencies toward average-cost pricing. Upward-sloping marginal cost curves lead to prices that are too low on efficiency grounds. Water-pricing decisions are related also to decisions about expanding the capacity of existing systems. Some communities are contemplating selling their water systems to private firms, with the hope that these firms will be better able to finance system expansions and upgrades. In some regions, the most important water resource issue at the present time is the use of water markets to reallocate water among users, especially between agricultural and municipal users. There are many questions about the extent to which these markets can work efficiently and fairly and about the appropriate role of public agencies in overseeing their operation. In the future the role of markets in allocating water will undoubtedly increase. One major change to which they will have to adapt is the rapidly rising values placed on the maintenance of instream water flows. In many parts of the world international water resources, i.e., those shared by two or more countries, are the objects of political struggle and uncertainty.

Notes

[1] Major examples are the Central Valley Project in California and the Central Arizona Project.

[2] It's interesting to recall that one of the earliest large western water systems was an administered system—that developed by Mormons in 19th-century Utah.

[3] Jean A. Bowman, "Groundwater Management Areas in the United States," *Journal of Water Resource Planning and Management*, Vol. 116, 1990, pp. 484–502.

[4] That this could be a problem with stringent reduction of water consumption is suggested by the recent experience in Germany; see "Day Humor," *Wall Street Journal*, Sept. 29, 2014, p. 1.

[5] This example is based on the assumption that the marginal cost of water is increasing. If it is decreasing, then pricing at marginal cost will lead to losses. One of the problems at the end of the chapter deals with this case.

[6] If groundwater aquifers are the source and recharge rates are slow, there may also be a user cost, as discussed in chapter 10, associated with drawing down what may be a nonrenewable, or partially nonrenewable, resource.

[7] An acre-foot is a quantity of water that would cover one acre of level ground to a depth of one foot. It amounts to about 326,000 gallons.

[8] Jedidiah Brewer et al., "Water Markets in the West: Prices, Trading, and Contractual Forms," NBER Working Paper 13002, Cambridge, MA, 2007.

[9] These water rights may be held by farmers individually or often by irrigation district organizations, groups who manage regional systems of canals and small impoundments to supply irrigation water to the region's farmers.

[10] In most real-world settings, of course, the situation is much more complicated. Production and delivery costs may differ between the two uses, for example. Or some of the water applied to farms may run off and provide some of the water withdrawn downstream for M&I purposes. We are using this very simple illustration to get the basic point across about the efficiency gains from water transfers.

[11] This incident was featured in the film *Chinatown*.

[12] Bonnie Colby Saliba and David B. Bush, *Water Markets in Theory and Practice*. Boulder, CO: Westview Press, 1987.

[13] Marcia Weinberg, "Federal Water Policy Reform: Implications for Irrigated Farms in California," *Contemporary Economic Policy*, Vol. XV, April 1997, pp. 63–73.

[14] In chapter 7 we discuss the use of property rights systems to solve natural resource allocation problems and considered the features that property rights and markets have to have to function efficiently. It is worth reiterating some of these ideas here, in the specific context of water markets.

[15] This is, in fact, a major problem in many states. See Charles W. Howe, "Increasing Efficiency in Water Markets: Examples from the Western United States," in Terry L. Anderson and Peter J. Hill, eds., *Water Marketing: The Next Generation*. Lanham, MD: Rowman and Littlefield, 1997, pp. 79–99.

[16] For a discussion of public goods, see chapter 6.

[17] Ines Dombrowsky, *Conflict, Cooperation and Institutions in International Water Management: An Economic Analysis*. Northampton, MA: Edward Elgar, 2007, p. 57.

[18] Remembering that the area under marginal curves is equal to the total.

Key Terms

administered water systems
average-cost pricing
declining block pricing
groundwater
instream flow protection
investment in water supply systems
prior appropriation water rights

riparian water rights
surface water
third-party effects
water markets
water rights transfers
water withdrawals/consumption

Questions for Further Discussion

1. Show that if the marginal costs of water supply are downward-sloping, then pricing so that marginal cost equals marginal willingness to pay means that the water company will experience losses. How might these losses be made up?

2. If water is a "necessity for the maintenance of human life," how can it be rational to price it the same way we would any economic good or service?

3. What are some of the potential "third-party effects" in the large-scale transferring of water rights from agricultural to urban areas?

4. What are some of the problems that a public agency might face in trying to provide oversight and guidance for water markets?

5. The eastern part of the United States has much more abundant water than the West. But per-capita water consumption in the West is higher than that of the East. Why?

Useful Websites

Information on the major federal water resource agencies:

- Bureau of Reclamation (http://www.usbr.gov)
- U.S. Army Corps of Engineers (http://www.usace.army.mil); a faster way to this material is (http://www.nap.usace.army.mil/sb/flood.htm)
- Natural Resources Conservation Service (USDA) (http://nrcs.usda.gov)
- The water resources division of the U.S. Geological Survey (http://www.er.usgs.gov), primarily involved with water resources reports and data
- Environmental Protection Agency (www.water.epa.gov)

Many state universities have water resource research institutes and centers, such as:

- Oregon State University (http://www.research.oregonstate.edu/research-centers-and-institutes-osu)
- Texas A&M University (http://www.research.tamu.edu/tag/water)
- University of California (ciwr.ucanr.edu)

There are many water-oriented public interest groups:

- American Rivers (http://americanrivers.org)
- North American Lake Management Society (http://www.nalms.org)
- American Water Resources Association (http://www.awra.org)

The Australian government has a good site that discusses transferable water entitlements:

- Environment Australia Online (http://www.environment.gov.au), in its publication "Evaluation of Findings—Environmental Incentives"

Selected Readings

Dombrowsky, Ines. *Conflict, Cooperation and Institutions in International Water Management: An Economic Analysis.* Northampton, MA: Edward Elgar, 2007.

Griffin, Ronald C. *Water Resource Economics: The Analysis of Scarcity, Policies and Projects,* Cambridge, MA: MIT Press, 2006.

Harrington, Larry W., and Myles J. Fisher, eds. *Water Scarcity, Livelihoods, and Food Scarcity: Research and Innovation for Development.* London: Routledge, 2014.

Pashardes, Panos, Timothy Swanson, and Anastasios Xepapadeas. *Current Issues in the Economics of Water Resource Management: Theory, Applications and Policies.* New York: Springer, 2005.

Pennington, Karrie Lynne, and Thomas V. Cech. *Introduction to Water Resources and Environmental Issues.* Cambridge, England: Cambridge University Press, 2010.

Rogers, Peter P. et al., eds. *The Water Crisis: Myth or Reality?* New York: Taylor and Francis, 2006.

Shaw, W. Douglass. *Water Resource Economics and Policy: An Introduction.* Northampton, MA: Edward Elgar, 2007.

Young, Robert A. *Determining the Economic Value of Water: Concepts and Methods.* Washington, DC: Resources for the Future Press, 2005.

16

Economics of Agriculture

Human beings have walked the earth for about 2 million years. A very short time ago, in comparative terms, they invented agriculture, the purposeful cultivation of domesticated plants and animals. Today agriculture is fundamental to the continued existence and welfare of the global population. It is a prime natural-resource-using sector, requiring inputs of land, water, air, and biodiversity. Discussions of the future of world agriculture revolve around two facts, or expectations:

- the expectation that in the next few decades human fertility will add two to three billion more people;
- and the expectation that future growth in agricultural productivity, already uncertain, will be doubly so because of changes in global climate regimes.

Among the countries of the world there is great variability in the status of their agricultural sectors. Some have developed tremendously productive systems, though there are questions about their long-run sustainability. The developing world is mixed; some countries have experienced impressive gains in agricultural productivity, others have not. In some countries subsistence agriculture is still a widespread practice. In others, the agricultural sector is changing readily in response to significant institutional and political changes in the economy at large.

In this chapter we take up some of the important questions of agriculture in the contemporary world. Some are discussed in the context of global climate change, including the demand/supply balance and its implications for **food security**. We will also discuss incentive issues that bear on the sustainability aspects of modern agriculture.

■ Historical Changes in Supply and Demand

If we look at the recent history of agricultural production and food availability in the broadest possible way, we can understand it as an ongoing dynamic interaction between the forces that increase production and those that increase consumption. Throughout the 20th century both demand and supply have increased. The most important factor behind the demand shifts has been demographic growth; more people demand more food. Factors pushing out the supply function are technological and institutional in nature: more productive biological stock, machinery, fertilizers, irrigation, business practices, and so on. Most notable is that technology has developed faster than population; thus supply shifts have outstripped demand shifts, so food production has more than matched population growth. The point at which these factors intersect is the **price of food**. For most of the previous four decades, agricultural prices have been reasonably level, with occasional upward spikes, especially in the last few years (see figure 16-1).

There have been, of course, regional variations in this history. There have been substantial increases in total output over the last few decades in Asia. These have been high enough to offset rapid population growth in many of these countries, so that per capita production also has increased rapidly in that part of the world. Total output in Latin America has also increased fast enough to offset population growth, as it has in Europe and North America.

On the down side are Africa and the countries of the former Soviet Union. In Africa, especially sub-Saharan Africa, total food output has increased over the last several decades, but not enough to match population growth, so per capita production has shown a marked decline. Eastern

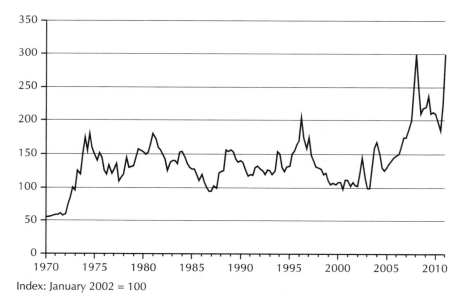

Index: January 2002 = 100

Figure 16-1   World Crop Price Spikes since 1970

Source: USDA, Economic Research Service, *Climate Change and Agriculture in the United States: Effects and Adaptation*, USDA Technical Bulletin 1935, 2012.

Europe and the countries of the former Soviet Union have seen a marked collapse of agricultural output, both total and per capita. These countries moved strongly toward large-scale industrial agriculture during the post–World War II years and up to the dissolution of the Soviet Union in 1989. Since then they have worked, to a greater or lesser degree, toward a return to an owner-operator type of agricultural structure. This has led to tremendous dislocation and disruption of agricultural production and distribution in these countries.

How will the future play out? World population is expected to continue increasing, until it tops out at about 9 billion people later in the 21st century. Will increases in food production keep up with demography, or will productivity growth in agriculture slacken? We are back to the question mentioned in several previous chapters: Is it more appropriate to be optimistic or pessimistic about future technological and demographic developments? Malthus set the tone of the debate over 200 years ago. Population growth, he said, would inevitably outstrip productivity growth, leading to widespread famine.[1] This has not come to pass yet, but perhaps it will in the not-too-distant future. Or is there something about the tendency of population growth to moderate, and the ability of human ingenuity to increase agricultural productivity, that will forestall this dismal forecast, perhaps forever? Opinions remain divided.

■ Food Security in a Time of Climate Change

If world population does indeed increase and peak at about 9 billion, world agricultural production would have to increase by about 35 percent to keep pace. This will have to be done under the added burden arising from global climate changes. Given these challenges, it has become common to think in terms of future **food security**. A food supply is secure when food of adequate nutritive value is available at reasonable prices. "Reasonable" in this sense means in real terms; that is, prices relative to income levels of the people in question.

The available food supply of any region can be written as follows:

$$\frac{\text{Food avilable for}}{\text{consumption}} = \frac{\text{Food produced}}{\text{locally}} + \frac{\text{Net food}}{\text{imports}} - \frac{\text{Food}}{\text{wasted}}$$

On a global basis, of course, net imports are zero, so food available is production minus waste. But as the region under consideration becomes smaller, food imports and exports will normally constitute an increasing element in total supply. We will consider aspects of agricultural trade in chapter 21. And we will not discuss the issue of food wastage. Suffice it to say that in many regions, particularly in the developing world, food security can be augmented by giving attention to the logistical system that handles food transportation, storage, and preservation.[2]

The expected impacts of global climate change include

- increasing mean temperatures
- increasing incidence of extreme weather events

- changed, for the most part decreased, water availability
- shifts in distribution of crop and animal diseases and insect pests

From climate models we know that these impacts will vary considerably from one region to another: harmful in some, reasonably neutral in some, and perhaps even beneficial in others. The ultimate impact will depend critically on the adaptive responses made regionally to these climate changes. According to a recent USDA report regarding U.S. agriculture:

> These adaptive responses may range from farmers adjusting planting patterns and soil management practices in response to more variable weather patterns, to seed producers investing in the development of drought-tolerant varieties, to increased demands for federal risk management programs, to adjustments in international trade as nations respond to food security concerns.[3]

While the general outlook on global warming is reasonably clear, it is also true that the particular impacts on specific regions remain probabilistic: known only with uncertainty. So it is unclear what specific shifts in agricultural practice will be favored in the future. But the uncertainty puts emphasis on having agricultural systems today that are flexible and adaptable to new conditions. In the remainder of this chapter, therefore, we will deal with a number of issues related to resource-using decisions of farmers and how these decisions can affect the adaptability and resiliency of current food-production systems.

■ Government Support Policies in Agriculture

From the brief discussion above, it is easy to understand the economic pressures that farmers have been under. Rapid technological advances shift supply and drive prices lower, leading to greater competitive pressure on farmers and consolidation of farms. Thus over the last four or five decades almost all developed countries have pursued public policies and regulations designed to provide aid and support for their farmers. The ultimate aim of these programs has been to lift farm incomes above those which would prevail in competitive markets with no control over the rate of technological innovation.[4]

Table 16-1 shows some of the major approaches that policy makers have used to shift income toward agriculture. They have often been used in combination. Continued attempts have been made through the years to reduce the levels of public support going to farmers, but this has been difficult, given the political realities of most countries.[5] There has been a trend, however, away from programs of supply restrictions, price supports, and input subsidies toward programs of direct income payments and crop price insurance programs.[6] One reason for this is a growing appreciation for the **economic distortions** that the earlier types of support programs produced. A distortion occurs when farmers shift their operations to take advantage of the particular provisions of public programs, introducing various types of

---

Table 16-1 Types of Income Support Programs that Have Been Used to Benefit Farmers

Price supports	Since technical change tends to drive agricultural product prices lower, some programs have been put in place that essentially guarantee certain minimum prices. This can be accomplished in several ways, such as price-based loans or payments to farmers and public purchase of farm commodities.
Supply restrictions	Restrictions are placed on total output or on the use of certain inputs, in an attempt to lower the supply of farm output so as to raise prices. In the United States the primary restriction of this type has been acreage restrictions.
Direct income payments	Farmers are offered direct payments from the public treasury to increase their incomes. Payments may be tied to certain parameters (e.g., payments related to size of the farm), or be designed to lift income by certain amounts.
Input subsidies	Costs of selected farm inputs are subsidized so that their effective prices to farmers are lowered. An example is the provision of large quantities of irrigation water at below-market prices.
Structural adjustment payments	Farmers are helped financially in making certain operational changes, such as putting some land aside into a conservation reservation, shifting to a new crop, or engaging in certain environmental practices.
Subsidized insurance	Covering partial or complete crop failures, or low prices.
Programs to aid small farmers	In the U.S. a new microloan program began in 2013, aiming to help small, family, beginning, or disadvantaged farmers with loans of $35,000 or less.

biases that, within a wider market context, are inefficient and cost-ineffective. Many of these distortions have influenced the impacts of agriculture on the quantity and quality of the underlying natural resource base.

Acreage Restrictions and Intensification

Many of the current characteristics of large-scale technologically sophisticated farming appeared in response to early government support programs. In the United States during the 1950s Congress sought to support farm incomes by instituting minimum prices for certain agricultural commodities such as corn, wheat, and cotton. The result was predictable: to take advantage of these price supports farmers boosted their outputs. But this led to **crop surpluses**; crops that could not be sold at the support level prices. This in turn led to a system of acreage restrictions. For each farmer the U.S. Department of Agriculture identified a certain number of acres, called their **acreage allotment.** Crops grown on the allotment qualified for the support price. Any crop grown on non-allotment acreage was not supported—it might actually have been penalized under some circumstances. These allotment restrictions had the predictable effect.

The total output of a crop farmer can be broken down:

$$\underset{\text{(TO)}}{\text{Total Output}} = \underset{\text{(A)}}{\text{Total Acres Harvested}} \times \underset{\text{(TO/A)}}{\text{Yield per Acre}}$$

The allotment programs sought to control total output by controlling the total acreage harvested. Farmers responded by putting their energies into increasing yields per acre—intensifying their agricultural production. **Intensification** of this sort has many forms: more fertilizers and pesticides, more use of machinery, adoption of higher-yield crop strains, more use of irrigation water, and so on. Thus farmers have had the incentive to move toward a low-acreage, high-intensification system, as compared to a higher-acreage, lower-intensification system that would have resulted if the acreage allotment system had not been put in place.

The relatively simple acreage restriction programs of the 1950s have become increasingly complicated over the intervening decades, as exhibit 16-1 makes clear. Today it is virtually impossible to tell what modern agriculture would look like if these public support programs had never been put in place. Although these programs are universally touted as aimed at

---

Exhibit 16-1 Current Cropland Programs and Definitions in the United States

Conservation Reserve Program (CRP) was designed to voluntarily retire from crop production about 40 million acres of highly erodible or environmentally sensitive cropland for 10–15 years. In exchange, participating producers receive annual rental payments up to $50,000 and 50 percent cost-share assistance for establishing vegetative cover on the land. The Federal Agriculture Improvement and Reform Act of 1996 (1996 Farm Act) limited CRP enrollment to 39.2 million acres any time through calendar year 2007.

Conservation Security Program is a voluntary program to provide financial and technical assistance to promote conservation practices on farms. Up to $1,954 million was authorized between 2006 and 2010.

Farmland Protection Program is a voluntary program to offer to buy development rights from farmers as a way of protecting agriculture. Provides for spending approximately $100 million a year in matching funds to states.

Commodity Price Support Programs include three primary types of payments: annual direct payments unrelated to production or prices, counter-cyclical payments that are triggered when prices fall below statutorily-determined target prices, and marketing assistance loans that offer interim financing and, if prices fall below statutorily-determined loan prices, additional income support.

In recent years, federal programs to subsidize ethanol production have involved tax incentives and renewable fuels standards that expand the market for certain agricultural crops.

Sources: Congressional Research Service, "Farm Commodity Programs: Direct Payments, Counter-Cyclical Payments, and Marketing Loans," Report RL33271, Washington, DC, 2006; Congressional Research Service, "Agriculture-Based Renewable Energy Production," Report RL32712, Washington, DC, 2007; Congressional Research Service, "Funding Levels for Conservation Programs in the 2007 Farm Bill," Report RL34178, Washington, DC, 2007.

enhancing public welfare, broadly considered, many are the result of **rent-seeking actions** on the part of various groups who have political access in the policy process. Agricultural policy has been especially prone to this over the years.[7] With the more recent growth of public concern about the preservation of natural and environmental resources, there is increasing concern about the distorted way in which modern agriculture has developed and a growing emphasis on moving toward income support methods that are less distorting. Among many developed countries, for example, there is a perceptible movement away from programs such as acreage restriction toward direct income payments. In theory these should reduce the distortions that characterize modern agriculture.

■ The Economics of Soil Productivity

Perhaps the most fundamental current requirement is the maintenance of soil productivity, on the grounds that soil of depleted fertility would be less amenable to future cropping changes that might be desirable. The productivity of soil is simply its power to produce crops in useful quantities, and is related to the physical and chemical characteristics of the soil itself together with the hydrological and meteorological systems in which it is situated. Loss of soil productivity has been a continuing concern around the world. Developed economies tend to be concerned with the long-run effects of modern agriculture on soil productivity. In developing economies, however, there is more concern about farmer incentives and the potential for "extracting" productivity to achieve short-run gains by farmers who are nearer to subsistence levels of living.

Problems of soil fertility have frequently been discussed within the framework of **sustainability.** Agricultural practices are "sustainable," according to this view, as long as they do not lead to diminished soil productivity over the long run. This perspective is useful in that it leads us to be especially watchful for practices that may undermine soil productivity irreversibly in the long run. But it is not an adequate concept for addressing the decisions that need to be made by farmers in actually managing their soil productivity. These decisions are **investment decisions;** they involve actions that reduce current incomes in return for higher incomes in the future. A sustainability perspective leads us to think of doing whatever it takes to hold the line against soil productivity loss. An investment perspective leads us to ask what constellation of actions leads to the **efficient level of productivity.** Furthermore, it is useful to think of soil productivity as a **renewable resource,** so that it makes sense to look for a **steady-state** usage pattern, that is, a level of soil fertility that is managed at a constant level through time. A constant level of productivity presumably satisfies the sustainability criterion; it satisfies the efficiency criterion only if this constant level of productivity is also the correct level in efficiency terms.

An Efficient Steady State

Think back to chapter 2, where we discussed the basic features of different types of natural resources in terms of a simple accounting equation:

$$S_1 = S_0 - Q + \Delta S$$

Let S_0 and S_1 now refer to soil productivity, the former being the productivity at the beginning of the year, and the latter being the productivity at the end of the year after all production operations have been concluded. A steady-state, or sustainable, situation is defined as $S_1 = S_0$, which obviously implies that $Q = \Delta S$. In this case, Q refers to the amount of soil productivity that is extracted from the soil during production, and ΔS refers to the amount of productivity added. In agricultural use, Q is determined by such things as choice of crops and cultivation techniques. Some crops, for example, demand more soil nutrients than others whereas other crops can help replenish certain soil qualities. Traditional plowing and harrowing can expose soil to substantial wind erosion; practices such as no-till or low-till cultivation can substantially reduce soil loss.

The term ΔS refers to the productivity that is returned to the soil during the growing season. This can occur in a variety of ways. Productivity may naturally replenish itself through geological and hydrological processes. Land in floodplains is subject to replenishment during spring flooding. Weathering processes and the decay of vegetation can add to the depth of topsoil, and hence to its productivity. Productivity can also be added by direct human action. Terracing can actually lift soil productivity permanently above its "natural" state; contour plowing can prevent soil erosion; fertilizers and cover crops can replenish nutrients; and so on. $Q = \Delta S$ means, therefore, that steps are undertaken to put productivity back into the soil equal to that which was taken out.

But the condition $\Delta S = Q$ is a condition for the steady state in terms of soil productivity. It does not tell us which steady state is the most efficient. In the absence of any externalities, the most efficient productivity level is that which leads to a maximum of net incomes accruing to farmers. We can envisage a relationship between maintained soil productivity and net farm incomes as pictured in figure 16-2. At low productivities, agricultural output is also low, so although it may not cost much to

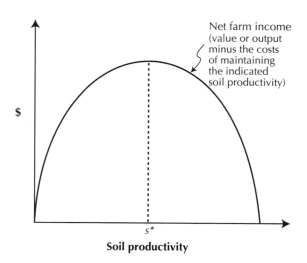

Net farm income (value or output minus the costs of maintaining the indicated soil productivity)

s^*

Soil productivity

Figure 16-2   Efficient Steady-State Soil Productivity

maintain productivity at this level, net farm incomes are low. At high soil productivities, total output is large but the costs of replenishing the productivity "drawdown" is very high, leading again to low net incomes. At an intermediate level of maintained soil productivity, indicated as s^* in the figure, net farm income is maximized.

Note several things. It is certainly not efficient to try to maintain soil productivity at a maximum, whatever that means. In effect there is no maximum. Productivity could always be increased with the right management practices, no matter how high it is to begin with. The appropriate action is not to try to maintain some *maximum* productivity, but to maintain the *efficient* level of soil productivity. Note also that nothing has been said about the initial level of soil productivity. If the initial condition is to the left of s^*, it implies a buildup of steady-state productivity, through such means as terracing, irrigation, or soil amendments. In this way agricultural land productivity as it is currently maintained may exceed the productivity that the land originally possessed. If the initial level of productivity is to the right of s^* on the other hand, some **disinvestment** in productivity may be called for.

■ The Economics of Monoculture

Future adaptability of cropping patterns in response to local climate changes will put a premium on having available alternative crops with suitable characteristics. It may also mean that farmers in different regions, now growing the same crop, will want to shift in different directions. Modern agriculture is based on a system of **monoculture**. This means several things. First, a very large proportion of the human food supply comes from a small number of crops. In particular, corn, wheat, rice, and potatoes account for a very large proportion of the total calories consumed by human beings, either directly or through the animals they support (especially corn). Many other crops that potentially could supply important amounts of nutrition have been overlooked or undeveloped.[8] Monoculture also refers to reduced **genetic diversity** within specific crops. The genetic makeup of crops determines their characteristics, such as potential yield, growth rate, and degree of resistance to diseases and pests. Most modern agriculture is based on a limited number of crop strains that have been developed through techniques of plant breeding and development, including the classical techniques of controlled growth and selection and more recently advances in **biotechnology.**

Preserving genetic diversity on the farm involves two phenomena: (1) developing new cultivars that have desirable genotypes and (2) getting farmers to grow a diverse portfolio of cultivars.[9] We focus on the second of these. Plant breeding has contributed to the development of new cultivars that have substantially higher potential yields than the older ones. The concern, however, is that through this breeding and adoption program we will lose **genetic diversity.** The newly developed varieties are genetically uniform within themselves. A widespread shift to these varieties could lead to a large proportion of the crop being susceptible to a particular disease or pest, resulting in widespread crop failure. This risk is reduced by developing cultivars of the crop that are genetically different, especially in terms of the genes that confer resistance to certain important diseases, present or future. Then farmers need to adopt and grow a reasonably broad portfolio of cultivars rather than only one or two. With a broad portfolio in use, the loss of any one cultivar through disease can most easily be compensated for by shifting to other available cultivars that do not have the same susceptibility.

Note that this is a problem of diversity, not a problem dealing with classic negative externalities from the choice of specific cultivars. If cultivar A has undesirable properties (perhaps it is insufficiently disease-resistant), its use could presumably be stopped with a simple regulation—assuming it could be enforced. But for diversity to prevail there must be a collection of cultivars available for farmers to choose among. This "collection" cannot consist of one approved cultivar, no matter how good it appears, because its exclusive adoption by all farmers puts us back in a condition of strict monoculture, which could easily be invaded by an evolving pathogen.

If public authorities rule out, by regulation, all unsatisfactory cultivars, how is it possible to get farmers to choose a diverse portfolio from among the group of cultivars that are approved? It seems highly unlikely that individual farm production portfolios could be identified and enforced by public authorities. Thus we must understand how farms choose their portfolios and how they may be influenced to choose more diverse portfolios. One way of thinking about this is in terms of the private and public benefits of the portfolio choices made by individual farmers. Suppose a number of cultivars are available for farmers to choose among. These cultivars vary in terms of their (disease-free) yields and their resistance to a certain disease. Left to themselves, farmers choose a portfolio of cultivars that maximizes their expected net incomes.[10] They probably will not choose the single cultivar with the highest disease-free yield, because this would expose them to an unacceptable level of risk. By also growing some cultivars with lower yields but also lower risks of loss, they can actually increase their expected long-run net income.

But there may be additional, external benefits from choosing a diverse portfolio of cultivars. A larger portfolio lowers not only individual risks, but also the risks to neighboring farmers. Diseases tend to spread beyond the borders of the fields where they first break out. Thus when one farmer lowers his risk, the risk to nearby farms also is lower. This implies that some portion of the total social benefits from a larger portfolio of cultivars will accrue as **external** benefits. And, as we mention many times throughout the book, when an activity produces external benefits, private decision makers—left to themselves—tend to undersupply the service relative to levels that maximize social benefits. Thus farmers, in the situation described above, will tend to select portfolios of cultivars that are less diverse than those called for by the criterion of social efficiency.

From an incentive point of view, the problem is that the external benefits produced by farmers who might choose a diverse cultivar portfolio normally do not accrue to them, nor does there seem to be any strictly private market arrangement that could be set up to accomplish this. Perhaps some type of public subsidy program is the answer: the subsidy could be linked to the number of cultivars a farmer grows. One way of administering the subsidy would be to offer price rebates on the purchase price of cultivars that farmers might not choose under normal circumstances.

■ Economics of Pesticide Resistance

Modern agriculture, and increasingly the agriculture of the developing world, is characterized by the use of relatively large amounts of chemical inputs, particularly fertilizers and pesticides. In 1940 U.S. farmers spent $44 million on pesticides; in 2007 this number was about $8 billion. Aggregate pesticide application rates (quantity applied per acre) increased until around the years 1981–1982, and since then have declined moderately. A large reason for the decline is that pesticide *quality* (potency, toxicity, and persistence) has increased, thus leading to a decline in *quantity*. There are wide differences of opinion on such basic questions as how public regulation has affected pesticide use, the economic benefits to farmers of using pesticides, and the specific environmental implications of pesticide-use practices.[11]

Pesticide use has usually been considered an environmental problem, especially as regards ecosystem contamination and human health impacts. But it also has important production ramifications. One of these is the problem of increased pest resistance stemming from the overuse of pesticides. Organisms evolve in directions related to the conditions of their environment. Higher pesticide levels create conditions leading to the evolution of organisms with greater resistance to the pesticides. Over time pesticide use can lead to greater pest resistance, which motivates higher levels of pesticide use, which spurs further resistance, and so on. Why would a rational farmer, realizing that elevated levels of pesticide use lead to greater pest resistance, not reduce his use of the substances in order to lower the likelihood of that happening? We have here an interesting and important problem of shaping incentives so as to harmonize individual behavior with the welfare of society.

To explore this, consider a simple example. Suppose there is a certain relatively small geographical region, for example, a particular valley, with several dozen farms, all growing the same crop, say, corn. The corn is attacked by a certain pest, which lowers yields and reduces incomes of the farmers in the region. Let us assume that the region is biologically distinct, in the sense that the pest population here is relatively independent of outside influences. Farmers use a particular pesticide to control the pest. The pesticide is quite effective, but there is a hitch. At high pesticide use levels, the pests develop a resistance that makes the chemical less effective. This decreases yields and lowers returns. If all farmers use low pesticide levels, resistance does not develop. The problem this presents is the following: although the level of pest resistance in the region is determined by the

aggregate quantity of pesticide used there, individual farmers have control only over the quantity of pesticide they apply themselves.

We now present some illustrative numbers to show how this shapes the **incentives** faced by individual farmers. The numbers do not correspond to any real-world situation, but they do show the relative levels of returns that would result from different courses of action, which is enough to explore the incentives inherent in this type of situation. We focus, then, on the returns available to one typical farmer in the valley. To simplify even further, suppose the farmer is faced with just two choices: to use pesticides in a small quantity or to use them in a large quantity. The incomes he would receive from each of these two strategies are shown in the following matrix:

		Other Farmers	
		Low usage	High usage
Farmer A	Low usage	$10	$5
	High usage	$15	$7

Note that the incomes to our farmer (Farmer A) depend on what the other farmers choose to do. That seems reasonable because the evolution of pesticide resistance is a valley-wide phenomenon linked to overall usage rates, not just the rates on one farm. Thus the returns to Farmer A depend in part on pesticide levels used by other farmers.

Suppose the farmer were to choose a low pesticide use rate. If others also use a low rate, the farmer will have a "payoff" of $10, whereas if other farmers use a high rate, the return will be only $5. This seems reasonable. If everyone sticks to a low use rate, resistance is slow, losses to pests are relatively low, and incomes relatively high. But if all other farmers choose high application levels, resistance is high and Farmer A suffers from being the only one who refrains from the higher use; he uses low pesticide levels in a high resistance situation.

Suppose instead that the farmer chooses a high application level. If everyone uses a high level, the farmer's income is $7. Large applications imply high resistance, lower yields, and therefore lower returns than if everybody were to keep their applications low. On the other hand, if all others use low pesticide levels, Farmer A would get a high return ($15) from using a high level, because the pests will have low resistance, and so with high application levels he will get rid of them all.

Note carefully how this affects the incentives facing our farmer. Regardless of what the other farmers do, Farmer A is better off choosing a high application level. If other farmers choose low application levels, Farmer A will have the highest returns if he applies at the high level. This strategy is also the best one if others use the high pesticide levels. The high application level is individually best under both circumstances. But if this is the incentive situation facing Farmer A, it is also the incentive situation facing each of the other farmers. Thus, we conclude that although individual farmers can be presumed to act rationally in terms of selecting the strategy with the highest expected payoff for themselves, the overall result is an outcome in which everyone has lower incomes. The individual payoff to the self-interest decision situation is $7, even though they could each get a payoff of $10 if somehow they would all use the lower rate.

We have seen this dilemma many times before in earlier chapters. **Open-access resources** present problems of this type. Users of the resource, in making their own individual decisions about whether and how much to use, contribute to an outcome in which the resource is overused in the aggregate. In the pesticide case we also have a type of open-access resource that gets overused. The resource in this case is the **susceptibility** of the pest to the pesticide. This quality of susceptibility is in fact a valuable resource that can be significantly degraded and even lost if overall pesticide use is too high. The **open-access externality** in this case stems from the fact that if an individual farmer chooses a high application level, the effects, in terms of its contribution toward increasing pesticide resistance, will be felt by him and by all the other farmers in the valley.[12]

Another revealing way of looking at this is with the concept of **public goods.** These are goods or services that, when made available for one person, automatically become available to others. There is no way of excluding others from enjoying the benefits of the good or service. Suppose every farmer is applying pesticides at the higher level. Why wouldn't individual farmers voluntarily reduce their pesticide usage? Because the impacts of individual cutbacks of this type are public goods; the benefits they produce, in terms of a small reduction in resistance, accrue equally to all farmers in the region, not just to the individual who makes the cutback. As we saw earlier, public goods tend to be undersupplied by individual actions of this type. Thus cutbacks in individual pesticide use will be undersupplied, which is the same as saying that the overall level of pesticide application will be higher than the socially efficient level.

To achieve socially efficient levels of aggregate pesticide use, some means must be found to get all farmers (or a significant fraction of them) to use the lower pesticide application rates and to refrain from trying to take advantage of this situation by opportunistically shifting to higher levels. There are several ways of doing this. One is to sponsor an agreement among the farmers themselves to use lower application levels. This could be a **voluntary agreement,** if it were possible to get wide-enough participation through this means. Perhaps if a voluntary agreement could be developed among 90 percent of the farmers, aggregate pesticide use could be controlled enough to preserve pest susceptibility at high levels. Perhaps the participating farmers could somehow sanction those who refuse to join the agreement, such as by controlling some other part of the overall process (e.g., the town grain elevator could refuse to accept grain from farmers who are not part of the pesticide program).

Of course **direct public regulation** is also an option. A regulation requiring lower pesticide use levels would have to be enacted by a political body with the appropriate jurisdiction (local, regional, or state), and this would then have to be enforced through such techniques as self-reporting by farmers, surveillance, and examination of pesticide purchase records. One problem with regulations of this type (and with voluntary agreements) is that the incentives are still strong for farmers individually to apply the higher levels, in this case surreptitiously. How often this happens depends in large part on the effectiveness of the enforcement of the regulation or agreement.

Another way of controlling individual pesticide use is through an incentive program such as a **tax on pesticide use.** The tax would have to be sufficient to lower the high usage return rates of the tabulation above to levels that are below the return rates for low usage levels. Since it is probably not feasible to tax each unit (pound or gallon) of the pesticide as it is applied, a tax here would probably have to be placed on the quantity of pesticide purchased. In effect the idea is to make the pesticide expensive enough that farmers will choose the low use levels automatically.

■ The Conflict over Agricultural Biotechnology

Plant and animal breeding to obtain improved stock has gone on for centuries. Traditional methods relied on a recurrent series of breeding and selection which, over generations, would evolve organisms with improved features. With recent developments in biology and genetics scientists are now able to manipulate plant genotypes directly, vastly decreasing the time it takes to produce varieties with improved characteristics. The ability to produce these **GMOs** (genetically modified organisms) appears to give us a quick way of producing organisms with improved features, such as greater pest resistance, higher yields, improved nutritional content, greater drought resistance, and so on.

Since they were first introduced in the mid-1990s, GMOs have become an important force in the agricultural sectors of some countries. A major share of the corn, cotton, and soybeans in the United States are now GMOs. Rapid adoption of GMOs has also occurred in Argentina, Brazil, China, Canada, and India. It would appear that GMOs provide an effective means for meeting the challenges of feeding the several billion more people that demographers predict in the next few decades, and the stresses that future climate change will produce.

But GMOs are controversial. Critics argue that developing GMOs essentially short circuits natural selection processes, potentially producing organisms that could disrupt ecosystems or damage human health. Some people regard GMOs as violating the ethical beliefs that underlie their feelings about how food should be grown and consumed.

Another major concern is the fear of monopoly control and pricing by producers of GMO seeds. There are only two or three U.S. companies in the business of producing GMOs, the most well-known being Monsanto. Since GMO seeds, and some of the processes that are used in producing them, are patentable, firms can potentially set discriminatory prices—that is, prices well above production costs.

The situation would appear to call for a substantial program of rigorous research into the impacts of GMO crops. And in fact an enormous amount of work on the issue has been done over the last several decades. But the research has been done within the context of a highly contentious and politicized public debate over the pros and cons of this biotechnology. The result is a growing body of study results, of varying quality and provenance, which can be cited in support of either policy position.

In the United States we are, in effect, pursuing a grand experiment in the introduction of a new technology that some people fear may have serious side effects. Although the benefits of biotechnology appear to be positive, less is known about possible long-run deleterious impacts. It is a situation we have faced many times in other dimensions—short-run benefits, the value and distribution of which are of course highly contested, but uncertain long-run costs. The principles of choice we have discussed elsewhere in this book are just as applicable here:

- When future benefits and costs are involved, the rate at which they are discounted to the present will determine how much they will impact present decisions. See the material in chapter 5.
- There is always a question about whether individual decisions, made in accordance with benefits and costs as they impinge on individuals, are optimal from the standpoint of society at large. This question applies to GMOs in the same way as it does to individual decisions about mono cropping and the use of pesticides.

■ Balancing Agricultural Productivity with Resource Conservation

Decisions made by farmers have an important impact on the quality of the land resource. The Food and Agricultural Organization of the U.N. (FAO) has laid out the main principles of what is called **conservation agriculture**. These are:

- minimum mechanical and chemical soil disturbances
- maintenance of soil fertility
- crop rotation and the minimization of monoculture[13]

We have dealt with most of these in this chapter, emphasizing especially how the incentives facing individuals can lead them away from, or toward, the satisfaction of these principles.

Equally as important are decisions about maintaining the stock of land in agriculture. This means:

- reducing the extent to which agricultural land impinges on other types of land use, e.g., land that has special ecological value such as wetlands
- minimizing the extent to which agricultural land is lost to other uses

The last point is especially important with regard to the rural-urban interface. Urban agriculture, farmer's markets, community-supported agriculture, and localized food supplies are concepts that have become increasingly popular in recent years. Thus the protection of agricultural land near urban areas is important. As we saw in chapter 14 on land use, this has been pursued largely through public efforts to reduce the value of converting land to non-agricultural uses. By itself, however, this does not serve to make agricultural production on the rural-urban fringe any more profitable. So while it may reduce the extent to which agricultural land is converted to urban uses, it does not reduce the extent to which agricultural production is abandoned on the fringe.

■ Summary

There is widespread concern, but by no means widespread agreement, about the ability of modern agriculture to feed the ever-higher levels of world population. Problems tend to be different among countries, particularly among developed, developing, and transitional economies. A prime source of concern is the impact of modern agriculture on the quantity and quality of the natural resource base on which it depends. Agriculture in the developed world has come to be heavily subsidized. These public programs are normally very complex and have introduced many distortions into the agricultural production system. For example, acreage restrictions in the 1950s and 1960s undoubtedly led to the development of intensive agriculture and vigorous efforts to increase per-acre yields. It is, however, virtually impossible to know what modern agriculture would look like if many of these programs were stopped. It is perhaps more instructive to focus on particular agricultural decisions and practices in order to understand the forces that shape them and how they might respond to change. In this chapter we looked at the management of soil productivity, decisions surrounding the system of monoculture, the use of pesticides in situations where pest tolerance may increase, and the advent of biotechnology.

Notes

[1] T. R. Malthus, *An Essay on Population*, London, 1798.

[2] According to a recent study, approximately 30 percent of food grown in the United States in 2008 was lost, which includes "natural" losses (e.g., shrinkage from moisture loss), and food actually wasted by consumers and food handlers. See Jean C. Buzby and Jeffrey Hyman, "Total and Per Capita Value of Food Loss in the United States," *Food Policy*, 37, 2013, pp. 561–570.

[3] United States Department of Agriculture, *Climate Change and Agriculture in the United States: Effects and Adaptation*, USDA Technical Bulletin 1935, Washington, DC, 2013, p. 2.

[4] This is not true of some countries of the developing world, which have sought to drain rents out of agriculture for use elsewhere.

[5] Over half of the budget of the European Union goes toward supporting farmers in its member states. It has proved impossible to reduce these support levels by any significant amount.

[6] Organization for Economic Cooperation and Development, "Agricultural Policy Monitoring and Evolution," *OECD Countries and Emerging Economies*, Paris, 2013.

[7] See Andrew Schmitz et al., *Agricultural Policy, Agribusiness and Rent-Seeking Behavior*, 2nd ed. Toronto, Canada: University of Toronto Press, 2010.

[8] See, for example, the discussion in Edward O. Wilson, *The Diversity of Life*. Cambridge, MA: Harvard University Press, 1992, pp. 287–298.

⁹ A variety, or "cultivar," is a subset of a species consisting of a group of cultivated plants having a clearly distinguished set of characteristics that are retained when the plant is reproduced.

¹⁰ To review the concept of expected values, see chapter 8.

¹¹ Some of these are reviewed in Jorge Fernandez-Cornejo, Sharon Jans, and Mark Smith, "Issues in the Economics of Pesticide Use in Agriculture: A Review of the Empirical Evidence," *Review of Agricultural Economics*, 20(2), Fall/Winter 1998, pp. 462–488.

¹² The growing resistance of bacteria to antibiotics is exactly parallel to this, and explains why antibiotics continue to be overused despite the problem.

¹³ Food and Agricultural Organization of the U.N., *The Main Principles of Conservation Agriculture* (www.fao.org/ag/ca/1b.html).

Key Terms

acreage restrictions (allotments)
agricultural supply and demand shifts
biotechnology
genetic diversity
GMOs
income support policies
intensification of production

monoculture
open-access externalities
pesticide resistance
steady-state soil productivity
sustainability
voluntary agreements

Questions for Further Discussion

1. How does the economics of managing pesticide resistance resemble the economics of fisheries management?

2. In establishing the efficient steady-state level of soil productivity, what role does the interest rate play?

3. What relationship do you see between the decisions by farmers on what portfolio of cultivars they grow and compulsory auto insurance laws?

4. The problem of reducing pesticide use to avoid the growth of pest resistance is actually a public good problem. What is the nature of the public good in this case? The cultivar choice problem can also be explained in these terms. What is the public good in this case?

5. How have government programs to support agricultural incomes in general led to an increase in monoculture—that is, a reduction in crop and animal diversity?

6. If a policy official wanted to show a high present value of net benefits for GMOs, how should the discount rate be adjusted? Conversely, to show low net benefits of GMOs, what discount rate should be used?

Useful Websites

Studies of agricultural markets and agricultural support programs in the United States:

- U.S. Department of Agriculture, Economic Research Service (http://www.ers.usda.gov)

- Agricultural Research Service (http://www.ars.usda.gov/main/main.htm)
- Natural Resources Conservation Service (http://www.nrcs.usda.gov/wps/portal/nrcs/site/national/home/)

For international material:

- Food and Agriculture Organization of the United Nations (http://www.fao.org)

Many state universities have departments of agricultural economics that sponsor research on a wide range of topics in agriculture; see especially their publications lists, including:

- University of Wisconsin (http://www.aae.wisc.edu)
- University of Wyoming (http://www.uwyo.edu/agecon)
- Kansas State University (http://www.ageconomics.k-state.edu/)

Selected Readings

Bluffstone, Randall A., and Gunnar Kohlin, eds. *Agricultural Investment and Productivity.* Washington, DC: Resources for the Future, 2011.

Gardner, Bruce L., and Gordon C. Rausser. *Handbook of Agricultural Economics* (two volumes). New York: North-Holland, 2002.

Just, Richard E., Julian M. Alston, and David Zilberman, eds. *Regulating Agricultural Biotechnology, Economics and Policy.* New York: Springer, 2006.

Lobell, David, and Marshall Burke. *Climate Change and Food Security: Adapting Agriculture to a Warming World.* New York: Springer, 2010.

Mendelsohn, Robert O., and Ariel Dinar. *Climate Change and Agriculture: An Economic Analysis of Global Impacts, Adaptation and Distributional Effects.* Northampton, MA: Edward Elgar, 2009.

17

Economics of Outdoor Recreation

In this chapter we examine a number of issues in the economics of outdoor recreation. "Outdoor recreation" in its most general sense involves all kinds of activities, from sitting in the backyard watching birds to deep-wilderness winter backpacking. We are primarily interested in outdoor recreation activities that are resource-intensive, that make use of forests, grasslands, lakes, and rivers. No clear dividing line separates resource-intensive activities from those that are not. But we do recognize that some, such as picnicking in a national or state park, are closely related to the quality of the natural resources with which visitors interact. Others, such as golf and jogging, do not place direct demands on natural resources, though they must use resources to some extent—land and water for golf courses and roads for jogging.

Outdoor recreation in many developed countries has grown rapidly in the latter part of the 20th century. Table 17-1 on the following page presents data for the United States on the number of people who participated in different types of outdoor recreation in 1982–83, and 2005–09, and the percentage change during this period. Keep in mind that over this time span the population of the United States increased about 22 percent, so one can see that most activities increased because of both increased population and increased participation rates. Note the relatively large increases in participation rates for walking, bird watching, hiking, backpacking, and camping and the decline in hunting. To some extent this may reflect the impacts of the environmental movement, which has tended to put greater emphasis on nonconsumptive uses of resources rather than the traditional consumptive uses.

A major impetus for the development of a separate economics of outdoor recreation is that, traditionally, much of the supply of outdoor recreation resources has been a public function, through national and state parks and forests and through the water resources made available with the building of large federally subsidized dams. Public authorities who control these resources need guidance for their decisions. In recent decades there has also developed a thriving **privately provided** market in outdoor recreation, from ski resorts to privately provided hunting and fishing, to whale watching and scuba diving resorts. So the economics of outdoor recreation now

Table 17-1   Participation in Selected Outdoor Recreational Activities, 1982–1983, 2005–2009

	Percent of Population Participating		Total Participants (millions)		Percent Change in Participants 1982–83 to 2005–09
	1982–1983	2005–2009	1982–1983	2005–2009	
Walking	53.0	84.1	91.9	194.2	111.3
Attend outdoor sports events	40.0	52.4	69.4	121.0	74.4
Outdoor concerts, plays, etc.	25.0	36.5	43.4	84.3	94.2
Bird watching	12.0	34.9	20.8	80.5	287.0
Day hiking	14.0	32.6	24.3	75.3	209.9
Outdoor team sports	24.0	26.9	41.6	62.1	49.3
Camping (developed area)	17.0	24.1	29.5	55.7	88.8
Canoeing/ kayaking	8.0	12.4	13.9	28.6	105.8
Hunting	12.0	11.5	20.8	26.6	27.9
Backpacking	5.0	9.8	8.7	22.7	160.9
Downhill skiing	6.0	6.4	10.4	14.8	42.3
Snowmobiling	3.0	3.8	5.2	8.7	67.3
Cross country skiing	3.0	2.1	5.2	4.9	−5.8

Source: Cordell, H. Ken, Gary T. Green, and Carter J. Betz, *Long-Term National Trends in Outdoor Recreation Activity Participation, 1980 to Now,* Internet Research Information Series, 2009.

includes questions about managing public reservations, the appropriate roles of public and private initiatives, and the management problems facing private firms operating in this space.

■ The Demand for Outdoor Recreation

Several different perspectives are important in studying the demand for outdoor recreation. One is to estimate the demand for a certain type of outdoor recreation activity among a defined group of people. Suppose we are a California company dealing in camping equipment. We would be interested in knowing how the demand for backpacking by the residents of California (or the country, if we were selling by mail-order or online) could be expected to grow over the next decade. We would want to estimate the impacts of anticipated growth in population, increases in income, and other factors we think might be important in determining how many people might be expected to engage in this activity. We might then want to determine the implications of this demand growth for the growth in demand for the specific products we expect to sell. This perspective is also of interest to the private individuals and public agencies who supply the parks and areas in which backpackers pursue their recreational activity.

Another perspective is what we might call the **facilities management** viewpoint. Suppose we are in charge of a particular park, current or proposed. We need to develop an understanding of the demand curve facing our single facility, which is affected by population, incomes, transportation services, and the presence of other competing or complementary facilities. A demand curve of this type is drawn in figure 17-1. The horizontal axis has an index of visitor-days, defined as the total number of day-long visits (e.g., two half-day visits make one visitor-day). Note that this is probably a great

simplification. Many parks produce a multiplicity of recreational services: day trips; overnight or longer visits; active recreational visits; sightseeing visits; and so on. But to have a tractable analysis, we must boil these down to a single "output" variable—thus the choice of visitor-days. The vertical axis has a monetary index, which will be used to measure the entrance price to visit the park. In many cases no entrance fee is charged. Of course, there still are other costs of visiting the park, namely, the travel costs of getting there. In this sense it is no different from any other good or service; even to buy a cantaloupe, one has to drive to the

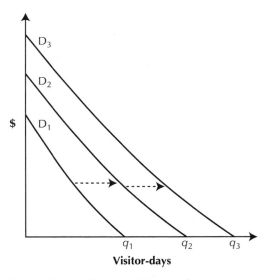

Figure 17-1   Demand Curves for an Imaginary Public Park

store. But travel costs usually loom much larger in visiting parks since they are usually a considerable distance from visitors' points of origin. The price indexed on the vertical axis, however, is the admission price visitors must pay to enter the park.

Each of the demand curves in figure 17-1 pertains to a different time period. These are **aggregate demand curves**, arrived at by summing together the individual demand curves of visitors to the park. We can assume that D_1 is the demand curve for some past year, say, 10 years ago, and that D_2 is the demand curve for the current period. Thus, D_3 is the **expected demand curve** for a future period, perhaps 10 years in the future.

What are the factors behind this shifting demand curve? A major one is **population growth.** Another is **income growth.** A third factor, actually a set of factors, is the cost of travel. Transportation **improvements** (e.g., building a new access road or linking it to the interstate system) or drops in the **price of gas** have the effect of shifting the demand curve to the right. And we must not forget the **taste and preference** factor; over time people learn more about outdoor recreation and come to appreciate it as a valuable source of psychic benefits in an increasingly urbanized society.

It is easy to hypothesize the existence of these demand curves, but difficult to estimate them in fact. It is especially difficult to measure how they have shifted over time. In the open-access experience of most public parks, detailed studies of demand have not been a high priority. This is changing as crowds have increased and interest grows in managing the access to, and use of, outdoor recreation facilities. In addition, economists have successfully developed methods for estimating recreation demand functions, like the travel cost method discussed in chapter 9.

Efficient Visitation Rates

In keeping with the idea used throughout the book, the **socially efficient visitation rate** is the rate that maximizes net benefits to society. If an area is a private operation, it presumably will be run at the visitation rate that maximizes net income. For this to be efficient in the social sense there must be no externalities, environmental or otherwise, stemming from the operation. We also have to have standard conditions with respect to public goods and the ability to exclude nonpayers.

We focus on publicly provided outdoor recreation facilities because historically these have been a predominating feature in the supply of these activities. Also, most public facilities historically have not required substantial entrance fees. If entrance fees are zero, i.e. open-access, the actual and expected numbers of visitor-days will be those shown as the sequence q_1, q_2, and q_3 in figure 17-1. The first is a historical number, pertaining to 10 years ago, the second shows visitor days this year, while q_3 shows the expected visitor-days 10 years into the future. There are several reasons for thinking that these do not represent socially efficient visitation rates. First, the costs of operating and maintaining the park are not being recovered through admission fees, but rather through some other means, perhaps through expenditures of tax monies collected from the citizenry of the relevant political district. In this case there is a disconnect between the people using the park and the people paying for it, so there is no reason to suspect that the willingness to pay of the marginal user corresponds to the marginal cost of accommodating that visitor. This is a requirement for efficiency, as we saw in chapter 5.

Another possible type of cost that is not covered if entrance fees are zero is the cost of resource degradation that may be related to visitation. In high-demand areas these costs can be significant, as is being encountered in ecotourist areas that draw large numbers of visitors.

Another reason for thinking that q_1, q_2, and q_3 are not socially efficient is the presence of **congestion externalities.** If admission prices are zero, we essentially have a situation of **open access.** Open access, as discussed in chapter 6, normally leads to use rates that exceed socially efficient levels. Recall the example of an open-access beach to show how congestion externalities arise. That example is perfectly illustrative of the situation facing open-access parks except that, in the latter, congestion externalities are likely to be even more important because activities such as backpacking are usually undertaken in the name of solitude, or at least a very low intensity level of activity.[1]

The quantities q_1, q_2, and q_3 of figure 17-1 show an increase in the open-access use levels of our park. Congestion externalities tend to increase as the demand curve shifts outward, and eventually, once visitation becomes very high, might choke off any further increases in visitation despite increases in population and other factors. This point has perhaps been reached in some national parks, when summertime visitor rates can be so high that physical capacities are reached. But in many other parks where visitation is less than what perhaps could be physically accommodated, questions have arisen regarding what the "optimal" visitation is and how it should be achieved.

To examine this question more closely, consider the model in figure 17-2. The curve labeled D is the normal market demand curve for visits to a public park. The point where this curve hits the horizontal axis (q_0) gives the open-access level of visitation; that is, the level that would pertain if no entrance fees are charged. Now suppose the marginal costs of operating the park are constant at a level of MC. If a price were charged equal to this amount, visitation would become q_1 visitor-days per year. This is not necessarily the efficient level of usage be-cause the curve D does not take congestion effects into account.

When the rate of visitation increases at a public park, the new visitors may cause congestion that lowers the value of the visitation experience not only for them but also for people who are already there. The nature of the congestion costs vary from place to place. For a wilderness area, congestion is connected to meeting other people on

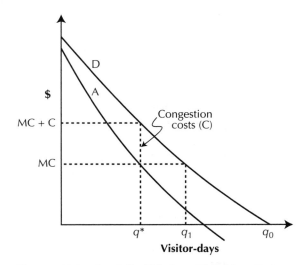

Figure 17-2   Socially Efficient Visitation Rates

the trail. For a ski resort, congestion is having to dodge other skiers on the slopes and waiting in line for the chair lift. For a picnic area, congestion means having all the good sites taken and having to put up with the sight and noise of neighboring groups. Ordinary demand curves do not account for these congestion effects because they are based on the willingness to pay of the **marginal user**. What we need is a demand curve of **net congestion effects;** that is, a curve that shows the marginal willingness to pay of the marginal user **minus** the congestion costs of existing users. These costs are essentially a reduction in the value of their visits caused by the entry of additional visitors. A demand curve adjusted for congestion effects is shown as curve A in figure 17-2. The height of D shows the willingness to pay of the marginal user; the height of A shows this marginal willingness to pay minus the congestion costs inflicted by the marginal user on existing users.

We now have a way of identifying the socially efficient use rate—it is q^*. But the curve D is the one that shows how visitation would vary with changes in the entrance fee. Thus, if we want to put into place a fee that will lead to a use rate of q^*, the fee must equal standard marginal costs (MC) plus congestion costs (C). This is shown as MC + C in the figure.

▪ Rationing Use

Open-space recreational areas come in all varieties: urban, suburban, wilderness. Most, however, are public in the sense of being financed and made available by a public agency: local, state, regional, national. For many, this argues for free entry: public facilities open to the public without a fee. The instinct for this is that open entry apparently gives equal weight to everybody; in particular it does not distinguish among people of different income/wealth levels. It is worth exploring this.

There are essentially four ways of managing entry to an area:

- Congestion cost
- First-come, first-served (FCFS)
- Limit entry to visitors with specific characteristics; e.g., only those who are town residents
- Entry price

The first of these has been the most common, especially in urban/suburban areas. Entry is limited only by the decline in the net benefits of a visit as congestion increases, as discussed above. A maximum visitation can be obtained either by FCFS, up to some limit, or by setting an entrance price sufficient to stop entry at the same limit. In fact, many suburban areas use a combination: an entrance fee to raise operating funds, with a cut off at some target maximum.

It is easy to understand that FCFS with an upper limit will yield a different subset of potential visitors than an entry fee. With no entry fee, the potential pool of visitors consists of all those who would derive positive net benefits from a visit. With a FCFS system, some random subset of the total pool would be allowed entry. Using a limiting entry fee would ration entry to those whose net visitor benefits exceeded the entry price. It is not impossible, but highly improbable, that these two means of rationing entry would yield exactly the same subset of visitors.

In addition, no, or low, fees with FCFS would have distributional implications, with income shifted from those who cover the cost of the facility, to those who visit. Costs are usually covered out of general or dedicated tax revenues. The distribution of benefits would depend importantly on the location of the area, for example location in a low-income urban neighborhood or an upper-middle income suburban location.

Rationing by Price

Entry fees to ration use have not been commonly used historically, except in private resource-based ventures such as downhill skiing. Thus, the provision of public parks and nature reserves has been seen as an important part of civic life and cultural identity, an activity that ought to be outside the market. This view is changing, however, under a number of influences. One is that admission fees may be a more appropriate and effective way of raising revenues to support the maintenance of park areas. Another is the rise of **ecotourism** as a potential revenue producer for developing countries, as well as for communities everywhere who are looking for ways to support public services. A third factor is that privately produced outdoor recreation is a fast-growing sector, and in this case entry fees are an integral part of the system. Finally, there is perhaps a growing appreciation of the fact that entry fees and the revenue they produce can provide a justification for expanding the system of parks and reservations in terms of both quantity and quality. The incentive for protecting resources is increased if that protection also yields a revenue flow. Perhaps one additional factor is the realization that access is already rationed by price to a very large extent, except that the price is in the form of travel costs. Those people who can afford the time and money to visit national parks and forests are the people who visit; those who cannot afford it do not.[2]

At the federal level there is a distinct trend toward charging entrance fees, although many areas remain open at no charge. Exhibit 17-1 (on the next page) discusses some of the fees that are authorized by current federal law. Entrance fees are also widespread in state public recreation areas. The primary justification for admission fees, in the eyes of the participating agencies, is to recover revenues so that more money can be put into developing, maintaining, and operating the sites. As we have seen above, this rationale leads to entrance fees that are too low for social efficiency if congestion is involved, and may also be too low to protect ecosystems in the reservations from excessive wear and tear by visitors. Although fees do indeed create a revenue flow, their primary justification is to ration the use of an asset that is scarce and to ensure that people who visit the parks value the experience more highly than people who do not visit.

Exhibit 17-1   Federal Public Recreation Site Entrance Fees

In 1995 Congress enacted the Recreation Fee Demonstration Program, which allowed some federal agencies, such as the National Park Service, to charge entrance fees. In 2004 this was replaced by the Federal Lands Recreation Enhancement Act (REA), which extended the authorization for entrance fees through September 2015. Legislation to extend such fees has since been introduced into Congress. The types of entrance fees used are the following:

- **Entrance fee**, used by the National Park Service (NPS) and the Fish and Wildlife Service (FWS), which normally cover entrance to entire parks or refuges.

- **Standard amenity recreation fee**, authorized for National Conservation Areas, National Volcanic Monuments, destination visitor and interpretive centers, and areas that meet specific amenity-based criteria.

- **Expanded amenity recreation fee** is a category that may be charged in addition to an entrance fee, or by itself, on lands managed by the NPS and FWS where the Secretary of the Interior determines visitors use a specific or specialized facility, equipment, or service. On lands managed by the Forest Service (FS) and the Bureau of Land Management (BLM), expanded amenity recreation fees may be charged only for facilities and services that meet defined criteria such as developed campgrounds, boat launches, equipment rentals, use of hookups for electricity, cable or sewer, reservation services, transportation, first-aid, and swimming sites.

- **Special recreation permit fees** mostly pertain to BLM and FS sites. Under REA, Advisory Councils and Recreation Resource Advisory Councils (RRACs) have the opportunity to review all non-commercial, individual special recreation permit fees. (Commercial and group special recreation permits, such as outfitting and guiding permits or recreation events, are not subject to review by the Advisory Councils and RRACs.)

- **Interagency recreation passes** provided by REA cover entrance fees for NPS and FWS sites and standard amenity fees for BLM, FS, Bureau of Reclamation, and Fish and Wildlife Service sites.

Source: Based on U.S. Department of the Interior, U.S. Department of Agriculture, *Federal Lands Recreation Enhancement Act: First Triennial Report to Congress Fiscal Year 2006*, Washington, DC, May 2006; National Park Service, *Reauthorization of the Federal Lands Recreation Enhancement Act*, http://www.npca.org/assets/pdf/Factsheet-Federal-Lands-Recreation-Enhancement-Act.pdf, accessed August 26, 2015.

Pricing and Total Revenue

A major rationale for entry fees in practice is to raise revenue, so it will be useful to clarify the connection between price changes and revenue changes. For any given price there is an associated quantity, as given by the demand function. Increases in price lead to decreases in quantity and vice versa. Since total revenue is simply price times quantity, an increase in price by a certain amount can lead to increases or decreases in total revenue, depending on how much quantity changes. Consider figure 17-3, the demand curve of an imaginary public park. At a fee of $12 per day, visitation will average 180, thus the total revenue, indicated by rectangle $b + c$, is $2,160. At a price of $14, visitation drops to 160, and total revenue (area $a + b$) increases to $2,240. Had quantity decreased by more in response to the higher price, total revenue could have decreased. If the demand curve was flatter, for example, so quantity decreased to 140 visitor-days, the new total revenue would have been $1,960, a decrease.

The critical parameter of a demand function, which determines whether total revenues increase or decrease (and how much) when prices change, is the **price elasticity of demand** (E_p). It is defined as:

$$E_p = \frac{\text{Percentage change in quantity}}{\text{Percentage change in price}}$$

and we use the following terminology:

if $E_p = -1$, we have unitary elasticity
if $E_p < -1$, we have a relatively **elastic** demand curve
if $-1 < E_p < 0$, we have a **relatively inelastic** demand curve

Note that when $E_p = -1$, the percentage change in quantity is exactly the same as the percentage change in price, and since total revenue is equal to price times quantity, it does not change in this case when price changes. On the other hand, if the demand curve is inelastic, quantity changes (in percentage terms) are lower than price changes, so total revenue will increase if price increases and will fall if price decreases. It is just the opposite when the E_p is elastic; in this case quantity increases (in percentage terms) exceed price changes, hence total revenue goes up with price decreases and down with price increases. So in figure 17-3, the demand curve was relatively inelastic between prices of $12 and $14; total revenue increased when the price increased.

Panel (a) of figure 17-4 (on the following page) shows three demand curves that differ in terms of their height and slope. Their shapes are derived both from the nature of the resource involved and the economics and demographics of the relevant population of demanders. Panel (b) of the figure shows the relationship between price and total revenue for each demand curve. In each case they are inelastic at low prices, thus total revenue increases as price increases. Each also reaches a

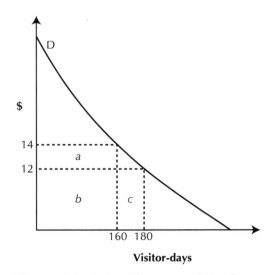

Figure 17-3   Price Changes and Total Revenue

point where the elasticity becomes unitary, except it is at a different point (a different price) in each case. These points are where the total revenue curves in the graph reach their maximum levels. At prices higher than this, the demand curves become elastic, which explains why total revenue declines as prices continue to increase.[3] Exhibit 17-2 discusses a research project that was undertaken to investigate the demand for visitation at three national parks in Costa Rica and the consequences of setting entrance fees at different levels. The researchers estimated, among other things, the level of entrance fees in the three cases that would maximize park revenues.

It should be emphasized that maximizing total revenue is not necessarily recommended as an appropriate strategy for national parks, forests, and other reservations. Social efficiency calls for maximizing net benefits, and the price-visitation combination that maximizes net benefits may not be the same as the one that simply maximizes total revenue. One major reason for this discrepancy is that environmental costs are included when determining social efficiency. They may or may not affect revenues in a consistent way. If willingness to pay by visitors is correlated strongly with the environmental quality of the sites such that environmental damage impacts the individual demand functions, then damage may be fully reflected in revenue losses. But visitors may not necessarily be sensitive to all types of ecological disruption, so willingness to pay may not be an accurate reflection of the ecological status of the park or reservation.

Another important factor in pricing park access is that parks and reservations normally exist as systems; states have multiple parks that they wish to manage in a coordinated fashion, as does the federal government with its network of national parks, for-

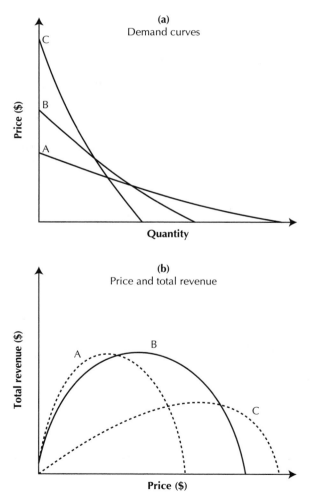

Figure 17-4   The Relationship between Price and Total Revenue for Three Different Demand Curves

ests, and monuments. In these cases it is probably not appropriate to price each independently in an attempt to maximize its own total revenues. Prices at the various reservations have to be established in a coordinated fashion, taking into account the demand interrelationships among them.

Exhibit 17-2   Pricing National Park Access in Costa Rica

Costa Rica has developed an extensive series of national parks, which are visited by large numbers of tourists each year. Earnings from ecotourism have become the country's largest single source of foreign exchange in recent years. Tourism is not distributed evenly among the country's parks. The three parks discussed below account for approximately two-thirds of foreign tourist visits in recent years. Until 1994, modest entrance fees were charged at these parks. On September 1 of that year fees for foreign visitors were increased by 1,100 percent, from 200 colones ($1.25 U.S.) to 2,400 colones ($15 U.S.). Fees for residents remained at 200 colones. This abrupt increase led to controversy between local groups and tourism operators and the rate-setting authorities, and to questions about what entrance fees were appropriate. A group of researchers undertook to examine the pricing situation, in particular to estimate the important features of the demand functions of ecotourists for visits to the three most heavily visited parks. Some of the results they obtained are as follows:

| | **Park** | | |
	Volcán Irazú	Volcán Poás	Manuel Antonio
Actual fee paid	$12.28	$9.85	$9.56
Average length of visit (days)	1.00	1.00	1.45
Maximum willingness to pay for a visit	21.75	21.60	24.90
Fee that visitors felt would be "appropriate"	6.48	6.77	7.37
Price elasticity of demand	−1.05	−2.87	−.96
Actual total revenues 1994–1995	427,307	669,940	431,371
Revenue-maximizing entry fee	7.06	9.28	13.59
Projected total revenues if revenue-maximizing entry fee had been used	$1,372,844	$675,447	$518,187

There are a number of interesting things about these results. Note that the price elasticities of demand are quite different for the three parks. In two of them the elasticity is near unity, while at the third demand is quite elastic. Note also that at one park the actual admission price was quite close to the revenue-maximizing one, at one park it was well below the revenue-maximizing price, and at the other the actual price was well above the revenue-maximizing price. By comparing the actual with projected revenues you can see how much additional revenue can sometimes be obtained with the appropriate price. It needs to be kept in mind, however, that revenue maximization is not necessarily the most appropriate goal for park managers to pursue.

Source: Lisa C. Chase, David R. Lee, William D. Schulze, and Deborah J. Anderson, "Ecotourism Demand and Differential Pricing of National Park Access in Costa Rica," *Land Economics,* 74(4), November 1998, pp. 466–482.

Differential Pricing

The real world, however, is obviously more complicated than the simple model above implies. Not all users or visitors are necessarily alike in terms of characteristics that affect their willingness to pay. This brings up the question of when it is justified, for efficiency and/or equity terms, to establish different prices for different users. Consider the following:

- Given the normal constraints on time and the extent of the normal workweek, the willingness to pay on weekends is often higher than that on weekdays, especially for less remote areas. Is it efficient and fair to charge different prices on weekends than on weekdays?

- Very often the same park or forest accommodates visitors who engage in different activities: some people are interested in backpacking and solitude, while others want easier access and are less in search of a "pure" wilderness experience. Is it efficient and/or equitable to charge different rates to people in the two groups?

- There are two public parks, alike in every way in terms of environmental values, but one is relatively close to an urban area and one is far away. Is it efficient and/or equitable to charge different entrance fees at these two parks?

Questions like these can get quite complex. We now try to develop some reasonably simple principles to help in thinking about the issues. Consider figure 17-5. This applies to a situation where there are two types of users of a park. One group has a demand curve labeled D_1, and the other has demand curve D_2. Note that the latter is steeper than the former; perhaps these are rock climbers, who have a relatively inelastic demand for this area, whereas the more elastic D_1 is the demand of day picnickers in the park. The **aggregate demand curve,** labeled D_t, is the horizontal summation of D_1 and D_2.

MC is the marginal cost curve, drawn horizontally on the assumption that the marginal cost of servicing all visitors is constant and the same for each visitor type. Let us assume that there are no congestion problems. Overall social efficiency requires that aggregate marginal willingness to pay be equal to marginal cost. This is achieved by

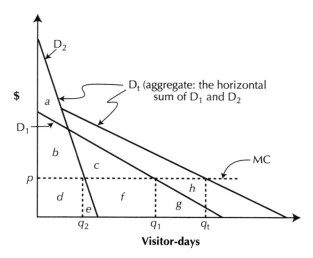

Figure 17-5 Efficient Pricing When There Are Two Classes of Visitors

setting price equal to marginal cost (p = MC) for both sorts of users. Total visitor-days then are q_t, and the visitor-days of each type are q_1 and q_2. Note that total revenue taken in just equals total costs (the area $d + e + f + g + h$). Of this total revenue, $d + e + f$ is paid by group 1 and d is paid by group 2. Net benefits accruing to group 1 are $b + c$; those going to group 2 are equal to $a + b$. Total net benefits are maximized (i.e., we achieve social efficiency) when the same price is charged to each type of user. Suppose we don't; suppose we charge $10 a day to type 1 visitors and $5 a day to type 2 visitors. This means that the marginal type 1 visitor values the visit at $10 while the marginal type 2 visitor values it at $5. It is not socially efficient to let the former in but keep the latter out. Thus, as long as the marginal costs of servicing individuals in the two groups are the same, there is no efficiency justification for charging different entrance fees.[4]

The obverse of this is also true, however. If the marginal costs of servicing people in the two groups are different, efficiency requires that they be charged different prices. In particular, prices should be higher to the group with the higher marginal cost, and lower to the group with the lower marginal cost. Setting p = MC for each subgroup of users achieves this result. An example might be that rock climbers require higher costs than picnickers because of the need for closer supervision, stand-by rescue and medical equipment, and so forth.

An example where there is a cost difference is when congestion costs differ from one time period to another. Many parks have capacity limits, either hard limits like a certain number of campsites or visitation levels where congestion externalities begin to take hold. Consider a very simple case of a park with a certain number of picnic sites, indicated as q_0 in figure 17-6. Suppose that the marginal costs of servicing the sites is quite low, set at the level MC in the figure. There are two demand curves: D_1 pertains to weekday visitors and D_2 is for weekend visitors. The latter is well outside the former because of the greater time availability that people have on weekends. Efficiency in this case requires two prices. During the week, set p = MC. In this case the average weekday visitation is q_1. But this price will not do for weekends, because

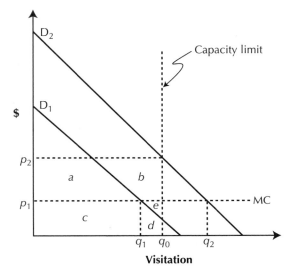

Figure 17-6 Peak Load Park Pricing

the quantity demanded at this price on weekends far exceeds the capacity of the park (that is, $q_2 > q_0$).

Parks might be under political pressure to charge the same rates during the weekend that they do on weekdays. In this case some type of nonprice rationing would be required to limit weekend use and to avoid situations where people without picnic sites tie up the park by milling around looking for an open site. Furthermore, if the price p_1 (= MC) were set on weekends, we have no guarantee that people ending up with picnic sites would be those who valued them the most highly. They could be simply the luckiest or the first ones to show up in the morning. Thus, to ensure a maximum of net benefits, we set p_1 = MC during the week, and p_2 during the weekends. You can see immediately that there is an extra element in this model. On weekends, total costs are equal to $c + d + e$, while total revenue from entrance fees is equal to $a + b + c + d + e$; the park is making a profit of $a + b$. In effect, this is a redistribution of income from the weekend park visitors to whoever ends up with these revenues, perhaps the general taxpayer if they go into a general account of some political entity. This creates an additional wrinkle. Suppose the park agency is under a political directive to operate as a **nonprofit.** Then it would have to resort to some means to avoid making the profit ($a + b$). There are two possibilities. One is to charge p_1 on the weekends but resort also to nonprice rationing, as mentioned above. Another is to inflate costs until they match revenues. By "inflate" we mean undertaking expenses that are not really needed to maintain the park at an acceptable level.

Pricing to Cover Fixed Operating Costs

Let us look at one last pricing issue. The examples in the previous section all had constant marginal cost curves at some level. This means that we assumed that total costs increased linearly with the number of visitors; each new visitor increased costs by exactly the same amount. But this is probably not an accurate assumption in some cases. Very often the operating costs of a public park are somewhat fixed in nature. To operate the park at all involves certain staffing and other costs, and these costs don't necessarily vary smoothly with the number of visitors that show up. Another way to say this is that, once the park is open and operating with the normal staff and supply costs, the **marginal cost** of accommodating an extra visitor is quite low, perhaps even zero in some cases. This is so at least up until the point where congestion begins, after which there are positive congestion costs.

Consider the case of zero marginal costs. Efficiency says to set price equal to marginal cost, and so here the entrance fee would be set at zero. But in this case, revenues are also zero, and the park is unable to cover its costs. What to do? In cases like this it may be useful to move in the direction of a **two-part price** system. In this kind of system the total visitation fee is broken into two parts, one part that is based on **current marginal visitation cost** (which in the example is zero), and the other part a **one-time-only seasonal payment** that gives individual visitors the right to have access whenever and however many times they choose throughout the year. The price of the seasonal pass is set (as closely as possible) so that it recovers the fixed operating costs of the park. For a person who visits the park just one time throughout the season, of course, the prices of the two permits meld into a single payment; it is only with multiple visits that the two prices become distinct.

■ Ecotourism

Tourists are a ubiquitous part of the modern world. **Ecotourists** are those whose visits are linked in some fashion to natural or environmental resources; the term covers essentially the same activities—touring, observing, participating—that we have discussed under the older term "outdoor recreation." Ecotourism can clearly be domestic, but perhaps has a stronger connotation of international travel, especially travel from countries of the developed world to visit the unique natural resource endowments of the countries in the developing world. Ecotourism is seen by people in some locales as a key element for stimulating economic development. On the level of incentives, it can elevate the value of natural assets that previously were outside the market, which may lead people to put greater stress on their conservation. If, through ecotourism, resources worthy of conservation can be increased in market value, then there will be less incentive for them to be deforested, converted to pasture or cultivation agriculture, or otherwise disrupted. Ecotourism has a number of important bioeconomic aspects.

Demand Estimation and Management

Many of the concepts discussed earlier in this chapter—demand estimation, revenue generation, and pricing issues—are directly applicable to ecotourism. If prices, such as park entrance fees or wildlife tour fees, are to be used to raise revenue or to protect sensitive resources from overuse, then knowledge of the relevant demand functions is useful and important. Private firms in the ecotourism industry have faced this problem all along and have presumably developed the necessary knowledge as a condition of staying in business. But the problem is relatively new in the public sector. Questions about access rights have traditionally been dealt with politically, which is where pricing decisions are addressed, at least initially. The situation is complex because countries are making many different types of resource reservations with important differences among them in terms of types of resources, objectives, and clientele. The list in table 17-2 on the following pages gives some idea of these differences for developing countries. Developed countries also normally have systems of national parks, wildlife refuges, and wilderness areas.

Table 17-2   Categories and Management Objectives of Protected Areas

Protected Area	Management Objectives	Examples
Scientific reserve/ strict nature reserve	To protect nature and maintain natural processes in an undisturbed state in order to have ecologically representative examples of the natural environment available for scientific study, environmental monitoring and education, and the maintenance of genetic resources in a dynamic and evolutionary state.	• Yala Strict Nature Reserve in Sri Lanka • Island of Barro Colorado in Panama • Gombe Stream National Park in Tanzania
National park	To protect relatively large natural and scenic areas of national or international significance for scientific, educational, and recreational use, under management by the highest competent authority of a nation.	• Royal Chitwan National Park in Nepal • Etosha National Park in Namibia • Iguazu National Parks in Argentina and Brazil • Volcán Poás National Park in Costa Rica
Natural monument/ natural landmark	To protect and preserve nationally significant natural features because of their special interest or unique characteristics.	• Angkor Wat National Park in Cambodia • Petrified Forests Nature Monument in Argentina • Gedi National Monument in Kenya
Managed nature reserve/wildlife sanctuary	To ensure the natural conditions necessary to protect nationally significant species, groups of species, biotic communities, or physical features of the environment when these require specific human manipulation for their perpetuation.	• Manas Wildlife Sanctuary in India • Most of the national reserves in Kenya • Biotope reserves in Guatemala • Marine reserves such as the one located in the Galápagos
Protected landscapes	To maintain nationally significant natural landscapes characteristic of the harmonious interaction of humans and land, while providing opportunities for public enjoyment through recreation and tourism within the normal lifestyle and economic activity of these areas	• Pululahua Geobotanical Reserve in Ecuador • Machu Picchu Historic Sanctuary in Peru • National Parks of England

Protected Area	Management Objectives	Examples
Resource reserve	To protect the natural resources of the area for future use and to prevent or contain development activities that could affect the resource pending the establishment of objectives based on appropriate knowledge and planning. Few countries have yet applied this category, but several resource reserves exist in Kenya, including Kora and South Turkana National Reserves.	• Brazil's Forest Reserves • Tahuamanu Protected Forest, Bolivia
Natural biotic area/ anthropological reserve	To allow the way of life of societies living in harmony with the environment to continue undisturbed by modern technology.	• The Gunung Lorentz Nature Reserve of Indonesia • Xingu Indigenous Park of Brazil • Central Kalahari Game Reserve of Botswana • Many protected areas in the South Pacific islands
Multiple-use management area/ managed resource area	To provide for the sustained production of water, timber, wildlife, pasture, and outdoor recreation, with the conservation of nature primarily orientated to the support of the economic activities (although specific zones can also be designed within these areas to achieve specific conservation objectives).	• Ngorongoro Conservation Area of Tanzania • Kutai National Park of Indonesia • Jamari and Tapajos National Forests of Brazil • Von Humboldt National Forest of Peru

Sources: International Union for the Conservation of Nature (IUCN), "Categories, Objectives, and Criteria for Protected Areas," in J. A. McNeely and K. R. Miller (eds.), *National Parks, Conservation and Development*, Smithsonian Institution Press, Washington, DC, 1984; J. Mackinnon et al., *Managing Protected Areas in the Tropics*, IUCN, Gland, Switzerland, 1986; as cited in Gardner Brown, "Wildlife in Developing Countries," in Partha Dasgupta and Karl-Gören Mäler, *The Environment and Emerging Development Issues*, Vol. 2, Clarendon Press, Oxford, England, 1997, p. 562.

Biological Impacts

There is a great deal of very legitimate concern that opening up resources to tourist impacts, especially resources that are ecologically sensitive, could lead to their long-run diminution in terms of quantity and/or quality. A strong desire to generate revenues could motivate visitation rates that are too high relative to some longer-run "sustainable" level. Or investment in infrastructure such as roads could open up resources that before had been protected by their remoteness. The concept of **sustainable ecotourism** has been suggested as the relevant guide for action.[5] This is certainly appropriate in the sense of making sure that ecological resources are not permanently damaged by tourism activities. But most ecotourism activities are connected with biological resources, and the question comes up, as it has repeatedly throughout the book, as to what the efficient stock of a resource is when used as an ecotourism resource. Virtually any level of tourism will affect the quantity and/or quality of a resource. The appropriate quantity and quality of a natural resource open to ecotourism will undoubtedly be different from what it would be if there were no ecotourism. The difference hinges on the trade-off between the values of the biological impacts and the economic values associated with the ecotourism. Furthermore, many ecotourism projects have been undertaken with the notion of providing a stimulus to economic development, which might become less resource-dependent in the future if it is successful. This raises the possibility that the optimal stock of an ecotourist resource is not steady-state, at least not yet. Rather, development may call for relatively heavy use in the short run and lower rates of use in the long run.

Institutional Issues

There are a range of institutional questions involved in the social management of ecotourism. One of the most important is the balance that should be struck between the public and private sectors. In many countries federal or regional governments are directly involved, for example, in managing access to national parks and wildlife refuges. In some cases (e.g., wildlife in Africa), private companies have formed to operate ecotourism activities in a market setting. In some cases units of local government function to some extent like private firms in managing local ecotourism.[6]

The best institutional arrangements in any specific case presumably depend on the details of that case—the resource involved and political and economic attributes of the countries. Some general principles may be possible, however. Ecotourism is based on market principles, in which supply must be directed at the demand; in this case, the demands of ecotourists. Not all resources that are valuable in some biological sense will be valuable to tourists in a market sense. It is clearly important that economically popular resources not be favored to the detriment of unpopular, but ecologically important, resources. When decisions are located in the private sector—that is, with private ecotourist firms—this problem comes under the heading of **external costs.** Decisions made in the public sector—that is, by public agencies responsible for ecotourist resources—may be made according to the narrow political interests of those in power, to the exclusion of other values that may be important in a wider social context.

The distribution of resource rents is also an important dimension of the institutional question. If ecotourism is undertaken in the name of economic development, it clearly makes a difference who accumulates the resulting rents. If they go to the state, they are used for purposes that state planners and politicians deem to be important. If they go to individuals locally, they are likely to be spent on entirely different goods and services. We have more to say about this in chapter 20, where we discuss natural resources and economic growth. Also, the motivation for many ecotourism projects is to provide incentives to conserve the resources in question as mentioned above. If this is to be successful, the rents must go, in large part at least, to those in the local population who have the power to conserve the resource. For example, the most effective way to stop poaching or deforestation by local people of public ecotourist reservations may be to direct some of the rents to these people.

■ Summary

In this chapter we focused on important issues in the economics of outdoor recreation. Many of these issues are connected to an understanding of the demand curves people have for outdoor recreation in general and for specific recreation sites. We looked at the general question of efficient visitation rates at a public park and brought in the problem of congestion externalities. A major part of the chapter dealt with the problem of how to ration use of public parks, which is becoming a much more difficult problem as populations and incomes grow. We considered nonprice rationing schemes and the use of entry fees to ration visitation. We looked at the relation of prices and total revenues, which hinges on the value of the price elasticity of demand, and also at questions of differential pricing and problems of pricing when marginal short-run visitation costs are very low, perhaps zero, but annual fixed costs must be covered. Lastly, we discussed ecotourism, including price policy, biological impacts, and the disposition of rents from ecotourism projects.

Notes

1 In many of the contingent valuation studies of willingness to pay for backpacking experiences, the likelihood of meeting other backpackers strongly affects the valuations expressed by respondents. One of the early examples is reported in Charles J. Cicchetti and V. Kerry Smith, "Congestion, Quality Deterioration and Optimal Use: Wilderness Recreation in the Spanish Peaks Primitive Area," *Social Science Research*, Vol. 2, 1973, pp. 15–30. See chapter 9 for a discussion of contingent valuation analysis.

2 As of 2014 the U.S. National Park Service charged entrance fees at about one third of its sites, particularly the most popular ones.

3 In Idaho, administrators of the state park system found that by lowering fees, total revenues increased. See "States Push Annual Park Passes To Raise Revenues," *Daily Hampshire Gazette*, May 29, 2014.

4 If the park agency wants to maximize revenues, on the other hand, it would probably want to differentiate prices. Charging higher prices to the group with inelastic demand would

increase revenues. Charging lower prices to the elastic-demand group also increases revenues from this source. This is what airlines do. Business travelers are group 2; "recreational" travelers are group 1. This practice is called price discrimination.

[5] See, for example, Erlet Cater and Gwen Lowman, eds., *Ecotourism: A Sustainable Option?* New York: Wiley, 1994.

[6] The well-known Campfire (Communal Areas Management Program for Indigenous Resources) program in Africa allows local communities, functioning collectively, to profit by selling access to local wildlife resources to safari operators.

Key Terms

congestion externalities
differential pricing
ecotourism
efficient visitation rates
elastic demand
inelastic demand
nonprice rationing

outdoor recreation demand function
peak load pricing
price charges and total revenue
price elasticity of demand
pricing to cover fixed costs
rationing through price
rationing use

Questions for Further Discussion

1. Suppose the demand curve for a public park is $Q = 80 - 2p$, where Q is the number of visitor-days and p is the entry price. The marginal cost of operating the park is MC = 10.

   a. What is the efficient level of entrance fee and the number of visitors at this fee level (assume no congestion problems)?

   b. At the price/quantity combination of (a), what is the price elasticity of demand for park visitation? (To find this, take a small change in price, say, $1. Figure out the elasticity with the change in quantity resulting from this price change. The percentage change in price and quantity is different depending on whether the price has gone up by one dollar or down by one dollar. Take the average of the two estimates.)

   c. What is the price-quantity combination that maximizes revenues, and what is the price elasticity of demand at this point on the demand curve?

2. If one rations the use of a public park with an entrance fee, we know that each user of the park values that visit at a level equal to or above the fee. If we ration by "first-come, first-served," what do we know about the visitors?

3. We talked earlier (see chapter 9) about measuring demand curves. How might we proceed if we want to measure congestion externalities associated with various outdoor recreation activities?

4. One reason for levying entrance fees at public parks is to generate revenues to help cover costs. What are the other reasons?

5. Suppose a natural resource area is set aside and designated as a scientific preserve open to scientists who study, for example, species diversity issues. Should scientists be charged for access to the area?

6. You have built a number of blinds that can be used to hunt or observe the migrating Canada geese in a spot on the main flyway. You have to estab-

lish a price to charge people for using the blinds. What considerations go into determining this price?

Useful Websites

Information on national parks, visitation data, and forecasts, as well as impact data on local communities:
- National Park Service, Public Use Statistics Office (https://irma.nps.gov/Stats)

Other federal agencies are also relevant:
- U.S. Fish and Wildlife Service (www.fws.gov)

Various studies about national and state parks:
- Resources for the Future (http://www.rff.org)

Information on national parks in other countries:
- National Parks Worldwide (http://nationalparksworldwide.com)

Relevant public interest groups:
- National Parks and Conservation Association (http://www.npca.org)
- The Wilderness Society (http://www.wilderness.org)
- National Fish and Wildlife Foundation (http://www.nfwf.org)
- The Trust for Public Lands (http://www.tpl.org)
- National Recreational Park Association (http://www.nrpa.org/)

General information on outdoor recreation and ecotourism:
- Great Outdoor Recreation Pages (http://www.gorp.com)
- The International Ecotourism Society (http://www.ecotourism.org)

Papers on the economics of outdoor recreation:
- Journal of Leisure Research (http://js.sagamorepub.com/jlr)
- Natural Resources Research Information Pages, "Outdoor Recreation Research" (www4.ncsu.edu/~leung/recres2.html)

Selected Readings

Clawson, Marion, and Jack L. Knetsch. *Economics of Outdoor Recreation.* Baltimore, MD: Johns Hopkins University Press for Resources for the Future, 1966.

Fisher, Anthony C., and John V. Krutilla. "Determination of Optimal Capacity of Resource-Based Recreation Facility," *Natural Resource Journal*, Vol. 12, 1972, pp. 417–444.

Hanley, Nick, W. Douglass Shaw, and Robert E. Wright, eds., *The New Economics of Outdoor Recreation.* Northampton, MA: Edward Elgar, 2003.

McConnell, Kenneth E. "The Economics of Outdoor Recreation," in Allen V. Kneese and James L. Sweeny, eds., *Handbook of Natural Resource and Energy Economics*, Vol. 2. Amsterdam: North-Holland, 1985, pp. 677–722.

■ ■

18

Economics of Wildlife Management

The various impacts of human beings on wildlife resources have become more frequent and more contentious in recent years. Continued demographic and economic growth has brought human work and dwelling places more directly into conflict with wild animals and plants. At the same time, these resources are becoming more highly valued for preserving ecosystem integrity, for providing unconventional inputs for human societies, and as sources of direct enjoyment for an increasingly urbanized population. On a more philosophical level, preservation of wildlife has to some extent become a rallying cry for those who believe it important that modern humans seek to reestablish their roots in the workings of the natural world.

Wildlife, in its most general sense, refers to living, nonhuman organisms that have not been domesticated. The line between what is domesticated and what is not is sometimes a little fuzzy, but for present purposes we don't have to be too precise. We deal with several important categories of wildlife in other chapters, in particular marine, forest, and diversity resources.[1] In this chapter we deal with wildlife issues from a somewhat different perspective, in particular those cases where the value of wildlife is not solely a function of its harvested value, but rather of the contributing role it plays in various wildlife-related activities pursued by humans. This includes, for example, sport hunting and animal watching. Another important wildlife-related topic is the control of **invasive species.** These are nonnative species that are introduced, either intentionally or unintentionally, into an area, which then disrupt and damage native ecosystems and the activities, such as agriculture, that depend on them. Defined broadly, wildlife issues could also include situations involving **existence values;** that is, the values to humans of knowing that certain wildlife are present, usually in adequate numbers, in a given area.

The chapter begins with a discussion of some basic questions concerning wildlife ecology, economic institutions, and public policy. It then treats a number of important wildlife-related issues: hunting, animal watching, predator control, and the control of wildlife markets. Several other wildlife problems are treated in other chapters: land-use restrictions and habitat control in the chapter on land economics and endangered species protection in the chapter on the economics of diversity preservation.

■ Wildlife Ecology and Human Institutions

We have seen that fisheries economics and policy essentially involve bringing together the ecology of fish populations with the economic incentives of human decision makers (see chapter 13). Wildlife economics requires the same approach. In this case, however, the interaction of the two—ecology and human institutions—may be more complicated because of wider variations in the animals and ecological niches in which they are found, the closer physical proximity that exists between terrestrial animals and humans, and the more complicated array of human motivations that characterizes noncommercial situations.

Population Growth Curves

Regardless of the objective of wildlife management—hunting, ecotourism, predator control—the critical relationship is the growth dynamics of the wildlife population of interest. A population increases, decreases, or remains constant due to a host of factors such as food availability, sex ratios, fecundity and mortality rates, and predation pressure. In 1942 Arthur Einarsen studied the way a population of pheasants grew after the species was introduced onto a previously uninhabited (by pheasants) island.[2] What he found is pictured in panel (a) of figure 18-1. For the first few years population increases were modest, but then the rate of change increased greatly. In 1941 the increment reached its maximum, and the next year it was lower. Assuming a continuance of this trend, it was expected that at some point, perhaps around 1946, the population of pheasants would meet its maximum, the carrying capacity for the habitat. After that the curve would flatten out, signifying no further increase.

What he observed in this case was apparently a phenomenon following a **logistic growth curve,** a relationship we encounter in chapter 13. It is an inverted U curve showing how the growth increment to a population is related to the size of that population. A logistic curve is depicted in panel (b) of figure 18-1. The annual increment of small populations is relatively low; it reaches a maximum at a population size of about 1,400 pheasants and then drops to zero at a population of about 2,600. Not all wild animals behave according to simple logistic models like this, but despite its simplicity it summarizes the basic population dynamics for many of them, as far as is known. Carrying capacity in this case is at about 2,600 animals, while 1,400 is the stock size that defines **maximum sustained yield,** the maximum quantity of the wildlife in question that could be harvested on a **sustainable** basis.

Several important points must be made here. First, although 1,400 is the population level that gives the maximum sustained yield, this strictly biological point of reference is not necessarily the stock that is optimal from a social standpoint. We saw in the case of the fishery that the commercial aspects of the problem—the market values of the fish and the costs of harvest—led to an economic optimum different from the biological point of maximum sustained yield. If we consider wildlife more broadly, we have to allow for the possibility of other sources of value, for example, value for **recreational hunting,** for **ecotourism** (wildlife viewing), for **biological diversity,** or simply **existence value.** These other sources of value could make it even more difficult to identify a socially optimal wildlife stock in any particular case.

We also must consider uncertainty, especially when we lack a very clear idea of what the growth curve looks like. Theoretically, if the growth function for any animal population were well known, it could be used to establish optimal harvest policies. The problem is that, in the real world, so many factors are at work that it may be very difficult, even with diligent research, to identify a simple relationship between stock size and the increment to that stock. Exhibit 18-1 illustrates this in the case of the wild turkey. The upshot is that management of many, if not most, wildlife populations has to proceed in the face of great uncertainty about underlying growth dynamics.

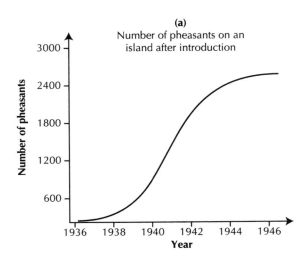

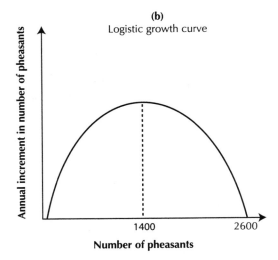

Figure 18-1   Growth of a Pheasant Population

Data Source: Arthur S. Einarsen, "Specific Results from Ring-Necked Pheasant Studies in the Pacific Northwest," Transactions of the Seventh North American Wildlife Conference, 1942, pp. 130–138.

Exhibit 18-1   Difficulties in Determining Wildlife Growth Relationships: The Wild Turkey

Hunting regulations were set cautiously after wild turkeys (*Meleagris gallopavo*) were reestablished successfully in much of the United States. Weaver and Mosby (1979) analyzed the effects of varying season lengths and bag limits by comparing population data for turkey flocks in two areas of Virginia. In a study area in the Central Mountains, the turkey population was estimated at 19,600 in 1963 and 29,400 in 1976, representing a gain of 50 percent. In an area of the Eastern Piedmont, turkeys numbered 20,700 in 1963, but the population declined by more than 13 percent to 18,100 birds in 1976. The harvest generally increased in the Central Mountain population; the average kill of 1,126 birds per year for 1959–62 increased to 1,794 for 1964–1968 and reached an average of 2,271 turkeys per year for 1969–1976. Conversely, harvests in the Eastern Piedmont declined from an average of 1,075 birds for 1951–1962 to 379 turkeys per year for 1971–1976. The results show that a reduction of the harvest to levels of about 2–3 percent of the autumn population did not halt a decline of turkeys in the Eastern Piedmont. Conversely, harvests of 8 to 10 percent did not prevent steady growth in the Central Mountain population. Therefore, hunting was not a factor causing a decline or preventing an increase, respectively, in these turkey populations.

Turkey populations in good habitat may prove resilient to large reductions. Rush (1973) described the effects of live trapping and removing turkeys for stocking in other areas. No detectable decline in the resident population could be detected, even though 38 to 43 percent of the autumn population of 350 to 400 birds was removed each year during a 10-year period. Turkey numbers in Michigan have continued growing concurrently with increased harvests of gobblers.

One might ask, if turkeys can withstand heavy hunting pressure, why were they so scarce 50 years ago? Factors apart from hunting apparently play a major role in determining turkey numbers, especially habitat conditions, disease, and weather. Therefore, beyond adjusting harvest rates, a full range of ecological conditions must be addressed in the management of wild turkeys.

Source: Eric G. Bolen and William L. Robinson, *Wildlife Ecology and Management,* Prentice-Hall, Englewood Cliffs, NJ, 1995, pp. 177–178. Data are from J. K. Weaver and H. S. Mosby, "Influence of Hunting Regulations on Virginia Wild Turkey Populations," *Journal of Wildlife Management,* Vol. 43, 1979, pp. 128–135, and G. Rush, "The Hen-Brood Release as a Restoration Technique," in G. C. Sanderson and H. C. Schultz (eds.), *Wild Turkey Management: Current Problems and Programs,* University of Missouri Press, Columbia, 1973.

Human Institutions and Values

The other side of the wildlife management and conservation issue is the array of human institutions and values that have shaped the historical development of wildlife law and management practices. Chief among the former is the institution of property rights. Terrestrial wildlife is just that; it exists on or close to the land surface. Property rights in land, therefore, have critical implications for the ways human beings have related to wildlife populations.

The dominant land-owning tradition in the United States is private property. Landowners have the legal right to devote their land to any lawful purpose they wish and to exclude trespassers—that is, those who enter without permission. The law governing the wildlife resource itself has evolved in a different direction.[3] Ownership of wildlife, in the sense of having the rights and responsibilities for its management, has become vested within political bodies, especially the state governments and more recently with the federal government. The reasons for this are depicted in the simple schematic in figure 18-2. The shaded areas in the figure represent the habitat of a particular population of wildlife, perhaps a certain animal or a plant of some distinct species. The dashed lines represent property boundaries as they have developed among the holdings of a number of private owners. Naturally, these are highly artificial; in the real world, boundaries and habitats take on all sorts of complicated shapes. But the simplicity allows us to see the concept clearly.

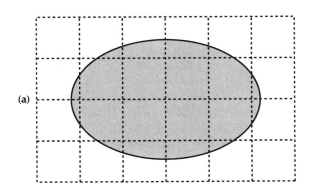

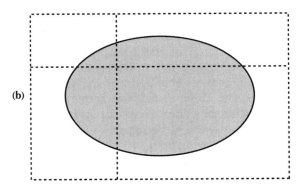

Figure 18-2   Schematic Representation of Wildlife Population Habitat as Compared to Property Boundaries

Panel (a) depicts a situation where the habitat of this population is broken up into many different property holdings. Put the opposite way, any one piece of property contains only a relatively small portion of the total habitat. Panel (b) is different in two senses. First, the number of property holdings is smaller, in this case just four. Second, just one property holding, the one in the southeast, contains the majority of the habitat. Panel (a) typifies the situation in early America: small land holdings relative to the geographic spread of wildlife habitats. In such situations it is useless to expect individual landowners, acting on their own, to engage in efficient wildlife conservation and management activities; each one owns such a small part of the overall habitat that uncoordinated efforts would likely prove fruitless. Effective wildlife management in this case calls for one of the following alternatives:

1. Coordinated action among the landowners achieved by agreement among themselves.

2. Action by some higher political body that has the power to make and enforce wildlife-related regulations.

The first of these may be difficult, depending on circumstances. The costs of trying to reach and enforce an agreement among landowners are called **transactions costs.** Factors that lead to high transactions costs in cases like this are the relatively large number of landowners, the possibility of **free riding,**[4] and the fact that not all landowners are likely to have the same views about the value and role of the wildlife in question.

In the United States, this state of affairs has historically led to two outcomes. One is that wildlife has tended to be treated as an **open-access resource.** Landowners individually had no particularly strong incentives to conserve wildlife, and so hunters and harvesters essentially had the freedom to take the wildlife without limit. Overharvesting resulted from both sport hunting by an ever-increasing population and by market hunting to supply game to the fast-rising urbanized part of the population. In 19th-century U.S. food markets, wild game was commonly available.

This state of affairs led to the second outcome, the assertion of control by state authorities over private actions that were decimating wildlife stocks. This included rules on hunting and prohibition of interstate shipments and sale of harvested game. Thus, now state wildlife authorities have primary jurisdiction over wildlife resources. Individual landholders may take steps to exclude hunters and other harvesters from their properties, but they do not have direct jurisdiction over the wildlife on their property in the sense of being able to enforce their own rules for hunting or otherwise harvesting it.

The historical wildlife situation in England, where much of U.S. law originated, was more like panel (b) of figure 18-2. There, private holdings were in general much bigger in relation to typical wildlife habitats. Thus the transactions costs of private wildlife management were relatively modest, and wildlife law in the United Kingdom came to be based on private ownership. That is, individual landowners are also endowed with property rights over the wildlife that inhabits their property.

Public Landownership and Management

There is a third way of dealing with the landownership problem: maintain or convert the land to public ownership, and then designate a public agency to manage the wildlife resources. Chapter 14, on land economics, contains information on the extent of public lands in the United States. Table 18-1 shows the federal agencies that are heavily involved in wildlife management. State agencies also oversee wildlife resources on state-owned land.

In a very general way there are two types of public lands on which wildlife issues are important. A variety of public areas, such as national and local parks, forests, wilderness areas, and the like, has been established for

Table 18-1   Partial Listing of Federal Agencies Having Responsibilities for Wildlife Management

Cabinet-level department	Agency name	Activities and responsibilities for wildlife
Interior*	U.S. Fish and Wildlife Service	Leading agency for conservation of migratory birds, certain mammals, and sport fishes; manages refuges and hatcheries; coordinates endangered species programs; administers federal aid to states; negotiates international agreements; works primarily from regional offices.
	National Park Service	Research and management of wildlife on national parks and monuments; coordinates Wild and Scenic Rivers System.
	Bureau of Land Management	Leading agency for managing lands in the public domain, primarily in western states; supervises multiple use, including wildlife, grazing, mining, recreation, timber, and watershed; about 55 percent of all federal lands are under Bureau of Land Management.
	Bureau of Indian Affairs	Trust for grazing, timber, water, and other resource management, including wildlife.
	Bureau of Reclamation	Leads programs for water development in western states; wildlife management and recreation considered in reclamation projects.
Agriculture†	Forest Service	Administers national forests and grasslands and wildlife thereon; research and management of all forest resources; fire protection and timber harvests are major concerns; regional experiment stations are activity centers.
	Soil Conservation Service	Publishes soil surveys; provides data and technical assistance for soil and water conservation; no research activities; funds small watershed projects and assists with habitat development on private lands; works primarily with organized districts.
Commerce‡	National Marine Fisheries Service	Provides management, research, and other services for living marine resources, including mammals and invertebrates as well as marine fishes; lead agency in managing offshore development as component of National Oceanic and Atmospheric Administration.
Defense§	Army Corps of Engineers	Major responsibilities for dredging, stream stabilization, and other developments of navigable rivers and coastal wetlands; issues dredge and fill permits authorized by Section 404 of the Clean Water Act.

* Other Department of the Interior agencies in one way or another involved with wildlife management include: Bureau of Mines, U.S. Geological Survey, Office of Surface Mines, and the Office of Water Research and Technology.
† Other Department of Agriculture agencies with wildlife-related activities include Animal and Plant Health Inspection Service, Agricultural Stabilization and Conservation Service, and Economic Research Service.
‡ Other Department of Commerce agencies with wildlife-related activities include the Office of Coastal Zone Management and the National Sea Grant College program; both are components of the National Oceanic and Atmospheric Administration.
§ Other Department of Defense agencies (e.g., Department of the Air Force) also manage wildlife and other natural resources on military lands.

Source: National Wildlife Federation (1987) as reported in Eric G. Bolen and William L. Robinson, *Wildlife Ecology and Management,* 3rd ed. Englewood Cliffs, NJ: Prentice-Hall, 1995, p. 477.

a variety of purposes, of which wildlife may be one. Other public lands, such as wildlife refuges, have been set aside specifically for the purpose of protecting wildlife resources. At the national level the latter is the National Wildlife Refuge System, which has grown to over 92 million acres of land and water since its inception in 1924.

Despite the fact that the primary purpose of wildlife refuges is to preserve the conditions that foster the health and welfare of wildlife species, refuge management frequently confronts the same questions that come up on other types of public preserves: whether, and to what extent, other objectives besides wildlife preservation should be pursued within the wildlife refuges. For example, a number of refuges allow cattle grazing, which is managed by the U.S. Fish and Wildlife Service through a system of grazing permits. Many refuges allow hunting; some allow timber cutting or mining. The basic question in these cases is how much of the non-wildlife-related activity to allow on the refuges.

The relevant laws on this issue[5] state essentially that the refuges may be used for other purposes as long as these are "compatible" with the major purposes for which the refuges were established. Conflicts about what is and what is not compatible are sure to increase in the future because people are placing higher values on wildlife preservation as a goal, because population and economic growth increase the pressure on refuge resources, and because of underfunding of the refuge maintenance and management operations.

■ The Economics of Sport Hunting

In colonial America commercial harvesting of terrestrial wildlife was an important source of food and materials (like deerskins and beaver pelts). In the marine world this continues to be true. The colonials discovered early on that with open access to wildlife stocks, commercial exploitation of wild animals could lead very quickly to stock reductions and scarcities. Their first response was to institute closed seasons and other regulations. Eventually, the states passed laws prohibiting the commercial sale of most wild animals. But although commercial hunting declined, sport, or recreational, hunting grew as a popular pastime in the United States and elsewhere.

In 2011 there were a total of 37.4 million participants in hunting and fishing activities in the United States (table 18-2). The most popular activity was freshwater fishing, followed by big game hunting. Total expenditures on hunting activities in 2011 were estimated at about $90 billion. The total number of people participating in animal watching that year was estimated at about 72 million, with $55 billion of related expenditures. Residential animal watching had three times the number of participants as nonresidential animal watching.[6]

We deal with commercial hunting, in effect, when we look at marine resource economics in chapter 13. The models we use there carry over to terrestrial commercial hunting, for example, the trapping of animals for fur. The value of the harvested product in this case is established on a market,

Table 18-2   Participation and Expenditures in Wildlife-Related Activities, 2011

	Number of participants (millions)	Expenditures ($ billion)
Sport fishing		
Freshwater	27.5	25.7
Saltwater	8.9	10.3
Sport hunting		
Big game	11.6	16.9
Small game	4.5	2.6
Migratory birds	2.6	1.8
Other	2.2	0.9
Total fishing and hunting*	**37.4**	**89.8**
Wildlife watching		
Residential	68.6	NA
Nonresidential	22.5	NA
Total wildlife watching*	**71.8**	**54.9**

* Totals do not equal the simple sum of constituent activities because people may engage in multiple activities.

Source: U.S. Fish and Wildlife Service, 2011 National Survey of Fishing, Hunting and Wildlife Associated Recreation, FHW/11-NAT (RV), Washington, DC, February 2014.

similar to the market price of fish. Recreational hunting has the added factor that its value is related not only to the wildlife harvested, but also to the satisfaction derived from engaging in the activity itself. In fact, in many cases the greater part of the value of hunting may stem from engaging in the activity rather than in the number of wildlife harvested.

Conceptually, however, we can approach it in a similar way. In figure 18-3 on the following page, panel (a) represents the **growth relationship** of the wildlife being hunted. It has the standard U-shaped relationship between the stock level and the annual growth increment, thus s_0 is the stock level that results in the long run if the animal (or plant) is not hunted. Any stock level lower than s_0 can be maintained indefinitely if the appropriate corresponding harvest level is correctly maintained.

An **effort-benefits** function for **recreational hunting** is shown in panel (b) of figure 18-3. It reflects the fact that people obtain benefits from the activity of hunting, not solely from the number of animals taken. By contrast, the figure also shows an "effort-revenue" function, where benefits are strictly proportional to the size of the catch. In that case we get a relationship that is a direct reflection of the underlying biological growth curve, which was the case in the model of a commercial fishery (see chapter 13). Note that the effort-benefits function and the effort-revenue function have the same end points; in the long run, hunters will not get benefits from hunting if success rates are always zero. But it is skewed to the right somewhat, because benefits arise from both the catch and the activity.

Figure 18-4 shows the effort-benefits function in combination with the function representing the costs of hunting; the former is labeled EB and the latter TC. The TC function is drawn under the assumption that each hunting day has the same cost. The open-access hunting level is e_1, which is very close to the zero-catch level of e_0. The latter is the effort level that drives the stock to, or near, extinction. Open access tends to be this close to the extinction point, to repeat, because hunters get benefits from the activity itself, not just from the catch. Because of excess effort levels, no net benefits are produced by this particular wildlife population at effort level e_1. Total costs are high enough that they exactly equal total benefits. The effort level that maximizes net benefits, on the other hand, is e^*. This is the level where the slope of the marginal cost curve (marginal cost) is equal to the slope of the EB curve (marginal benefits). Note that the efficient point involves lower levels of hunting but higher benefits than the open-access effort level.

High effort levels associated with open access suggest that effort or the catch rate must be controlled in some way. Historically, authorities have tried to do this through command-and-control regulations. **A closed season** is one of these. The hope behind limiting the length of a hunting season is that the number of hunting days will be reduced. How much this attains that objective, as opposed to simply compressing a given number of hunting days into a shorter time span, is an open question. In many places public authori-

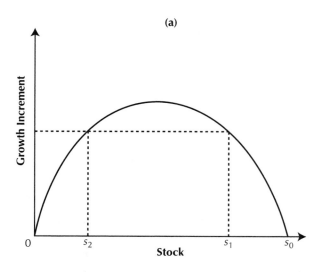

(a)

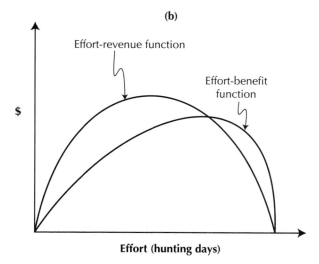

(b)

Figure 18-3   Stock-Growth and Effort-Benefits Functions for Recreational Hunting

ties use lotteries to control hunting effort. The state of Maine has a lottery to distribute moose-hunting permits, as does Wyoming for distributing permits to hunt elk. Massachusetts uses a lottery to issue deer-hunting permits for certain state-owned land.

Another common way of trying to reduce the impacts of open access is publicly enforced **bag limits;** that is, a limitation on the number of wildlife that may be taken per trip or per year. A way of modeling this is to see it as a shift back in the effort-benefits function. By setting a bag limit, authorities attempt to reduce the benefits accruing to hunters on a typical hunting trip. In figure 18-5, this is shown as a shift from the outer to the inner effort-bene-

fits function (from EB_1 to EB_2). The open-access hunting level moves from e_1 to e_2. How much this changes depends on how much the effort-benefits function changes in response to the catch limitations. If the bulk of the benefits of hunting come from the activity rather than the size of the catch, the relationship does not change much and the level of effort does not change much. The bag limit reduces the yield from a given number of hunting days. So though the effort level is reduced only modestly, the equilibrium size of the stock increases. From an economic standpoint, however, the fact that there is open access, even with bag limits, means that the effort level is still too high and net benefits are still zero. It is theoretically possible to lower the bag limit sufficient to shift the effort level back to e^*, even with open access. Net benefits would still be zero, however.

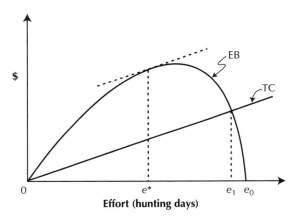

Figure 18-4   Efficient and Open-Access Hunting Levels

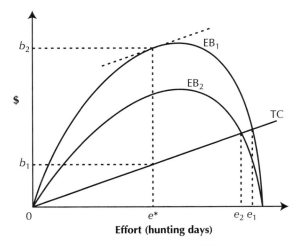

Figure 18-5   Policies for Controlling Hunting

Private Ownership

Why doesn't the public wildlife management agency simply charge a price for access to the wildlife sufficiently high to shift effort levels back to e^*? State fish and game agencies typically sell hunting licenses or permits, but the prices of these are normally kept quite low for political reasons. Thus, hunting access is usually regulated through command-and-control regulations, such as bag limits, gear restrictions, and establishment of open seasons.

Private landowners, on the other hand, have the right to restrict access to their property. A possibility that presents itself, therefore, is for private landowners to charge hunters for access to resident stocks of wildlife. Assuming the landowners are motivated to maximize their net incomes (which is actually the resource rental value of the wildlife stock), they would charge exactly the price that is needed to reduce effort to e^*. The economically efficient effort level e^* is the same effort level that maximizes the net incomes of the owners. The net income obtainable to the owners is an amount equal to $b_2 - b_1$.

With the population and income changes of recent decades, and with diminished stocks of many wildlife populations because of open-access problems, it is not surprising that privately provided hunting has become popular in the United States and elsewhere. It is widespread in the southwest as well as on commercial timberland of the southern states.[7] A market for hunting big game on private land has also developed in many states of the American West and on a number of Native American reservations in the West. In this sense, the United States is catching up with Europe, where markets in privately provided hunting and fishing opportunities have existed for some time. Privatized hunting is also growing in Africa.

One important element of these markets is a factor we discussed above, the patterns of property rights in comparison with the location of the habitat for the game animals in question. Suppose there is a pattern similar to panel (a) of figure 18-2. Here the bulk of the habitat is divided among a large number of landowners, each of whom owns only a small part of the total area. Privatizing hunting would require all the landowners to get together and agree on goals, procedures, and especially on how the total revenues would be shared among themselves. The transactions costs of doing this may simply be too high to overcome, especially if the projected revenues are not particularly great. If there is only a modest number of landowners, however, transactions costs may not be excessive. In some parts of the world new businesses have appeared whose specialty is contracting with a sufficient number of contiguous landowners to put together a large hunting territory, then managing the territory as a private hunting preserve.

The reservation of land for market-regulated hunting of wild, free-ranging animals blends into what can be called **game ranching,** where active management steps are undertaken to enhance the value of the wildlife stock. Such management practices as supplementary feeding, selective culling, and predator control may be used to increase the value of the stock of game animals. Of course, to do these things effectively, it is important that the firms or agencies doing the managing have control over most of the habitat of the target wildlife.

These developments have raised the inevitable question of whether state game regulations (bag limits, for example) should apply to privately provided hunting operations, since the private facilities have presumably addressed the open-access problem, which is the raison d'être for the regulations. Since state-level regulations and regulatory bodies have become strongly institutionalized, however, there is unlikely to be a very rapid evolution in this direction.

The models used above are extremely simple and unrealistic in many ways. We use them simply to explore some of the basic aspects of recreational hunting. One factor that is common in the real world, but overlooked here, is that there usually are other wildlife species, both plant and animal, that interact with the species being hunted. These other species may also be hunted, or perhaps are valuable in other ways, say, for habitat control or animal watching. The relevant effort-benefits function now becomes much more complex, because a relationship that contained all social benefits associated with hunting this species have to take into account all these other impacts. This can be a problem in both publicly and privately provided hunting arrangements.

■ Wildlife in Suburban Areas

In most parts of the world urban areas are growing both demographically and in terms of area. For the most part it is a process of **suburbanization,** in which growth occurs on the fringes of expanding urban areas to satisfy peoples' demands for single-family dwellings with an attached amount of surrounding space. Thus low-density housing developments commonly spread slowly, or sometimes rapidly, into lands that were previously uninhabited or used for farms. One effect of this has been to bring people into contact with the wildlife that were living on the suburban fringe. Coupled with this is the fact that in some parts of the country, such as the Northeast, changes in rural landscapes (e.g., the abandonment of farms) has allowed the reestablishment of some species in areas from which they previously had been pushed out. This has added to the likelihood of human/animal contacts as suburban development spreads.

There are two major dimensions of this phenomenon: (1) the biology, ecology, and population dynamics of the particular animal species at issue and (2) the human demography and attitudes that determine the social benefits and costs of animal populations in the suburbs. In extremely simple terms, we have pictured these two dimensions in figure 18-6 on the next page. Panel (a) shows the standard model of population growth. It shows essentially that without managing the particular animal in question, its population settles at something around k_0. Population levels lower than this can be realized, but only by pursuing some amount of harvesting or stock reduction. Keeping the population at a level of k^*, for example, requires that Δk^* of the animals be removed each year.

The population level k^* is chosen for a reason, as we can see by looking at panel (b) of the figure. This schematic presents the marginal benefits (marginal willingness to pay) by suburbanites at different stock levels and also the marginal costs associated with different population levels of the animal in question. The benefits function (labeled MWTP) summarizes peoples' attitudes about wildlife. It shows that they place a high initial value on this animal and that the value of a marginal animal declines as the animal population grows. This value is based on such factors as **existence value, hunting value,** or **viewing value.** The relationship—its height and shape—clearly depend on the particular animal involved (deer vs. skunks, for example) and the size and characteristics of the human population involved.[8]

The marginal cost curve (labeled MC) shows the social costs of this stock of wildlife. Costs could arise from several factors. The animals could bring about changes in the ecosystem sufficient to produce costs for humans—for example, changes to a surface water system produced by beaver dams. Health costs may occur in some cases, such as threats of Lyme disease from tick-carrying deer and rabbits. A major cause of damage in some regions is collisions between animals and automobiles. Physical threats to pets and children may be at issue, or perhaps damage to agricultural crops. Whatever the source of the costs, the MC curve is meant to encompass all those relevant to

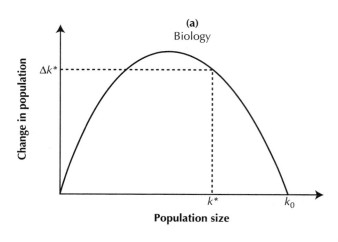

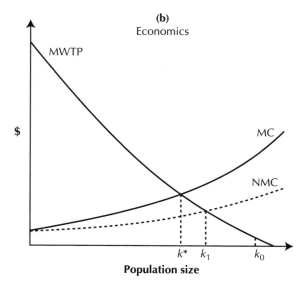

Figure 18-6   Wildlife in Suburban Areas

the case at issue. On the basis of the marginal benefits and marginal cost curves indicated, the efficient animal population size is k^*. This is substantially below the nonintervention level of k_0, but in different circumstances and with different animals, of course, the relationship of these two stock levels could be quite different.

As it stands, the analysis says nothing about the actual costs of managing the animal stock or of removing a portion of the animal population if necessary. This can be a contentious issue in itself, because many people and groups are committed to their views of humane treatment of animals, which may rule out certain approaches to animal removal. One way of modeling this is by deducting removal costs from the MC curve pictured. As a community moves to a lower population size, it does not experience a savings in cost indicated by the original MC curve, but by this amount minus the control costs. This yields a **net MC curve** (labeled NMC), sketched in the figure as a dashed line under the MC curve. The new dashed marginal cost curve intersects the MWTP curve at k_1, which is to the right of k^*, indicating that when control costs are included, the efficient population size of the animal is somewhat larger than when these costs are not taken into account. Exactly what these removal costs are is open to question. A substantial economic sector has developed over the last few decades comprised of firms that specialize in animal removal, from single nuisance animals (e.g., skunks) to large numbers of animals such as deer. Another approach has been to create open seasons where culling is done by sport hunters (see exhibit 18-2).

Exhibit 18-2   Sport Hunting to Manage Bears

Northern New Jersey has experienced a rapidly growing black bear population, as the animals seek food in the growing communities of the region. The response was to establish, over the objection of animal-rights advocates, a six-day bear hunting season, to run for five consecutive years starting in 2010. The first year, 592 bears were taken; since then the harvest has declined, as has the number of reported bear/human incidents.

In New York a ten-year program was established that substantially increased the length (to 16 days) of the bear season, and opened new areas where hunting is allowed. The objective of the plan is to decrease the bear population in the Catskills, and hold it steady in the Adirondacks.

Source: Lisa W. Foderaro, "Trying to Lure Hunters as Bears Get Too Close," *New York Times*, October 13, 2014, p. A15.

■ Distributional Issues in Restoration and Predator Control

In the analysis of the previous section we assumed that members of a particular suburban community were both the recipients of benefits and the bearers of costs associated with wildlife control. In many wildlife management programs, however, there is a major difference between groups of interested people: some groups being primarily beneficiaries and others being primarily bearers of cost.

In Minnesota the reestablishment of the gray wolf has been quite successful; as of 2008 there were well over 2,900 wolves in the state, and steps were being taken to delist the animal as an endangered species. This program is quite similar in concept to many other wildlife restoration programs. It confers existence-value benefits on a widely dispersed group of people, both inside and outside of the state. And it leads to substantial costs for a relatively small group, in this case ranchers and farmers who experience depredation of their domestic livestock. Many cases involving the endangered species fit this type of pattern: diffuse benefits, concentrated costs.

The basic structure of the problem is depicted in figure 18-7. The horizontal axis measures the stock size of an animal in a particular community, while the vertical axis contains a monetary scale. People who receive benefits from this stock are divided into two groups: a local group and everybody else. The local group consists of people who live in the vicinity of the animal community; $MWTP_L$ depicts the benefits this group receives from this wildlife. It could be expected to contain both market-type benefits (stemming from, for example, net revenues from animal-spotting businesses) and nonmarket benefits. Ranchers in Florida whose livestock may be threatened by the Florida panther also appear to gain some satisfaction from knowing that panthers inhabit their lands.[9]

$MWTP_N$ represents the valuation of this animal by all nonlocals. We would suppose that this is primarily existence value, though some will be viewing value also by people who visit the area. Both MWTP curves are of traditional shape, that is, downward-sloping to the right.

The curve labeled $MC_L = MC_N$ represents two marginal cost curves—the marginal cost curve for the locals is assumed to be the same as for the nonlocals. Remember these are aggregate marginal cost curves for the two groups. Thus, although the damage per person is undoubtedly higher among the local group, there are fewer of them. And although the costs per person (e.g., in terms, say, of lost hunting values) are much lower for outsiders, there are far more of them

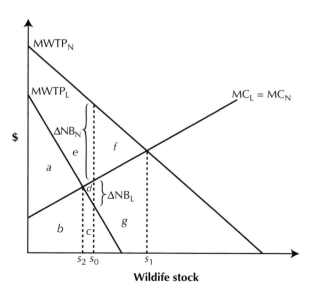

Figure 18-7   Wildlife Restoration

than there are locals. Thus, the two marginal cost curves have been drawn the same, so as to keep the graph relatively uncluttered.

The model shows a substantial discrepancy between the stock levels that are efficient from the standpoint of the local community and from the standpoint of the nonlocal group. These are, respectively, s_2 and s_1. The overall social efficiency level lies between these two points. If current stock levels were to the left of s_2 or to the right of s_1, there would be agreement between locals and nonlocals for building up the stock with a restoration program in the first case, and for reducing the stock in the second case.

But there would be conflicts for any stock level between s_2 and s_1. Suppose the actual stock level was s_0. Locals would be improved (i.e., their net benefits would increase) by a move to the left, whereas nonlocals would be improved by a move to the right. It's possible to determine the gains and losses from the diagram. For a small increase in the stock at s_0, nonlocals experience a gain equal to the distance between $MWTP_N$ and MC_N, shown as the distance ΔNB_N (for change in net benefits to the nonlocal group). Locals experience a reduction in net benefits equal to ΔNB_L. Since $\Delta NB_N >$ ΔNB_L, overall social efficiency calls for an increase in the stock size. As the stock size increases, ΔNB_N diminishes and ΔNB_L increases, and at some stock size they come into balance. This identifies the socially efficient size of the animal population.

How different s_0 and s_1 are, how much adjustment of the actual stock is required, and how much difference there is between net benefits to the two different groups obviously depend, at least conceptually, on the shapes and slopes of the different curves. Even though we don't know them exactly, they can still be used to help us think about cases of wildlife management. In Alaska, state officials planned a wolf-control project to reduce depredation of the state elk herds. In effect, they planned in accordance with the $MWTP_L$ and MC_L curves, as depicted in the figure, with little recognition that there might be a $MWTP_N$ curve well to the right representing the values of people in the rest of the country for the existence of wolves in Alaska. After a notable political backlash from this nonlocal group, the Alaskan authorities were essentially forced to return to the drawing board and develop new plans.

Another idea that presents itself just from the logic of the diagram is the possibility of compensation. Suppose the initial population is at s_0. For a small increase in the stock size, $\Delta NB_N > \Delta NB_L$, implying that compensation could be paid by the nonlocals to the locals to cover their loss in net benefits and still leave positive net benefits for the nonlocals. In fact, compensation could be used to reduce the political opposition that locals might express for the program. In the Minnesota restoration program, for example, compensation is paid to ranchers for livestock killed by the wolves.

These are abstract notions, however, until they can be filled in with actual numbers from surveys or other types of economic analyses. An illustration is available from a national survey to assess the net benefits stemming from the reestablishment of wolves in Yellowstone National Park.[10]

The researchers surveyed 335 local people (defined as people who lived in the three-state region of Wyoming, Montana, and Idaho) and 313 nonlocal individuals, asking them questions about willingness to pay for wolf restoration in Yellowstone. The mean response levels of the surveyed individuals were then blown up to regional and national dimensions by using state and national population numbers. The results are shown in table 18-3.

Table 18-3   Benefits and Costs to Local and Nonlocal People from Wolf Restoration in Yellowstone National Park

	Local	Nonlocal	Total
Mean WTP* of supporters	$20.50	$8.92	
Mean WTP of nonsupporters	$10.80	$1.52	
Estimated number of supporters	391,204	50,152,416	50,543,620
Estimated number of nonsupporters	340,522	25,774,290	26,114,802
Total WTP of supporters†	$160,553	$8,956,130	$9,116,683
Total WTP of nonsupporters†	$68,718	$784,322	$853,040
Net benefits	$91,835	$8,171,808	$8,263,643

* WTP = willingness to pay.

† These numbers are calculated by assuming a perpetual income stream, discounted at 7 percent, that gave a present value equal to the one-time payments that respondents indicated as their willingness to pay. They are also adjusted to reflect an estimate that *actual* willingness to pay is only 28.6 percent of *stated* willingness to pay; this is based on the researchers' previous work on the relationship between stated and actual WTP.

Source: John W. Duffield and Chris J. Neher, "Economics of Wolf Recovery in Yellowstone National Park," Transactions of the Sixty-First North American Wildlife and Natural Resource Conference, 1996, pp. 285–292.

The respondents were broken into supporters and nonsupporters of the wolf restoration. If we assume that the willingness to pay by supporters represents benefits, and willingness to pay by nonsupporters[11] represents costs,[12] then we can interpret these numbers in terms of the areas shown in figure 18-7. Benefits to locals ($a + b$ in the diagram) are $160,553, and their costs (b) are $68,718, leaving net benefits of $91,835. For nonlocals, benefits ($a + b + c + d + e + f + g$) equal $8,956,130, while costs ($b + c + d + g$) are $784,322, leaving a net of $8,171,808. Note, again, how much larger the net benefits are for nonlocals as compared to locals. This is because the total number of nonlocals essentially swamps the number of locals, and so the net benefits to nonlocals is the most important determinant of overall net benefits. Note further, however, that net benefits to locals are at least positive.

■ Public Policy and Wildlife Markets

The harvesting of wildlife, as well as much of the nonconsumptive appreciation of wildlife, is usually governed by, or influenced by, what happens in markets. This is clearly true of commercial harvesting, but it also is increasingly true of noncommercial activities. The commercial packaging of sport hunting and fishing on private lands is a growing activity, as is eco-tourism. What is more, illegal markets often thrive in places where conservation regulations cannot be enforced with vigor. This means in many cases that we must look to the operation of both legal and illegal markets for an understanding of the forces both pushing toward or away from conservation. An understanding of these markets can give us valuable perspective on how best to conserve wildlife resources in ways that are efficient and equitable.

To illustrate this let us look at two elements of African wildlife, the elephant and the black rhinoceros.[13] Several decades ago these animals were widely hunted for elephant ivory and rhino horn, which had high value in world markets. But growing scarcities of the animals led to concern about their long-run survival prospects. Conservation groups such as the World Wildlife Fund and the International Union for the Conservation of Nature were instrumental in getting a ban on rhino horn (1977) and later on elephant ivory (1989). The bans were carried out under the Convention on International Trade in Endangered Species.

The market ban was implemented to take away the incentives for hunters to kill these animals for their horn and ivory. In fact, the ban on ivory has been quite successful, leading to substantial increases in elephant numbers and greatly reduced concern for their long-run survival.[14] The rhino horn ban, however, has been a disaster for the black rhino. Illegal rhino hunting ("poaching") has continued and even grown in intensity, enforcement has been insufficient, and black rhino populations have continued a precipitous decline.

The question is: Why the difference? Why has the ban worked with one animal and not with the other? There are big differences between the factors affecting the supply and demand for ivory and those affecting rhino horn. The differences can be seen in figure 18-8 on the following page. Panel (a) shows very generally the situation in the ivory market, and panel (b) illustrates the horn market. Each model contains two supply (marginal cost) curves and two demand (marginal willingness to pay) curves. In each case, D_1 is the demand curve prior to the ban and D_2 is the demand curve after the ban. The bans, in other words, reduce the demand for the products in world trade. Accompanying the bans are laws making it illegal to hunt the animals in question. This raises the harvest marginal cost curves in the two cases, from the lower one, which is applicable before the ban, to the upper one, labeled S (poachers). The regulations against hunting, in other words, do not end the activity; they just make it somewhat more expensive because of the possible costs of getting caught and punished; in effect, they shift up the supply functions.

The major underlying difference between the two markets is the slopes of the demand curves. In the ivory market it is relatively flat, whereas in the horn market it is quite steep. The basic reason for this is that there are relatively good substitutes for elephant ivory, but not for rhino horn. Ivory is used primarily for tourist carvings and for such specialty items as piano keys.

These items have relatively good substitutes; in fact, an environmental group was instrumental in helping develop a plastic substitute for ivory piano keys. Good substitutes result in a relatively flat ivory demand curve, because modest price increases will cause many consumers of ivory to shift to substitute materials. So when the ivory ban is put in place, demand shifts back and supply shifts upward; the overall increase in market price is modest, but there is a large drop-off in quantity bought and sold. The ban, in other words, produces a substantial drop in quantity at a relatively small increase in price.

The rhino horn market is different. The demand for rhino horn comes mainly from its supposed medicinal value. In some Asian countries there are many medicinal recipes for which rhino horn is an essential ingredient; in effect it has no ready substitutes. The impact of this is that the market demand curve for rhino horn is quite steep. Increased prices do not lead to substantial decreases in quantity demanded. Thus, the ban on rhino horn has a very different impact from the one on ivory. The rhino horn demand curve shifts back because of the ban, and the supply function shifts upward to the illegal poachers' supply. There is a large increase in price for rhino horn, and a relatively small drop in quantity sold and bought. The ban does little, then, for reducing the quantities of rhino horn traded, so the rhino remains threatened by high rates of harvest.

Of course situations of this type can change. In recent years, for example, the huge growth in the middle-income population of China has

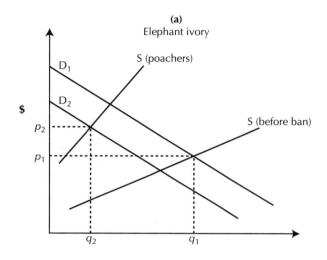

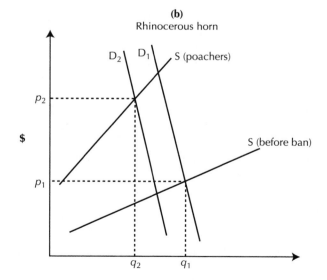

Figure 18-8   The Markets for Elephant Ivory and Rhinoceros Horn

fueled a substantial increase there in the demand for authentic ivory. The result is predictable: increases in prices and quantities supplied by illegal hunting. So much so that some countries, such as the United States, have put in place additional restrictions on the domestic ivory trade.

The major lesson from this discussion is that simple attempts by regulators to intervene and change the way a market operates can have very different impacts, depending on the basic structure of supply and demand factors in those markets. This should be a cautionary note that market intervention, to be at all successful, has to proceed with good knowledge of the parameters of the markets affected—not only the primary market in which intervention is carried out, but also of markets for closely related goods and services.

■ Summary

Wildlife management issues have become much more prominent in recent years. Increasing population growth has brought about greater contacts between humans and wildlife, and value changes among wealthier populations have given wildlife a higher priority in public decisions. Managing wildlife efficiently and effectively requires information from wildlife biologists combined with that from economics and other social perspectives. Wildlife law has developed in ways consistent with other dimensions of social change. In the United States, wildlife has been regarded as essentially an open-access resource, available to whoever gets there first. Open access, coupled with habitat loss, has led to substantial declines in many species of wildlife. This has led, among other things, to an expanded system of wildlife refuges here and elsewhere. It has also led to the growth of private provision of wildlife access for hunting or viewing. The management of wildlife in suburban areas is an increasing problem. Wildlife restoration and predator control programs have important distributional characteristics, usually consisting of benefits that are spread widely among a population and costs that are borne by a relatively small subgroup of the population. An investigation of several African wildlife restoration programs highlighted how important it is to have knowledge about the markets that one is trying to manage.

Notes

[1] Each of these has wild and domesticated components; aquaculture is the domesticated part of fisheries; commercial tree farms are the domesticated part of forestry; conventional plant breeding may be the domesticated part of diversity.

[2] Arthur S. Einarsen, "Specific Results from Ring-Necked Pheasant Studies in the Pacific Northwest," Transactions of the Seventh North American Wildlife Conference, 1942, pp. 130–138.

[3] Dan Lueck, "Property Rights and the Economic Logic of Wildlife Institutions, *Natural Resources Journal*, 35(3), 1995, pp. 625–670.

[4] To review the concept of free riding, see chapter 6.

[5] Primarily the National Wildlife Refuge System Administration Act of 1966, as amended.

[6] Residential animal watching is defined as an activity that takes place within 1 mile of home.

[7] Robert K. Davis, "A New Paradigm in Wildlife Conservation: Using Markets to Produce Big Game Hunting," in Terry L. Anderson and Peter J. Hill, eds., *Wildlife in the Marketplace,* Rowman and Littlefield, 1995, pp. 109–125.

[8] For any species there may be indirect sources of value. These are animals (or possibly plants) that are not particularly valuable to humans in themselves, but either support or diminish other species that are so valued. Mice may not be particularly desirable themselves, but they may be highly valued because they support other animals, such as foxes and hawks. In such cases the social value inherent in marginal willingness to pay is a derived value. The social value of the species is derived from the social value of the supported species that is essentially transmitted through the biological linkages connecting the different species in a particular ecosystem.

[9] David S. Maehr, *The Florida Panther: Life and Death of a Vanishing Carnivore,* Island Press, Washington, DC, 1997.

[10] See John W. Duffield and Chris J. Neher, "Economics of Wolf Recovery in Yellowstone National Park," Transactions of the Sixty-First North American Wildlife and Natural Resource Conference, 1996, pp. 285–292.

[11] This is the willingness to pay by nonsupporters to have the restoration stopped or abandoned.

[12] This basically assumes that no individuals will experience both benefits and costs from the restoration.

[13] The inspiration for this example comes from Gardner Brown and David Layton, "Saving Rhinos," paper given at the meetings of the Association of Environmental and Resource Economists, Annapolis, MD, June 1997.

[14] This is a judgment from the standpoint of the international community; the judgment from those African communities who might see elephants more as a potential source of economic wealth might be different.

Key Terms

bag limits
closed seasons
distributional impacts of
 wildlife management programs
existence, hunting, and viewing values
game ranching
management of suburban wildlife

open-access resources
private provision of
 wildlife benefits
recreational hunting
suburbanization
wildlife biology

Questions for Further Discussion

1. If access to a hunting area is rationed by price, we can be sure that the level of visitation that results will maximize the social net benefits of the activity. If the same activity level is determined by lottery, however, we cannot be sure of this. Explain why not.

2. The bioeconomic models used in wildlife economics are based on biological growth processes. How would the basic model change in a case like recreational trout fishing where the replenishment process is one of stocking by humans?

3. In determining the optimal stock levels for suburban wildlife, whose preferences should count, everybody's or just the people living in the particular suburb under analysis?

4. Suppose an elk herd is to be managed for the benefits it produces for hunters. Would you expect that management decisions would be different if a public agency is in charge of the operation as compared to a private firm?

5. For the situation depicted in figure 18-4, the state is going to use a lottery to choose e^* hunters who will each be allowed to hunt one day. If the state wishes to maximize the amount of revenue it can obtain from this system, what price should it set for each permit?

Useful Websites

The primary federal agency for wildlife resources:

- U.S. Fish and Wildlife Service in the Department of Interior (http://www.fws.gov)

Virtually all states have wildlife agencies, e.g.,

- Montana: Department of Fish, Wildlife, and Parks (http://fwp.mt.gov)
- California: Department of Fish and Wildlife (https://www.wildlife.ca.gov)
- North Carolina: Wildlife Resources Commission (http://www.ncwildlife.org)

Public interest groups provide useful information on policy issues and a wide range of wildlife populations:

- National Audubon Society, especially for birds (http://www.audubon.org)
- World Wildlife Fund (http://www.worldwildlife.org)
- National Fish and Wildlife Foundation (http://www.nfwf.org)

A number of organizations are devoted to specific species or populations, for example:

- Ducks Unlimited (http://www.ducks.org)

Selected Readings

Anderson, Terry L., and Peter J. Hill, eds. *Wildlife in the Marketplace.* Lanham, MD: Rowman and Littlefield, 1995.

Brown, Gardner. "Wildlife in Developing Countries," in Partha Dasgupta and Karl-Gören Mäler, eds., *The Environment and Emerging Development Issues*, Vol. 2. Oxford, England: Clarendon Press, 1997, pp. 555–573.

Duke, Joshua, and Jun Jie Wu, eds. *The Economics of Wildlife Conservation.* Oxford, UK: Oxford University Press, 2014.

Lueck, Dean. "Ownership and Regulation of Wildlife," *Economic Inquiry*, Vol. 29, 1991, pp. 249–260.

Oldfield, S., ed. *The Trade in Wildlife: Regulation for Conservation.* London: Earthscan Publications, 2002.

van Kooten, G. C., and E. H. Bulte. *The Economics of Nature: Managing Biological Assets.* Oxford, UK: Blackwell, 2000.

19

Economics of Biodiversity Preservation

Not too long ago the word "biodiversity" did not exist. Now it is a household word and a major focus of research in biology and ecology.[1] It refers to the variation that exists at all levels of biological organization: variation among individuals in a species, among species in a community, among communities in an ecosystem, and among ecosystems themselves. This variation is critical to the continued existence of life itself, not only the lives of the millions of organisms that make up the biological world, but also the life of the top predator in that world, human beings.

The normal, very long-run cadence of biological existence is that species develop, exist for a few million years, and then disappear. Over the billions of years that life has existed on earth, therefore, almost all species that once existed have become extinct. But evolution is relentless and profuse. Thus at the present time more species are alive on earth than ever before. Why then should the disappearance of species, a major phenomenon within diversity change, be a problem today? It is a problem because we (humans) apparently have touched off a new and massive species die-off. In the prehistory of the world there have been other times when biodiversity disappeared in a major way. Paleontologists have identified five previous periods during which there was a major, rapid spasm of species extinction. The last one, about 65 million years ago, killed off the dinosaurs and many marine and flying reptiles. Today's decline is different in that it is not the consequence of some catastrophic natural event like the striking of an asteroid, but the result of massive human demographic growth and the resultant technologies of economic maintenance and expansion. Although much of the popular press, as well as scientific attention, has focused on diversity among animals, diversity loss among plants is also a threat.

What can economics say about diversity preservation? Many people think it can't, or shouldn't, have much to say on the subject. When the U.S. Congress enacted the original Endangered Species Act in 1973, it specifically forbade bringing economic considerations into decisions about protecting specific species. And many biologists believe that economics, with its focus on the study of **trade-offs,** is not suitable, either analytically or morally, as a framework for studying biodiversity problems and making decisions about biodiversity resources.[2]

In this chapter we consider biodiversity protection and conservation using the analytical tools of economics. Usually in analyses of this type we start with concepts and principles, and then proceed to a discussion and evaluation of recent public policy initiatives. It might be interesting in the present case to reverse this order. Accordingly, we start off with a discussion of the U.S. Endangered Species Act. This alerts us to some of the difficulties that stand in the way of effective diversity preservation, which then opens the way for addressing some principles that might be applicable to this sphere of public policy.

■ The Endangered Species Act

The best-known effort in the United States to preserve biodiversity is the **Endangered Species Act of 1973** (ESA). Several previous federal statutes had addressed species preservation.[3] Among other things, these forerunner acts authorized the federal government to purchase land for the preservation of threatened species and to preserve these habitats "insofar as practicable." This language in effect allowed the relevant public agencies to weigh the **expected benefits** of species protection with the **expected costs** of that protection.

The ESA was enacted in the early 1970s—a time of strong environmental activism at the federal level when a number of other major environmental laws were passed. The spirit of that time among many political participants was that the environment needed massive new protection regardless of the cost. The ESA was written accordingly. It basically said that federal agencies were to protect endangered and threatened species at all costs, notwithstanding any questions about the "practicability" of their actions. The law also says that the determination that a species is threatened or endangered is to be made strictly on grounds of biological science and that private individuals everywhere are prohibited from "taking" individuals from any species designated as endangered.

To gain protection, a species must be **listed** as "endangered" or "threatened." An individual, agency, or any other entity may propose a species for listing. After negotiating an involved process of data gathering, public hearings, and comments, the secretary of the interior[4] may list the candidate species as endangered or threatened. When a species is listed, it is critical to specify its habitat—the geographical area that is essential for its survival. The administering agencies, the U.S. Fish and Wildlife Service and the National Marine Fisheries Service, must then develop **recovery plans,** detailing the actions required to bring about the recovery of the listed species. Species residing in domestic or foreign lands and waters may also be listed.

The ESA has been controversial throughout its history and probably will continue to be so. Shortly before it became law, a small fish, the **snail darter,** was found in waters below the construction site of a new, large, federally financed dam being constructed on the Little Tennessee River. Construction on the dam was halted by court order, the judge essentially saying that it really didn't matter how big and economically important the dam would be, or how small and apparently inconsequential the snail darter was, the clear language of the ESA required the protection of species—any species—at all costs. The subsequent fight in Congress and the U.S. Supreme Court led to the 1978 amendments to the ESA. They created a cabinet-level committee (nicknamed the **God Squad**), which can grant exemptions to the provisions of the ESA if the project:

1. Is of regional or national significance
2. Has no reasonable or prudent alternatives
3. Is one that clearly outweighs the alternative

Although the committee originally voted against the snail darter exemption, Congress did approve an exemption, and the dam project went forward.

Controversy and conflict over the Endangered Species Act have usually involved absolutes and extremes, one side stressing the need to do whatever it takes to avoid ecosystem collapse, and the other side talking about economic collapse if the law is enforced. Although the original act precluded economic considerations in the actual listing decisions, one way they were smuggled in was in the language applying to the development of habitat protection plans. The secretary of the interior, in specifying a critical habitat for an endangered or threatened species, may take economic factors into account and may, for example, exclude a particular region from designation as critical habitat if the benefits of doing so outweigh the costs. This is not enough to mollify the critics of the ESA, however. What seems to have gradually become clear is that the main issue is not the total social cost of preserving endangered species, but how these costs are distributed. Although the benefits of the law are distributed widely throughout society, its costs are concentrated on a small but vocal minority. We return to this later.

It also has become clear that attacking the problem species by species may not be the best way of carrying out the intent behind the law. Rather, the focus should be on preserving strategic ecosystems as a whole. This, and the cost distribution problem mentioned above, led the Clinton administration to aggressively pursue an idea called **habitat conservation plans** (HCPs) on private lands, where 80 percent of endangered species are to be found. These are voluntary, binding agreements between private landowners and public agencies. Landowners agree to undertake some conservation efforts on their properties, perhaps leaving large amounts undeveloped or particularly sensitive portions untouched. In return the agency agrees to let the landowner use some portion of the property, even if it leads to an **incidental taking** of some endangered or threatened species. The government further agrees to refrain from enforcing new regulations on the property throughout the life of the plan (perhaps several decades) even if new biological information later becomes available suggesting that further steps are needed to protect a species.

Needless to say, HCPs are controversial. Many in the environmental community feel that they don't provide sufficient species protection; many landowners are still leery of the idea of trying to conclude permanent agreements with highly politicized public agencies. And many ecologists are concerned that the system does not recognize the need for continued flexibility as more biological information becomes available and nature continues to respond in unpredictable ways, as it often does.

Has the ESA been effective? Table 19-1 shows a box score, as of 2015, of listed threatened and endangered species. A total of 2,221 species have been listed, of which 1,568 were domestic; 1,210 of these domestic species were listed as endangered, 358 as threatened. Of the 1,210 endangered domestic species, 726 were plants, 484 were animals. The relevant federal agencies have endangered species divisions that consider new listings, but budgetary limitations place a limit on the rate with which this can be accomplished. Of course the listing process has also become filled with political controversy over the years. Notice also from table 19-1 that, of the total 2,221 species listed as endangered or threatened, just over half (1,158) have recovery plans.

Beyond the simple box score, have the listings made sense in terms of which particular species have been listed and which have not? The U.S. Fish and Wildlife Service has been criticized for being overly political in its listing decisions, but given the dearth of hard information on values, costs, and other factors weighing on these decisions, it's hard to see how they could be otherwise. Studies clearly seem to show that, other things equal, if an animal is a mammal or a bird, it has a better chance of being listed than if it is a reptile or an amphibian.[5] This bias is described with the term **"charismatic megafauna,"** which are large, usually attractive species that for one reason or another capture the attention and affection of the public, like wolves, bald eagles, whooping cranes, and the like.

Despite this bias, can it be said that the Endangered Species Act has been effective? Views differ of course, often greatly, depending on which side of the political issue one happens to be. Two economists who have studied the law and its implementation offer the following assessment.

> Measuring the effectiveness of the Act requires one to decide when to declare victory. Should it be when a listed species is taken off the list? When a declining trend is reversed? When the rate of extinction is slowed? When critical habitat is protected so as to prevent species from declining to the point of being considered for listing? Although the answers to these questions are unclear and notwithstanding our pleasure from keeping favorite species like the bald eagle around, only one with modest expectations would give the Endangered Species Act a high performance rating.
>
> Since the inception of the Act in 1973, 11 species of more than 1,000 listed have recovered and have been removed from the list, including the

Table 19-1 Species Listed as Endangered and Threatened, 2015

Group	United States			Foreign			Total Listings (US & Foreign)	US Listings with Active Recovery Plan*
	Endangered	Threatened	Total Listings	Endangered	Threatened	Total Listings		
Mammals	74	26	100	255	20	275	375	63
Birds	79	21	100	215	17	232	332	86
Fishes	93	70	163	19	3	22	185	104
Reptiles	14	23	37	69	20	89	126	36
Clams	75	13	88	2	0	2	90	71
Insects & Arachnids	73	11	84	4	0	4	88	53
Snails	34	12	46	1	0	1	47	29
Amphibians	20	15	35	8	1	9	44	21
Crustaceans	22	3	25	0	0	0	25	18
Corals	0	6	6	0	16	16	22	0
Animal Subtotal	**484**	**200**	**684**	**573**	**77**	**650**	**1334**	**481**
Flowering plants	694	155	849	1	0	1	850	646
Ferns & Allies	28	2	30	0	0	0	30	26
Conifers & Cycads	2	1	3	0	2	2	5	3
Lichens	2	0	2	0	0	0	2	2
Plant subtotal	**726**	**158**	**884**	**1**	**2**	**3**	**887**	**677**
Grand Total	**1210**	**358**	**1568**	**574**	**79**	**653**	**2221**	**1158**

* There are 602 distinct active recovery plans. Some plans cover more than one species, and some species have separate plans covering different parts of their ranges. Plans include only listed species that occur in the United States.

Source: U.S. Fish and Wildlife Service, "Summary of Listed Species, Listed Populations, and Recovery Plans," http://ecos.fws.gov/tess_public/pub/boxScore.jsp.

eastern states' brown pelican, Utah's Rydberg milk-vetch, and the California gray whale. Species downlisted to threatened from endangered include the Aleutian Canada goose, greenback cutthroat trout, Virginia round-leaf birch, and bald eagle. According to the Environmental Defense Fund, less than 10 percent of the listed species have exhibited an improved status and the status of four times that amount is declining. For example, the population of Attwater's prairie-chicken, listed in 1967, has dropped to 42 in 1996 from 2,254 birds in 1975. The ratio of declining species to improving species is 1.5 to 1 on federal lands, and 9 to 1 on private lands.

Funding for the endangered species program of the Fish and Wildlife Service has failed to keep pace with the number of listed species, with the result that the real budget per species is 60 percent of its 1976 level. The Office of Endangered Species has inadequate funds to assay the status of about one-third of the listed species.[6]

How the Endangered Species Act fares in the future will depend on the ebb and flow of political events in federal and state governments. We must back away from the political controversies and consider the phenomenon as a problem of social choice. What factors determine the extent to which decisions made to protect endangered species will or will not advance overall social welfare? There are many who regard this as an overly "human-centric" approach to the problem. Drawing a line in the sand—"all species have a right to exist"—is heroic, but not the way real people live. As far as we know, humans are the only creatures on the globe that are blessed, or cursed, with the ability to make decisions by consciously looking at alternatives and choosing the one that is in some sense the best. How should we choose in this case?

■ The Noah Problem

A good way of tackling this question is to consider the **Noah problem.**[7] This is essentially a parable that can be used to focus on the core issues of biological diversity preservation and the factors to be considered when making preservation decisions. Noah has been told of the coming flood. He and his sons and daughters have constructed an ark which, though immense, is not unlimited in capacity.[8] They now select species of animals and plants to put in the ark.

But there are simply too many species in total to put in the ark. One might conclude simply that a bigger ark is needed, but the same problem would arise because literally all the world's species cannot fit in an ark. Nor is postponing the flood a practicable alternative, since this is out of Noah's hands.

The question is: Which species should Noah load onto the ark before battening down the hatches? He could just accept them on a first-come, first-served basis, or just select those which look cute and cuddly, as the U.S. Fish and Wildlife Service is accused of doing. Or he could employ a more complicated **decision rule** to make the determination. Of all the species extant, he needs a means of deciding which should be allowed aboard and which should not. If he wishes to pick species so as to maximize social welfare in some sense, what criteria should he use for the selection? Noah's choice problem is analogous to society's problem in choosing species preservation programs. Consider the factors affecting the benefits and costs of including particular species. On the benefit side there are two types of factors:

1. The effect that including a species on the ark will have on its survival probability

2. The social value of the species, using whatever criteria are important for measuring social worth

On the cost side we have:

3. The social opportunity cost of including the species

Let us consider each of these factors.

Impacts on Survival

A critical first piece of information needed is **survival probabilities,** on and off the ark. In Noah's case we could perhaps assume that any species included on the ark will assuredly survive, while any species off the ark would just as assuredly disappear. The assumed survival probabilities, in other words, are 1.0 and 0, respectively. This is not an accurate reflection of reality, at least today. In real-world species protection programs survival probabilities are hardly ever at such extremes; rather they are intermediate, and the question becomes how much will they be increased by particular types of conservation programs or decreased by certain habitat-disrupting activities.

It's important to emphasize this perspective. If we are designing species conservation programs, we ought to consider survival (or alternatively, extinction) probabilities **with and without** the programs. Suppose we have two species, A and B. If no efforts are made at preservation, species A has a 100-year survival probability of 30 percent (i.e., a 70 percent chance of becoming extinct during the next century), whereas for B the survival probability is 10 percent. Suppose we have $1 million to spend on just one preservation program (that is, Noah has room for just one more species on the ark). Which species should we spend it on? You might think that species B ought to be chosen, because it is the most highly endangered. But suppose the best-designed preservation programs in the two cases would increase survival probabilities to 90 percent for A and 20 percent for B. We can double the survival probability of B, but triple it for A. If we can only afford one program, which should it be?

Survival probabilities, with and without various types of preservation programs, are the province of biologists and ecologists. Enormous progress has been made in understanding biodiversity relationships and the population dynamics of some species. It's clearly too much to expect that survival probabilities soon will be available for a large number of the world's species. In fact, nobody knows with a high degree of accuracy yet how many species actually exist. So survival probabilities may be hard to come by, except for certain individual species that attract a lot of political and scientific interest, such as whooping cranes and spotted owls.

Having said this, however, we must stress that **some general notion** of survival probabilities—for individual species or perhaps groups of species in a region, and the way they are impacted by human activities of different types—is important in making reasonable decisions about diversity preservation. Noah can make the choice between A and B in two ways, by flipping a coin or by trying to reflect on the qualities of the two species and what inclusion or exclusion from the ark would mean for each of them.

The Benefits of Survival: Individual Species

What is the social value of a species? This is a controversial question. We could try to avoid it. Noah might try to make a decision based on something other than species value; for example, by looking at species survival rates, as mentioned above. He would select the species whose survival probability was increased the most by inclusion on the ark. With two similar species, this might be reasonable. But suppose species B is a domesticated animal used as an energy source, say, a horse, while species A is a nasty microorganism, such as the smallpox bacteria. It's unreasonable to treat them as equal in value. We could treat this strictly as a scientific exercise. Noah could admit species that in his judgment, as an ecologist, would contribute most to an ecosystem that functions in a certain way. But this would appear to smuggle human values into the problem, because Noah would be making decisions on the basis of his vision of a desirable world. Thus the logic of intelligent species diversity preservation requires that we consider the value of species—that is, the benefits that would flow from species preservation.

The value of a species can be broken down into two parts:

1. The value of a species in itself
   a. commercial, or market, value
   b. nonmarket value
2. The value of a species because of its relationship to other species

The first of these is relatively easy to think about, at least conceptually, though it may be very difficult to measure in practice. There are certain obvious sources of value for particular wildlife species. Certain species have a commercial value when harvested, such as fish; or when linked to ecotourism, such as whale watching. Recreational use may also be consumptive or nonconsumptive, like hunting vs. bird watching. Among plants, certain wild species may have value because they have useful genes, which when transferred to commercial crops impart desirable properties in terms of characteristics such as disease resistance or growth rates. A much-emphasized source of commercial value is as a basis for pharmaceutical products. Examples include the rare rosy periwinkle, which is the source of an effective drug to treat leukemia, and the Pacific yew tree, which is the source of a drug to treat ovarian cancer. It is relatively easy to measure the economic value of commercialized species, because people register their willingness to pay in organized markets for food, medicines, and outdoor recreation.

But while numerous individual species have been discovered ex post facto to contain chemicals useful to humans, the real question in species preservation is how we make decisions about the preservation of species with **unknown characteristics.** Here we run into a variant of what is called in economics the **diamond-water paradox.** Something that is very valuable in total need not be valuable on the margin. Water is necessary for life, both biologically and, in practical terms, for public health. Diamonds are not necessary in the same way; apart from a few industrial uses they are primarily devoted to jewelry. Yet diamond prices are very high while the price of a gallon of water is, in general, very low. Prices, in other words, do not seem to reflect biological realities. The answer to this riddle is that prices reflect **marginal value,** not **total value.** In graphical terms, marginal value is the height of the marginal willingness-to-pay curve at a point, whereas total value is the area under the curve up to that point. It's quite possible to have an item, like water, which has a relatively low marginal value but a very high total value. And vice versa, as in the case of diamonds.[9]

Let us apply this to the phenomenon of **species prospecting.** Suppose that we are looking for a particular chemical compound for a specific pharmaceutical use and that once we have found it in one species, we won't have to look any further. We might call this the **needle-in-a-haystack** type of search. Now suppose that there are 1 million species and that we believe one of them contains the substance we are seeking. If it is found, it will generate benefits of $100 million per year. We are able to sample 100 species per year to see if they contain the substance having this quality. Obviously, the probability that we will find it this year is 100 in 1 million, or .0001. Suppose now that one of these 1 million species is in danger of going extinct this year. How much should we spend on trying to preserve this species? The value is $100 million times the probability that this species contains the required compound. If it is true that only one species has the material, this latter probability is 1 in 1 million. Hence the value of the one endangered species is $100. Note that this is a small fraction of the value of the substance once it is found. Suppose we have reason to think that there are about 10 species out of the total of 1 million that might contain the substance we seek. In this case the value of the threatened species is even smaller, because there are potential substitutes for it if it becomes extinct and if it contains the substance we are looking for.

These conclusions stem importantly from the assumption that species prospecting[10] is a needle-in-the-haystack phenomenon. But reality may be more complicated than this. If one species is found to have a desirable property, investigators might want to look at related species in the hope that they also have useful characteristics—perhaps the same substance as contained in the first species but which in the related species is much less costly to obtain. Finding one needle in the haystack strongly suggests that there may be other valuable needles in the general vicinity of the first one. In this case the probabilities discussed above are altered in a way that gives the marginal species greater value.

The fact that the marginal species has relatively modest value does not imply, however, that we can sit back and not worry about species loss. For one thing, the rate of species loss is important. If, as some have claimed, 20,000 species are on the brink of extinction,[11] this would be very much more than a marginal change. We come back to this theme below.

The other factor that has to be taken into account in valuing species is **nonuse,** particularly **existence,** value. People value the fact that species are preserved. They are willing to pay for preservation programs even if there is no particular market value attached to the species. They probably value particular species more than others; they are also likely to express an existence value for all species, without distinctions among them.

If, in the end, we could come up with a measure of the total (marginal) value, from all sources, for each species, Noah's course of action would be clear. Knowing these estimated values, he could then calculate the value per unit of space that each species would have on the ark (note that this allows for different space requirements for each species) and load those with the highest value up to the point where the ark is filled. Analogously, a public agency could act so as to maximize the social value of species preservation given the size of its budget.

The Diversity Benefits of Survival

That benefits flow from the preservation of individual species is undeniable; that benefits are different for different species is also probably true, though somewhat more controversial. But species diversity is essentially about **collections of species,** not individual species. So **diversity-related benefits** of a species come, in some fashion, from the contribution a species makes to the diversity of a collection of species. There are two questions to explore: (1) What are the benefits of diversity; for example, what is better about having a population with a diverse set of species rather than one that is relatively nondiverse, and (2) what contribution does an individual species make to the diversity of the population of which it is a member? We deal first with the value question.

Suppose you are stocking a first-aid kit. Right now it contains two items, bandages and aspirin. Your budget allows you to buy one additional item this year. What should it be? If you were quite sure that in the year to come the only medical problem you will encounter is little finger cuts, you might buy more small bandages. But you don't know this; in fact, you realize that there are lots of different problems you may encounter and you don't know which will occur with certainty. Under the circumstances you might put a high value on diversity—that is, adding something to the first-aid kit that is different from what is already there, for example, an antiseptic cream to put on cuts and abrasions.

In species preservation the same principle may hold. There is value in preserving differences, or diversity, among species. Noah has already loaded species A, and now species B and C come along. Species B is quite similar to A, while species C is very different from A. Noah might want to load species C on the grounds that it will make the ark more diverse. We are speaking here of **insurance.** If the future is uncertain, as it always is, then it is also uncertain what qualities will have the greatest value when that future arrives—hence, the value of preserving sets of species, or organisms, with diverse qualities. The diversity itself is a source of value.

Apart from the insurance value of preserving a diverse nature, there are good biological and ecological reasons for doing so. These are related to the role that diversity plays in maintaining the health of natural ecosystems. One important dimension of ecosystem health is **resilience.** An ecosystem is resilient to the extent that it reestablishes old ecological parameters after a major disturbance. A resilient grassland reestablishes itself after experiencing a severe drought over several years. There are many aspects of resilience—for example, how fast the reestablishment occurs and how closely the new ecosystem resembles the old. But resilience clearly is one of the factors that determines the ability of an ecosystem to deliver services of value to human beings.[12]

Exactly how diversity affects resilience is a complex biological question. There are many dimensions of diversity and many dimensions of resilience. This is a case where economic valuation of resilience may be easier to determine than its biological aspects. Consider figure 19-1. Suppose an agricultural area suffers some type of ecological disruption. One effect of this disruption is the shifting of marginal costs of agricultural production upward, from MC_1 to MC_2. In the face of constant prices (P, assumed to keep the problem simple) output and incomes decline, the former from q_1 to q_2, and the latter by an amount equal to $b + c$ per year.[13] As long as the higher cost function prevails, incomes are $b + c$ lower than they were before the disruption. The economic face of resilience is regaining these net benefits as the ecosystem recovers its former parameters and productivity. The recovery trajectory could be fast or slow, direct or circuitous, human-aided or not.

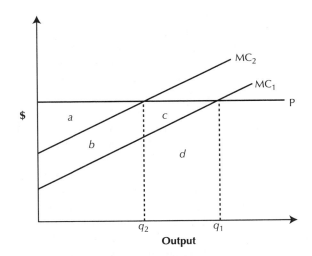

Figure 19-1   Cost Implications of Ecosystem Disruption and the Value of Resilience

■ Cost-Effective Biodiversity Preservation

Credible estimates of the social value of biodiversity are very difficult to produce, even though we all recognize that the values exist. This suggests that we fall back to the perspective of **cost effectiveness.** Cost-effectiveness analysis takes a physical measure of diversity and then tries to figure out the maximum amount of that measure that could be obtained with a given budget or cost or, equivalently, the minimum cost of achieving a given amount of diversity as expressed by the diversity measure we have chosen. The Noah problem can be cast in this form. The "budget" in this case is simply the size of the ark; given this, the goal is to maximize the amount of diversity among the animals that are loaded.

To give this problem a measure of concreteness, let us deal with the issue of habitat protection. Preserving habitats is not the only way of protecting species; control of legal or illegal hunting, the control of animal predators, and raise-and-release programs can also be effective. But habitat protection is clearly the prime strategy in most cases. This brings up the following question: On the assumption that there is a limit on the resources that can be devoted to habitat protection and that there are many candidate sites for protection, which particular sites should be chosen? This is known as the **optimal reserve site selection problem.** The nature of the problem is easy to see. Suppose there are 100 candidate sites and we can only preserve 10 of them. There are in fact 17.3 trillion different sets of 10 sites that can be drawn from a total of 100. Some way must be found to determine the best 10 sites in terms of their contribution to diversity conservation.

Hot Spots

Diversity is sometimes equated with simply the **number of species** present in a collection; a situation is more diverse the larger the number of species it contains.[14] By this criterion Noah would be correct simply to maximize the total number of species loaded onto the ark. This would lead to questionable results, because it would mean that species taking up less room would be favored; large animals and plants would be less valuable. Noah could maximize his plan by loading mostly microorganisms.

The idea of **species hot spots** is based primarily on species numbers. Hot spots are identified as regions containing relatively large numbers of species in small areas. Myers, for example, has listed 18 hot spots around the globe; collectively they occupy about 0.5 percent of the earth's surface, but he estimates that they contain about 20 percent of all extant species.[15] The biggest advantage in using number of species as an index of diversity is that it is simple. It implies a very straightforward action plan; if you want to conserve diversity, save as many species as possible, with one species as good as any other. But a simple rule like this may not give the best results. Consider table 19-2.[16] This shows the species present in four candidate reserve sites, A, B, C, and D. There are 6 species in total. Sites A and B contain species 1, 2, 3, and 4. Site C contains species 1, 2, and 5, and site D contains species 3, 4, and 6. Suppose the sites are all equal in terms of the costs of preservation. If we follow a simple hot spots approach, we would preserve sites A and B. The optimal set of sites, however, consists of sites C and D. The latter have fewer but more unique species, whereas sites A and B have more

Table 19-2   Example Showing the Failure of the Hot Spots Approach

| | Potential reserve sites | | | |
	A	B	C	D
Species present	1	1	1	3
	2	2	2	4
	3	3	5	6
	4	4		

species, but they are the same for both sites. Instead of a simple hot spot rule, therefore, it would be better to have a rule that adds sites based not only on the number of species but also on their uniqueness.

A modified hot spot approach is possible. One example is nicknamed the "greedy algorithm."[17] Select first the site that has the greatest number of species. Then select sites sequentially that add the greatest number of additional species to those already represented. Although this procedure usually works fairly well, it does not guarantee that the selected sites in aggregate preserve the greatest number of species. In table 19-2, for example, this algorithm would end up with either site A or site B in combination with either site C or site D.

Sites can also differ in terms of the relative abundance of species, which may be important to take into account. Suppose one area has 5 species, each of which has 20 percent of the total individuals in the area, whereas another area also has 5 species but 1 accounts for almost all the individuals and the others have only 1 individual in each. Ecologists have developed the notion of **species abundance,** in which not only the presence or absence of a species is recorded but also its relative abundance, expressed as the proportion of total individuals in the area belonging to this particular species.[18] One way of constructing a diversity index from these abundance proportions is:

$$D = \frac{1}{\Sigma\, p_i^2}$$

where D = the index
p_i = the proportion of the ith species in the area under study

If there are 5 species and each is equally abundant (i.e., each species accounts for 20 percent of the total individuals in the sample), this index simply gives the total number of species, 5. But the number drops if the distribution is skewed, that is, if one species represents a disproportionately large share of the individuals in the sample. A measure like this may be useful for some purposes, but it might be misleading in certain cases. On the one hand, it may not decrease much at all if a species that is very low in abundance becomes extinct. And if an extinction is accompanied by a reshuffling of the abundance of the remaining species, the index actually could go up. This might run counter to most people's notion of diversity, which is tied closely to specific extinctions.

Scientists have looked beyond indexes like D above to develop measures that better represent the diversity of a set of species and, thus, the loss in diversity when one or more of the species becomes extinct. The main requirement of a better index is that it be based on some notion of the **relative importance** of different species in an area. For example, if the extinction of one species affects the survival probabilities of many other species in the area, but not vice versa, then the extinction of that species may be regarded as more important than the extinction of one of the other species.

Another important feature of a single species is its **genetic distinctiveness.** Suppose, for example, that a region contains 5 species of a certain genus of beetles. Suppose, further, that we have examined the genetic makeup of each species and determined how unique each is, in the sense of containing genes that the other species do not. We could measure how closely the species are related to one another in terms of the complement of genes they carry, and then develop an index of diversity based on these relationships. An index of this sort would show a big drop if a species became extinct that had no close genetic relatives, but it would show only a small drop if a species with a close genetic relative goes extinct. Suppose we are unsure which particular genetic characteristics might be valuable in the future, for example, in providing material for advanced medicines. Then we might want to adopt a strategy of preserving as broad a collection of genetic material as possible. So the loss of a species with more unique genes would count as a bigger loss of diversity than one with genes common to many species. Exhibit 19-1 discusses a study of this type, focusing on wild cranes.

The analytical and data problems of reserve site selection continue to need the work of scientists, but practical steps must be taken by groups and agencies that are facing the problem now. The Nature Conservancy, a national organization that raises money to buy and conserve sensitive resource areas, has developed a ranking system for guiding its decisions about sites to purchase.[19] Two main types of information are used: the biodiversity present at a site, and the probabilities that the biodiversity would survive if the site were protected. Thus, a prospective site gets a higher

Exhibit 19-1   Cost-Effective Biodiversity Preservation

There are 15 species of wild cranes in the world. If the United Nations, for example, were to have a sum of money to devote to crane preservation, which species should it target? Martin Weitzman, of MIT, developed a theoretical approach to diversity preservation and applied it to this problem. The first type of information needed was extinction probabilities, the probabilities that the species will become extinct at some time in the next 50 years, given no additional preservation efforts. The probabilities, shown in the tabulation, are estimates made on the basis of several factors—most especially the pressures on the habitats and flyways used by the different species.

Crane species produce direct-use values, such as those for bird watchers and hunters. The North American whooping crane, for example, is the basis of a substantial tourist business. But suppose we wish also to take diversity into account. Suppose we wish to direct our preservation budget so as to encourage the preservation of genetic diversity among them. Cranes have been well studied among biologists, and Weitzman was able to get data on the DNA of the 15 species. In particular he was able to calculate the genetic distances among the species based on certain dissimilarities in their DNA. Preserving diversity in this case, therefore, amounted to preserving species that have the most dissimilar DNA. From the DNA he was able to estimate the impacts on overall crane diversity of improving the survival probability of each. These diversity impacts are also shown in the tabulation. Note, for example, that although the Siberian and whooping cranes have about the same extinction probabilities, preserving the former would have a much greater impact on overall crane diversity than would preserving the latter.

The next logical step in this kind of analysis would be to introduce cost estimates of preserving the different species of cranes. These would undoubtedly vary widely because the cranes exist in very different locales and migrate over very different regions. But cost data of this type are almost impossible to get at the present time (the author of the study rightly concludes that gathering cost data of this type should be a high priority of environmental research).

Even without cost data, however, some interesting conclusions are revealed. The Siberian crane is in a class by itself. Not only does it have a high extinction probability, but it has no close genetic relatives among other crane species. The sandhill crane, on the other hand, is quite secure (very low extinction probability). Yet there is a greater payoff in diversity preservation from making the sandhill even more secure, than one would get in any other species, even the threatened whooper. This is because the sandhill has no close genetic relatives, while the whooping crane has several.

Crane Information

Common Name	Scientific Name	Geographical Range	Extinction Probability	Diversity Impact
Black crowned	*Balearica pavonina*	Central Africa	0.19	8.7
Grey crowned	*Balearica regulorum*	South-East Africa	0.06	14.1
Demoiselle	*Anthropoides virgo*	Central Asia	0.02	7.0
Blue	*Anthropoides paradisea*	South Africa	0.10	4.8
Wattled	*Bugeranus carunculatus*	South-East Africa	0.23	7.8
Siberian	*Grus leucogeranus*	Asia	0.35	10.3
Sandhill	*Grus canadensis*	North America	0.01	11.1
Sarus	*Grus antigone*	South-East Asia	0.05	4.7
Brolga	*Grus rubicunda*	Australia	0.04	6.5
White-naped	*Grus vipio*	East Asia	0.21	9.2
Eurasian	*Grus grus*	Europe, Asia	0.02	1.3
Hooded	*Grus monachus*	East Asia	0.17	1.4
Whooping	*Grus americana*	North America	0.35	4.5
Black-necked	*Grus nigricollis*	Himalayan Asia	0.16	5.8
Red-crowned	*Grus japonensis*	East Asia	0.29	2.9

Source: Martin L. Weitzman, "What to Preserve? An Application of Diversity Theory to Crane Conservation," *Quarterly Journal of Economics,* Vol. 108, February 1993, p. 161.

ranking (higher priority for purchase) if it contains a large number of species or other diversity attributes and/or if the survival probabilities of the species would be greatly improved if the site were protected. A site that meets both criteria would, of course, come out with a very high priority for purchase and protection. The U.S. Fish and Wildlife Service has developed a system called **gap analysis** (GA) to give more scientific backing to its habitat preservation programs. GA makes use of a variety of techniques (satellite mapping, on-site evaluations) to locate areas of biodiversity, especially in relation to areas currently in public ownership or under some existing type of habitat preservation. Those areas found to contain high-biodiversity resources but not covered by current land preservation programs are given high priority for protection.

▪ Costs of Diversity Protection

We have mentioned several times that rational diversity preservation must take preservation costs into account. It is worth addressing this in more detail, particularly since there are many people—for example, the political representatives who passed the Endangered Species Act—who think otherwise. It is easy enough to see the logic of considering costs. Suppose there are three potential reserves that might be protected and that each has the same value in terms of whatever index of diversity is used, but that there are different costs associated with preserving them. In particular, suppose the costs are $100, $60, and $40, respectively, for the three sites. It is obvious that if we have a total budget of $100, we can preserve far more diversity by saving the last two sites, since with our budget we can afford both of them, than if we put our whole budget into preserving just the first of the sites. Consideration of costs will inevitably push us toward sites that, other things equal, are less expensive to preserve.

The social costs of preservation consist of two major parts: (1) the **social values** that are lost when restricting use of the designated habitat sites, and (2) the **direct costs** of managing the sites once the restrictions have been introduced. Most of the lost social values are the lost values of production of commodities and services that preservation no longer allows. For example, this could be the lost value of timber production, agricultural output, or recreational values for activities that are incompatible with preservation. If the land is currently in private ownership and there is an active land market, these opportunity costs may be reasonably well estimated by looking at the changes in property prices before and after the restrictions are put in place. This brings up an important point when public purchase of habitat is involved. If the public agency purchases land outright for inclusion in a habitat preserve, it will presumably have to pay the full market price for the land in question. This is the **cash cost** of the acquisition. If externalities are associated with the private land use, the cash land cost may have to be adjusted to get the true social opportunity cost of the acquisition.

Economic Incentives and Habitat Preservation

Habitat preservation is clearly the key to biodiversity preservation. On public lands key players are the relevant public agencies, which have to include biodiversity preservation along with whatever other objectives history or the political process has given them. But most endangered species, and by extension biodiversity, are on private land. So a critical question is what kind of public regulation or institutions, if any, are appropriate to achieve efficient levels of biodiversity preservation on private lands.

Consider figure 19-2, which represents the cost-and-revenue situation of a single farmer. The horizontal axis shows the quantity of farm output produced, which is sold by the farmer at a price of p. The farmer's private marginal cost curve is labeled MC_p. This producer maximizes net income at an output rate of q_1 since this is where the private marginal cost curve intersects the price line.

Suppose that, starting with this situation, biologists discover certain threatened or endangered species on the farmer's property. Suppose also that it has been possible to value the amount of habitat destruction that the farming operation causes and to relate this damage to the quantity of farm output. This is a heroic assumption in the practical world, but it allows us to explore the conceptual aspects of the problem. This gives us a new social marginal cost curve, labeled MC_s, which encompasses both MC_p and the habitat damage.

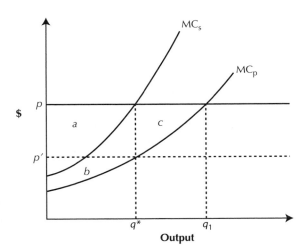

Figure 19-2   Analysis of Policies to Protect Endangered Species Habitat

The output level q_1 exceeds the socially efficient output q^*. Let us consider the different ways of reducing output to this lower rate. If we think generally in the tradition of the Endangered Species Act, the first idea that comes to mind is simply to pass a law requiring that output be reduced to q^*. This is the traditional **command-and-control** approach, with enforcement carried out by our standard regulatory institutions. But although this approach conforms with tradition, it does not address the incentive aspects of the situation. At q^* the farmer has a strong incentive to increase output because the output price is so much higher than private marginal production costs at that point. Prior to the regulation, the farmer's net income was $a + b + c$, whereas afterward (assuming complete compliance) it is $a + b$, meaning that income at q^* is c less than it would be at q_1. This shows the source of the perverse incentives that have in some cases worked against the effectiveness of the Endangered Species Act. If the particular endangered species were not found on the farm, the regulation would not be in force and the income of the farmer would be the full $a + b + c$. It is essentially worth c to the farmer to be rid of the organism(s) in question, assuming that she gets no benefit herself from these species. This may be enough to motivate the farmer to get rid of the species before they are discovered publicly.[20]

Observers of the ESA have pointed out for some time that although its benefits may be widely distributed throughout society, its costs are concentrated on those private parties unlucky enough to own land that is the habitat of endangered species, such as the farmer whose situation is depicted in figure 19-2. What is at issue, then, is not necessarily whether total benefits exceed total costs, but how the costs and benefits are distributed. A plan that has positive net benefits overall may nevertheless be vigorously opposed by some people or groups if they end up bearing a disproportionate amount of the costs. One can approach this at two levels: One can argue about who really owns endangered species or who has what rights, or one can simply treat it as a practical problem that reduces the effectiveness of the ESA. If we were to take the latter course, it suggests that the landowner depicted in the figure be **compensated,** in whole or in part, for the lost income caused by the regulation.[21]

Compensatory payment programs of this type are quite common in some countries (see exhibit 19-2). In general they take the form of contractual agreements between landowners and public agencies to refrain from certain practices or otherwise change their operating procedures in return for a payment. The exact terms of the contract—its amount and the activities it affects—have to be worked out on a case-by-case basis. This type of approach holds real promise. At the same time, we must recognize the problems that have to be solved if they are to be effective, for example: (1) paying landowners for actions they might have taken voluntarily, (2) agreeing on the size of the payment, and (3) monitoring to make sure landowners in fact act in accordance with the agreements.

Another possibility for addressing this problem is to develop a **market** for the services of the endangered species, so that its conservation by landowners and others would have a commercial rationale—that is, so the compensation to the landowner will come through revenues on the market. Perhaps the endangered species involved have **ecotourism** value in the sense that people are willing to pay the landowner for opportunities to observe or photograph the organism. Or perhaps it is a plant that has possible medicinal value that a pharmaceutical company is willing to pay the landowner to conserve. Assume that these species values are directly related to the quantity of agricultural output. In the model, this change would imply a new price line. The price for the agricultural crop is p, but since each unit

Exhibit 19-2   Examples of Compensation Programs for Landowner Activities Aimed at Diversity Conservation

United States: Conservation Resource Program

Initiated in 1985, the program gives incentives for farmers to enter into contracts to change the land use for specific plots in order to enhance their value for the preservation of biodiversity resources. The program incorporates competitive auctions to ensure that regulators obtain maximum benefits from a given budget.

Australia: The Tasmanian Forest Conservation Fund

A program design to protect old-growth forests under high threats for loss; employs inverse auctions to reduce the costs of obtaining habitat conservation benefits.

Indonesia: Program to reduce the incidence of sedimentation from coffee plantations

Auctions are used to obtain accurate assessments of coffee growers' willingness to accept payments of specific amounts to enter into a soil conservation contract.

Sweden: Program to compensate farmers for a reduction in land under conservation

Annual payments are made for multi-year contracts, typically four years, with payment rates depending on soil type and the estimated values of protected biodiversity resources.

Austria: Program aimed primarily at farmers that involves private contracts to protect landscape or grants for the establishment of new biological resources or ecosystems

One requirement is that the new landscape and ecosystem resources must be guaranteed for at least 20 years.

Switzerland: Program to convert 12 percent of the country's cultivated area to protected status

Started in 1993, payments to farmers are based on a scale of rates which depend on the type of land involved. The payments specify agricultural and land-use practices that must be followed to qualify.

For further information see Organization for Economic Cooperation and Development, *Scaling Up Finance Mechanisms for Biodiversity*, OECD, Paris, 2013; *Paying for Biodiversity: Enhancing the Cost Effectiveness of Payments for Environmental Service*, OECD, Paris, 2010.

of this output would cause a loss in market value of the endangered species of some constant amount, the new effective output price is now p', which is p minus the species value (in other words, $p - p'$ is the value of the endangered species, expressed as a function of agricultural output). In this case the normal profit-maximizing incentive of the landowner would lead her to reduce agricultural output to the socially efficient level, or in other words, to undertake a socially efficient amount of species conservation.

How feasible is it to create markets in order to produce this kind of incentive effect? The ecotourism market appears to be the most promising. One problem with ecotourism is that, in the animal world, it frequently focuses on large, popular animals. Many animals, on the other hand, are pests to humans, for which willingness to pay may actually work in the wrong direction. Furthermore, the millions of small animals such as insects, or even microscopic organisms such as bacteria, are not likely to be attractive enough to support tourist enterprises of any size, except in isolated instances.

■ Summary

Biodiversity refers to the variation that exists at all levels of biological organization: individual, species, and ecosystem. Efforts to understand and preserve biological diversity have become a major focus within natural resources analysis and policy. In the United States much of that focus has been on the Endangered Species Act, which has been politically controversial and modestly successful in terms of conservation. From a conceptual standpoint, we presented the Noah problem, the issue of which species to include in the ark when space is limited. The answer depends on the value of individual species, on the relation of the species to others in terms of its contribution to biological diversity, and on the value of the diversity. Since the latter element is extremely hard to measure, effort has instead been devoted to cost-effective diversity preservation; that is, maximizing diversity preservation for a given expenditure of resources. This depends critically on the definitions that are used to express diversity, as well as on extinction probabilities and preservation costs. In practical terms, diversity preservation means habitat preservation. This brought up the problems of optimal reserve site selection and the use of incentives to help protect sites in private ownership.

Notes

1 The work of Edward O. Wilson has done much to spread the concern about diversity loss and its consequences. See his award-winning book, *The Diversity of Life*, Harvard University Press, Cambridge, MA, 1992.

2 See, for example, many of the papers in E. O. Wilson, ed., *Biodiversity*, National Academy Press, Washington, DC, 1988.

3 In particular the 1916 National Park Services Act, the Endangered Species Preservation Act of 1966, and the Endangered Species Conservation Act of 1969.

4 The actual criteria the secretary of the interior is supposed to use in listing an endangered species are: (1) present or threatened destruction of habitat, (2) overutilization of the species, (3) disease or predation, (4) the inadequacy of existing legislation, and (5) other natural or man-made factors.

5 See Andrew Metrick and Martin L. Weitzman, "Conflicts and Choices in Biodiversity Preservation," *Journal of Economic Perspectives*, 12(3), Summer 1998, pp. 21–34.

6 Gardner M. Brown, Jr., and Jason F. Shogren, "Economics of the Endangered Species Act," *Journal of Economic Perspectives*, 17(3), Summer 1998, p. 10.

7 Not to be confused with the Noah principle, which has been put forth by David Ehrenfeld, a biologist, on the assumption that Noah had room enough for anything. It says that all species, without exception, should be protected at all costs, and especially without regard to human values. See D. W. Ehrenfeld, "The Conservation of Non Resources," *American Scientists*, Vol. 64, 1976, pp. 648–656.

8 According to the Bible it is $300 \times 50 \times 30 = 450,000$ cubits^3, where a cubit is the length of the forearm to the tip of the middle finger, or about 18 inches. So the ark was about 1.5 million cubic feet, or roughly the size of a modern destroyer.

9 The apparent counter-parable to the diamond-water paradox is the airplane rivet story. Individual species extinctions are likened to pulling individual rivets out of an airplane. For a while nothing happens, because there is a redundancy in the number of rivets in the airplane. So the persons popping the rivets develop a false understanding of the value of the marginal rivet; since the airplane still flies, it must be true that the marginal rivet has no value. A point

is reached, however, where one more popped rivet leads to a catastrophe. But airplanes are not nature. Airplanes are designed by humans, and one trade-off that is analyzed carefully is the number of rivets (strength) vs. weight (speed). Other things equal, more rivets make the airplane stronger, but slower. It would be foolish to start popping rivets when you know the number of rivets is already optimized. It probably won't take many, as several air crashes have revealed. The fact that there are few redundant rivets in airplanes does not generalize to the natural world.

[10] "Species prospecting" is the name given to the search for beneficial properties of wild species that might be useful, say, in agriculture or pharmaceuticals.

[11] Christine Dell'Amore, "20,000 Species Are Near Extinction," *National Geographic*, Dec. 16, 2013. news.nationalgeographic.com/2013/12/131216.

[12] C. S. Holling, D. W. Schindler, Brian W. Walker, and J. Roughgarden, "Biodiversity in the Functioning of Ecosystems: An Ecological Synthesis," in Charles Perrings et al., eds., *Biodiversity Loss: Economic and Ecological Issues*, Cambridge University Press, Cambridge, England, p. 54.

[13] Revenue decreases by $c + d$, whereas costs decrease by $d - b$; the net change is therefore $b + c$.

[14] We are speaking of species diversity, but the same principle could hold at any level: the number of different individuals within a given species, of ecosystems within a geographical area, and so on.

[15] Norman Myers, "The Biodiversity Challenge—Expanded Hot Spot Analysis," *Environmentalist*, 10(4), 1990, pp. 243–256.

[16] This example is taken from Stephen Polasky and Andrew R. Solow, "Conserving Biological Diversity with Scarce Resources," Marine Policy Center Woods Hole Oceanographic Institution, April 1997.

[17] An algorithm is a mathematical procedure that one follows, like a recipe, to solve particular numerical problems.

[18] See, for example, Robert E. Ricklefs, *The Economy of Nature*, 4th ed., W. H. Freeman, New York, 1997, p. 516.

[19] As a part of its Natural Heritage Program.

[20] See, for example, the cases discussed by Charles C. Mann and Mark L. Plummer, *Noah's Choice: The Future of Endangered Species*, Knopf, New York, 1995.

[21] This is not a new proposal. The 1930 American Game Policy, a public statement developed by a committee of experts under the direction of Aldo Leopold, contained a section on "Inducements to Landowners." It suggested subsidies to rural landowners to provide wildlife habitat and hunting access. See Wildlife Management Institute, *The North American Wildlife Policy 1973*, WMI, Washington, DC, 1978, p. 39.

Key Terms

biodiversity resources
charismatic megafauna
diamond-water paradox
endangered species act
gap analysis
greedy algorithm
habitat conservation plans
incentive-based habitat protection

incidental taking
Noah problem
preservation costs
reserve site selection
species abundance
species hot spots
survival probabilities

Questions for Further Discussion

1. What is the difference between endangered species preservation and species diversity preservation?

2. What are the different ways that "success" under the Endangered Species Act might be measured?

3. What is the difference between describing the Noah problem as a benefit-cost problem and as a cost-effectiveness problem?

4. There are 10 small balls of equal size, but different color, in one urn, and 10 balls of the same color, but unequal size, in another. Which collection is more diverse?

5. A farmer is to be offered, on a take-it-or-leave-it basis, a sum of money as compensation for taking certain actions to preserve an endangered species of wildlife on the farm. How might you determine the minimum offer that could be made and still have the farmer accept the agreement?

Useful Websites

Economic studies of various facets of biodiversity preservation:
- Resources for the Future (http://www.rff.org)
- World Resources Institute (http://www.wri.org)
- The International Society for Ecological Economics (http://www.isecoeco.org/)

Information, including country summaries, of activity under the International Convention on Trade in Endangered Species:
- Wildnet Africa (http://www.wildnetafrica.com)

Information on developing economic incentives for biodiversity preservation:
- International Union for Conservation of Nature, Economics of Biodiversity (http://www.iucn.org/what/biodiversity)

Other sites:
- Audubon Nature Institute (http://www.auduboninstitute.org)
- Natural Resources Institute (http://www.nri.org)

Selected Readings

Helm, Dieter, and Cameron Hepburn. *Nature in the Balance: The Economics of Biodiversity*. Oxford, UK: Oxford University Press, 2014.

Kontolean, Andreas, Unai Pascual, and Timothy Swanson. *Biodiversity Economics*. Cambridge, UK: Cambridge University Press, 2007.

Ninan, K. N. *The Economics of Biodiversity Conservation: Valuation in Tropical Forest Ecosystems*. London: Routledge, 2006.

Perrings, C. *Our Uncommon Heritage: Biodiversity Ecosystem Services and Human Well Being*. Cambridge, UK: Cambridge University Press, 2014.

Polasky, Stephen, ed. *The Economics of Biodiversity Conservation*. Burlington, VT: Ashgate, 2002.

Section VI

NATURAL RESOURCES IN INTERNATIONAL PERSPECTIVE

This last section addresses natural resource issues from an international perspective. Chapter 20 discusses resource decisions in developing countries, which have similar objectives to those elsewhere but which are normally undertaken in different institutional and political settings. Chapter 21 deals with the impacts of globalization on natural resource decisions, particularly those related to the growing flow of international trade in natural resources.

20

Natural Resources and Economic Growth

At present there are almost 200 countries or recognized national political units in the world, and they vary enormously in almost every dimension: economic, social, demographic, and political. They also are diverse in their natural resource endowments, in terms of the type, quantity, and quality of resources within their borders. In this chapter we take a brief look at a huge subject: the role of natural resources in those countries of the world in which there is special emphasis on economic growth and development.[1]

It has become customary to sort the countries of the world into several categories. **Developed countries** are those that have made successful transitions to industrial and postindustrial economies, with relatively slow demographic growth and relatively high levels of social welfare, and where the primary focus is on continued economic growth to match, at least, population growth. In the **developing world,** on the other hand, growth in per capita income and wealth has tended to lag behind those achieved in the advanced economies. Table 20-1 on the following page presents relevant data for certain broad demographic regions of the world. Of course, these regional aggregates hide the experiences of different countries. Some individual countries have been quite successful in laying the institutional and social groundwork for economic growth. In others, income growth has been almost nonexistent in recent years, and the political and social changes needed in order to produce economic development have been delayed. Within many countries there have also been great differences from one region to another in terms of economic growth.

■ The Institutional/Demographic Context

A catalog of natural resource issues with which developing countries are grappling would be extensive and would include the following:

- Managing the exploitation of nonrenewable resources, such as oil and minerals
- Managing commercial forest resources and the conversion of forest-land to other uses
- Preserving wildlife stocks that have varying local, regional, and international significance
- Maintaining the optimal stock of agricultural soil productivity
- Developing and utilizing water resources in efficient and equitable ways
- Maintaining efficient levels of marine resources

But this list looks similar to a list of resource problems facing developed countries. How different are these problems in the developing world as compared to those encountered in developed countries? Do we need special models and analyses to study them in place of, or in addition to, the ones we have discussed so far? The best answer to this is probably the following: Most of the underlying concepts discussed so far are as applicable to developing countries as they are to the developed world. Notions of efficiency, incentives, the importance of the distribution of net benefits, overexploita-

Table 20-1   Population, Economic Indicators, and Life Expectancy by Demographic Region

	Population (millions)		GNI (PPP) per Capita*	GDP Annual Growth Rate (%)	Life Expectancy at Birth	Energy Consumption Per Capita**
	2013	Est. 2050	2012	2007–2011	(years)	2011
World	7,137	9,727	11,690	3.8	70	74.8
Asia	4,302	5,284	7,800	7.5	71	52.0
China	1,357	1,314	9,210	12.3	75	78.0
India	1,277	1,652	3,840	6.9	66	19.8
Russia	144	132	22,760	6.0	70	209.3
Western Asia (Middle East)	251	405	15,090	5.8	73	140.1
Europe	740	726	28,870	1.2	77	134.9
Northern Africa	208	316	6,260	5.7	70	42.1
Sub-Saharan Africa	926	2,185	2,240	6.3	56	17.4
North America	352	448	49,800	1.4	79	258.0
Latin America and Caribbean	606	780	10,870	6.7	75	57.9
Oceania	38	58	30,590	7.5	77	NA

* GNI (PPP) = gross national income in purchasing power parity divided by mid-year population.
** Expressed as million Btus. Asia region for energy excludes central Asia.

Sources: Population Reference Bureau, *2013 World Population Data Sheet*, Washington, DC, September 2013 (http://www.prb.org/pdf13/2013-population-data-sheet_eng.pdf); U.S. Energy Information Administration, *International Energy Statistics*, Washington, DC, accessed July 2014 (http://www.eia.gov/cfapps/ipdbproject/iedindex3.cfm?tid=44&pid=45&aid=2&cid=regions&syid=2005&eyid=2009&unit=QBTU).

tion of open-access resources, the important role that property rights play, and the occurrence of market failure and government failure are all ideas that are as important in the developing world as they are in the developed. But in developing economies the **institutional landscape** can be quite different, leading to an intertwining of political, social, and economic elements in very complex ways. For example, in our discussion of forestry economics in chapter 12, we use a simple model for showing how efficient decisions are related to, among other things, interest rates. We essentially assume that there exists a financial market, separate from the timber market, that can accommodate financial transactions in ways that efficiently complement whatever decisions are made about harvesting trees. This kind of institutional assumption is often not tenable in developing countries.

Another example is the **labor market**. In chapter 13 we examine the efficient effort levels for a fishery and conclude that in open-access situations, attaining efficiency normally requires reduced effort; some of the fishers have to exit the industry. The implicit assumption is that these people could find alternative employment elsewhere. But what if they could not? In many developing countries employment opportunities are scarce; under these circumstances it may not be desirable to reduce effort on a local fishery, even if open access has led to high use levels.

A third point of difference is that in many developing countries, elements of the natural resource endowment are relied upon to provide a major impetus for economic growth. Petroleum and mineral deposits, agricultural land, forests, hydropower, and wildlife resources in many countries are considered sources of growth. So there are important questions regarding the nature of the connection, if there is one, between resources and growth, and the ways resources should be used if the objective is to stimulate economic growth. In this chapter we take up some topics regarding the linkage between natural resources and economic growth.

Still another issue is the impact of growth on subgroups within countries, particularly on the poor. We normally define growth as increasing per capita incomes, but we need to think also about how it impacts people across the spectrum. Increasing average income in a country doesn't necessarily imply that incomes are rising for everyone or whether, if they are, they are all going up in the same proportion. **Pro-poor economic growth** is a concept of growing interest among analysts and policy makers, though there are differences of opinion as to what it means and, especially, how to bring it about.[2]

■ Natural Resource Decisions in Developing Countries

A major theme we have stressed throughout is that to understand how people use natural resources we must first understand the incentives they face. Incentives are the individual benefits and costs that accrue to people as a result of their decisions. These incentives explain why people choose certain alternatives over others, and especially why they use natural resources the way they do. They also explain why the decisions made by individuals may not be conducive to maximizing the welfare of society as a whole. This is especially true of decisions that lead to excessive rates of natural resource use. This logic extends from diagnosis to prescription; changing how resources get used is accomplished most effectively by changing the incentives people face.

The importance of this idea can be appreciated by reading exhibit 20-1. It discusses two agricultural situations, one in Kenya and the other in Ethiopia. In the former, colonial policies seriously undermined the ability of local farmers to increase agricultural production. Since independence, however, incentives have been put in place that have led to substantial increases in agricultural output. In the Ethiopian case, on the other hand, heavy taxes and property rights problems have led to impoverishment and soil degradation.

But if we relay the same message in earlier chapters, why devote another chapter to it here? The primary reason is that the political, social,

Exhibit 20-1   The Importance of Individual Incentives: A Tale of Two Countries

The histories of two adjoining countries, Ethiopia and Kenya, highlight the difference that economic institutions make, especially with regard to their impacts on agriculture incentives.

Machakos is a semi-arid district in Kenya with a poor-to-middling climate for agriculture. The country was governed as a colony of Great Britain until 1963. As such, the best agricultural land was reserved for Europeans; natives were forbidden to grow cash crops. With restricted land access and lack of market incentives, the region was characterized by heavy soil erosion and declining yields. This changed when Kenya became an independent republic.

Today, Machakos is substantially more productive, with the successful introduction of cash crops, greater use of fertilizers, and more soil conservation projects. The fundamental changes after independence involved new rural institutions:

- Lower land taxes
- Secure land tenure for individuals
- Infrastructure development that gave access to international markets
- Availability of finance

Today a productive agriculture sector supports substantially larger populations than before these changes were instituted.

Recent studies of Ethiopia, on the other hand, reveal many areas where agricultural productivity growth has lagged behind population growth, leading to soil degradation and food scarcities.

In 1974 a communist state system was established. Private land rights were abolished and large-scale collectivization projects were pursued. Peasant farmers therefore lacked secure rights to the land and strong incentives to improve productivity. Moreover, incentives did not exist to adopt improved agricultural technology, and there were few programs to develop soil conservation techniques and make them available to farmers. One result was a massive famine that was alleviated only through outside aid.

Source: For further information see John Heath and Hans Binswanger, "Natural Resource Degradation Effects of Poverty and Population Growth Are Largely Policy-Induced: The Case of Colombia," *Environment and Development Economics,* February 1, 1996, pp. 67–68.

and institutional settings in many developing countries are very different from those of the developed world.[3] In particular, people in developing countries often do not have access to clearly defined, specialized economic institutions for handling different aspects of economic activity. In developed countries, for example, well-developed institutions handle banking and other financial transactions, insurance, social security, and the transfer of real assets such as land. In developing countries, on the other hand, these institutions often do not exist. Consider the following:

- In sub-Saharan Africa many farmers do not have access to efficient rural banks and credit markets. This leads them to carry larger numbers of cattle as insurance against droughts. But larger herds lead to extra strain on grazing lands, which results in soil degradation.

- In developing countries there is typically a lack of institutions for what in developed countries are called welfare systems—systems that help maintain minimal income levels for those who would otherwise fall below subsistence levels. This means that welfare systems must be arranged through customs and practices regarding resource use. One way this has been done historically is to maintain a resource (e.g., firewood or water) on an open-access basis, which the poor can resort to in times of need. Open-access resources, in other words, are primarily devices for welfare assurance. We have seen the conditions of overuse that often result from open-access arrangements.

- In many poor countries it is difficult for families to eke out a living from a natural resource base of low productivity. In this case children are essential to help in this production, and small families are at a disadvantage. Thus, resource scarcities may lead to higher fertility rates, which exacerbate the scarcities.[4]

■ Incentives and Political Power

In the developed world, democratic political institutions that are reasonably distinct from economic ones lead to individuals and groups contending for influence over the processes of public policy. In developing countries, on the other hand, political power is often still in the hands of small groups, who can use it directly to gain direct or indirect control of natural resources and of the wealth this makes possible. Thus, although the behavior of individual resource users is a function of the incentives they face, it is in the political arena that rules and procedures are established that shape these incentives. Suppose, for example, that political authorities set high income tax rates on farmers, essentially to transfer agricultural rents from the people who created them to those with the power to set the taxes. Under some circumstances this could lead farmers to mine the fertility of the soil as they try to maintain subsistence incomes in the face of a growing population. This is an incentive problem: High taxes lead to overuse of resources. But it is also a political problem: The authorities have too much arbitrary power and can set high tax rates that the farmers cannot escape. Note also the Kenyan case mentioned in exhibit 20-1; colonial authorities at one time made it illegal for Kenyan farmers to raise certain cash crops. This is not so much an incentive problem as it is a problem in the exercise of political power.

Thus, the incentives facing individuals are determined by the de facto rules under which people operate, and those who control the political system have the power to establish, change, and enforce the rules. The motives of those in power are not necessarily to ensure that a country's natural resources are used in a way that maximizes social welfare. In many cases they aim to create conditions that allow them, or their allies, to capture a large portion of whatever resource rents are produced.

Note also the term "de facto" rules. Countries in the developing world often have weak enforcement institutions, so that **extralegal** resource-using actions are not at all unusual. Many countries, for example, have regulations in place to manage timber harvesting. All too often, one runs into cases where large timber companies, often but not always foreign, harvest timber illegally and escape penalties because of weak enforcement actions.

Having stressed the political dimensions of resource use, however, we nevertheless focus in the rest of the chapter on matters of social efficiency, or the maximization of social net benefits. Clarity in these matters may help to promote the political and institutional changes that welfare-improving economic growth and development require.

■ Property Rights

Nothing can be more fundamental to incentives than **property rights.** A property right is essentially an empowerment that establishes the conditions under which a person, or group of people, can utilize a natural resource. They determine the values that resources have in different uses to different people, and therefore the incentives they have to use the resources in different ways. These are abstract notions, so let us consider a concrete example. In many developing countries low-income farmers are often observed making decisions that lead to soil erosion and reduced productivity of their land. Why would farmers willingly pursue a course of action that undermines the productivity of the resource that is their lifeblood? One major reason could be that their property rights to the land are insecure or **attenuated.** Suppose there is a reasonably good possibility, because of political uncertainties in their country, that they could be dispossessed of their land, either because they might be physically removed from it or because they may not be able effectively to stop encroachers. The incentive effect here is owners avoiding the costs of maintaining long-run fertility—"mining" the current fertility because the land is likely to be lost anyway in the long run.

People are not motivated to conserve a natural resource if the benefits accruing to them from conservation are lower than the costs. Property rights are the terms of empowerment that determine how these benefits and costs will be distributed. There are two main factors in this determination:

1. The social rules establishing who has the legal right to the benefits and who has the legal responsibility for the costs.

2. The economic costs to resource owners/users of excluding other potential beneficiaries from the benefits and costs arising from the use of a resource.

In developed economies, property rights economics normally focuses on the legal specification of the rules of resource use, because these countries usually have reasonably effective systems of legislatures, courts, police, or land survey techniques with which property rights can be defined and enforced. Even in these cases, however, there can be differences between the way a property right is legally specified and the way it is actually used. Many landowners, for example, though having complete and secure rights to their land in the legal sense, may find it simply too costly to keep people from entering "their" property and enjoying some of the benefits of its use.

In the developing world, on the other hand, property rights are typically much more complicated. In some countries or regions, formal legal rules and institutions are scarce. In these cases there is greater reliance on **customary rules** and private means of enforcement, such as social norms and pressure. It means also that extralegal exploitation of natural resources can occur fairly commonly. In some developing countries, for example, illegal timbering by private interests on state land has contributed to large-scale deforestation; in these cases the states have been unable or unwilling to stop the encroachment.

A useful way of classifying property rights is in two categories: individual and collective. **Individual** rights are those exercised by single persons, or perhaps by single families. **Collective** rights, on the other hand, are exercised by some type of group, perhaps a clan, a community, or the central state itself. In pastoral and arid regions, much property, especially of resources, is held communally, with the local village or clan establishing rules for its use. In these settings, however, personal property (like tools or homes) is usually held as individual property. There are many situations around the world in which one part of a resource flow (e.g., hunting or food gathering in a forest) is controlled communally, while other parts (e.g., timber plots) are held as individual property. The appropriate balance between collective rights systems and individual rights systems has been a matter of controversy around the world. On the one hand, many state farms and other collective agricultural enterprises have been dismantled in recent years in favor of individual farm businesses. Fisheries also trend toward individual ownership. On the other hand, most forests in developing countries are owned and controlled by state agencies.

Some of the specific property rights problems characterizing natural resource use in developing countries are the following:

1. The prevalence of open-access situations

2. Insecure tenure that reduces natural resource user costs

3. Inadequate markets through which resource owners can capture the full value flows associated with resource conservation

4. Inequality in the distribution of resource property rights

Open Access and Rent Dissipation

We have dealt several times with the issue of **open-access resources** and the dissipation of resource rents to which it leads. The open-access problem is thought to be particularly severe in many developing countries with respect to marine, forest, grazing, wildlife, and water resources. When access to a resource is open to all, **open-access externalities** exist, incentives to conserve are weakened, and resource overuse often results. Traditional societies have often exploited their resource base with communal property institutions, arrangements where resources are open to use by members of the local community but closed to outsiders. Thus, local resources have often been used in common by small, relatively homogeneous, but somewhat marginalized social groups. Open-access resources serve mainly as a community welfare support system. Disadvantaged members of the community may receive support essentially by gaining access to the natural resource commons. In more recent times, population pressures and resource scarcities have combined to put pressure on these communal open-access institutions. This in turn has focused attention on finding some means for solving the open-access problem, such as private property, state control, or new communal institutions for managing the resources. Open access has often been evaluated in terms of its implications for resource overuse. If we focus on economic growth, we also should stress **rent dissipation.** Growth requires that resource rents be invested in productive forms of capital. But without rents, there can be no investment—at least not from this source. Exhibit 20-2 depicts an example of this.

The Absence of Markets

We have mentioned before that natural resource owners may not face a complete set of markets for all the service flows stemming from the resource. This is a problem in the developed world as well. A forest owner may face a well-functioning market for harvested timber, but little or no market for the amenity values or flood control values produced by the forest. In such cases the decisions of property owners will be biased toward those outputs for which markets exist. This problem is also encountered in developing countries.

Coastal wetlands in many tropical and subtropical countries often contain mangrove forests. These ecosystems support diverse communities of flora and fauna, the harvested products of which have important value. The mangrove forests also produce valuable ecosystem services such as flood control. But they are also under demand in many places for filling and conversion, either to intensive agriculture or to urban development. Private owners of these areas must compare the value of services the mangroves can produce in their natural state with the price they could get if the land were sold to developers. A careful study in Fiji estimated the following values for natural resource products produced by a mangrove forest area:[5]

1. Forest products gathered on site (e.g., firewood, game animals, fruits): $F9 per hectare per year

2. Fishery products harvested off site (fish that make use of the mangrove for an essential part of their life cycle, but are actually caught elsewhere): $F150 per hectare per year

---

Exhibit 20-2   Rent Dissipation and Economic Growth

Safi is a small port community in Morocco, about 100 miles southwest of Casablanca. The primary livelihood of its people is fishing, in particular a sardine fishery. Each night a large fleet of sardine boats ply the waters proximate to the town, and each morning the catch is off-loaded and trucked to market. The operations are extremely labor-intensive, boat crews are large, off-loading is via long (4–6 people) bucket brigades, and the docks are alive with men engaged in all sorts of tasks, besides large numbers of onlookers.

Let us look again at the economics of open-access resources like this sardine fishery. The figure shows the typical fisheries effort-yield function, and the open-access equilibrium effort (e_0), assuming the cost curve labeled C_0. The families of Safi are quite normal: couples form, children are born, the population increases. With few alternative enterprises, the rising population increases the local labor supply. Analytically, this shifts the cost function, actually pushing it downward because of the surplus labor with few alternative job opportunities. Effort levels are increased, stocks are driven lower, and the sardine fishery is in a permanent state of low stocks and productivity.

Clearly, this is not conducive to economic growth, or even to maintaining present income levels of an increasing population. The only way we can turn this situation into one that promotes growth is to invest in other forms of capital, both nonhuman and human, that will lift the productivity of the growing population of the community. But here is the bind. How are we to make these investments? Rents in this fishery have been totally dissipated because of open access. Total costs are equal to total revenues; there is no surplus to devote to other investments.

To promote growth, then, two things must happen. First, some means must be found to limit effort levels. This could be any of the ways we discuss in earlier chapters: voluntary cooperative action by groups of fishers themselves, public regulation of some sort, ITQs, and so on. Second, some means must be found to transform some or all of the resulting rents into investment that will ultimately provide employment and incomes for the young people of Safi.

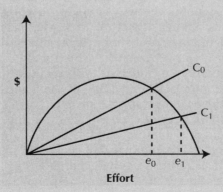

Thus, a substantial part of the values generated by the mangrove forests, which would be lost if they were converted, is realized by fishers, for whom the mangrove essentially provides nursery services for the harvested fish in their younger stages. But there is no way for mangrove owners to realize a return on these services; they have substantial social value, but no value to the individual owners. The market in which the demanders and suppliers of these services could conclude transactions on quantities and prices does not exist.[6] Thus, although the mangrove forest owners may have clear and uncontested title to their land (actually wetland), they are likely to be biased toward development because this provides higher individual returns than those arising from its use as mangrove forest.

Property Rights, Distribution, and Investment

One common feature of property rights in developing countries is a highly skewed distribution of ownership, in which a relatively small number of people own a large fraction of the country's resource capital. This is very directly an issue of equity; most people would regard it as unfair if 95 percent of the land in a region were owned by 1 percent of its population. What a fair distribution of natural resource assets might be is a matter of ethics and politics. But a skewed distribution of natural capital can have important productivity effects, in both short and long runs. Large amounts of land or other resources that are owned by few people are not likely to be used as intensively as they would if they were more evenly distributed. More than that, the expenditure of resource rents, and hence the long-run impacts on growth, are affected by property ownership distributions. If rents accrue largely to a small group of owners, they are likely to be spent on things that enhance their own consumption and status and not on investments needed for long-run development. If rents are more broadly dispersed among the population, they are more likely to be spent on such things as education and investments that increase productive efficiency.

■ Sustainable Growth

Sustainable economic growth is clearly a complex phenomenon, with major interactions among a host of demographic, technological, political, and institutional factors. At bottom, economic growth in any country is related to the growth and use of its productive capacity relative to the growth of its population. Productive capacity is a function of both the quantity of productive inputs (labor, capital of the traditional sort, natural capital) available to the economy and the productivity of those inputs in turning out useful goods and services. In this context, therefore, growth requires increases in the quantity of inputs and/or in their productivity. We thus have a way of linking natural resources with economic growth. Natural resources can be thought of as **natural capital,** the quantities and qualities of which are provided by nature. Human beings may make use of this capital, combining it with other inputs to produce goods and services.

Do countries with relatively abundant natural resources find it easier to develop economically than countries with scarce natural resources? We know by casual observation that natural resources are not **necessary** for growth, because we see many countries (Japan, Singapore, Korea) that have achieved high growth rates despite relatively poor natural resource endowments. And we know natural resources alone are not sufficient for growth, because some countries (Nigeria, Venezuela, Zambia) with very substantial resource endowments have experienced very tepid growth in the past several decades.[7]

The fact that many countries with abundant resource stocks have been unable to turn these into economic growth, and in fact may have experienced economic decline, has led some to posit the existence of a **"resource curse."** The thinking here is that something about the presence of abundant natural resources depresses growth rather than encourages it. This idea is contested, however.[8] One reason for this is that history clearly shows us many cases where natural resource endowments, national or regional, have been instrumental in supporting economic growth. Botswana has used its diamond resources to provide the impetus for growth. Iceland has grown by using its fishery resources. Many countries have been successful in developing agricultural sectors to help spur national economic growth.

The way to achieve **sustainable growth** in the face of the declining availability of a natural resource is to augment the quantity/quality of nonresource capital inputs. How much alternative capital must be substituted for the diminished natural resource capital? This depends on the relative productivities of the different input types, which depends on the technological and institutional situation in which the country finds itself. This is a matter of preserving the overall productive capacity of an economy.

■ The Control and Management of Resource Rents

If per capita income is to be maintained or increased, especially in the face of population increases, any disinvestment in natural resources must be offset, or more than offset, by investment in other forms of productive assets. This essentially requires a source of monetary resources with which to invest in these alternative assets. One of the most obvious places to look for these investable resources is **natural resource rents.** There are two essential parts of this process:

1. Using natural resources in ways that maximize their rents

2. Channeling those rents into productive investments

We talk throughout the book about the conditions that resource-use decisions must meet in order to maximize resource rents. Rent maximization, as a goal, is just as applicable to developing countries as to the developed world. For the rest of this chapter we focus on condition 2 above: the disposition of the rents.

Those who initially capture the rent may be any one, alone or in combination, of the following:

1. Owners of the resource, perhaps private nationals, national governments, or foreign parties of one type or another

2. Private firms engaged in extraction, whether local, national, or foreign

3. Public firms engaged in extraction, usually national firms of the country where the resource resides

4. Illegal firms, foreign or local, large or small

Note that one entity could fall into several of these categories.

The disposition of resource rents can be depicted with the following schematic:

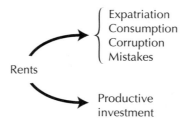

A portion of the rents may flow out of a country as **revenues accruing to foreign companies** involved with the extraction of resources. In some cases rents are distributed as **payments to individual citizens** (or perhaps small local groups), which some observers have recommended as a way to make sure the funds do not get siphoned off in corrupt practices, as well as a means to address serious wealth inequalities that often exist in developing countries. In many cases resource rents have been used as a major source of repayments by governments to **foreign creditors,** a use that has sometimes led to objections by people who see this as detracting from the need for current social expenditures. Resource rents may also be used to finance **general government expenses,** which may account for the oversized public sectors of many developing economies.

Rents may also be siphoned off into channels of **corruption, which include** illegal and usually invisible payments to public and private officials. It may sometimes be difficult to distinguish between true corruption and payments made in connection with projects and plans that are unrealistic, inefficient, and of little promise—for example, when a government invests rents in an agricultural development project that has little chance of success.

Finally, there are various investment flows to which resource rents may be directed, including investments in **public infrastructure** and **firms and industries** producing an array of goods and services. Distinctions are sometimes made between hard infrastructure (ports, roads, airports) and soft infrastructure (schools, health clinics). The latter are frequently referred to as investment in **human capital**; that is, investment in the skills and capacities of the citizenry. One good thing about human capital is that it perhaps is less subject to appropriation by political authorities than other forms of wealth. In addition, human capital investments can impact other important dimensions of the overall problem. It is clear, for example, that investments in health, education, and training, especially for women, can have important impacts on fertility rates. Thus, if a portion of natural resource rents is spent on investment in education, it can lead to a substantial decline in the population growth rate, which in turn will lower future demands for natural resources.

In some cases the channel for disposition of resource rents is simple and straightforward, as in the direct expenditures of rents that private or public extracting firms make: direct spending on health clinics or schools, direct investments in auxiliary industries, and so on. But the main channel is through public agencies of one type or another whose mandate is to accumulate and disperse the rents. The first is usually accomplished through taxes, royalties, fees, or other instruments, and the latter through specialized agencies or programs for making and monitoring expenditures. A key player in this process is normally a country's banking system. It is during this transfer process, usually under control or influence by political authorities, that a portion of the resource rents can be diverted, stolen, wasted, or otherwise misappropriated. Recent years have seen greater efforts directed at making this whole process more **transparent** and easier to monitor.[9]

■ The Volatility of Resource Rents in Developing Countries

A difficult and ongoing problem confronting countries who might think of using resource rents to spur economic growth is the fact that these rents can be very volatile over time. This is because of the volatility of natural resource commodity prices on international markets. The 1970s and 1980s saw massive changes in petroleum prices, with large run-ups followed by substantial declines. There was a boom in coffee prices in the latter part of the 1970s. Prices of copper and phosphate increased sharply in the late 1970s and early 1980s, then fell back to earlier levels, and since have risen again sharply. In the latter 1950s many commodities, including copper, rubber, and petroleum, declined fairly sharply. But in the 2000s they have bounced back up, fueled especially by the vast increase in demand for these materials in China.

Figure 20-1 on the next page shows the long run (1962 to today) performance of an index of world primary commodity prices. This index is a composite of major minerals, agricultural, and forestry prices. One can see two major patterns: (1) a long-run trend downward until the end of the 20th century and (2) the tendency for substantial fluctuations around the trend. Recent decades saw peaks in the early 1970s and in 1980, 1988, 1995, 2007, and 2010, followed by rapid decreases. A primary reason for the cyclical price swings is the fluctuations in investment in extraction and processing facilities. When prices strengthen, optimism among investors leads to rapid upswings in investment that often overshoot, leading to overcapacity, market surpluses, and price collapses.

In a world where natural resource commodity prices fluctuate rapidly and strongly, it is hard to develop a sustainable program of public or private growth-producing investment programs based on natural resource rents.

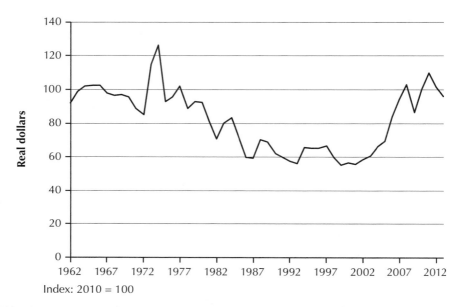

Index: 2010 = 100

Figure 20-1   Commodity Price Index (non-energy) in Real 2005 Dollars

Source: The World Bank Group, *Commodity Markets Pink Sheet,* 2013 (http://go.worldbank.org/ 4ROCCIEQ50).

When prices increase and rents are high, spending them may not get the close scrutiny it should; projects may be undertaken without adequate benefit-cost analysis. When resource commodity prices fall, projects undertaken earlier may have to be put on hold, or perhaps financed out of risky borrowing.[10]

Many countries (both developing and developed) have created **sovereign wealth funds**, basically savings (and investing) accounts, in which to deposit resource rents. Often these accounts are held in countries with more developed and transparent financial markets, in hopes that they can be insulated from political interference and the rent seeking they might attract if left on deposit at home.

■ Summary

Most of the world's population is located in developing countries, those that are trying to achieve faster rates of economic growth that will eventually lead to levels of economic welfare characteristic of the developed world. Many, though not all, of these countries have economies today that are heavily dependent on natural resources, especially agricultural resources. There are two important linkages that need to be considered closely: the contribution that natural resources can make to economic growth and the impact of growth on the quantity and quality of the stock of natural capital. Many concepts and models presented in previous chapters are as relevant in developing countries as they are in the developed world, but there are also some important differences. One is that in many developing countries a full set of reasonably efficient economic institutions may not be present; for example, capital markets that resource owners can rely on in making decisions about optimal holdings of natural capital stocks. With nonrenewable resources, economic growth clearly requires that disinvestment in resource stocks be compensated for by investments in other types of productive capital. With renewable resources and growing populations, it is also true that natural capital, which in this case can be used in a steady-state fashion, should be supplemented with nonnatural capital. The most obvious source of funds to invest in nonnatural capital is natural resource rents. Thus, the maximization of rents, and its distribution to those who would invest it productively, is perhaps the most central problem in the relationship of natural resources and economic growth.

Notes

1 A distinction is sometimes made between economic *growth* and economic *development*. The former refers to increases in income and wealth per capita, whereas the latter also includes other social changes that accompany growth such as developments in education and health care, and demographic factors that moderate population growth. For our purposes we need not dwell on this distinction.

2 See the papers in Machiko Nissanke and Erik Thorbecke, *The Impact of Globalization on the World's Poor: Transmission Mechanisms,* Palgrave Macmillan, New York, 2007.

3 It is worth reiterating here that although we use just two categories, developed and developing, the countries within each category vary greatly in terms of many important social and economic characteristics. In a review chapter we paint with a very broad brush, using analyses that are generally, but not universally, applicable to all countries.

4 For an extended discussion of such resource problems in developing countries see Partha Dasgupta, *An Inquiry into Well-Being and Destitution,* Clarendon Press, Oxford, England, 1993.

5 Cited in John A. Dixon and Padma N. Lal, "The Management of Coastal Wetlands: Economic Analysis of Combined Ecological-Economic Systems," in Partha Dasgupta and Karl-Gören Mäler, *The Environment and Emerging Development Issues,* Vol. 2, Clarendon Press, Oxford, England, 1997, pp. 399–423.

6 You will recognize the main problem, which is that the nursery services are essentially public goods. Given the way that the fish grow and later disperse, it is not possible to make nursery services available to one fisher without making them available to all the others.

7 *Necessary* conditions are conditions that must hold in order for a certain result to occur. *Sufficient* conditions are conditions that will produce the result if the conditions hold. A necessary condition need not be sufficient, and a sufficient condition need not be necessary.

8 For discussion of the "resource curse," see Richard M. Auty, *Sustaining Development in Mineral Economies: The Resource Curse Thesis,* Routledge, London, 1993; Jeffrey D. Sachs and Andrew M. Warner, "The Curse of Natural Resources," *European Economic Review,* Vol. 45, May 2001, pp. 827–838; Andrew Rosser, *The Political Economy of the Resource Curse: A Literature Survey,* Institute of Development Studies, 2006.

9 Transparency International (www.transparency.org) is an NGO set up to encourage this. See also the British Extractive Industries Transparency Initiative (www.eitransparency.org/section/abouteiti).

10 See, for example, I. M. D. Little, *Boom, Crisis and Adjustment: The Macroeconomic Experience of Developing Countries,* published for the World Bank by Oxford University Press, New York, 1993.

Key Terms

collective property rights
customary rules
developing/developed economies
human capital
national income
natural capital

natural resource rents
natural resources and growth
public infrastructure
resource "curse"
sovereign wealth funds
technological development

Questions for Further Discussion

1. Are natural resources necessary for economic growth?

2. Discuss the pros and cons of creating a "development fund" into which revenues are put from the sale of natural resource commodities, with the proceeds to be used for development projects. What are the alternatives to such a fund?

3. How does one reconcile the idea of economic growth, in terms of increasing per capita incomes, and steady-state use rates of renewable natural resources?

4. Many people tend to boil down the development/resources relationship as: large population and high population growth rates, fixed resource base, thus resource degradation and scarcities. Discuss this line of thought.

Useful Websites

Links to websites on the theme of sustainable development:

- Tom Tietenberg's sustainable development online bibliography (www.Colby.edu/personal/t/thtieten/sustainbiblio.html)
- International Institute for Sustainable Development (http://www.iisd.org)

Public agencies and organizations:

- The World Bank (www.worldbank.org)
- Organization for Economic Cooperation and Development, Green Growth and Sustainable Development (http://www.oecd.org/greengrowth/)
- United Nations Sustainable Development (http://sustainabledevelopment.un.org)
- Inter-American Development Bank: Sustainable Development (http://www.iadb.org/en/inter-american-development-bank)

NGOs:

- International Institute for Energy Conservation (www.iiec.org)
- International Organization for Sustainable Development (www.iosd.org)
- World Business Solutions for a Sustainable World (http://www.wbcsd.org/home.aspx)

- International Institute for Environment and Development (www.iied.org)
- National Council for Science and the Environment (http://www.ncseonline.org)

Scientific journals:

- *Ecological Economics* (http://www.journals.elsevier.com/ecological-economics/)
- *Environment and Development Economics* (http://journals.cambridge.org/action/displayJournal?jid=EDE)

Selected Readings

Auty, Richard M., ed. *Resource Abundance and Economic Development.* Oxford, England: Oxford University Press, 2001.

Barbier, Edward P. *Natural Resources and Economic Development.* Cambridge, England: Cambridge University Press, 2005.

Collier, Paul. *The Plundered Planet.* New York: Oxford University Press, 2010.

Dasgupta, Partha. *An Inquiry into Well Being and Destitution.* Oxford, England: Oxford University Press, 1993.

Hendrix, Cullen S., and Marcus Noland. *Confronting the Curse: The Economics and Geopolitics of Natural Resource Governance.* Washington, DC: Peterson Institute for International Economics, 2014.

21

Globalization and Natural Resources

Fifty years ago less than 10 percent of total global output entered into trade among countries. Today (2015) this proportion stands at about one-third. This is the statistical face of globalization, the "shrinking" of the world that is bringing its 190-odd countries into even closer contact and interdependence. It is not new; trends toward closer connections among the diverse people of the world have gone on probably from the beginning of human civilization. But industrialization—and the subsequent massive reductions in transportation costs for people, goods, and information—has greatly reduced the effective distances among people.

■ Dimensions of Globalization

Our task in this chapter is to investigate the effect of globalization on the utilization, and conservation, of natural resources. But first let us be clear about what globalization actually is. Globalization has a number of dimensions:

- Increasing trade among nations. Over the last 60 years the annual growth rate of total economic activity in the world has been about 3.5 percent; the annual growth rate in total global exports has been about 6.2 percent. In other words, international trade has grown about twice as fast as overall economic growth. Economies are becoming increasingly interconnected through trade.

- Interconnectedness of financial markets. Money and other financial assets can be, and are, moved around the world very rapidly. The flows are large, and they can be volatile, moving into and out of a country so fast that they can destabilize economies, especially those that are relatively small by international standards.

- Movements of people. Every year millions of people in the world migrate from one country to another (and there are even more movements within countries). The moves are in response to many things, but a primary factor is economic migration, where people move from one country to another in search of better economic prospects. Demographic factors (e.g., differentiated fertility rates) are also important here.

In addition to these very direct and obvious impacts of globalization there are others that perhaps are less obvious:

- Changes in economic institutions. Globalization is often thought to involve a general predisposition for shifting economic activity toward private sector and market-oriented institutions. This has been stressed especially in the developing world, where substantial factions of national economies have been run by state-owned and/or operated firms. On the other hand, a huge impetus to global trade has been the ascendency of China, which has encouraged the growth of **managed trade** using large public, or combination of public/private, enterprises.

- Significant realignments in political power. Many observers feel that globalization will have important local political impacts, especially shifting political power away from national governments and toward international bodies. Two types of institutions are singled out: multi-national companies and international policy bodies. By opening up their economies to the full forces of international commerce, nations may give large international companies (the multinationals) greater power over domestic economic policy, at the expense of local authorities. This would not necessarily be bad if these multinational companies had the interest of the local citizenry at heart, but they normally do not.

- Globalization may also shift political power toward large international agencies such as the World Bank, the International Monetary Fund (IMF), and the World Trade Organization (WTO).

- Greater inequalities in income and wealth. A major point of contention on globalization is whether it is leading to greater levels of **economic inequality** among and within countries. Critics say it does; others say it doesn't. In fact, the distribution of income and wealth and its connection with trade and economic development has been much studied. While there have been small changes in the worldwide distribution of wealth over the last fifty years, they are nowhere near the extreme changes that took place in the first half of the 19th century, when some countries were embracing the industrial revolution aggressively.

- Cultural and economic homogenization. The term "cultural homogenization" means increased attachment to the "cultural products" of the developed world, especially American products. Likewise, economic homogenization usually refers to a situation in which people strive to achieve a material standard of living characteristic of the developed world as opposed to the local, subsistence-based economies of much of the developing world.

■ Trade and Natural Resources

The aspect of globalization that interests us here is international trade in natural resources. In 2013, about one-third of the total commodity trade in the world consisted of natural resources, interpreted broadly—that is, including both extracted resources and harvested items such as fish and forest products. About 70 percent of these resource exports consist of fuels and mining products.[1]

Global trade in natural resources has a number of unique characteristics:

- Natural resources are not evenly distributed among the countries of the world; some countries have abundant natural resources, and others have few. For example, more than 90 percent of world oil reserves are in just 15 countries. This means also that countries differ markedly in the extent to which they are affected by resource trade. Some have huge resource exports, while others have little; many developed countries have economies that rely heavily on imports of natural resources, including "virtual resource imports," i.e., products with high resource content that are imported into countries with resource scarcities. See table 21-1.

- Natural resources and trade therein are heavily involved in the complex processes of economic development. Nature is often the key asset

Table 21-1   Natural Resource Exports and Imports, as Percent of Total Country Merchandise Exports and Imports, Selected Countries, 2008

Country	Resource Exports as Percent of Total Merchandise Exports	Country	Resource Imports as Percent of Total Merchandise Imports
Canada	39.0	Japan	45.9
Norway	77.8	India	42.9
United States	11.0	Korea, Rep of	41.8
United Arab Emirates	52.1	Taipei, Chinese	34.5
Russian Federation	72.9	European Union (27)	33.6
Australia	61.1	Singapore	29.7
European Union (27)	9.2	China	29.2
Singapore	20.0	Indonesia	29.1
Bolivarian Rep of Venezuela	95.8	Thailand	27.9
Saudi Arabia	90.0	United States	27.0
Kuwait	95.2	Turkey	25.1
Algeria	98.8	Brazil	24.7
Angola	100.0	Australia	18.2
Iran	84.2	Canada	16.5
Nigeria	92.2	Mexico	13.1

Source: World Trade Organization, *World Trade Report 2010: Trade in Natural Resources*, Washington, DC, Tables 2 and 3, pp. 207–208.

of the poorest countries. Managed properly, it can power the forces of economic development. But there can be many ways in which it works in the opposite direction as we discussed in the last chapter. Resource trade also has the potential in many cases to exacerbate political/economic conflicts among and between exporters and importers.

- Many natural resources around the world are in the public domain; either explicitly owned by governments, as in the case of sub-soil resources, or essentially owned by nobody, as in some deep sea resources. Ambiguous ownership contributes to contention, sometimes actual combat, over the rents arising from resource production.[2]
- Markets for natural resources often have relatively inelastic supply and demand curves. Thus small shifts in these curves can create big price changes. In addition, many such resources can be stockpiled, leading to uncertainty about future supplies which also contributes to volatile prices. In earlier chapters we have mentioned this factor, and demonstrated it graphically (see figures 10-8, 11-2, and 20-1). For countries that are dependent on resource exports this creates major problems for macroeconomic continuity and stability.

■ Trade and Resource Conservation

For our purposes, the most fundamental question is this—Does international trade help, or hinder, efforts to achieve the conservation of natural resources? Figure 21-1 depicts the essentials of a typical situation: a country in which there is a domestic market for a resource, and an international market where the resource trades at a world price. Domestic market demand is labeled D, domestic supply S, and the international market price I. In the absence of international trade, q_1 units would trade at p_1. But with international trade, total production in the country would be q_2, of which $q_2 - q_3$ would be exported. The local, domestic, price would be set by the international market.

So the primary effect of trade in this type of case (where international prices

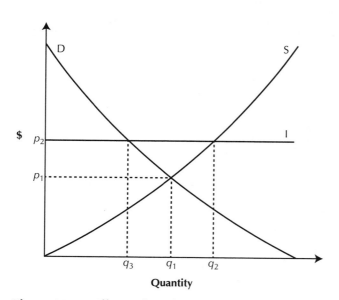

Figure 21-1   Effects of Trade on Output and Prices

exceed domestic prices that would pertain if there was no trade) is to inten-sify production. It also raises domestic prices. On the surface, trade clearly appears to work against resource conservation, if by "conservation" we mean "lower rates of use." Throughout the book, we have used as a criterion the socially efficient rate of resource use, which can be distinguished only in reference to the configuration of social benefits and costs of the situation we are analyzing. If D, S, and I truly represent the complete set of benefits and costs to the society involved, then q_2, the quantity with trade, would repre-sent the socially efficient rate of output for that country as it engages in for-eign trade, in this case exports. We have discussed repeatedly the conditions that must be met to achieve this socially efficient rate of output.

First and foremost is lack of **external costs**. Virtually all instances of resources extractions involve potential externalities, for example:

- Timber harvesting can impact local or regional hydrological regimes, such as flood frequencies.
- Open-pit mining operations can affect local topography, with scenic and habitat implications.
- Petroleum well operations can impact local water quality.
- "Fracking" in some locations can apparently encourage local earth-quakes of varying intensities.
- Farm-raised fish can sometimes escape and contaminate the geno-types of nearby wild fish.

The shift from q_1 to q_2 represents output that is slated for export. In the United States, the standard scenario would be that new or existing private firms undertake the necessary steps: (1) resource development, (2) produc-tion, and (3) transportation. When referring to other countries, especially resource-rich developing countries, the scenario can be substantially more complicated. The added output destined for export may be produced by a domestic private firm, a public firm, or a firm (private or public) of foreign origin. The capital mobility of globalization has led to a situation in which much of the resource production is done by firms that are not owned by the nationals of the country in which the activity is taking place. It is likely that the incidence of external costs, and the ability of authorities to control them, will vary with the ownership of the firms doing the production. A foreign firm may be more prone to disregard production externalities than a domes-tic firm. We discussed an instance of this in chapter 1. A closely related requirement for efficiency is lack of **open-access externalities**, which brings up questions of sovereignty, ownership, and control of natural resources.

Resource Sovereignty, Ownership, and Control

Sovereignty means the right of having governance over. It is generally agreed that countries have sovereignty over all resources lying within their borders. A very stringent notion of sovereignty is that **domestic prices** of a resource ought to reflect conditions of domestic supply and demand. Then trade automatically would be a violation of sovereignty, because with trade domestic prices track world prices.

There are many situations in the world in which sovereignty over important resources is ambiguous or contested. Many of these are related to ocean resources, as exhibit 21-1 indicates. **Ownership** is the legal right by somebody—the owners—to exclude nonowners from the resource. Ownership can lie with public or private entities, and can be the subject of lively markets, or political initiatives, by which it is shifted among parties. Ownership is not identical with **control**, which consists of having the power, legally and technically, to use the resource as one wishes, to the exclusion of others. There are many places in the world where natural resources, under the sovereignty or ownership of one party, are nevertheless put in use by others who have the power to do so.

Exhibit 21-1   Issues of Natural Resource Sovereignty

Until the 20th century, a country's sovereignty extended only out to a 3-mile limit from shore. In the 1982 United Nations Convention on the Law of the Sea (UNCLOS), the idea of the "territorial sea" was established. Most countries now claim sovereignty over a territorial sea with a breadth of 12 miles. Many states claim an additional 200 miles as an exclusive economic zone (EEZ).

Within the EEZ, the coastal state enjoys "sovereign rights for the purpose of exporting and exploiting, conserving and managing the natural resources, whether living or non-living, of the waters superjacent to the sea-bed and of the sea-bed and its sub-soil, and with regard to other activities for the economic exploration and exploitation of the zone, such as the production of energy from water, currents and winds" (Article 56, UNCLOS). The UNCLOS also gives countries the rights and responsibilities with respect to protection and preservation of environmental resources in the EEZ.

Source: World Trade Organization, *World Trade Report 2010, Trade in Natural Resources*, p. 178.

Governance Issues

We notice from figure 21-1 that having exports implies that net incomes, a large part of which may be natural resource rents, are greater than they would be in the absence of the exports. We have explained (see chapters 5 and 20) the requirement for sustainability in resource use: that resource rents be reinvested in other types of production assets. And this puts the spotlight on the **governance** question: the extent to which public oversight and regulation of resource production can be pursued without rent seeking and corruption. **Rent seeking** means efforts by people to gain control of the regulatory process in order to gain greater control of the flow of resource rents. **Corruption** means using illegal means, such as bribery, to gain access to rent streams and the natural resources that can produce them.

All of these factors strongly suggest that globalization of natural resource markets will lead to socially efficient and equitable levels of resource extraction *only* if the governmental and regulatory aspects of the participating countries are able to deal with the higher resource values.[3] There is, in addition, the challenge of attaining sustainable resource use which, as we have seen (chapters 10 and 20) is a matter of directing resource rents into investments in non-resource capital.

In addition, the analysis of figure 21-1 shows current prices as they relate to the interplay of current supply and demand. In international resource markets, however, prices were historically set through long-term contracts negotiated between buyers and sellers. So the interplay of supply and demand, as depicted in the graph, can be obscured. In recent years many more of these international resource prices have been set by trading on organized markets,[4] which in fact may be one reason for the higher price volatility recently.

■ Public Policies of Resource-Trading Countries

Historically, most countries have thought about foreign trade from a mercantilist point of view: encourage exports, limit imports. This encouraged a focus on import restrictions, either tariffs or quantitative restrictions, to improve trade balances. Most international efforts to foster trade improvements, such as those of the World Trade Organization, have concentrated on motivating countries to reduce restrictions on imports.

In contrast to this, many countries that export natural resources have sought to improve their situations by imposing restrictions on exports, especially by imposing taxes on exported items, and sometimes by imposing outright quantitative restrictions. This has especially been the case with natural resources, which account for about a third of the cases where export taxes have been imposed.

Several justifications have been used historically to justify export controls. Most importantly, perhaps, is the view that, by penalizing exports, a large quantity of the resource will stay home, which will benefit the local economy through lower prices. Domestic food prices are often the target here. Another recent example is the export restriction by China on its rare earth exports, to ensure supplies for its own industries.

Taxes on resource exports have also been common. A major rationale for these is that it can be a source of government revenues, which can then be used for local infrastructure, for example improved roads. Another rationale has been that by keeping a larger proportion of output at home and at a lower price, it encourages the development of domestic resource-processing industries, with the attendant benefits of employment and economic growth. Still another reason why nations sometimes resort to export taxes, with negative connotations in this case, is that they can create pots of money that can then be appropriated by members of the politically connected elite.

Export Taxes

What happens when a country installs an export tax; in particular, what happens within that country? Of course the real world is complex: many countries, many goods, many different types of markets, many different types of political leaders, and so forth. But we can consider the economics of a simple case.

Figure 21-2 displays an analysis of the situation where a single country, assumed to be a relatively small part of the total international market for a traded natural resource, institutes an export tax on its own exports. The local demand and supply functions are as indicated, and initial world demand is shown as p_0; it is horizontal to indicate that this country is small relative to the total world market, so it could sell any amount of this resource at a price of p_0. Before the export tax, the total quantity supplied by this country is q_0, of which q_1 is sold domestically and $(q_0 - q_1)$ is exported.

Now an export tax equal to $(p_0 - p_1)$ is introduced. What this means essentially is that now producers in this country will receive a price of p_1 for exports (the world price net of the tax). On the assumption that the domestic industry consists of a group of competitive suppliers and demanders, the domestic price will also go down by the amount of the tax. Suppliers will initially prefer to offer their supply to local, untaxed markets rather than international, taxed markets. The effect of this will be to increase domestic supply and drive down domestic prices by the amount of the tax, so that suppliers ultimately will be obtaining the same price on either market.

The new, after tax, results will be total domestic supply q_3, of which q_2 is sold in country and $(q_3 - q_2)$ is exported. In addition, the domestic taxing

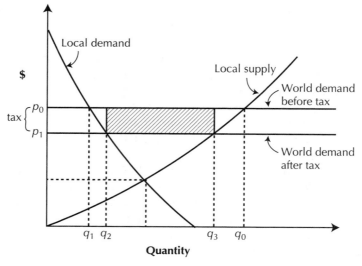

Figure 21-2   Analysis of a Tax on Exports

authorities collect revenues equal to the area of the box identified by $(q_3 - q_2)$ and $(p_0 - p_1)$.

Without going much more deeply into these results we can see a couple of things: local suppliers are worse off because the price they can get for their commodity goes down; local demanders are better off because the price they have to pay goes down. And local tax authorities, or whoever gets the benefit of the tax revenues, are better off because of the tax. What factors determine how much these amounts are in relative terms? One is the price elasticities of local demand and supply; in effect, how steep the demand and supply curves are. Another is the importance of exports relative to the size of the local market; if this country exports most of this commodity the costs to producers will outweigh the gain to consumers; the opposite would be true if exports are a small percentage of total output.

■ Modes of International Governance in Resources Trade

The main international institution governing trade is the World Trade Organization (WTO). Its purpose is to establish rules and procedures governing trade, and thus stimulate economic activity related to international trade. It is especially aimed at reducing the barriers to trade, to get nations to refrain from putting tariffs and quotas on imports or subsidies on exports, and in general to move toward conditions of free trade among the world's nations, almost all of which are members of the WTO. One section of the WTO agreement also outlaws what are called "nontariff barriers" such as excessive inspection requirements, excessive product specifications, and the like. But there is a very broad list of conditions that are exceptions to WTO rules; one is that governments are allowed to set restrictions in order to achieve the "protection of human, animal or plant life or health," and the "conserving of natural resources."

Many natural resource groups and interests feel that WTO efforts to relax trade restrictions undermine a country's individual ability to protect important natural resource assets by acting against those who would damage these assets. A well-known controversy along these lines has been the U.S. import ban on tuna coming from Mexico, on grounds of protecting dolphins in the eastern Pacific tuna fishery. The Marine Mammal Protection Act (MMPA) became law in the United States in 1972. One of its major objectives is to minimize the killing of marine mammals during commercial fishing operations. In the eastern Pacific Ocean, certain species of dolphins accompany schools of commercially valuable tuna, and if the tuna are caught using certain traditional methods, large numbers of dolphins will also be caught and killed. The MMPA governs U.S. tuna-fishing practices to prevent, or reduce, the incidental dolphin kill. It also restricts imports of yellow fin tuna from other countries that use standard purse-seine techniques, unless their dolphin kills are within 1.25 times the U.S. average for the same.

The United States imposed a ban on tuna imports from Mexico in 1990, citing these MMPA provisions. The GATT (General Agreement on Tariffs and Trade, the precursor to the WTO) dispute resolution panel ruled that this was a violation of the rules governing trade restrictions. Nevertheless, Congress enacted the International Dolphin Conservation Act of 1992, prohibiting the importation of any tuna that was not "dolphin safe"; that is, caught by methods that did not result in dolphin deaths.

Since then there has been an ongoing struggle between interests who would like to see these import restrictions relaxed and those who want them continued. The former maintain that the restrictions are not only counter to the WTO agreement, but ineffectual; furthermore, they say, there are better ways of reducing dolphin deaths, such as working with the fishing fleets of other nations to help them develop better procedures for reducing dolphin deaths. Supporters of the trade restrictions believe they are still an effective way to enhance overall protection for dolphins. Another issue is that dolphin-safe fishing methods may have negative impacts on other species of fish as well as sea turtles.

In addition to the general activity under the WTO, there are additional institutional means for dealing with resources trade. A brief review of terminology will aid your understanding of the next section.

International agreements come in several forms:

- A **convention** is an agreement in which countries define a problem and jointly commit to addressing it, but without specifying exactly the concrete steps that will be undertaken to meet its objectives.

- A **protocol** is an agreement that attempts to fill in some of the details of a convention: what specific actions signatories will undertake, what institutions will be established to implement the agreement, and so on.

- A **treaty** is a fully developed agreement specifying problems, actions to be undertaken by signatories, steps to be taken under implementation and enforcement, and so on.

- A **bilateral agreement** is one entered into by two countries to manage a particular resource. For example, the China-Australia Migratory Bird Agreement, and the Columbia River Treaty between the U.S. and Canada.

- **Multilateral agreements**, as the name implies, are agreements among groups of countries with the objective of managing an important resource. This includes **regional agreements**, which are groups of propinquitous countries whose concerns focus on a resource of local interest.

Trade Agreements

Bilateral and multilateral agreements are instruments that go beyond the rules of the WTO, and deal with specific trade issues of the countries making the agreement. From the standpoint of the United States and its neighbors, one of the most important is the North American Free Trade Agreement (NAFTA), an agreement negotiated among the United States, Canada, and Mexico primarily to reduce tariffs and other barriers to trade among the three countries. NAFTA is meant to stimulate the economies of these three countries by expanding markets for the goods and services they produce, or might produce in the future. Natural resource concerns played an important role in the NAFTA negotiations. There were, and still are, substantial differences of opinion about how NAFTA impacts resources in the participating countries. Indeed, differences of opinion on this matter split the environmental community. Sierra Club, Greenpeace, and others were against it; Audubon, World Wildlife Fund, the Environmental Defense Fund, and others were in favor of it.

Commodity Agreements

International commodity agreements are efforts in which both exporting and importing countries develop a joint plan for managing the trade of a specific resource commodity. They are usually aimed at reducing price fluctuations and establishing trade protocols that work to the benefit of both sides of the trading link. They sometimes involve the establishment of buffer stocks, and usually some degree of commitment to manage production and exports.

Commodity agreements were very popular in the post-World War II trading world, and were thought to be effective devices for regulating the resources trading on which many developing countries depended. Their popularity has since diminished, though some continue to exist, such as the International Agreements on Coffee, Cocoa, Sugar, Olive Oil, and Tropical Timber. The reality is that the interests of exporters and importers are usually opposed, so it is difficult to find agreements that have benefits for both.[5]

Resource Cartels

An "international resource cartel" is a term given to an agreement among exporting countries to act together to support the price of a particular resource. OPEC (Organization of Petroleum Exporting Countries) is the prime example. The objectives are normally to produce higher and more stable international prices, and the normal means are production and export quotas. Many resource cartels have been formed; few have been successful in producing substantial price increases, and very few have lasted beyond several years. The main reason for the failure of international cartels is cheating by some members, i.e., surreptitiously expanding production and exports beyond the limits set by cartel authorities.[6] In addition, cartels, being attempts to manipulate a market, automatically provide the incentive for countervailing actions by importers, such as:

- diversification of sources
- lowering resource intensities
- developing substitutes
- negotiating long-run contracts
- building up buffer stocks
- augmenting supply through recycling

Bilateral Investment Treaties

Agreements between two countries designed to facilitate and systematize the flow of direct investment from one to another are called **Bilateral Investment Treaties (BITs)**. They are often used in natural resource projects, where firms in one country invest in facilities to produce, process, and/or transport natural resources in another country. They are meant to address the strategic tactical issues created when investors commit to projects which are then under the regulatory control of another country. Key objectives are to agree on a set of rules governing both investors and the host country, and provide protection against expropriation—direct or indirect—through regulation. A key issue in BITs is whether they substantially reduce the control a country has over its own resources, by weakening its legal ability to control its production. In recent years there has been something of a backlash against BITs, especially among developing countries.

Natural Resource Agreements

Finally, there are formal agreements among countries designed to manage specific resource issues. They are formal in the sense that they utilize the full machinery of diplomacy and ratification among signatory countries. There are hundreds of such agreements currently in effect, though of course they vary greatly in terms of their effectiveness. Many of these are regional, such as:

- Convention on the Conservation of Nature in the South Pacific
- Regional Convention for the Conservation of the Red Sea and Gulf of Aden Environment

There are also many global agreements, acceded to by all, or a large majority, of countries. Examples are:

- Convention on Fishing and Conservation of Living Resources of the High Seas
- Convention on Biological Diversity
- Convention on the Protection and Use of Trans-boundary Watercourses and International Lakes
- FAO International Undertaking on Plant Genetic Resources

About 20 of the multilateral agreements include trade provisions. One of the most important is the Convention on International Trade in Endangered Species.

Convention on International Trade in Endangered Species of Wild Fauna and Flora

Roughly 5,000 animal species and 28,000 plant species are protected under the international Convention on International Trade in Endangered Species of Wild Flora and Fauna (CITES). CITES came into force in 1975.

Under it, each country is supposed to establish its own permit system to control the movement of wildlife exports and imports. It is also supposed to designate a management body to handle the permit system and a scientific body to determine whether trade is likely to be detrimental to the survival of the species. Species are separated into three classes:

1. Species threatened with extinction, in which commercial trade is banned and noncommercial trade regulated.

2. Species that may become threatened if trade is not held to levels consistent with biological processes, for which commercial trade is allowed with conditions.

3. Species that are not currently threatened but for which international cooperation is appropriate, for which trade requires permits.

The endangered species trade is considered by many to be a qualified success, although much more remains to be done, especially in improving national permit processes. There are some simple lessons to be derived from considering this type of trade restriction, which we will pursue by looking at an international supply-and-demand model of an endangered species. The same conclusions can apply to other cases, such as export restrictions on logs to protect rain forests. Consider the market model of figure 21-3. This shows the world, or aggregate, supply and export demand conditions for a species of wildlife. The supply function is based on the costs of hunting, transporting, processing, record keeping, and so on, necessary to bring the wildlife to the point of export. It is an aggregate supply function made up of the supply functions of the various countries in which that species grows. The demand function shows the quantities that the export market will take at alternative prices. The intersection of the two functions shows the market price and quantity of this type of wildlife that will be traded in a year's time.

Two types of trade constraints could be used to reduce the quantity of this species moving in international trade: export controls and import controls. Each will reduce the quantity traded, but they will have very different impacts on price. Export controls work by essentially making

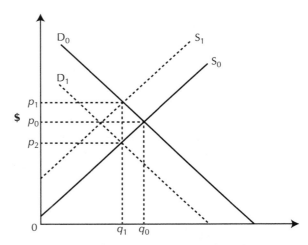

Quantity of Trade in an Endangered Species

Figure 21-3   Effects of Trade Policy on the International Market in Endangered Species

exporting more costly, which has the effect in figure 21-3 of shifting the supply function upward from supply curve S_0 to supply curve S_1. The result of this is a reduction in quantity traded, in this case to q_1. The amount that quantity falls depends on the extent to which the supply curve shifts up and also on the slope of the demand function; the steeper this slope, the less will quantity contract. But this approach to trade reduction also leads to an increase in price, from the original price p_0 to p_1. This price increase could have several impacts, depending essentially on property rights. Imagine a case where the endangered species is subject to private ownership, either by individuals or by small, well-defined groups. Perhaps the habitat of the species is under private ownership, for example. The higher price for the species now becomes a signal for its owners to be more concerned about its safety and welfare because, in this circumstance, efforts at conservation will have a direct market payoff.

The added price will have the opposite effect, however, when property rights in the endangered species are ill-defined or completely absent, which is the usual case. Most of the habitats for the world's endangered species are common property, in the sense that either everybody has the right to enter or harvest the animal or plant, or that, as in public parks, authorities are unable to keep people from taking the species "illegally." We saw, in chapter 6, the problem to which common-property resources are prone: because other users cannot be kept out, nobody has an incentive to conserve the resource. It's either use it or lose it to some other harvester. The increased price for the endangered species in this case will work against conservation. It will encourage higher rates of extraction, higher rates of poaching on common-property habitats, and thus higher pressure on the endangered species.

Controlling imports, however, drives the price downward. Import controls have the effect of reducing the demand for the imported species. In figure 21-3 this leads to a backward shift in demand, from D_0 to D_1. This has been drawn so as to give the same quantity reduction as before. But in this case the price drops to p_2. The effect of this price decrease is to decrease the incentives discussed in the previous paragraphs. In particular, where endangered species are subject to common-property exploitation, the lower price would lead to reduced pressure to harvest and less rapid population decline. Something of this sort has happened recently as a result of an international ban on ivory imports. The ban has led to a substantial drop in the world price of ivory, which has reduced the pressure of poachers on the elephant in many parts of Africa.

■ Summary

The chapter commenced with a brief catalogue of the various dimensions of globalization. It then focused on trade in natural resources, referring first to the unique factors characterizing this trade, and then analyzing the extent to which trade impacts natural resource conservation and efficient levels of resource use. We then referred to specific policies that trading countries often pursue, looking specifically at the effects of export taxes. The chapter then discussed briefly the many forms of joint action that countries use to regulate international trade in resources. It ended with a discussion of the trade provisions of the Convention on International Trade in Endangered Species of Wild Fauna and Flora.

Notes

[1] Consult the statistical reports of the World Trade Organization for voluminous data on international trade, especially their recent volume, *World Trade Reports 2010, Trade in Natural Resources.*

[2] In recent years we have seen the rise of what are called "conflict resources," where rents are being diverted to support armed conflict among groups jousting for economic and political goals. See John-Andrew McNeish, *Rethinking Resource Conflict*, Chr. Michelsen Institute, Norway, Sept. 17, 2010.

[3] These arguments are made strongly in Joseph E. Stiglitz, *Globalization and Its Discontents*, Norton, New York, 2002; and Paul Collier, *The Plundered Planet*, Oxford University Press, New York, 2010.

[4] Such as the Chicago Mercantile Exchange, the London Metal Exchange, the Tokyo Commodity Exchange, and the Dubai Gold and Commodity Exchange.

[5] A technical way of describing this is to say that such agreements usually are "zero-sum," which means that what is gained by one party is lost by the other; in other words, there are no "win-win" outcomes.

[6] For a review of general cartel experience see Margaret C. Levenstein and V. Y. Suslow, "What Determines Cartel Success?" *Journal of Economic Literature*, Vol. 44, 2006, pp. 43–95.

Key Terms

bilateral investment treaties
CITES (Convention on International Trade in Endangered Species of Wild Fauna and Flora)
commodity agreements
conventions

export taxes
natural resources agreements
protocols
resource cartels
resource sovereignty
trade agreements

Questions for Further Discussion

1. Redraw figure 21-1 to illustrate a country that produces a natural resource and exports 95 percent of it.

2. Change the model of figure 21-2 to show a tariff on an imported item rather than a tax on exports. What is the impact on domestic consumers?

3. Which of the many aspects of globalization do you think will have the greatest impact on natural resource use around the world?

4. How might bilateral investment treaties work against resource conservation in exporting countries?

Useful Websites

Links to websites on the theme of globalization:

- Extractive Industries Transparency Initiative, EITI (https://eiti.org)
- World Trade Organization, WTO (http://www.wto.org)

Selected Readings

Collier, Paul, and Anthony J. Venables. "International Rules for Trade in Natural Resources," *Journal of Globalization and Development*, 2010, 1(11), pp. 1–19.

Feldman, David Lewis, ed. *The Geopolitics of Natural Resources*. Northampton, MA: Edward Elgar, 2011.

Fisher, Carolyn. "Does Trade Help or Hinder the Conservation of Natural Resources?" *Review of Environmental Economics and Policy*, 2010, 4(1), pp. 103–121.

Ruta, Michele, and Anthony J. Venables. *International Trade in Natural Resources: Practice and Policy*. World Trade Organization, Staff Working Paper ERSD-2012-07, March 2012.

Stiglitz, Joseph E. *Globalization and Its Discontents*. New York: Norton, 2002.

Vandevelde, Kenneth J. *Bilateral Investment Treaties History, Policy, and Interpretation*. Oxford, England: Oxford University Press, 2010.

World Trade Organization. *World Trade Report 2010, Trade in Natural Resources*. Washington, DC: World Trade Organization, 2011.

Name Index

Subject Index